Monaca aka Phillipsburg

A Beaver County River Town

Volume II of II

by Sandy Davis

Table of Contents for Volume II

Monaca Municipal Building

George Washington Town Plaza

C. J. Mangin Community Center

Borough of Monaca Flag

Tidbits of information

Interesting Monaca Ordinances

Monaca Water Works

Water Tanks

Monaca Reservoir

Monaca Wharf / Boat Landing

Riverfront Park   and Pump House Park

MONACA BOROUGH

Monaca Municipal Building – 926 and 928 Pennsylvania Avenue

The Municipal Building has a history of its own and Monaca has always taken pride in its city building. In 1895, the first municipal building was erected at a cost of $5,000. The first floor of this building housed the police station, the fire department, a polling precinct, and a vault where all the borough records were kept. Later the council room was moved to the large room on the second floor which was used as a meeting place for organizations and public gatherings. There was also an office for the chief of police and a room for the burgess where he could hold court when the occasion demanded. The outside of the building was of brick and in almost a square shape. J. A. Snyder was the architect and A. H. Lindsay was the contractor for this city building. Prior to this first municipal building being erected, the borough's business was transacted in an older frame building located on Eighth Street; but it soon outlived its usefulness.

1905

City Building, Monaca, Pa.

| Mateer Bros. Meat Market | Boro Building | photo from old postcard |

For those fond of genealogy............

In 1841 L. F. LeGoullen was the Burgess, Justice of the Peace and Manager of the
Seminary.   Council was Israel Bentel, Christian Authenrieth, Jacob Schaefer.

The first council in 1895 when the first municipal building was erected consisted of
James A. Irons/Chief Burgess, W. A. Miksch/President, Samuel D. Hamilton/Secretary,
Harry C. Glasser/Treasurer, Hirman Hicks, George Winkle, the Hon. John T. Taylor,
W. J. Cain, and George W. Weinman.

In 1898 the Borough Officers were:
J.M. Kirk/Burgess, S.D. Hamilton/Clerk, H.C. Glasser/Treasurer, J. W. Ramsey/Street
Commissioner, James Arbogast/Chief Fire Department, Dr. J. J. Allen/Health Officer, J. A. Irons,
J. R. McClurg/Justices of the Peace, F. Smith/Constable; and Councilmen – Pres. J. W.
Moorehouse, George Harbison, William Rambo, Paulus Koehler, David Fisher, David Kay,
John Dietrich.

In 1902/03 William W. Morgan was Burgess and Justice of the Peace and Harry C. Glasser was a Beaver County
Commissioner.

In 1936, a large brick addition was added to the rear of the original building, with oak wood finish. Carlisle and
Sharrer, architects of the Beaver Valley and Pittsburgh prepared the re-construction work; Cook-Anderson Company
was awarded the general contract.   Early in 1937, the addition was officially opened.   As of 1937, the police car
could be driven directly into the garage adjoining the new police headquarters, the prisoners unloaded and taken to
the borough jail.   Before this new system, prisoners were taken from the police car in full public view in front of
the municipal structure.

Rear view of the municipal building in 1940 showing vehicular entrance

Also in 1937, the front and sides of the original building were resurfaced with a covering of limestone. With the new addition to the building, by 1940, the entire first floor then housed the office of the Burgess, the police headquarters, a fire apparatus room, the borough garage, and a water meter repair department; the second floor of the original building was occupied as headquarters and a recreation room by the fire department. This area was furnished and equipped by the fireman and included pool tables, a radio, and reading and lounging nooks. There was a spiral stairway leading to the firemen's rooms on the first floor. The firemen had their own toilets and showers, too.

in 1954

1960s
Photo courtesy Beaver County Historical Research and Landmarks Foundation

The area of the second floor of the new addition was a large, nicely furnished and well-equipped council chamber, offices of the borough secretary, tax collector, borough engineer, and a room occupied by the Ladies' Auxiliary to the Fire Department. The auxiliary room had a well-equipped kitchen for use by the firemen and ladies as needed. The Woman's Auxiliary paid for the furnishings of the rooms as well as installation of window shades, floor coverings, kitchen equipment for the firemen's and Woman's Auxiliary kitchen.

The newly fitted borough building had two entrances, one on Pennsylvania Avenue and the other through a paved alleyway, giving entrance to the office of the Burgess and Police Department and the street department. There were four cell blocks. The garage was large enough for all of the borough trucks and street cleaning equipment.

In late Jan /early Feb of 1937 the Monaca Junior Woman's Club moved the Monaca Public Library to a room on the first floor of the municipal building. They were using the room formerly occupied by the Monaca tax collector. The public library was an exclusive project of the Junior Women's club and they were very pleased to have a home for the library and approximately 1,500 books.

Once again – for the history/genealogy buffs: as of Feb 8, 1937, Monaca Council
consisted of..... William Riddle-President, Glen F. Wilson-Borough Secretary,
C. W. Weinman was Borough Treasurer; and members --First Ward: John
Jacober and George E. Lay; Second Ward: E. G. Groleau and A. Howard Brown;
Third Ward: Earl Carnahan and T. D. Walker; Fourth Ward: William Riddle and
Harry Lavery; Fifth Ward: George Cain & Philip Petrie; John A. Johnston was Burgess.

Monaca Council made the decision at their Monday, Jul 10, 1961, meeting to purchase property for a new public parking lot on Pennsylvania Avenue. It was recommended by an appointed committee to purchase the Batchelor and Gormley properties, located between the Borough Building and the Keystone Building on Pennsylvania Avenue. There were buildings on the two properties and there would be a cost for the purchase of the properties, the demolition of the existing buildings, and the cost of paving and preparing the parking lot. One of the buildings was the old Penn Theatre / Roxy Theatre building (which when standing on Pennsylvania Avenue, would have been located to the right of the borough building). The parking lot would provide for at least 35 parking spaces with meters installed, generating additional income for the borough and helping to pay for the parking lot project. There were eventually two parking spaces designated for the police cruisers and another space with free 10-minute parking for those conducting borough business; all others were metered.

Ground was broken on Wednesday, Nov 2, 1994, for the current Monaca municipal building. The first building was erected at a cost of $5,000 in 1895 and the new building, in 1994, was at an estimated cost of $1.25 million.   This new building was erected on the site of the public parking lot which was located beside the old municipal building. It was a one and a half storey, red and light tan building housing the fire and police departments and the borough's administrative operations.   The Monaca Council made the decision to erect this new building rather than spending almost $1.4 million to bring the old structure up to state building codes; not to mention the more than $1,500 monthly costs they spent in just utilities.

Once they completed the new building, the old one was demolished and a new parking lot was put in its place; which means both were the reverse of where they were previously situated.   The borough paid for the construction of the new municipal building by selling "citizen growth bonds" which came in smaller denominations than bonds usually do; this permitted more people to be purchase some and have the opportunity to participate in the project.   Council hired two Pittsburgh engineering firms to help build their new structure; as well as H.H. Reich Engineering to perform HVAC air balancing in the new building and to provide testing of the heating and air-conditioning systems.

Photo courtesy Beaver County Historical Research and Landmarks Foundation
The former Municipal Building with the new Municipal Building erected adjacent
to it on the property that was formerly a public parking lot.

The new building was completed and things were being moved into new borough building Nov 5, 1995.

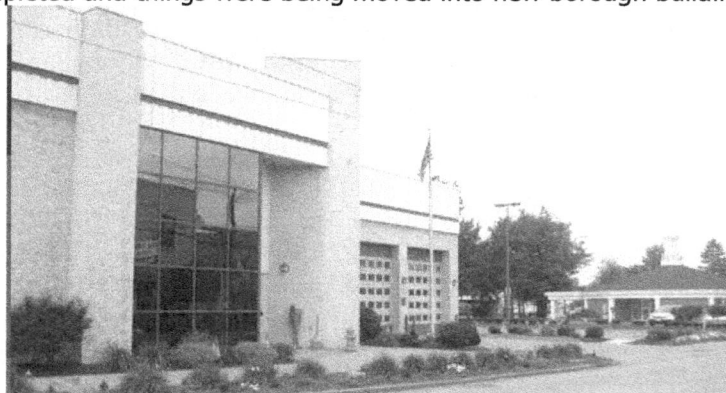

Council did preserve one item from the original municipal building – the stone that was outside the old building with the letters etched in it that say "Municipal Building."   They were incorporated into the new building as a way to preserve a little bit of the town's history.

Monaca Borough Officials - Sep 1911

Standing: Peter Raymer-Street Commissioner; E. B. Steiner-Borough Clerk; G. Miller, Dr. D. C. Moore, J. D. Wagner-Councilmen; Chief of Police Con Crowley.   Seated: J. A. Miller, F. D. Baldwin-Councilmen; Burgess W. W. Morgan; George V. Mullen-Councilman, C. M. Wagner-President of Council

Sep 1911   Chief of Police – Con. Crowley

John A. Johnston

John A. Johnston – In 1940, John retired to private life after serving Monaca for 16 years as Burgess and 18 years as a Justice of the Peace.   He first came to Monaca in 1880 when only 13 years old where he began to work in the Phoenix Glass Company; he advanced quickly in the company and was recognized as an expert glass worker.   For 2 years he was head of the police department. In 1922, he was elected as Burgess and he succeeded H. H. Morgan as Justice of the Peace.   He also held the position of tipstaff at the Beaver County court house for several years.   He married Jenny T. (Baker) and they had 5 children; several years after Jenny died, he remarried to Mrs. Edith Baily of Monaca.

*** *** *** *** ***

Miscellaneous Borough Information and Titbits of Information

George Washington Town Plaza

This is drawing of the planned fountain/plaza area.   George Washington School building would have been located in the mid to upper right side of this drawing.

Built between 1980 and 1990

Borough of Monaca Flag

Red   White   Blue
With blue print

The Borough solicited people to submit designs to be considered for becoming the official flag of Monaca Borough. In 1976, Council adopted a design created and submitted by Tammi Temple, who at that time was in the seventh grade at the Monaca Jr. High School (became C. J. Mangin Elementary).

C. J. Mangin Community Center

Monaca created a Community Center using the former original High School building (which then became the Junior High School and lastly was the C. J. Mangin Elementary). The building, located on the corner of Tenth Street and Indiana Avenue, had been vacant since 2009 and in 2011 was bought from the Central Valley School District for $1. Usage of the building was to be a multipurpose community center with the gymnasium and auditorium at that time being used by Central Valley Youth Wrestling, Central Valley Fast Pitch Softball, and the Monaca Youth Baseball League. Hopes in 2011 were for the building to be further used as the home of the Monaca Emergency Operations Center and the Monaca Public Library; rentals would be available for parties, showers, birthdays, and meeting place of other organizations.

As of early 2016, there was an elevator being installed in the building and I believe the only activity in the building was a day care center which was occupying a portion of the building.

*** *** *** *** ***

Tidbits of information:

There was a toll bridge at Monaca in 1899 / 1900 because an article stated that kids were ice skating along the shore just up from the toll bridge.

Another article stated there was a 3-cent toll to cross the bridge.

_____

Council Decisions..............
The first of Sep 24, 1900, the Monaca borough council passed an ordinance granting a right-of-way through the borough for a branch of the Consolidated Street Car Company to have a line running up Ninth Street from the Ohio River Bridge to Pennsylvania Avenue and thence east along Pennsylvania Avenue to the Opalite Tile Company's plant.
At the same meeting in Sep 24, 1900, it was approved to erect a new business building with the front facing Ninth Street and adjoining the Hotel Monaca building. It would be a three storey building constructed of iron, brick and stone. The basement would contain three storerooms, a room for dynamo, engine, and heating apparatus, and three cellars. The first floor would contain three large storerooms (18 x 70)– the second floor a stage and large auditorium – the third floor a lodge room (55 x 57), necessary anterooms, and closets. The 2nd floor theatre would be one of the coziest little play houses found in Western PA with two entrances – one from Ninth Street and one from the side.
(This building became known as an opera house, but more popularly known as the Citizen's National Bank Building, the Business Hall, the Business Building, and/or Campbell's storage building.)

_____

There was a need for a lamp lighter in 1903.

_____

May 12, 1903 - Businesses on Pennsylvania Avenue between Tenth and Fifteenth Streets presented a petition. It stated "The gutters have become so foul and full of debris, as to be obnoxious to the smell and sight, and a regard for health makes its early abatement an absolute necessity."

_____

Robert D. Lindsay, tax collector - opened an office early Jul 1906 on Pennsylvania Avenue with N. Wurzel, Jr.

_____

Monaca Indians organized their first football team on Oct 5, 1903, and wanted to hear from other
        90-pound teams in the county for games:
    Players – Fred Glasser RH, John Wagner LH, Dave Cain C, Glenn Glasser QB, Nat Zitzman RE,
    E. Zitzman LE, Emmett McMillan RT, Howard Shanks LT, Harrison Ramer RG, George Mellon LG,
    R. Laverty Manager, F. Glasser Captain.

————

1903 - There was another petition circulated from the residents of Monaca Heights who were asking "...that a new school house be erected on Monaca Heights, so as to better accommodate the children in that growing community." It claimed that by Jan 1, 1904 there would be at least twenty-five families residing on Monaca Heights.

————

1907 – Pennsylvania Avenue was being paved with bricks by the Ira W. Logan Company of Rochester.

————

At age 21, Max Barnett was elected a member of Monaca borough council; in 1911, that meant he was the youngest councilman in the state of Pennsylvania.

————

In 1911, there were …..
        two banks   two building and loan associations   paved streets
        churches   P & LE RR Co.   plans for an American Express Co.
        The 3 miles of roadway between Monaca and Aliquippa needed to be completed to make a
                continuous boulevard from Monaca to Pittsburgh.
        Completion of a sewer system (that emptied into the Ohio River below the water works).

————

There was a Light and Street Committee in 1913. This committee was responsible for having the old gas street lights abolished and replaced with electric lights.

————

In 1913, Washington Avenue and Pennsylvania Avenue extension were paved.

————

William W. Morgan was Monaca Borough Justice of Peace in 1920; he was then living on Pennsylvania Avenue.

————

This may be interesting, too…………………….affected who could and what could be sold, bought, etc. on Sundays.

You can check it out more if you research the Superior Court of Pennsylvania - Act of Apr 22, 1794 – section 1 and the preamble to this – passed Sep 25, 1786.
        The best way to summarize all this was that all worldly employment was prohibited and the burden of a defendant, or anyone who was questioned as to not upholding the Act, was to show that the work done was rather a work of necessity. For the most part, almost all business was shut down on Sundays. Violators of this Act were not given a trial by jury either; they were just tried by a magistrate. It is safe to say that if you were a merchant or had a business that handled any of these types of products or did these services, you should always be on the good side of your local magistrate, just in case.
        After finding a 1910 newspaper article about some Monaca business men being charged by a pastor for violations because they supposedly "sold" and did not just "give" ice cream products to some residents, I did some researching. So, it seems that you could go in, get a fully prepared meal, but not have a milk shake with your hamburger, a tall cold glass of root beer, nor have pie or ice cream sundae as dessert.

An "act for the prevention of vice, immorality, and of unlawful gaming and to restrain disorderly sports and dissipation."
Persons could be brought up on charges for serving or selling certain things on the Sabbath:

- Spirituous liquors.
- Ice cream, butter, butter products.
- Baked goods.
- Furnishing drinks, such as soda water or lemonade.
- Selling of cigars- even to guests of a hotel.
- Sunday newspapers (it was stated they were a convenience, and not a necessity, it was considered a performance of "worldly employment" to sell, deliver, etc.).
- Managing and operating of a steamboat for the purpose of conveying excursions was "worldly employment" and prohibited.

Then I looked up some of the legal information and found the following............

Pennsylvania State Reports Containing Cases Decided by the ... Volume 21   Some persons were found guilty of not obeying the law; they challenged their convictions, but all were upheld and accompanied with this exert:

> Therefore, Section 1. Be it enacted &, That
> from and after the 1st day of August next, if any person shall do
> or perform any worldly employment or business whatsoever on
> the Lord's day, commonly called Sunday, works of necessity and
> charity only excepted, or shall use or practise any unlawful game,
> hunting, shooting, sport, or diversion whatsoever, on the same day,
> and be convicted thereof, every such person, so offending, shall,
> for every such offence, forfeit and pay four dollars, to be levied
> by distress ; or in case he or she shall refuse or neglect to pay the
> said sum, or goods and chattels cannot be found whereof to levy
> the same by distress, he or she shall suffer six days' imprisonment
> in the house of correction of the proper county : *Provided, always*,
> That nothing herein contained shall be construed to prohibit the
> dressing of victuals in private families, bake-houses, lodging-houses,
> inns, and other houses of entertainment, for the use of sojourners,
> travellers, or strangers, or to hinder watermen from landing their
> passengers, or ferrymen from carrying over the water travellers or
> persons removing with their families on the Lord's day, commonly
> called Sunday, nor to the delivery of milk or the necessaries of
> life before nine of the clock in the forenoon, nor after five of the
>
> clock in the afternoon, of the same day.

There seemed to always be a pastor or particularly "interested" parishioner looking over every one's shoulder to be sure the law was upheld and reported to the authorities. Some things never change, do they.

––––––––

An article in The Pittsburgh Gazette Times – Aug 5, 1915, (page 5) stated that there were current rumors among real estate dealers in Monaca that the United States Steel Corporation, the Baldwin Locomotive Works, and the Bethlehem Steel Company were dickering for large acreage in Monaca. It was reported that 65 acres of land in the eastern end of the town (that would be going toward Aliquippa) were to be bought, along with a 12-acre plot of the old Freedom Oil Works.

––––––––

On Nov 24, 1914, after a second election, the court decreed that the larger southern section of Beaver County be known as Center Township. Eighteen years later, the remaining portion of Moon in the north was annexed by Monaca, becoming the Fourth and Fifth Wards (Monaca Heights and Colona Heights).

––––––––

It was often advertised and spoken of that two particular areas and their road ways were used for Sunday drives by the Monaca townspeople.

One roadway was from Monaca and Moon Township to Bellowsville (Potter Township) was known as the Beaver and Frankfort grade. It was described as having "the Ohio River on one side and a wildly romantic natural forest on the other." It was shaded by overhanging branches. There were clay mines to see, a log cabin, ravines, and runs to enjoy.

The other scenic drive was Elkhorn Run where the stream wound its way back and forth on either side of the road with wooden bridges to cross and presented numerous waterfalls. The roadway had almost perpendicular cliffs and anywhere you look you'd find some type of tree or shrub or ferns with fronds several feet long, as well as rhododendrons perfectly placed to complete the view of nature's virgin forest.

Oct 2, 1930
Plans to raze houses located near the approach of the Monaca/Rochester bridge were being made and work on beautifying the area, too.

_____

During the depression, there was an area down by the docks called Shantytown for those persons who could not pay their rent; almost every town in the area had their own "Shantytown" during the depression.   People lived in shacks and grew their own food in gardens.   There were bean lines at 5th Ward Fire Hall, too.

_____

Borough Building
Jul 14, 1961 – first discussed the parking lot and later in 1961, Monaca Council adopts proposals for off
       street parking lot near borough building.

Apr 23, 1962, was the date bids for the parking lot would be opened.

_____

Apr 12, 1966, was the first day of a period with free parking in Monaca; they were discontinuing the use of parking meters on Monaca Borough streets.   There would be free parking for 2 hours between 9 am and 9 pm.   Meters in the municipal parking lot were still used during this "free parking" time.

_____

Feb 9, 1979
    Phoenix Glass wanted to redevelop the Monaca area.   This involved 48 home owners, 32 tenants, and 26 businesses which included 22 rooming houses.   The land involved was south of Pennsylvania Avenue (toward the hill) between Sixth Street and 100 feet east of Ninth Street and south of Spruce Alley between Ninth Street and beyond Hall Street.   Phoenix had about 10 acres; with the expansion plans, it would add another 11 acres. Tenants were told they might receive up to $4,000 to relocate, while businesses might be eligible for up to $10,000.   In addition, each property would be appraised by two or three independent appraisers and would be given fair market value for the property.
    Monaca Council did approve the redevelopment because all buildings were leveled.   Only the American Legion building remained at the corner of Sixth and Pennsylvania Avenue.   CVS built a new pharmacy on the property close to the corner of Ninth Street and Pennsylvania Avenue by the Phoenix entrance.   All other property currently sits idle, empty, or as a parking lot.   Phoenix did not really erect any type of buildings on these properties along Pennsylvania Avenue, which had once been full of historic buildings and businesses.

_____

1980 – almost all the buildings on one side of Pennsylvania Avenue in the 600, 700 and 800 blocks were razed for Phoenix project of revitalization.

_____

Mar 15, 1988 - Approved an old house on Pennsylvania Avenue to be razed to provide 40 off street parking spaces.   It was formerly a pizza shop.

_____

Baker's Landing, PA was post office of Moon Township – adjacent to the borough.
It was located in the area along the river close to what was Pittsburgh Tube, then Metcon (2015).

_____

Economic Development

Monaca Borough has been actively undertaking policy and project initiatives to expand its economic development potential. These efforts date back to the 1992 Comprehensive Plan which specifically recommended supporting the diversification of its commercial and retail community, including in the central business district of the downtown. In addition, the Comprehensive Plan specifically targeted the goal of directing economic development to the underutilized industrial areas along the Ohio River and increasing the recreation opportunities along the river. Increasing pedestrian and bicycle circulation throughout the downtown and along the Ohio River would expand the economic reach and convenience to the residents in the downtown area, as well as increase their access to regional resources.

Monaca Borough's industrial Brownfields* area is approximately 90 acres consisting of eleven Brownfields properties mostly consisting of former steel mill related industrial lands. Private developers, community leaders and borough officials have identified this area for potential mixed-use riverfront redevelopment with public river access. Monaca very recently was working with Beaver County to explore the adoption of a new riverfront redevelopment district zoning overlay for its riverfront lands. The ability to create a new mixed-use zone in this area, which accommodates complete public access along the river's edge with a potential trail connection such as the proposed Ohio River South Shore Trail (ORSST), would have a significant economic impact on Monaca and would also represent a major shift in riverfront land use along this stretch of the Ohio River. The major identified Brownfields parcels in the project area include: The Moor Industrial property, The Colona Transfer property, The Beaver County Corporation for Economic Development (BCED) property, and McClymonds Coal Transfer.

* "A brownfield is a property, the expansion, redevelopment, or reuse of which may be complicated by the presence or potential presence of a hazardous substance, pollutant, or contaminant. It is estimated that there are more than 450,000 brownfields in the U.S. Cleaning up and reinvesting in these properties increases local tax bases, facilitates job growth, utilizes existing infrastructure, takes development pressures off of undeveloped, open land, and both improves and protects the environment."

*** *** *** *** ***

Ex-burgess dies

ELVA BITTNER MASSEY
...In 1959 photo...

Elva Bittner Massey. Beaver County's first woman burgess, died late Wednesday afternoon at the Medical Center of Beaver County.

Mrs. Massey had been appointed to succeed her husband, William Massey, as burgess of Monaca when he resigned in 1956 due to illness. He died in 1969.

Mrs. Massey had been a longtime resident of Monaca, but resided at the Beaver Valley Geriatric Center at the time of her death. She was 88.

She was a member of Redeemer Lutheran Church, Monaca; American Legion Post 580 Auxiliary; was a charter member of Monaca No. 1 Volunteer Fire Department Auxiliary; and belonged to numerous other organizations.

Funeral arrangements are being handled by the Harper J. Simpson Funeral Home, Washington Avenue, Monaca.

from 1983 newspaper

Sidewalk Basements   aka   Sidewalk Vaults

This was something new to me, but in exploring and having building owners share and giving me tours of their buildings, it was discovered that even Monaca, although considered a smaller town in comparison to say Pittsburgh, had these structures.   A "Sidewalk Basement" is basement space that is built underneath a city sidewalk, in front of the foundation wall of a building; considered underground urban spaces.
Most commonly called:
- **"Sidewalk Basement"** - appears to be maybe the third most popular name.
- **"Sidewalk Vaults"** - probably the most popular name found in other websites.
- **"Sub-Sidewalk Basement"** - a more technical name, usually used in official construction
-       descriptions.
- **"Hollow Sidewalk"** - appears to be popular in Seattle, Portland, and Sacramento, New York City.

They were built primarily in the 19th and early 20th centuries (and probably the 18th, too) to be used as entrances, storage space, coal bins, elevator shafts, and other uses.   Some were designed as basement corridors, and related architectural subterranean include stairs from the sidewalk and windows and doors into basement shops.
Evidently, extending building basements below adjacent sidewalks was not uncommon in many cities and was quite typical for industrial neighborhoods.

Vaults usually were constructed to permit immediate access to building utility/delivery areas without having to enter the building proper.   Many historic industrial city neighborhoods will reveal a lot of hints to and uses of open spaces below, including obsolete coal chutes (often filled in with mortar), stairways, manholes, diamond-patterned or bullet glass set in cast iron frames, steel diamond plate, sidewalk elevator hatches, and thick granite slabs spanning from curb to building line.

Signs, views, and clues to show there are/were sidewalk basement / sidewalk vaults in a building:

This drawing shows many of the tell-tell signs to know if there is a basement area under the of a sidewalk area.

These two pictures show the evidence of former entrances to sidewalk basements/sidewalk vaults.

Building owners were expected to maintain the vaults and many time were taxed for their use by the city who owned the property under rules of revocable consent.   As sidewalk delivery of coal waned, and coal bins (typically housed in vaults) were no longer needed, building owners often closed off or even filled in the vaults to prove non-use and therefore be removed from the tax.   Access to basement areas also began to fade away with the installation and usage of elevators and more accessible machinery.

The sidewalk basements I investigated are classifiable into two types by roof form: brick arch and stone slab. These may appear to be an earlier and later method of construction, but there is no chronology apparent.   The floor in these areas are/were usually paved with brick. Entrance to the vault areas differed in many ways:

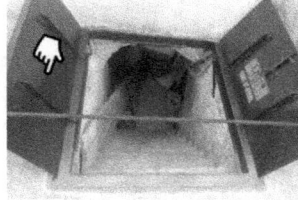

Sometimes access was via a stairwell.   Note the arched doorways.

And yet, sometimes there are/were no steps leading down to the area; the space existed below the sidewalk but access to it was strictly from the inside of the building/basement.   Evidence of it is grill work on the sidewalk area to vent the space below.

Don't forget to look down next time you are strolling along a sidewalk, you may find evidence of one these sidewalk vaults / sidewalk basements.

Here are two pictures of at least one sidewalk basement/vault that still exists in Monaca.

*** *** *** *** ***
*** *** ***

Interesting Monaca Ordinances

Oct 9, 1919
Ordinance No. 193
   Moving building and structures was a quite common practice ....

An ordinance of the Borough of Monaca prohibiting the erection of wooden or frame buildings, tin or iron-clad wooden buildings or structures, on Pennsylvania avenue, from Ninth street to Fifteenth strreet, and on Ninth street from Atlantic avenue to Pennsylvania avenue, in the Borough of Monaca; also prohibiting the erection or construction of any wooden, frame, tin or iron-clad wooden addition to any building now upon the above mentioned parts of said avenue and street; and likewise prohibiting the moving of any such building or structure as aforesaid upon the above mentioned parts of said avenue and street and providing penalties for such construction or moving of any such building or additions aforesaid; and providing for the removal thereof; also prohibiting the construction of any building of any character within the Borough of Monaca without first receiving a written permit for such purpose from the Secretary of the Council and providing penalties for erecting any building without first obtaining such written permit.

Be it enacted and ordained by the Burgess and Town Council by the Borough of Monaca, and it is hereby enacted and ordained by the authority of the same:

Section 1. That it shall be unlawful after the passage of this ordinance for any person or persons, firm, partnership, corporation, or organization, to erect or cause to be erected or constructed, any wooden or frame, tin or iron-clad wooden or frame dwelling house, shop, ware-house, store, carriage house, stable, garage or other building whatsoever within said borough, upon, or to move any such building upon, or to make or cause to be made or constructed any wooden or frame, tin or iron-clad wooden or frame addition to any building of any kind now upon any lot or lots of land fronting or abutting on Pennsylvania avenue from Ninth street to Fifteenth street, or on Ninth street from Atlantic avenue to Pennsylvania avenue, within one hundred feet of the lines of the above mentioned parts of Pennsylvania avenue and Ninth street.

Section 2. Any person or persons, firm, partnership, corporation or organization violating any of the provisions of Section One of this ordinance shall, upon conviction thereof before the Burgess of said Borough, or any Justice of the Peace thereof, forfeit and pay, for the use of said Borough, the sum of not less than fifty dollars nor more than one hundred dollars, in the discretion of the Burgess or Justice of the Peace imposing the same, per day for each and every day that such building or addition thereto remains upon the above mentioned parts of said Pennsylvania avenue and Ninth street, after notice in writing from the Secretary of the Town Council to remove the same; and in default of the payment of the said penalty and costs of prosecution, the person, or persons so offending shall be committed to the Borough Lockup for a period not exceeding forty-eight hours, or to the County Jail not exceeding thirty days, in the discretion of the Burgess or Justice of the Peace aforesaid.

Section 3. If any person or persons, firm, partnership, corporation or organization, erecting or causing to be erected, or moved upon, any lot or lots of land, fronting or abutting on the above mentioned part of said Pennsylvania avenue or Ninth street, within one hundred feet of the lines thereof, any wooden, frame, tin or iron-clad wooden or frame building, or erecting or causing to be erected, any wooden or frame, tin or iron-clad wooden or frame addition to any building, in violation of Section One of this Ordinance, shall neglect or refuse to remove or cause the same to be removed within forty-eight hours after notice in writing from the Secretary of the Town Council to remove the same, it shall be lawful for and the duty of the High Constable or other officer of the said Borough, designated by the Town Council, to remove or cause to be removed such unlawful structure or addition at the cost and expense of the person or persons, firm, partnership, corporation or organization erecting or maintaining such illegal structure as aforesaid; which structure is hereby declared to be a public nuisance; and such cost and expense of removal shall be recoverable, including costs, at the suit of the said Borough before any Justice of the Peace therein, as debts of like amount are now recoverable by law.

Section 4. It shall be unlawful for any person or persons, firm, partnership, corporation or organization to erect or cause to be erected any building or structure within the limits of the Borough of Monaca without first having obtained from the Secretary of the Town Council a written permit for so doing, for issuing which the said Secretary shall be entitled to receive, for the use of the said Borough, the sum of one dollar for each new main building and fifty cents for each addition to a main building, such sums to be for the services of the Secretary in issuing such permit.

Section 5. Any person or persons, firm, partnership, or organization violating the provisions of Section Four of this Ordinance shall upon conviction thereof before the Burgess of said Borough or any Justice of the Peace thereof forfeit and pay for the use of the said Borough a fine of not less than five dollars nor more than twenty-five dollars, in the discretion of the Burgess or Justice of the Peace imposing the same; and in default of such payment the person or persons so offending shall be committed to the Borough Lockup for a period not exceeding twenty-four hours or to the County Jail for a period not exceeding five days. And such offender shall also in addition to such fine pay the costs of the proceeding instituted for the recovery of the same.

Section 6. All ordinances and parts of ordinances inconsistent herewith are hereby repealed.

Enacted and ordained into an ordinance of the said Borough of Monaca this 5th day of July, A. D. 1919.

DAVID J. MITCHELL,
President of Council.

Attest:
HENRY MIKSCH,
   Secretary of Council.
Approved this 5th day of July, A. D. 1919.

RICHARD J. MAWSON,
10|3-10-17   Burgess.

This particular ordinance passed in Monaca on Jul 20, 1908, will give insight to the conditions, some of the more common sites, and the basic atmosphere of what it was like to be living in Monaca at that time. Take the time to read through this ordinance and be transported back to brick streets, gas lights, hitching posts, and horse and buggy traveling.

Ordinance No. 128

An ordinance providing for and requiring the grading, paving and curbing of Fourth street hereinafter described, and assessing a portion of the costs of the same on the owners of the property abutting thereon.

Two-thirds of the owners of property representing not less than two-thirds in numbers of feet on the properties fronting or abutting on Fourth street, hereinafter described to be paved, having petitioned the council of the Borough of Monaca, under and in accordance with the provisions of the Act of Assembly, approved the 23rd day of April, 1889, entitled, "An Act authorizing the Council of Incorporated boroughs to require the paving, curbing and macadamizing of streets or thoroughfares or parts thereof, and assess a portion of the costs of the same on the owners of property abutting thereon and providing for the collection of the same". Therefore:

Be it enacted and ordained by the Town Council of the Borough of Monaca, and it is hereby enacted by authority of the same:

First. That Fourth street in said Borough, beginning at Atlantic avenue and extending to Pennsylvania avenue, being a public highway laid out and opened in said Borough, be graded, curbed and paved.

Second. That the width of the driveway on said Fourth street from Atlantic avenue to Pennsylvania avenue shall be twenty nine feet.

Third. That the curb shall be set at the outer edge of the pavement of the driveway at each side thereof, for the protection thereof, and of the sidewalks which curb shall be of good hard sandstone with six inch face, not less than two feet in depth, at least three feet in length, dressed on top, face and jointed at least eight inches, properly dressed on one side to receive the bricks of the pavement of the driveway, and on the other side, the bricks of the sidewalk, and properly and firmly set to conform to the grade of the street. All curb now set in said street that does not conform to the foregoing requirements shall be changed so as to comply therewith or supplied by new curb if necessary to comply with said specifications.

Fourth. All gas lamps, hitching or other posts, and all telegraph, telephone, electric light, electric street railway poles and all other poles shall be removed from the driveway and placed immediately in the curb line so as to leave the driveway clear and unobstructed between the curbs. And the individuals or companies owning or using said posts shall remove the same at their own expense within ten days after notice served upon said individuals or companies or their proper officers to remove the same.

Fifth. All gas or other pipes in said street shall be laid or placed not less than two feet below the grade thereof, and in such portion of the street as the council may direct. And where said pipes now laid therein do not conform to these requirements, the parties or company owning, using or controlling such pipes shall within ten days after notice requiring it to be done, place the same at the proper depth or in the location required. All taps or openings of gas mains or pipes shall be made and service pipes carried therefrom to a point inside the property line where the same is to be used, before the foundation for the pavement is made. And no disturbance of the street after it is paved shall be permitted for the laying of service or other pipes for gas, unless under special circumstances where it could not reasonably have been laid before the paving of said street, and then only by resolution of council, duly passed and placed upon its minutes. All laying, changing or lowering of pipes shall be done in a skillful, careful and substantial manner, and wholly at the expense of the party owning, using or controlling the same, and the ditches shall be re-filled with gravel to sub-pavement grade.

Sixth. All sewers and water pipes on said street shall be laid and placed in accordance with the ordinance for that purpose provided, and each party or property owner connecting with sewers or using water from water mains shall at his or her own expense lay proper service pipes or sewers underneath the side walk to connect with principal service pipe and sewers, and at such depth and in such manner and under such conditions and restrictions as to the taking up and putting down of the sidewalk as council shall require. No additional taps for sewers or water main or service pipes therefrom shall be made or laid after the street is paved, except by resolution of council duly passed and entered upon its main or service pipes therefrom shall be made or laid after the street is paved, except by resolution of council duly passed and entered upon its minutes. All water hydrants shall be removed from said street.

Seventh. All costs and expenses of grading and paving of the driveway, curbing, changing, renewing or repairing the curb on Fourth street above described, shall be borne, apportioned and paid as follows: Two-thirds thereof by the owners of property abutting thereon, according to their foot frontage, and the balance or one-third of the costs thereof shall be paid by the borough; and the portion of said two-thirds to be paid by each of the owners shall be determined and collected under and in accordance with the provisions of said Act of Assembly, of April 23rd, 1889, and

all the residue of said cost shall be paid by the borough as aforesaid.

Eighth. All ordinances or resolutions or parts thereof inconsistent with the provisions hereof, be and are hereby repealed.

Ordained and enacted into a law in Council this 20th day of J..., 1908. CHARLES M. WAGNER
Attest:— President of Coun
E. B. STEINER,
Secretary of Council.
Approved this 20th day of J..., 1908. PAULUS E KOEHLER
Burg
Jul22-29aug5.

25

POLICE

FIRE DEPARTMENTS
Monaca Volunteer Fire Department – No. 1
Colona Volunteer Hose Company   aka
Monaca Fifth Ward Volunteer Fire Department – Company No. 5
The Monaca Heights Chemical Fire Company   aka
Monaca Heights Fire Company   aka
Monaca Heights Volunteer Fire Department – No. 4
Center Township Fire Companies
The Potter Township Volunteer Fire Department
Grenade fire extinguishers

POLICE

MONACA BOROUGH POLICE DEPARTMENT

Monaca hired its first policeman in 1883.

William Hunter was the first policeman in the Borough of Monaca.

He was named on Jan 1, 1883, and served until 1888.

John Shroads was the "one-man police force" – named in 1901 and served to 1906 when he became chief and Frank M. Hays was named patrolman.

John A. Johnston served for 2 years as head of the police force.

1915 – John Iben joined as a patrolman.

In 1918, he became police chief and served until 1940.

1937 – the boro police force included a chief and two patrolmen.

John Iben – Chief – Dan Liston and Mike Fronko patrolmen.

1940 – Dan Liston became chief – he had served on force since 1937.

1942 – three more men were added to the force.

1954 – The department had 9 on the police force....

Dan Liston – Chief (in his 38th year of service).

Mike Fronko – Asst. Chief.

Allen Henry, John Stuehling, John Kaloons, Lawrence Fitzsimmons, Paul Smith, John Mottes, and John Iben.

Chief of Police Shroads and Constable Hays arrested a drunk yesterday. He was put in the bastile and later at a hearing before Burgess Koehler, received the usual dose administered in such cases.

from Aug 1906

M. B. FRONKO   DANIEL J. LISTON   JOHN IBEN

In this 1940 picture – Daniel Liston – Chief; John Iben and M. B. Fronko - Patrolmen

Monaca Police Department   1990

Also, well known as a Monaca Police Chief was Lawrence "Rocky" Conti.   He was named Chief by Monaca Borough in Aug of 1974. In a surprise move in Jan 1975, council demoted him to Lieutenant and named James Kovac, a part-time patrolman to the chief's position.   Bowing to public pressure, he was reinstated in Feb 1975 as Chief once again.

*** *** *** *** ***

FIRE DEPARTMENTS

1902 picture of the horse drawn fire department wagon.

BCHR&LF

This 1954 picture is of the Monaca Borough fire trucks. This ladder truck was a 1953 American LaFrance. (It cost about $32,000 and was paid off in one year.)

Chiefs of Monaca's Three Fire Companies in 1940

| Floyd Milligan | Daniel S. Vogt | Robert M. Winkle |
| Fifth Ward Company | Company No. 1 | Fourth Ward Company |

Tradition passed down indicates there was a "bucket brigade" that existed as early as 1892, but no records exist to verify this information. The first fire company was organized in Felix Lay Hall (Sixth Street and Pennsylvania Avenue) on Oct 6, 1895. Minutes of the first meeting stated that R. D. McGeary was the first president and Samuel Hamilton was the first secretary; there were twenty men as members. The minutes of the next meeting stated, they chose the name "Monaca Volunteer Fire Company No. 1" and they had set thirty as the maximum number of members.

Some of the early members included: James Arbogast, Forquer Smith, D. B. Winkle, Herman Morgan, John Dietrich, Clyde Irons, Dave Burry, Washington Potter, and John Potter.

Some of the first presidents of the company included: R. D. McGeary (resigned in 1897); Fred Patton (1897 to 1904); and then William Berringer.

Prior to 1904, members wore rubber boots, coats, and helmets that were purchased by the company.

In 1905, the Monaca Fire Company had thirty-five members and for the first time they adopted uniforms; they also purchased a hose wagon.

After a portion of Moon Township was annexed to the Borough of Monaca in 1903, the two former Moon Township Fire Companies became part of the Fourth and Fifth Ward areas of "the heights." The council then appointed George E. Dietrich as the chief of all fire departments in the Borough. They also set the maximum number of firemen to receive pay at any fire event to now be thirty-five for the main company and fifteen for each of the two ward companies.

Monaca Volunteer Fire Department – No. 1

– 926 Pennsylvania Avenue, now 928 Pennsylvania Avenue
Applied for a charter on Oct 7, 1905; it was granted Dec 23, 1905.
1895 to 1906 a hand drawn cart was used.
1906 – Council granted permission to use part of the municipal building for stables in 1906; a team of horses was purchased from the Homestead Fire Company; and they got a horse drawn cart. The horses were kept in Paulus Koehler's barn until the new stable was completed. The brick stable was erected in early 1907 – it was ready for use for the horses mid Apr 1907. The firemen took turns and were responsible for feeding and grooming the horses.
1904 – a fire bell was obtained and used till 1930 when an alarm was purchased.
Oct 1906 – a new team of horses was purchased.
1918 – the company disposed of the hose team and purchased new equipment. The first "motor" fire truck was a Brockway unit of the La France Company of New York. D. J. Mitchell and Henry Miksch made the trip by train to pick up the truck, then drove it back to Monaca.
1928 – a modern La France fire truck was purchased
1930 – a modern ladder truck with a 65-foot aerial was also purchased
1930 – when Moon Township was annexed in December, the Fourth and Fifth Ward companies became part of Monaca's Fire Department.

2016

The aerial truck of the Monaca Fire Department was the largest/longest in the lower valley and was the pride and joy of the company.   It was the highlight when exhibited in parades throughout the Tri-State area and won numerous awards at firemen's parades in competition with similar pieces of apparatus.   Due to its length, there was a driver needed at the rear of the extension to aid in the steering of the vehicle.   It was 65 feet long and purchased in 1930 at a price tag of $16,000.   The ladders on the extension portion were raised from a platform at the rear of the truck and they pivoted to give a larger field of operation for the machine.   It was always a fun thing to watch this truck driving in parades as the front portion of the truck would remain in the middle of the roadway or street while the driver at the rear of the truck would cautiously weave the back portion from one side of the street to the other side. Young and old alike looked forward to this display.

It is very hard to read, but on the side, above the rear wheel, it has "Monaca V.F.D. No. 1" on it and also "Monaca, PA" lettered on the front of the truck.   This vehicle is from the late 1950s.

Monaca No. 1 VFD River Rescue

Colona Volunteer Hose Company – 800 Jackson Avenue, Monaca Heights

> 1903 J. W. Reid headed a group of interested citizens from the area that called themselves
> Colona, Moon Township, and they formed a Volunteer Fire Department.
>> o   The Colona Volunteer Hose Company joined the Western Pennsylvania Fire Association in 1903.
>> o   John W. Reid was the president of the company from 1903 until 1930.
>
> Colonial Steel Company donated the lot and building and fire plugs were located at proper
> intersections for fire use.
>
> The first apparatus for this company was a two-wheeled hand-drawn hose reel. It was used until
> 1906 when a hand-drawn wagon was purchased requiring an addition to the building.
>
> 1917 – equipment and wagon bed were mounted on a Ford chassis.
>
> 1927 – the Ford truck was discarded and a modern equipped apparatus was purchased.
>> o   A truck that could carry 40-gallon chemical tanks, two hand chemicals, and 1000 feet of two-
>> inch hose.

> *The first officers of this company were: President-J.W. Reid; Vice President-C.B. Shrum;*
> *Chief-W. J. Dinsmore; Secretary-Treasurer-Ray Carnahan; Trustees- George Kolp,*
> *William Woodfield, and William Peterson.*

> The Colona Volunteer Hose Company became ....

Monaca Fifth Ward Volunteer Fire Department – sometimes called Company No. 5 – 800 Jackson
Avenue – Monaca Heights

> The name was changed when this portion of Moon Township was annexed to Monaca Borough
> in 1930.   In 1965, the Company purchased a La France Pumper.

The Monaca Heights Chemical Fire Company - corner of Taylor Avenue and Bechtel Street

Nov 17, 1912 – the decision to begin this fire company was decided at a citizens' public
meeting held on the "Heights" – it would provide protection for the "hill."

Jun 1, 1913 – a 50-gallon chemical engine was purchased from funds that had been raised.

A small hose house was built and a fire bell was purchased from Heckman Bros.

The lot at corner of Taylor Avenue and Bechtel Street was purchased and a 24' x 40' building
was erected.   A bell tower was attached and the fire bell installed.

Chartered - Jun 5, 1925.

Jun 1925 – a new 1000 feet of hose, a new truck equipped with
four forty-gallon chemical tanks, and two hose reels were purchased.

Dec 1930, when the township was annexed to the Borough, a water supply was assured. The
truck was then changed and had a combination chemical and hose equipment.

The first officers were: President-Frank Rambo; Secretary-E.E. Elmer;
Treasurer-W. A. Dalzell; and Chief-R.M. Winkle.

After the annexing occurred, this fire company became known as…………….

Monaca Heights Fire Company – Fourth Ward - 913 Taylor Avenue – Monaca Heights
aka   **Monaca Heights Volunteer Fire Department – No. 4**
– corner of Taylor Avenue and Walnut Street   Monaca Heights

This company was originally referred to/called - Moon Twp. Fire Department prior to Dec 1930, when
the Monaca Heights area was annexed into the borough.

The original fire hall building was on the corner of Taylor and Bechtel Street (1031 Bechtel).

1964 - a new building was completed.   The old one storey frame fire hall was sold to the sole
bidders Ronald and Joan Ciccozzi. The Ciccozzis planned on using it for storage and
display purposes for their refrigerating and air conditioning business.

Former station building at corner of Bechtel Street and Taylor Street.

current

1913 Monaca Heights VFD   Taylor Avenue

***   ***   ***   ***   ***
***   ***   ***

With Center Township and Monaca bordering each other, they also often aid each other as needed in the times of emergencies. Many of the families of Monaca and Center Township are inter-twined in one way or another, so I included just a bit of information for general purposes.

Center Township Volunteer Fire Department

Center Township Fire Co. No. 1 – 3385 Brodhead Road
> Organized in the Bluebird Dance Hall on Brodhead Road in 1929/1930.
>> (This dance hall stood in the vicinity of the current Lincoln Homes area – Mike Meiter's property.)
> Chartered on November 25, 1930. Jack Coombs was elected as the first President of the company and Mike Meiter was named chief.

Center Township Fire Co. No. 2 – 108 Grandview Avenue
> Organized Mar 1943.
> Homer Morgan gave piece of land to the Company on Grandview Avenue.
> Well known businessman in Monaca and then in Rochester Max Barnett's father, Morris's home was moved to Sylvan Crest when the Monaca-Aliquippa Boulevard was being built over the Barnett property. This house became the first building of the Volunteer Fire Company No. 2 Sylvan Crest when it was donated in 1944 by the County Commissioners.
> In 1948, the men bought cement block and built the current front part of the fire hall.
> The original 2 stall garage/station was completed in 1971 and has since been remodeled.

Center Township Fire Co. No. 3 – 110 Van Kirk Road
> Organizational meeting held Jul 1946 to form this Company.
> 1948 building was erected on Monaca Road – Van Kirk area. Then the current building was erected on VanKirk Road.

1960 – all 3 of Center Township's fire departments organized into one unit to operate more efficiently instead as 3 separate companies. They became the Center Township Volunteer Fire Department but still have the three separate station numbers, separate locations of the fire halls, and separate trucks at each station.

*** *** *** *** ***
*** *** ***

Grenade fire extinguishers

It is quite ironic to me that the glass fire grenade was created to be helpful; were considered to be practical for fire safety over a hundred years ago and are now found to be VERY dangerous and toxic to humans today if they are still filled with carbon tetrachloride.

These types of extinguishers were manufactured and used between 1870 and 1910. The grenade resembled a ball-shaped light bulb but was larger. It was also produced in a tear-shape and a rolling pin shape. Homes, business, and all public buildings were installing these glass fire grenades. The glass was thin enough to be easily shattered when thrown into a fire or onto flames. Most of the preserved grenades I have been shown or have seen from Monaca and the surrounding areas are the upside-down tear shaped models and the majority of them were the *Red Comet* extinguishers made by Red Comet Incorporated in Littleton, Colorado.

The liquid inside each of the bulbs was either a water and salt solution and had bicarbonate of soda or muriate of ammonia added to the solution. Others were filled with carbon tetrachloride**. Carbon tetrachloride, which is now known to be a VERY dangerous chemical, causes damage to the lungs, liver, kidneys, and the brain; it is easily absorbed into the body through the skin and lungs. Carbon tetrachloride is now banned and considered a quite hazardous material. People of the 1800s were not aware of the health dangers that came with it.

Whichever solution or liquid was used in the bulb, there was a cork and cement used at the bottom to keep the contents from evaporating.   These extinguishers were made to be used like a military grenade, to be thrown at the fire to put it out.   The design of the bulb, with its long neck, allowed it to be easily grasped. Companies made them in a variety of colors, including red, greenish yellow, green, cobalt blue, and clear. The bulbs were made to fit into a wall rack or holder.   Many of the extinguishers used in the common household or smaller businesses would have been from 5 7/8 inches to 8 ¼ inches high/long.   They would be embossed with the manufacturer's name.

> **If you have one of these** antique extinguishers in your possession and it is still
> filled with the liquid AND it does not specifically state that it contains the salt water
> solution, then you will <u>not</u> find any buyers for it !!   Even the Antique Road Show has
> banned people from bringing them onto their sites due to the danger and hazardous
> materials they contain!   You should have the extinguisher disposed of professionally;
> contact your municipal environmental officer or fire marshal for specific instructions on
> how it should be handled and where it can be disposed.

Example of the label found on one of the globes.........

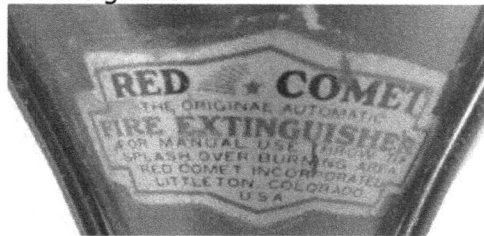

Some samples of the shapes and styles by different manufacturers.............

Catapulted "Bomb" Puts Out Fire

A GLASS "bomb" fire extinguisher throws itself into the flames when heat melts a plug to release spring tension in the wall bracket. When catapulted, the bursting bulb spreads an extinguishing fluid to smother flame.

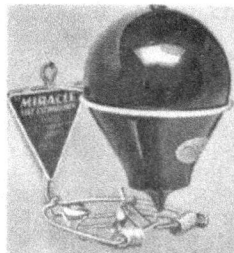

Fire extinguisher is hurled into flame when heat melts alloy plug.

The ad "Catapulted "Bomb" Puts Out Fire" particularly interested me. It states that the bulb filled with fluid "throws itself into the flames when the heat melts a plug"; that the bulb containing the liquid is "hurled" into the flames ....well..............

1. If the plug would hit the bottle, wouldn't that strike alone just break it?
2. If it did indeed release the bulb and supposedly hurl it, well, just how far could it honestly have gone?
3. If by luck it did get thrown by the holder/device, the name "bomb" would be quite appropriate because goodness forbid a person was in range and got hit with it.
4. With probably less than a pint of liquid, how much of a fire could this extinguish I F it was lucky enough to actually land on the flames?

This type of extinguisher was supposed to smother.   Now – what do you suppose was the mixture of chemicals to create a large enough fog to extinguish flames?   It appears it wasn't exactly a fog as in smoke, but rather a "fog of water."   It appears that this type of extinguisher would have been similar to the invention of the soda-acid extinguisher, where a cylinder would contain 1 or 2 gallons of a mixture of water and sodium bicarbonate.   Within the cylinder would have been a suspended vial that contained concentrated sulfuric acid.   The vial that contained the acid was broken (by one of two means depending on the type of extinguisher - one way involved the use of a plunger that broke the acid vial, the second way involved the release of a lead bung that held the vial closed). When the acid was mixed with the bicarbonate solution, carbon dioxide gas would be produced and this would pressurize the water.   The pressurized water would then be forced from the canister through the nozzle or a short length of hose. The acid was neutralized by the sodium bicarbonate.   This type of extinguisher would have been hung from a wall bracket or even from a ceiling.

Another type of fire extinguishing used by Monaca businesses was the Grinnel Fire Sprinklers.   Specifically, they were installed in the Batchelor Building at 1026 Pennsylvania Avenue in the late 1920s/by 1930.

This a sample of a 1930 Grinnell Fire Sprinkler (brass with red glass in middle)

Another style - a manual sprinkler head (brass with purple glass in middle)

A 1929 Grinnell Decorative fire sprinkler head(brass)

*** *** *** *** ***
*** *** ***

MONACA WATER WORKS

1880 – with the destruction of the Bridgewater pier of the Cleveland and Pittsburgh railroad bridge, it was discovered there was a river of pure water beneath the bed of the Ohio River.

Water works building- 1890   Courtesy BCHR&LF

1895 – Monaca's municipal water plant was installed.
It consisted of eight artesian wells, a brick pumping station, 750,000 steam pump, pipe lines, and a 500,000-gallon reservoir.

1898 – it became necessary to install a much larger steam pump which pumped directly from the river.

Monaca Water Works former structure.

1902 – a filtering crib was placed under the bed of the river – 300 feet from shore and then 75 percent of the water to Monaca was obtained from the underflow and 25 percent through gravel and sand under the river bed.   A 14" raising main direct to the reservoir was laid.

Late 1920s   Photo courtesy Borough of Monaca

1932 – the Allaire Water Company's plant at Colona was purchased by the Monaca Borough and Monaca
       water was supplied to Colona in 1933.

1933 – a P.W.A. grant (which was the first P.W.A. project in Pennsylvania) let the Borough extend service
       to the Fourth and Fifth wards and built a booster station pipe system.
       (Public Works Administration)

1940 – the W.P.A. project was nearing completion.   New stone-faced pump house - 2 stories.
       (Works Progress Administration)

Over all the years after the formation of Phillipsburg and Monaca, floods plagued those along the Ohio River. Few
of the previous floods had any significant effect on the Water Works or the pumps housed within until the St.
Patrick's Day flood of 1936.   This particular flood forced Monaca officials to disconnect the pumps and dynamos
and "by a system of blocks" raised them about 25 feet out of the flood water levels.

Once the flood water receded and an evaluation of the situation was completed, it was determined that raising the
pumps and dynamos permanently above the flood level reached in this 1936 event should be done as soon as
possible.   The W.P.A. was once again utilized and in 1939 the project was approved.   In addition to raising the
dynamos of both pumps some 14 feet, the whole pump house was faced with stone, reroofed, and the interior was
altered and rearranged for more economical water production and distribution.   When the project was completed,
the building was a work of art.

In a project a few years prior to the 1939 improvements on the Water Works building, the W.P.A. was approved to
do some other projects including retaining walls, a fountain, and lily pond.   While doing these other projects, a
band stand and grotto was also constructed of cut and dressed stone on the same level as the current Water Works
building.   Its design resembled a mini castle, as does the current Water Works.

Fun Fact: The Monaca Water Works newest structure had   the nickname of Castle on the Rhine.

View looking from river

View looking from Atlantic Avenue   Courtesy BCHR&LF

A portion of Monaca Heights was once called Dockter's Heights. There was a new line from the pump house completed in 1908.   It was referenced as *Dockter's Heights* in Moon Township up until 1911 – then usually just as Monaca Heights.   See Locations section for more on Dockter Heights.

*** *** *** *** ***

Water Tanks

There is a very large water tower on Tew Street / Blaine Street off Marshall Road, Monaca Heights.
        Originally erected at this site prior to 1977 when it was renovated and eventually replaced with
        the current tank.

Monaca first built the 300,000-gallon water tank on Monaca Heights.   There was a police radio antenna on the top of tank.   This water tank provides storage for the water usages of Monaca residents, businesses, and industries. The pumps for this tank were operated only at night. In the summer they were operated seven nights per week. The original tank was replaced with a new 500,000-gallon water tank for storage in Feb 1990.   There is a separate tank on Kermiet Drive, too.

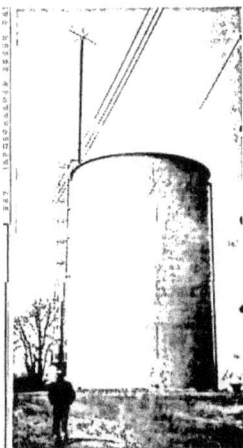

1977   2015
Tew St/Blaine Street off of Marshall Road

Tank on Kermiet Drive

Monaca Reservoir

It is located on Taylor Street, Fourth Ward (Monaca Heights).   There was a reservoir on Monaca Heights
  as early Mar 17, 1910 when a watchman was hired.   This reservoir connected with the Monaca
  municipal water works; it was originally a W.P.A. project.
A new reservoir was put into use in Sep/Oct 1941 – construction for it started in the fall of 1940.
  It was located / adjoined the old reservoir.
There are two open air reservoirs at this location – a 1.7 million gallon and a 1.5 million gallon – both
  surrounded by a 6-foot wire fence and barbed wire above the fence.
As Mar 1984, it was reported that Monaca was the only Beaver County community which still stored water
  in open-air ground reservoirs.
The reservoirs are now (2015) covered.

Entrance to protected, fenced in reservoirs on Monaca Heights

Aerial view of two reservoirs

*** *** *** *** ***
*** *** ***

MONACA WHARF / BOAT LANDING

with
Riverfront Park   and   Pump House Park Information

From the very beginning of Phillipsburg and Monaca, it has been associated with the Ohio River as shown with
Phillips and Graham's boat yard.   The borough has been associated with the river in one form or another from
industrial ties, to recreational, to transportation. If you are from the Beaver Valley, you just know the river in some
form.   With that being said, I have included just a brief introduction of information of how the Ohio was accessed,
calmed, or utilized; how the river has always been involved in the growth and development and improvement of
Monaca.

The Monaca Borough Council approved construction of a wharf or boat landing along the Ohio river in 1889,
opposite the pump house. At that time, it was sometimes called "hog back."   When there was any type of freight
shipped by water or for the loading and unloading of passengers, this wharf was used.

Jun 24, 1930, the borough of Monaca passed an ordinance (No. 295) for the widening and extension of Saw Mill or
River Street.   This was enacted so there would be access to a better water supply and for providing for municipal
wharf purposes.   The Saw Mill or River Street was located between Ninth Street and ran along the Ohio River to
the Pump House location, with the width from the Ohio River to the shore lines of all the lots along that portion of

Atlantic Avenue; some of the properties close to Sixth Street were affected also. The Borough of Monaca, under the power of eminent domain, appropriated and condemned the land for widening this Saw Mill or River Street. This meant that the owners of property along that stretch of Monaca who would have already established any type of beach front, wharf, or boat landing of their own would lose that right with the property now being considered the Borough of Monaca as owners. The Borough Solicitor was authorized to handle all cases if the involved property owners refused or failed to agree with this ordinance or with any amount given them for damages or loss resulting from the same ordinance.

The W.P.A. took on enlarging the current wharf as one of their 1933 projects. Even though the actual size of the wharf was considerably shorter, the War Department granted the wharf to have a maximum length of 1,000 feet. Once completed, the new wharf in 1933 was 800 feet long, it had a river wall that was 21 feet high, a terrace wall 14 feet high and the "wharf proper" was over 60 feet wide. It was made of 7,000 perch of cut stone. (a "perch" is a unit of measurement commonly used in older customs and was equal to 10 feet; in stone work it would indicate cubic feet/inches –one perch = 16 ½ feet long, 18 inches high and 12 inches thick).

Although NOT Monaca's, here is an image of what a stone wharf would have looked like.....

See the W.P.A. section for more projects and improvements made in Monaca.

By the mid 1900s, the 1933 wharf had long since been abandoned and disappeared. This area of the Ohio River had become quite popular with local boaters and/or fishermen and was used with great frequency. In the spring of 1995, there was nowhere on the Monaca side of the Ohio River between the Emsworth and Montgomery Locks for anyone to launch a boat. Monaca manager, Tom Stoner, wanted to change all this and envisioned an Atlantic Avenue/Monaca Riverfront Park, therefore starting the campaign to reach that goal. In May of 1995, the Department of Community Affairs (DCA) awarded $100,000 to the borough for the $300,000 riverfront park project. The Riverfront Development Committee also committed to about $150,000 meaning the completion of the park project was within site. There was to be a double boat launch in place and the whole area cleaned up. The borough slowly acquired about six and a half acres needed for the project; some of the land already owned by the borough, the remaining being purchased from the railroad company.

The location of the new Atlantic Avenue Riverfront Park is in the western end of the borough, at the end of the Atlantic Avenue with the Monaca-Bridgewater P & LE train bridge looming over the property. The bridge holds its own historic value being among one of the oldest train bridges in the country. The site's second phase of improvement was to have the launches in place, a pedestrian walkway, a 20 foot by 28 foot pavilion, the access road and parking lot in place. Mr. Stoner had this dream for more than 10 years and finally his vision of improving the 6+ acre site came true. There was a ceremony to celebrate the official opening of the Monaca Riverfront Park; with a paved roadway and parking lot and launch area, along with a large new pavilion. As of 1997, there were still finishing touches being added to the park, but for all general purposes, it was officially opened for business May 31, 1997.

There is a future plan to have boat docks right at the bottom of a steep hillside where the water is 25 feet deep right off the shoreline.   Another future phase of the Riverfront Park is to dredge the Markey's Run, a natural tributary that starts in Center Township and empties into the Ohio at the Monaca Riverfront Park site, and build inland docks.

The area surrounding the pump house has existed as a park for years, at one time housing a basketball court and used for many activities. The new 3-acre park replaces the aging basketball courts that had crumbling asphalt and swing sets that had become rundown.

Monaca Riverfront Park   aka   Pump House Park

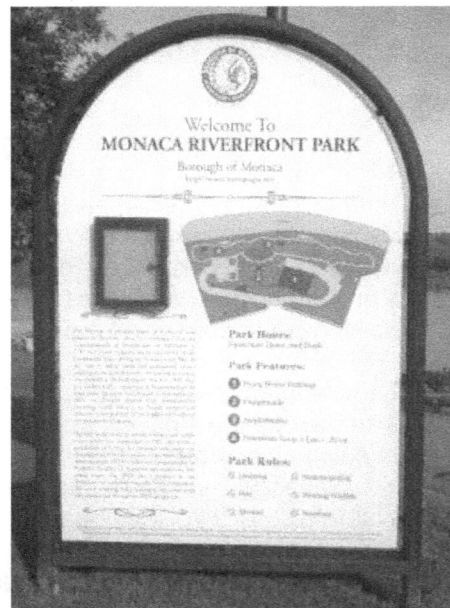

*** *** *** *** ***
*** *** ***

EDUCATION and SCHOOLS

First Ward School

Third Ward School

Marshall Road School

Fourth Ward School

Fifth Ward School

George Washington Junior High School

Senior High Schools

Early Graduating Classes for Monaca

Monaca Schools' progression

Center Township Schools

Potter Township Schools

Central Valley School District

Soldiers' Orphan School

Thiel Hall at Phillipsburg

Garfield Business Institute

Info-Age Computer School of Beaver County

Penn State / Pennsylvania State University

Community College of Beaver County

Beaver County Vocational Technical School

Education

From the time Monaca was called Phillipsburg, education was always important and received the proper attention.

When the New Philadelphia Society was still in Phillipsburg, there was a little red brick school house built to educate the children. It was erected on the triangular shaped lot between Fifth and Sixth Streets. It was built in 1840 and had been torn down in 1884. There was another frame building erected on this lot between 1840 and 1850 and was known through the years as the "Ark." Records indicate it was painted white with green shutters on the windows. The curriculum taught in the Ark consisted of instruction in reading, writing, and arithmetic. Although the other red brick building was torn down in 1884, the Ark survived much longer. When the First Ward School was built, the Ark was purchased by Rev. W. G. Taylor and was moved to property on the low 900s on Pennsylvania Avenue where it was set up and used as the public hall. Once the Ark was moved and the other building was torn down, there was a beautiful large gazebo built on the triangular lot.

In the earliest recorded school board meeting records of Jun 12, 1871, it was found where two schools were to be opened for the ensuing year; both the brick and the frame (Ark) schools were to be used with the first day of school in each on Oct 16, 1871. The Jun 15, 1872, minutes instructed both teachers to teach the American language to all pupils. A meeting on Jan 29, 1876 authorized the teachers to designate what each pupil must study and they were also authorized to expel any who refused.

Higher education was always important to Monaca residents and officials. Even though the first school board was established in 1866, minutes of their meetings were not found between 1866 and Jul 1896. On Jul 7, 1896, the Board approved to establish a "Rudimentary High School" to accommodate all those who wanted to continue their studies; they would offer Algebra, Rhetoric, Physical Geography, and Higher Arithmetic with others being added as needed. (Rhetoric is the art of effective or persuasive speaking or writing, especially the use of figures of speech and other compositional techniques.) The first principal of the high school was W. W. Reno. He was succeeded the next year by Frank W. Smith. Mr. Smith became ill, so on Oct 26, 1899, D. C. Locke was elected to fill his unexpired term.

The Ark building was used as a school, once it was moved to Pennsylvania Avenue it was used as the town hall, by the Presbyterian Church, and then used as a restaurant and residency. It was purchased along with an adjacent vacant lot by Louis Stoll and was torn down for him to build a new theatre building in 1926.

Can I find pictures of it or street views of it or the exact location of where it was set after it was moved from the other end of town -- no. I can only go by the address of the Hackett restaurant and then the information of the theatre that Mr. Stoll built at 922 Pennsylvania Avenue.

The official name of the town and post office was changed from Phillipsburg to Monaca on Sep 20, 1892, but the school district did not officially change the name to "Monaca School District" until Oct 1, 1892. Professor Barnes was the principal of the Monaca common schools, followed by R.S. Nagel, C.A. Moore, and John Dunn; the Supervising Principal in 1956 was Philip H. Petrie.

The following were listed as School Directors in 1898:

J. R. Gormley-President	Dr. J. J. Allen
W. J. Mellon	G. Lindsay
John T. Taylor	Thos. Rambo

Following is an account of the school buildings of Phillipsburg / Monaca.

Schools

First Ward School – 800 block Pennsylvania Avenue (between Eighth and Ninth Streets)
1884 to 1961 – razed 1980

The School Board voted at their Sep 27, 1880 meeting to buy one-half acre of land on
Pennsylvania Avenue (then called Fourth Street) from Justus Merkel for $535 to build a
new four room school house.

The Board accepted a bid by Charles Lais on May 10, 1882 of $5,646 for a four-room building of
red brick to be erected on the ½ acre lot purchased in 1880. This building was the
First Ward School. It was finished in 1884.

S. E. Barnes was hired the first principal at $40 per month.

1891 – Jun 15, approval was given for an additional four rooms to be added to the existing
building due to the growth in population. The addition was completed in 1892 and
the school then consisted of 8 classrooms and was used as a grade school.

Professor D.C. Locke was the principal prior to 1908; E.R. Gehr was the principal beginning 1908.

1924 was the last year for a graduating class out of First Ward School –it became strictly
an elementary school then.

1956 – Mrs. Grace I. Patterson, Principal

It was vacated in 1961 but not razed until the end of Jul 1980 to make way for the revitalization
program and the rebuilding of the Phoenix Glass Company plant.

Photo courtesy BCHR&LF

In this picture -- Dr. Milliron's home/office would have been to the left of the school building;
an alley, then the Kemmer Hardware storeroom would have been to the right side.

First Ward School Building – front view.

Another view of the ivy-covered school building.

The picture above is the alley way that ran between the First Ward School building and the former Kemmer Hardware storeroom.

Pennsylvania Avenue is running left to right along the bottom of the picture; Ninth Street is pictured on the left of the Doyle's building.   The alley beside the school went from Pennsylvania Avenue back to the former section of Pacific Avenue (now property of Phoenix) and it would have begun just past the cars in the picture below.

The pointer in this picture is indicating the steeple of the First Ward School building.   Ninth Street is on the left edge of the picture – Kemmer's is on the right side of the picture and the alley would have been on the left side of the former Kemmer building.   As of 2016, CVS Pharmacy occupied this area.

Third Ward School – Indiana Avenue & Fifteenth Street

1906 to 1964 - building still standing (converted to apartment building).

> 1904 – Dec 23, a contract was given to McDonald and Hartman firm for the new Third Ward School building. It was a 12-room school building; used for grade school children.

This new building was located on the corner of Fifteenth Street and Indiana Avenue (2016 – apartment building) and was finished in 1906.

> 1906 – Feb 22, the high school was transferred to the Third Ward School.
>
> 1911 – Converted to house grade school and high school students.

Between the First Ward and Third Ward schools, there was a calculated total of 700 students.

> 1912 – chemistry desks and cupboard were purchased and added to the already improved Chemistry and Physic labs. The high school students had four-year courses.
>
> 1916 - Due to the steady overcrowded conditions, it was necessary to erect a two room portable school building in back of the Third Ward building.
> At the Aug 10, 1916 meeting, the building contract was given to William Mecklem.
>
> 1918 - Sept - it was necessary to lease the second floor of the Bank Hall for school purposes. It was divided into four class rooms.

The W.P.A. and P.W.A. *(Works Progress Administration and Public Works Administration – these were part of "New Deal" in 1933)* aided in beautifying the schools and grounds and making repairs where needed. They installed cut stone for a retaining wall around the Third Ward building.

> 1956 – Mrs. Elizabeth S. Smith, Principal.
>
> 1964 – the George Washington Building was converted into an elementary building to accommodate the elementary students from the Third Ward School which was closed.

Corner of Indiana Avenue (pictured along bottom left) and Fifteenth Street (just out of picture on right)

The Third Ward School was later sold and made into apartments.

2016 photo   Converted to apartments
Indiana Avenue runs along bottom of picture; Fifteenth Street to the right

Marshal Road School – (#1999) Marshall Road, Monaca Heights

It was located on Marshall Road, between Blaine Road and Cascade Road on Monaca Heights. This school was an elementary school building.

The W.P.A. and P.W.A. *(Works Progress Administration and Public Works Administration – both part of "New Deal" in 1933)* aided in beautifying the schools and grounds and making repairs that were needed to the schools and/or the athletic field.

The W.P.A. also aided in the grading of a regular size football field and several tennis courts were made ready at the Marshall Road athletic field area. They installed cut stone for a retaining wall around the school building. In total, the W.P.A. work was $73,700.

1956 – Margret Vetter, Principal.

1975 – the School Board voted to close the school by 1976 and move all the current fifth and sixth grade Monaca Height students to the two newer buildings (the Fourth and Fifth Ward Schools).

May 21, 1984 – the school was demolished and the property was going to be developed. One, two, and three bedroom apartments were built. The property is now Spring Run Apartments.

Marshall Road Grade School

2014 view of former location of school

Fourth Ward School – 1135 Walnut Street, Monaca Heights

1953 – Oct – The Beaver County School Board approved the proposed site for a new school building.

1954 – Jun -The directors approved locating the new Fourth Ward elementary school directly at the rear of the old building.   Previous plans were to have the new building erected at the extreme rear of the property.   With the new approved plan, it was not necessary to dismantle the old school while the new building was being constructed.   The six room building was of light brick; had glass block windows, glazed tile of different colors was used throughout the interior with no more than two rooms having the same design.

1956 - A new Fourth Ward School on Monaca Heights would be a six-room elementary school. The six-room school would be built on the same site of the present four room frame school building which would be razed when the new building was constructed.   Mrs. Knapper, Principal. The new Fourth Ward was originally built to replace the Fifth Ward School. This school was one floor, had 6 classrooms and an all-purpose room.

Jun 1992 – the School Board voted to close the Fourth Ward School and reopen the Fifth Ward School. It was to house first through fifth graders.

When the school closed, it had been housing grades 4, 5, and 6 with a total estimated students in all three grades of 130.

2013 – former school was converted into apartments.

There was a school erected on the Welch Plan, Monaca Heights. O. H. Locke was principal in 1908.
All records indicate that Welch Plan school house became the Fourth Ward School since the Welch Plan of homes was located within the area of Fourth Ward.   In 1904, Prof. Joseph Thomas taught in "the school" on Monaca Heights.   It has been stated that his tradition was to give each of his pupils a pound of fine candy on the last day of school before each summer vacation.

Welsh Plan aka Fourth Ward School Building

New Fourth Ward School building being erected (original Fourth Ward School is in background).

View of the back of the completed new Fourth Ward School.

View of front of former Fourth Ward School in 2015 – converted into apartment complex in 2013.

Fifth Ward School – corner Jackson Street and Ridge Road, Monaca Heights /2590 Ridge Road
First building was constructed about 1902/1903.
Located on Monaca Heights (by youth baseball field).
Original structure housed children in grades one and two – it was a 4-room wooden structure.
The first building was replaced with new structure shortly after 1955; it had two floors and eight
    classrooms.
1956 – Mrs. Cora M. Hezley, Principal.
1958 – The new Fifth Ward School was also built on Jackson Street – Monaca Heights.
1975 – the current fifth and sixth grade students were moved from the Marshall Road school
    and placed in the Fourth and Fifth Ward schools.
1983 – the Fifth Ward School was closed to elementary students. Arrangements were
    made for the primary grade students from the Fourth and Fifth Ward schools to attend
    classes in the upper floor of the junior high and all fourth and fifth grade students from
    the hill would attend the Fourth Ward School. The Fifth Ward School building was
    rented to the Info Age Computer School and Garfield Business School.
1992 – Fifth Ward School was re-opened.

Note:
The Moon Township school directors decided to open a school at the new town of Colona. The old Jackson
residence was to be remodeled and made suitable for school purposes for the winter of 1902 and in 1903 as a new
building was to be erected. The Jackson's residency was located in the area of what became Fifth Ward on
Monaca Heights.

Colona School House – (was there in 1910) In 1926, the Colona School had grades one to five – Monaca Heights
students.

All this information indicates this school became Fifth Ward School.

courtesy BCHR&LF
Two views of former Fifth Ward School Building

Front view of the Fifth Ward school building built in c 1955/56.

Rear/side view.

Extra Fact: *In 1912, due to a case of scarlet fever at Colona – the school was closed one Thursday and Friday to be fumigated.   School / classes were resumed on Monday.*

George Washington Junior High School – Pennsylvania Avenue & Eleventh Street
  The building was erected in 1930-31 during a time period of financial crisis.
        It was built in the Art Deco/Modern style which was a current trend in public buildings
        of that era.   It was a rectangular two storey, yellow brick building.
  The lots needed to build the school were owned in 1931 by Agostine Tufano and the
        Presbyterian Church of Monaca.
  The school opened in Sep 1932 as the George Washington Junior High School.
        The first floor had six classrooms, an office, and a wood shop.
        The second floor had eight classrooms, two kitchens, and a cafeteria.
        With major cutbacks being made in budgets, the Domestic Science (home ec.) and
            Manual Training (wood shop and mechanical drawing) rooms were not equipped
            and therefore, not used at first as classrooms.
  1956 – Mr. Christy J. Mangin, Principal.
  1964 – the George Washington Building was converted into an elementary building to
        accommodate the elementary students from the Third Ward School which was closed.
        -    The Third Ward School was later sold and made into apartments.
        These rooms were utilized by the American Red Cross organization during that time.
  It was later used as an elementary school before it was sold to private developers in 1971.
  This particular school building was a part of the most significant growth and development period
        of Monaca which was between 1895-1935.   The area east of Ninth Street along
        Pennsylvania Avenue became the downtown business district.   The school was a
        prominent feature in the heart of the downtown area.
  The Borough of Monaca sold the building to a man in Bridgeville, then purchased it back from
        him so it could be razed and the property be used to develop a fountain plaza.
  Before the building was razed, it was used by the Melchiorre Distributors and Penn Supermarket
        as a warehouse . It was scheduled to be demolished by Aug 15, 1986.

George Washington School (Entrances facing Eleventh Street).

Side view of the right side of the school, facing Pennsylvania Avenue.

Rear view of the school (looking at building from Maple Alley)

Some pictures of the inside of the George Washington School building shortly before being demolished in 1986.

Typical classroom

First floor corridor

one of the two sets of stairs between floors

Senior High Schools – Indiana Avenue & Tenth Street

Prior to 1922, the School Board anticipated the overcrowded conditions to continue, so they purchased a large plot at Tenth Street and Indiana Avenue. It was really too small to consider building a school on, so while examining other locations, J.M. Davis and Morris Barnett came forward and offered to provide the additional ground needed since they both owned lots adjacent to the other larger lot.

1925 - the new Senior High School was built with the capability of holding up to 500 pupils. It was located on the corner of Indiana Avenue and Tenth Street.
With the cost being below the estimate, the board found they had sufficient funds to provide some kind of athletic field. They purchased the property of Miss Maggie Smith on both sides of Indiana Avenue between Fifteenth and Sixteenth Streets. This property was already in a nicely graded shape of an amphitheater form.

1939 – the bleachers at the athletic field were destroyed by fire in the summer of 1939. There was a W.P.A. project planned to provide for building modern concrete ones. This project was to include a structure with concrete stands and built-in dressing rooms. Red tape delayed the start of the project and it was not completed until the 1941 season.

1956 – Eudore G. Groleau, Principal.

1964 – this former high school building became the new junior high school. (It was eventually renamed the C. J. Mangin building and became an elementary school.

1976 - the school building on Indiana Avenue was rented to the Beaver Valley Christian Academy.

Senior High School Building   (10th Street on bottom left, Indiana Avenue on bottom right)

The former senior high building was later renamed the C. J. Mangin Elementary Building.

1942

Building was renamed......

C. J. Mangin Elementary School – 998 Indiana Avenue

1977 – this once senior high, then designated a junior high building, on Indiana Avenue was completely renovated to accommodate K through 6 grade students who were once in the George Washington building.

The last school building to be erected by the Monaca School District was their new high school in 1964 on Ella Street and Allen Avenue (Monaca Heights).   It was built on a 41 acre site close to the Stephen Phillips Homes. In 1977 a new wing was added to this school building and both high school and junior high school students were then housed in the school.   The former Junior High School (once the senior high building) on Indiana Avenue was completely renovated to accommodate K through 6 grade.

This school building is currently the only former Monaca school being used as a school for district children and following the merger of Monaca and Center, it became the Central Valley Middle School.

*** *** *** *** ***

Early Graduating Classes for Monaca.................

1898 - The first Monaca High School commencement was held in 1898 in the Monaca Rink (which later became Paul's garage, L & M Market, Mesta Industrial Roofing at 823 Pennsylvania Avenue); consisted of 4 girls in the graduating class – Maggie Varner, Myrtle Carey, Modina Carey, and Elizabeth Craig.   Miss Lily Carey was the first high school principal.

1899 – 2nd graduating class:
James Moore, Clara Frank, Mae Cain, Blanche Johnston, Rosena Bock

1900 – 3rd graduating class
Harry O. Glasser, Robert D. Lindsay, Homer White, Howard Fronk, Libbie Lay, Agnes Thompson, Agnes McGreary, and Vera Taylor

1901 – 4th graduating class:
Mowrey P. Simpson, William Fisher, Mary Hood, Bessie Holloway, Nellie Sweet, and Gertrude Householder

1902 – this class was not graduated until 1903 due to the recommendation that courses of study be extended to a three-year period.

The 1903 and 5th graduating class consisted of only 3 students:
J. H. E. McMillan, Olive May Moore, and Ethel Shillito

1904 – the commencement exercises were held in the YMCA hall. Seven students graduated:
Clara Dixon, Helen Carey, Marie Schier, Lydia Frank, Marian Love, Charles Dixon, Leonia Rosenbaum

1910 – no students graduated.

1911 – one student graduated.

1912 – six students graduated.

1912-13 school year – four students were in senior year, they were sent to Rochester High School and graduated from there.

1914 – 14 students graduated – an unusually large class.

1916 thru 1926 – 151 were graduated, with no class larger than 22.

*** *** *** *** ***

Chronological and condensed information of the Monaca Schools:
(There are no written records, so *tradition* is used for the information on the very early schools.)

1840 – first public or common school was built of red brick. It was torn down in 1884.

1850 – second building was of frame construction, painted white with green shutters on the windows.
- This building was located on the triangular plot of the ground now known as the "Band Stand Lot" which was on the triangle lot at the corners of Fifth and Sixth Streets.
- 1882 / 1883 - This building was purchased by Rev. W. G. Taylor and moved to a location on Fourth Street (now Pennsylvania Ave) and fitted up as a public hall.

1871 – the earliest recorded school board meeting is that of Jun 12, 1871, when it was decided to open two schools.   Both the brick and the frame were to be used.   Both schools were to commence on Oct 16, 1871.

1872 – Jun 15 minutes, state that both teachers were to teach the "American" language to all pupils.

1876 – Jan 29 minutes - the teachers were given authority to designate what each pupil must study and they were authorized to expel any who refused.   It was also presented to divide the town into wards.

1878/1880 – The P & LE railroad came to town and with it growth in the population.

1880 – the Board voted on Sep 27, 1880 to buy one-half acre of land from Justus Merkel on Pennsylvania Avenue (this was still called Fourth Street then), paying $535. It was purchased for the purpose of building a new school house of four rooms.

1882 – Phoenix Glass Company also came to Monaca – again more growth.
  The Board accepted a bid by Charles Lais on May 10, 1882 of $5,646 for a four-room building of red brick to be erected on the ½ acre lot purchased in 1880.   This building was the First Ward School.   It was finished in 1884 – S. E. Barnes was hired the first principal at $40 per month.
  With the new First Ward School constructed, the wooden structure built in 1850 was sold to Rev. W. G. Taylor who moved it to Pennsylvania Avenue (back then it was named Fourth Street) and it was used for the public hall.

1891 – Jun 15, approval was given for an additional four rooms to be added to the existing building (First Ward School) due to the growth in population.   The addition was completed in 1892.

1892 – the first high school was organized and taught by W.W. Reno.
  Phillipsburg became Monaca and the name of the school district also changed on Oct 1, 1892 to the Monaca School District.

1896 – Jul 7, it was approved to establish a Rudimentary High School for the accommodation of those who had completed the present courses and any others who desired pursuit of higher studies. Those studies included Algebra, Rhetoric, Physical Geography, and Higher arithmetic and would be accomplished over a two year period.

1903 – Mid May – a petition was circulated among the residents of Monaca Heights to be presented to the Moon Township school board asking that a new school house be erected on Monaca Heights. The petition stated that this school would better accommodate the children in the growing community area. (Fourth Ward School)
  In Sep 1903, the board voted to alleviate even more crowded conditions and the first floor of the Lay building was rented.   (Lay building – corner of Eighth Street and Indiana Avenue.)

1904 – Dec 23, a contract was given to McDonald and Hartman firm and the new Third Ward School building; a 12-room school building was built and finished in 1906; it contained grade school children.   This new building was located on the corner of Eighth Street and Indiana Avenue.

1906 – Feb 22, the high school was transferred to the Third Ward School.

1912 – chemistry desks and cupboard were purchased and added to the already improved Chemistry and Physic labs.

1916 - Due to the steady overcrowded conditions, it was necessary to erect a two-room portable school building in back of the Third Ward building.   At the Aug 10, 1916 meeting, the building contract was given to William Mecklem.

1918 - Sept - it was necessary to lease the second floor of the Bank Hall on Ninth Street for school purposes.   It was divided into four class rooms.

1922 - At a special citizens' meeting, Mar 7, it was approved to build yet another new school building. John H. Phillips, a Pittsburgh architect, was hired. The board had already purchased a large plot at Tenth Street and Indiana Avenue from Mrs. Fanny (Sweet) Dodd in anticipation of needing more school buildings.   James M. Davis and Morris Barnett held title to properties adjoining this plot and offered to provide the additional ground. This building served as the high school until 1964.   (Later dedicated as C. J. Mangin School.)

1925 - The new Senior High School was then built with the capability of holding up to 500 pupils. With the cost being below the estimate, the board found they had sufficient funds to provide some kind of athletic field.   They purchased the property of Miss Maggie Smith on both sides of Indiana Avenue between Fifteenth and Sixteenth Streets.
  This property was already in a nicely graded shape of an amphitheater form.

1930 – The large area of Moon Township in the Monaca Heights area was annexed to Monaca Borough, thus adding two new wards, the fourth and fifth.   The school age children from this area had attended schools in Rochester, but now the school board took action to accommodate them within the Monaca schools.

1930 – Dec – the Board once again discussed the need for more room due to overcrowding; and the need for erecting a junior high school came about.   The board hired the firm of Bradley and Stetson of Aliquippa.   The Presbyterian church property on the corner of Pennsylvania Avenue and Eleventh Street was purchased and later other adjoining property was acquired.

As with many other businesses, areas, and schools over the entire nation in the early 1930s, there was a financial crisis. Monaca was no different. The Great Depression took its toll on all areas of life. A large part of the school tax of 1930-1931 had not been paid and more than ½ of 1931-1932's were still outstanding.   The district had to stop the purchase of all new equipment and the teachers even had to suffer with a reduction in their salaries.
     Teachers received payment in "script" or "baby bonds" instead of paying them in "real money," but local merchants were understanding enough and they accepted these as payment for teachers' purchases whenever possible.

1931-1932 school year brought drastic financial woes for the district.
     No new books were purchased and salaries of the teachers were reduced to the minimum.

1932 – Monaca was rebounding and in 1932 was found to be in solid financial standings again. During 1932, the buildings on this plot were removed and the George Washington School was built and opened on Sep 1932.   The cost was $125,000 for the George Washington School.

Even though no new schools but the George Washington building were added in Monaca, overcrowding was an ever-present condition.   During the 1931-32 school year the junior high students were brought to the high school building; this made almost 800 pupils were housed in a building intended for 500 students.   The auditorium in the H.S. building was partitioned with curtains, the gym was also partitioned, both areas then being improvised class rooms.

In 1937 and 1940 – there were seven school buildings and an athletic field:

In Jan 4, 1937, the system was divided into four departments – Kindergarten for preschool children (80 students); Elementary for grades 1 to 6 inclusive (980 students and 31 teachers); Junior High for grades 7 to 9 inclusive (494 students and 14 teachers); and the High School for grades 10 to 12 inclusive (328 students and 15 teachers). Phillip H. Petrie was supervising principal of the Monaca Public Schools and Clinton M. Puff was the Jr-Sr high school principal.

1947 - The district added a unique offer to their students – A Biology Camp which was held at Raccoon State Park – the students would stay three days and nights at a camp.   It taught the campers first hand experiences of biology.   This program continued for several years.

1953 – Oct – The Beaver County School Board approved the proposed sites for a new school building. A new Fourth Ward School on Monaca Heights would be a six-room elementary school. The six-room school would be built on the same site of the present four room frame school building which would be razed when the new building was constructed.

1954 – Jun -The directors approved locating the new Fourth Ward elementary school directly at the rear of the property of the old building.   Previous plans were to have the new building erected at the extreme rear of the property.   With the new approved plan, it was not necessary to dismantle the old school while the new building was being constructed.   The building was of light brick, glazed tiles of different colors were used throughout the interior with no more than two rooms having the same design.
     Oct – The Monaca School Board approved application for a new elementary school building to be constructed to replace the present Fifth Ward Building. The new building was to be a four-room structure similar to the new Fourth Ward Building in Monaca Heights.

1956 – There were two grade schools to be constructed – the Fourth Ward Building on Walnut Street in
Monaca Heights (it was a six-room structure with an all-purpose room) and the Fifth Ward School.
As of 1956……Monaca had 7 public schools and one parochial school:
St. John the Baptist School – 1336 Virginia Avenue.
Senior High School – (C.J. Mangin Building) Indiana Avenue and Tenth Street – Eudore
G. Grouleau/ Groieau, Principal.
Junior High School – (George Washington building) Pennsylvania Avenue and Eleventh.
Street – Christy J. Mangin/Principal; Philip H. Petrie/Supervising Principal
(superintendent) had his office in this building.
Fifth Ward School – Jackson Street – Mrs. Cora M. Hezley/Principal.
Fourth Ward School – Walnut Street – Mrs. Knapper/Principal.
Marshall Road School – Marshall Road – Margret Vetter/Principal.
Third Ward School – Indiana Avenue and Fifteenth Street – Mrs. Elizabeth Smith/Principal.
First Ward School – Pennsylvania Ave. and Ninth St.– Mrs. Grace Patterson, Principal.

1957 – The Monaca, Center, and Potter School Districts formed a jointure in compliance with the State
Department of Public Instructions promotion of overall reduction in the number of school districts
in the Commonwealth.
The 1957 jointure was fair – the agreement provided that each community pays for every
student in the jointure. If Center Township has more students in the schools, it pays more – if
Monaca has more, it pays more; and the same with Potter.   Dr. Harry Fink was the supervising
principal during this jointure. It was known as the Monaca Area Joint Schools.   If it would be a
merger, that would be the fifth union school district, governed by one school board and financed
under one tax structure; if no merger – then it would continue to operate under the present
jointure system.

1957 - The new six room Fourth Ward Elementary Building was erected. (to hold 180 students).

1958 – The new two level, eight room Fifth Ward Building was built. – Jackson Street, Monaca Heights
(to hold 240 students).

1958 - Integration of Center Township elementary students into Monaca elementary schools was started
in 1958 for the first time.   This allowed Center Township students to have a full day of classes
for the first time in many years.   There were three elementary schools in Monaca that the
Center students were attending.   There were 12 members of the joint board (seven from
Monaca and 5 from Center) who all favored the union district proposal – two of the members
opposed holding referendum on the issue in Oct 1958.   (It was still a jointure at this time.)
This jointure only lasted until 1960 when it was dissolved because neither side could agree on
the site for a new high school.   Therefore, Monaca chose a site and built their own high school
building, as did Center.   Although Monaca was left to stand alone once out of the jointure,
Center still had the possibility of merging with Potter and becoming partners.

1964 – The new Monaca Senior High School was opened.   Erected on 41 acres on Monaca Heights.
The former high school on Tenth and Indiana became the junior high school for 7th to 9th grades.
The George Washington Building was converted into an elementary building to accommodate
the elementary students from the Third Ward School which was closed.

1975 – The school board hopes to close the Marshall Road school by 1976 and move all the current fifth
and sixth grade Monaca Height students to the two newer schools (Fourth & Fifth Ward).

1977-78 – Revisions were made and a new wing was added to the high school and it became a junior-senior
high school.
The old junior high (once senior high) building on Indiana Avenue was completely renovated to
accommodate K through 6 grade students who were once in the George Washington building.
The George Washington Building was sold, the Borough rebought the building, and then later tore
it down; the land was used to build a park.

1983 – the Fifth Ward School was closed to elementary students. Arrangements were made
    for the primary grade students from the Fourth and Fifth Ward schools to attend classes in the
    upper floor of the junior high and all fourth and fifth grade students from the hill would attend
    the Fourth Ward School.   The Fifth Ward School building was rented to the Info Age Computer
    School and Garfield Business School.

1984 – May 21 – the Marshall Road School was demolished; property was owned by Mitchell's
    Contracting Corp. and property was going to be developed. There were seven lots in all included
    in this sale.   There were one, two, and three bedroom units of apartments built.

1990 – Monaca School District had only 4 schools:
        C. J. Mangin Elementary – 998 Indiana and Tenth Street.
        Fourth Ward School - Allen Avenue, Walnut Street, Elm Street on Monaca Heights.
        Elementary wing of the junior high – Seventeenth Street and Indiana Avenue.
        Monaca Junior-Senior High School – on Monaca Heights.

1992 – The Monaca School Board voted at a Jun meeting to close the Fourth Ward Elementary School
        and to re-open the Fifth Ward building.   With the Fourth Ward only having one floor
        and 6 classrooms, the Fifth Ward was bigger with two floors and eight classrooms.
    Monaca School district still had but 4 schools – just a little change:
        C. J. Mangin Elementary – 998 Indiana Avenue and Tenth Street.
        Fourth Ward School was closed and Fifth Ward school on Jackson was re-opened.
        Elementary wing of the junior high – Seventeenth Street and Indiana Avenue.
        Monaca Junior-Senior High School – on Monaca Heights.

2007 – In the fall of 2007, the Center Area and Monaca school boards both approved resolutions to
    complete a historic merger. It was the first voluntary merger of school districts in Pennsylvania.

2009 – The voluntary merger between Monaca and Center Township was completed.   As of 2015, the
    merger proves to have gone smoothly and is going very well. The newly formed school district is
    named Central Valley School District. Center Township's former junior and senior schools
    complex buildings at 106 Baker Road Extension, Center Township, Monaca was made into the
    new high school for grades 9 through 12.   The Monaca Borough's former junior / senior school
    complex at 1500 Allen Avenue, Monaca Borough became the newly merged districts' Middle
    School for grades 6 through 8.   The former Center Todd Lane at 113 Todd Lane, Center
    Township became Todd Lane Elementary for children in grades 3 through 5 and Center Grange
    Primary school at 225 Center Grange Road, Center Township held that name and houses
    students K through grade 2.

*** *** *** *** ***

Some of the past Supervisory Officials in the Monaca School District

Supervising Principals – P. H. Petrie (prior to 1960), Dr. Harry E. Fink (1960-61), Dr. Marcus W. Davies (1961-64),
C. J. Mangin (1964- _);   Superintendents – C. J. Mangin (1969-1977), Anthony P. Cerilli;
High School Principals – M. Fritz Carey, E. R. Gehr, S. C. Henderson, L. H. Peterson, C. P. Shorts, A. M. Sytull, P. J.
Cook, H. E. Pebly, F. W. Henck, E. Laubauch, E. G. Groleau, Dr. Harry E. Fink, F. W. Crawford, Anthony P. Cerilli;
Junior High School Principals – C. J. Mangin, Anthony P. Cerilli, Joel Carr, Michael Siget, Roland Delaney, Robert
Wagoner.

*** *** *** *** ***

Center Township Schools

This information is included because Monaca and Center Schools have been 'connected' over the years.

Phillipsburg, Moon, Monaca, Center – they all tend to mesh together during the course of time for one or more various reasons. History books tend to state the Moon became Center Township, but part of Moon became annexed to Monaca and is now the part of Monaca Borough known as Monaca Heights. There are areas of Center that go down to the Ohio River, where the dividing properties are still sometimes quite gray, especially in historic references with the area called Colona.

With all that being said, I am going to throw in a brief history on the one room school houses that I found information on while researching and writing my book on Center Township. These one room school buildings may have never seen a Monaca resident, but I can almost guarantee that there were cousins between Monaca, Moon, Center that would have attended one or more of the schools I have listed.

Fun fact: There is(was) a Beaver County One Room School House Association
This group of former one room school house students continued to hold reunions
for many years.

Once Moon Township / now Center Township, there were 5 one room school houses......................
    Simon Field School House – Brodhead Road (across from current water tanks) Center Twp.
    Bunker Hill School House – By Bunkerhill Church.
    Davis School House – On Chapel Road, Center Township.
    Alcorn School House – (2nd building) – corner Brodhead Road and Marshall Road, Center.
    Vankirk School House - Van Kirk Road, Center.

Central School-
    This school was built in the mid 1930s, a few years prior to the Consolidated school being built.

Center Grange Elementary aka Consolidated Elementary – 225 Center Grange Road, Center
    Center still used two one room buildings – Vankirk and Alcorn.
        The original Center Grange Road school building closed as a school house at the end of the 1986/87 school year and was used by the Beaver Valley Intermediate Unit (BVIU) and other organizations for many years before being torn down; a new primary school was built in 2007.
Center Grange Primary School
    Newly constructed in 2007. Currently used as the primary school of Central Valley Schools.

Todd Lane Elementary – 113 Todd Lane, Center Township
    This school building was constructed in 1971 and renovated in 1995.

Senior High School – 160 Baker Road Extension
    This school building was constructed in 1960 and was home to students in grades 7 through 12. The first graduating class was in 1965

Junior High School - adjoined the former Senior High building by a long hallway. Now serves as an extension to the Central Valley Senior High School building.

As previously written, Center Township was involved in a brief school jointure with Monaca between 1958 and 1960.

In 1971, Potter Township joined Center; the Potter Township School District and Center Township School District became known as the Center Area School District.

In 2009 the first schools to voluntarily merge in Pennsylvania were the Monaca Area School District and Center Area School Districts forming the current Central Valley School District.

So...................currently..............................

Central Valley High School

In 2009 plans were finalized for a voluntary merger of the Monaca and Center Area School Districts. The newly formed school district was named Central Valley School District. As of 2016, the merger proves to have gone smoothly and is going very well.

Following this merger..........

.....The former Center High and Middle School building is now the Central Valley Senior High School with students in grades 9 through 12; 160 Baker Road Extension.

.....The former Monaca Jr.-Sr. School building is now the Central Valley Middle School for grades 6, 7, and 8 students; 1500 Allen Avenue.

......The Todd Lane Elementary School building is now still named Todd Lane Elementary with students in grades 3, 4, and 5; 113 Todd Lane.

......The Center Grange Primary School also is under the same name as prior to the merger with Monaca for kindergarten, first, and second grade students; 225 Center Grange Road.

*** *** *** *** ***

Following the merger in 2009, the new mascot for the Central Valley Schools became the Warriors.

The Monaca School District was formerly called the Indians.

A full colored mosaic tile Indian portrait was on the outside of the Monaca Jr. Sr. High School building. The former mosaic Indian mascot was removed and replaced with the new mascot - the Warriors.

The Center Township School District's mascot was formerly the Trojans.

Did you know................

In Jun of 1968 when Center Township was in need of building a new elementary school, that the Center Township School Board had to have authorization and approval from both the Monaca School Board and Potter Township Board before they could proceed with construction plans?

Why................well........The authorization to build was necessary from both Monaca and Potter boards because the three districts were placed by the county board in the same administrative district. This meant that if there would be any merger between Potter and Center, Monaca and Center, or all three districts – then Potter and/or Monaca would then also be responsible for the financial obligation generated by Center for the new elementary building.

Potter and Monaca boards eventually did give their approval, and the new elementary building was erected in Center Township.

More proof that Monaca and Center and Potter areas, residents, and schools seem to keep being tied together even without, or prior to formal jointures or mergers.

*** *** *** *** ***
*** *** ***

Soldiers' Orphan School - Pennsylvania Avenue Extension and Fourth Street
(these were formerly Factory Street and Hanover Street)

Dec 1865

The first soldiers' orphan school in Pennsylvania. Was needed as a direct result of the Civil War.
There were many hurdles to be conquered ---

The state would not provide grounds, buildings, books, nor furniture.

It required $20,000 for 30 acres of ground, buildings, furniture for house and school rooms, books, apparatus, etc.

A small amount of money was paid for each orphan for board, clothing, schooling, books, doctor & medicines -- that was.....$115 each under 10 years - $150 each over 10 to 16 years old.

The workers for 150 orphans would require 20 assistants to be paid out of the small amount allotted.

The organizer and supervisor for the proposed school became the Rev. William G. Taylor, D.D.
Dr. Taylor accepted the challenge and began to accomplish the huge task.
Dec 1865 – bought the former Water Cure (which had closed, but became a summer resort).

Repairs were made, it was enlarged, and it was furnished appropriately.

Four storey dwelling was added (34 x 44 feet), an additional school room, a chapel, a boys' hall, a girls' hall, and 41 acres of ground were also bought.

In 1870 and 1873 more acreage was bought to make a total of 210.

The hall included laundry, bakery and additional cook room.

Dr. Taylor bore the expenses of all the above - $48,000. He also tastefully decorated all the buildings – old and new. The girls' parlors and music rooms were furnished with Brussels carpets, chairs, piano and an organ in the chapel. It was felt that "taste" was essential to instill culture in the girls and boys.

The state prescribed eight grades as the extent of the educational course. Dr. Taylor had four grades of a mathematical and scientific course, and one-fourth of the orphans were able to finish these four grades.

No student was promoted unless his standing was at least 75. In 1874, the state inspectors found that the average standing of students in the school to be 93. These results were achieved with the help of the teachings of Prof. S.H. Piersol.

The laws of health were carried out by Dr. Taylor, too. Proper food for physical and mental growth was provided, as well as all clothing fitted and adapted, including well fitting shoes. The children maintained cleanliness of body, house, school rooms, wash and out houses. The buildings were very well lit, had excellent ventilation, and the children were permitted 9 hours of regular sleep.

The boys received one hour regular military drilling, play time in the morning, noon, evening and recess in addition to their class room time and daily duties.

The girls also received daily classroom time and under the guidance of Dr. Taylor's wife, each girl acquired a systematic and practical knowledge of domestic work, including classes in scrubbing, washing, ironing, housecleaning, dining-room work, dishwashing, cooking, all kinds of baking, mending, darning, plain family sewing, dressmaking, bonnet trimming, housekeeping, sweeping, bed making, arranging rooms and parlors. Dr. and Mrs. Taylor did daily inspections.

Every room, kitchens, and washrooms were open for the inspection of visitors (under the guidance of a member of the institution. These visitors were welcome all days except Sunday from 8 am until 5 pm.

Dr. Taylor had a Bible class for his family, all students and employees. He did not employ any individual who declined to attend the Sunday services. He was also the general head and superintendent of the school.

His wife was supervisor of the general household and departments presided over by other women employees.

Employees of the school over the years included:

Prof. W. G. Taylor
Prof. Scudder H. Piersol – academic head of teaching force

Teachers:

A. G. Thorne	David McAllister	J. S. Steele	R. F. Thompson
J. N. Biers	James M. Phillis	Miss Lizzie Dever	Miss Lizzie Rollings
	Miss Mary M. Taylor	Miss Maggie Krossen	

Superintendents of the boys

| J. Niel | P. Bromwell | P. Auishouse | Henry Turner | W. P. Badders | E. H. Crandall |

Matrons were Miss N. W. Thompson and Miss Minnie Cole

Superintendents of Sewing Department

| Miss Mary Chambers | Miss Ella Mann | Miss M. McLaren | Mrs. L. L. Brown |
| Mrs. J. J. McGinniss | | | |

Tailor – J. Braun

Superintendent of kitchens

| Mrs. M. J. Hoyte | Mrs. L. Turner | Mrs. A. M. English | Miss S. Feustermacher |
| Miss Eunice Brown | Miss Julia Echies | | |

Superintendent of children

| Miss Rachael Wilson | Miss Sue Work | Miss Ada Grandey |

Laundresses   Mrs. C. Lloyd and Mrs. C. Frank

General Caretaker – Mrs. James W. Taylor

Farmers and Gardeners

| Benjamin Stute | James Smith | John Hughes | William Kaler |
| Joseph Garrett | A. Yount | | |

Shoemakers – C. Pfancuch and A. Blott   Butcher – C. Erbeck

Physicians – David McKinney and D. S. Marquis

Six hundred and seventeen orphans were cared for with over 200 of whom required medical attention upon arrival.   The yearly average number of students was about 140.

This drawing is a view of the boys Marching on/along Hanover Street (now known as Fourth Street) and the road on the left side was then Factory Street, now known as Pennsylvania Avenue Extension that leads out of town, heading toward Brodhead Road/Center Twp.

A view of the upper building that faced onto what was Hanover Street, now Fourth Street. Pennsylvania Extension (known as Factory Street) would have been to the left of this picture.

This is an actual photograph of the school, not a drawing.   Little Beaver Historical Society

The building on the left sat on the same area where the current Sewage Plant of Monaca now sits and is the building that burned down in 1876.   The larger building on the right of the picture was still standing when they were constructing the RR tunnel coming into Monaca.   You can see quite a few of the children on the porch roof; there are also some on the lower porch and standing around the building.

Note all the buildings on the hillside behind the school. They were all torn down when the railroad tracks were laid in that area.   For orientation…. the Beaver Valley Alloy Company is currently just on the other side of where these buildings once stood.   The roadway that is running horizonal in front of the school buildings was Factory Street (now Pennsylvania Avenue Extension); the road coming toward the bottom of the picture was First Street (now Pennsylvania Avenue).

During the temporary absence of Dr. Taylor, on Aug 22, 1876, the main building accidentally caught fire and was totally destroyed.   It was a loss of $25,000, but the insurance would only pay $10,300.   This loss caused the school to close after 10 and ½ years of successful business.   The closing was due to the heavy expense involved in erecting a new building, the shortness of time, and the 2 ½ years of the first contract still remaining.   Thus, the Soldiers' Orphan School ceased forever.   The attendance at the time of the fire was 180 students.

The photo below shows entering Monaca on former Factory Street (now Pennsylvania Avenue Ext) and the empty lot area of the former portion of the school that burned in 1876 (smaller pointer). To the top, left of the photo is the remaining Soldiers' Orphan's building (larger pointer).

A view of construction taking place on the Pennsylvania Avenue RR arch - 1903

Little Beaver Historical Society

NOTE: As with so many of these older photographs, if you take time to look closely, so many other aspects of Monaca are revealed. Ex. The original steeple of the German Lutheran Church can be seen (top right); a small shelter was once located within the cemetery (right side); one of the towers of the Ohio River bridge is visible (top right); Water Cure/Thiel College/Central Hotel tower is visible just to the left of the larger pointer.

The 1870 census sheets showed the following at the Soldier's Orphan School:
William Taylor-Professor, Clara Taylor—wife of Wm.; Mary M. Taylor 20-teacher; the Taylor's other children: Elizabeth, Eleanor, James, John, Harry; Kate Baker—seamstress; Mary Hogt—cook; John Hughes—laborer; James Neil 70—teacher; Nancy Thompson 48—teacher; Robert Thompson 24-teacher

ORPHANS' SCHOOL – 1870 Census

Name	Age	Sex	Race	Status
Maxwell Hiram	14	M	W	at School
Maxwell James	11	M	W	at School
Marquis William	14	M	W	at School
Moore John	13	M	W	at School
Murphy William	15	M	W	at School
Mullen Samuel	13	M	W	at School
Olcott James	15	M	W	at School
O'Brien Thomas	13	M	W	at School
Powel Albert	13	M	W	at School
Patterson John	9	M	W	at School
Patterson James	8	M	W	at School
Taufer John	13	M	W	at School
Murphy Fred	11	M	W	at School
McKee John	12	M	W	at School
Rollings George	13	M	W	at School
Reed John	11	M	W	at School
Riddle George	12	M	W	at School
Rutter John	11	M	W	at School
Rutter James	9	M	W	at School
Southward Thomas	15	M	W	at School
Solsby James	12	M	W	at School
Solsby Thomas	15	M	W	at School
Stevens William	13	M	W	at School
Temple John	15	M	W	at School
Wike Wesler	14	M	W	at School
Wike Albert	10	M	W	at School
Ray Frank	10	M	W	at School
Young John	12	M	W	at School
Young Jesse	10	M	W	at School
Mullen Drusilla	14	F	W	at School
Muller Nancy	12	F	W	at School
Nelson Lydia	15	F	W	at School
Nelson Sarah	13	F	W	at School
Olcott Delphine	13	F	W	at School
O'Brien Mary	11	F	W	at School
Patterson Nancy	13	F	W	at School
Purvis Allice	12	F	W	at School
Prentice Elizabeth	13	F	W	at School
Prentice Martha	11	F	W	at School
Prentice Sarah	9	F	W	at School
Heasley Frances	15	F	W	at School
Hershey Malissa	12	F	W	at School
Hoit Ada E	15	F	W	at School
Howel Mary	15	F	W	at School
Hutchison Eva	15	F	W	at School
Hart Martha	11	F	W	at School
Hart Adalade	9	F	W	at School
Jenkins Sarah	12	F	W	at School
Kruse Anna	10	F	W	at School
Magee Margaret	14	F	W	at School
Marquis Lucy	15	F	W	at School
Marquis Ella	12	F	W	at School
Renolds Loretta	15	F	W	at School
Renolds Ida	14	F	W	at School
Reed Isabel	15	F	W	at School
Reed Rebecca	14	F	W	at School
Shafer Laura	14	F	W	at School
Temple Mary	14	F	W	at School
Thompson Mary	14	F	W	at School
May Elenor	15	F	W	at School
Young Harriet	14	F	W	at School
Young Mary	12	F	W	at School
Zerby Emma	14	F	W	at School
Jones Laura	13	F	W	at School
Allen Sarah	12	F	W	at School
Brown Eunice	14	F	W	at School
Bennet Eliza	16	F	W	at School
Bremmer Harriet	11	F	W	at School
Bitner Mary	13	F	W	at School
Bitner Martha	11	F	W	at School
Bitner Anna	8	F	W	at School
Burgess Jane	15	F	W	at School
Burgess Mary	11	F	W	at School
Burns Susan	10	F	W	at School
Cook Anna	14	F	W	at School
Cole Amanda	15	F	W	at School
Cole Irene	14	F	W	at School
Cole Carrier	12	F	W	at School
Carney Eliza	13	F	W	at School
Carney Jennie	12	F	W	at School
Craven Martha	8	F	W	at School
Dawson Amanda	15	F	W	at School
Dolr Malissa	14	F	W	at School
Ewing Malinda	11	F	W	at School
Ewing Sarah	8	F	W	at School
Fulconer Sarah	15	F	W	at School
Grubaugh Mary	12	F	W	at School
Grancly Francis	15	F	W	at School
Grancly Celia	13	F	W	at School
Guthrie Clara	10	F	W	at School
Hanson Julia	8	F	W	at School

Thiel Hall at Phillipsburg - 129 Fourth Street (originally called Hanover Street)
Dec 1865 - a Lutheran Institution of higher learning of the Pittsburgh Synod was established; it became known as Thiel College – 1866.
- It was founded as a coeducational institution in 1869 at Greensburg, PA as the result of a meeting at the Lutheran Church Pittsburgh Synod convention between Dr. William Passavant and A. Louis Thiel.   It would become a college to serve western Pennsylvania.
A. Louis and Barbara Thiel gave $4,000 to his pastor, Rev. G. A. Wenzel, D.D. to start the school.   The Thiel's made their gift because they wanted to "give back" and share their profits made from investments in the oil region in western Pennsylvania.   Their $4,000 would be equivalent to over $60,000 nowadays.
Reverend Dr. William Passavant was chosen because he campaigned for organizing a Lutheran college in the region for many years; with this passion, he was more than willing to become involved.
In the spring of 1866, the former Water Cure building / Hotel of Cimotti was purchased; later an adjoining house and lot were also bought.   The former hotel and ballroom received the title of *Thiel Hall*.
Sep 1, 1870 - Thiel College was officially incorporated and opened.
The College was located where the current Monacatootha Apartments now stand (2016).

The hotel and ballroom were set aside for religious services, to the sacred purpose of Christian education.
Professor (Rev.) Giese, of Milwaukee, and five students were the first instructor and students of the school.
      Rev. W. Kopp was added to the staff by the close of the first year.
      Rev. H. E. Jacobs D.D., L.L.D., assisted by Prof J. F. Feltshans of PA College, Gettysburg were hired when Rev. Giese accepted a call to NY.
Sep 1871 - Thiel College in Phillipsburg (Monaca) was moved to the Academy Building in Greensville, PA.

courtesy of the BCHR&LF

Formerly the Cimotti and Central Hotel – became Thiel College, founded by Reverend W. A. Passavant in Phillipsburg (Monaca) in 1866.
    (Note the "Central Hotel" sign on the right-hand side of the building.)

Courtesy Beaver County Historical Research and Landmarks Foundation

This photo shows one of the dormitories used for Thiel College - at 200 Fifth Street Monaca.
(This building would have sat along the block where the Monacatootha Apartment building now sits on Fifth Street.)

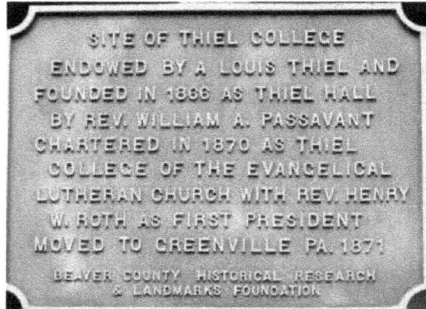

SITE OF THIEL COLLEGE
ENDOWED BY A LOUIS THIEL AND
FOUNDED IN 1866 AS THIEL HALL
BY REV. WILLIAM A. PASSAVANT
CHARTERED IN 1870 AS THIEL
COLLEGE OF THE EVANGELICAL
LUTHERAN CHURCH WITH REV. HENRY
W. ROTH AS FIRST PRESIDENT
MOVED TO GREENVILLE PA. 1871
BEAVER COUNTY HISTORICAL RESEARCH
& LANDMARKS FOUNDATION

This plaque is located at the corner of Fourth Street and Pennsylvania Avenue.

The 1870 census enumeration had the following listed for Thiel College:

Butcher's Business College – Reeves Building, Beaver Falls
       This became known as Garfield Business Institute and they had a branch in Monaca.

Garfield Business Institute –2590 Ridge Road
1977 to 1990
       1895 - Originally known as Butcher's Business College in Beaver Falls.
       It became known as Garfield College, Business College and was in the Reno Building at 170 Madison
          Street in Rochester by 1917. They were then located in the Reeves Building in Beaver Falls
          and opened for class in Aug, 1977 in Monaca on Marshall Road.
       In May 1985, they moved to the former Fifth Ward School building at 2590 Ridge Road where it
          was located as of Aug 1990.

———

Info-Age Computer School of Beaver County – 2590 Ridge Road (the old Fifth Ward
1990 to?   Elementary building),
       Founded in 1984 by Dr. Anthony J. Meta and several associates.
       It was privately owned.   A sister school to Garfield Business Institute.

Garfield Business Institute — **Info-Age** COMPUTER SCHOOL

PRESENTS AN

OPEN HOUSE

WHEN: Wednesday, May 15, 1985, at 7:00 p.m., and Saturday, May 18, 1985, at 11:00 a.m.

WHERE: 2590 Ridge Road, Monaca, Pennsylvania, 15061. Formerly the Monaca Fifth Ward Elementary School.

WHO: New High School Graduates and others interested in modern Secretarial and Business Programs; parents, friends, educators, business people welcome.

WHY: See our modern State-of-the-Art equipment and facilities. Hands-on demonstrations in our computer labs. Review our modern up to date curriculum, financial costs, job placement program, and other facts about the New Garfield Business Institute.

HOW: Call (412) 728-4050 to tell us you are coming. Refreshments served.

Get A Head Start On Your Career,
GO GARFIELD!

Just for general information – Garfield Business Institute was then located in New Brighton and in 2006 I found – "ADVANTAGE TRAINING, INC. (formerly GARFIELD BUSINESS INSTITUTE) 430 Corporation Drive Aliquippa, PA 15001."

Other local colleges

Although the following educational institutes are not located in Monaca Borough, some of them have been in existence since the mid 1800s and many residents of Monaca have attended and received their continued educational learning at them.

Beaver County Commercial College – opened in about 1902

BEAVER COUNTY COMMERCIAL COLLEGE, Beaver, Pa.

We teach Bookkeeping, Shorthand and Typewriting, and all other commercial branches practically. Business men recognize the merits of our school and apply to us for office help. Fall term opens August 30th. Write for catalogue. **W. P. POLLOCK, Principal.**

1909 ad

———

There were two colleges found in 1917 that residents of Monaca may have attended:
       Duff's College – Business College – 7ths Avenue and 10th Street, Beaver Falls.
       Westminster College – College – New Wilmington, PA

———

Geneva College – Beaver Falls

Geneva College opened its doors on Thursday, Apr 20, 1848.   It was originally founded and named as "Geneva Hall" in honor of Geneva, Switzerland, the center of the Reformed faith movement.   This college was originally located in Northwood, Ohio, moving to Beaver Falls in 1880.   Several locations for the new site of the institute were considered before the "College Hill" neighborhood in Beaver Falls was decided upon.   The land at the site of the current college campus was donated by the Harmony Society.   Old Main is the oldest building currently on the campus; it was completed in 1881.   By 1865, the college was listed as being fully co-educational, due to opening a Female Seminary just three years after it began.   It also opened its doors to freed southern slaves in about 1865, "an uncommon practice during the post-Civil War period."

————

Community College of Beaver County -   1 Campus Drive, off Poplar Drive, Center Township

Very often referenced as CCBC.   Originally formed and located in Freedom, PA.   They leased a few floors of the Freedom National Bank building along with 17 vacant storefronts for classrooms and offices.   CCBC moved to Center Township and began to create its own campus in 1971.   In 1976, the Golden Dome was built.   CCBC added an aviation building in 1990; the Aviation Sciences Center is located in Beaver Falls, PA. Later in the spring of 2017, the college completed a renovation program which completely updated the campus.   CCBC celebrated their 50th anniversary in May, 2017.

————

Penn State / Pennsylvania State University – Beaver Campus - Brodhead Road, Center Township

Opened in 1965.   The college admitted 97 students for its first semester.

Campus sits on property that once was the Hartenbach family home and farm and The Beaver County Tuberculosis Sanitarium (see Medical section for more on the Sanitarium).

The building that served as the administration building for Penn State from 1965 through 2004 was the original building of the Sanitarium.

University Drive entrance off Brodhead Road (by duck pond)

————

Beaver County Vocational Technical School   aka   Beaver County Career and Technology Center

Located at 145 Poplar Drive – Center Township

The following information was taken directly from their web page:

(Their wording gave a much clearer explanation of what they do/offer.)

"The Beaver County Career & Technology Center is a full-time career and technology center that serves the youth of Beaver County in Pennsylvania. The Beaver County CTC officially opened its doors in the fall of 1978 under the name of the Beaver County Area Vocational Technical School. The school is located in Center Township (Pennsylvania)   adjacent to the Community College of Beaver County.

The Beaver County CTC is dedicated to providing programs consisting of high quality, cutting-edge technical training integrated with a strong academic education and an emphasis on critical thinking, problem-solving, decision-making, and team-building skills. The curriculum is closely tied to the needs of business and industry. Through twice-yearly Craft Committee meetings, advisors guide program development to assure that the curriculum and equipment match the needs and standards of employers. Employers tell us what skills are needed for success in their fields and those are the skills we teach. Instructors align course curriculums with the skills employers need for employees to be successful."

They offer a tuition-free education to high school students from all of the fourteen Beaver County School Districts through citizens' and businesses' taxes.

*** *** *** *** ***
*** *** ***

Library

Post Office

LIBRARY

The Monaca Public Library had a few locations before becoming situated in 2000 at 609 Pennsylvania Avenue.

In 1937, the library occupied a room in the old part of the municipal building when it was at 926 Penna Avenue. The library moved into a room on the first floor that was formerly occupied by the Monaca tax collector. The library was a project of the Monaca Junior Woman's Club and started in Dec 1933. Club members were in the library each evening to supply patrons with books. There were approximately 1,500 books for both children and adults in the library in 1937.

Wagner Memorial Library / Monaca Public Library – corner of Eighth Street and Pennsylvania Avenue
　　　　　Establish in 1933.
　　　　　First located in the Mullen Building – located Twelfth Street and Pennsylvania Avenue.
　　　　　1937 moved to the Municipal Building on Pennsylvania Avenue.
　　　　　1940 the Monaca Junior Women's Club still had control of the library.
　　　　　1970 to 1973 the library was closed while it relocated to 1018 Pennsylvania Avenue.
　　　　　1981/1982 it relocated again into the Wagner home at 319 Eighth Street and was
　　　　　　　　renamed Wagner Memorial Library.
　　　　　　　　The house was donated by Dr. John Wagner of Pittsburgh as a memorial to his family.
　　　　　　　　o　1990 a gazebo was added to the property.
　　　　　Wagner Memorial Library closed its doors for good the first of Jul 29, 2000.
　　　Now called *Monaca Public Library* was relocated once again to 609 Pennsylvania Avenue /
　　　　　　corner of Pennsylvania Avenue and Sixth Street. Opened at this location Aug 1, 2000.

1018 Pennsylvania Avenue location.　　　　　　　　　　　　Photo courtesy BCHR&LF

Former Wagner home and former location of the Monaca Library (faces Eighth Street).

Location of the Monaca Library (2015).
Corner of Sixth Street and Pennsylvania Avenue (former Graeser building).

The library has once again moved locations ----- as of mid 2017, it is located on the 2nd floor of the C. J. Mangin Building – corner of Indiana Avenue and Tenth Street.

*** *** ***

POST OFFICE

1856 – first post office of Phillipsburg was established under the name of Water Cure.
      Although the name of the town was Phillipsburg - that name had to be changed because there was another town in PA with the same name.

     The first location was most likely the Water Cure Sanitarium since Dr. Clement
      Baeltz was the manager of the Sanitarium and Dec 6, 1956 he was appointed the first postmaster. Many publications state it was first located opposite the old cemetery on Pennsylvania Avenue and this was the location of the Sanitarium.

1858 to 1881– the post office location was in the Knapper Building - now 111 Fourth Street (was the Knapper home, then the Bechtel home).

Jul 20, 1892 – the post office name officially became Monaca / Borough of Monaca.

Sep 1903 – petition was passed around requesting the removal of the local post office from its present location to the new Keystone Improvement Company's Building (Keystone Building) at 1016 Pennsylvania Avenue.

1906 to 1934 - was located in the Keystone Building, then to the new Batchelor Building.
      David Kay 1906-1907   George Carner 1916   Mrs. Ida Kay 1907-1913
      George Weinman 1916-1922   Lenore Pipes 1913-1916   Frank Dindinger 1922-1934

In Nov 1914, electric lights were installed in the post office to replace the gas jets.   This improvement was hailed "with delight by local folk," who in the past years had trouble reading the "combinations of their letter boxes after dusk."

Jul 1, 1917 – city delivery was established.

Jan 16, 1928 – mounted delivery service was set up for Fourth and Fifth Wards.

Sep 8, 1928 – resolution asking the federal government to erect a modern post office as adopted since the post office was housed in a leased storeroom.
      ....no building was erected exclusively for the post office.

Aug, 1930 - the Batchelor Furniture Building at 1026 Pennsylvania Avenue........across Pennsylvania Avenue from the post office's 1963 building location. (This Pennsylvania Avenue location became Callaghan's Pharmacy which had been at 310 Ninth Street.) While located in the new Batchelor Building on Pennsylvania Avenue, there was the post office and a large storeroom on the 1st floor the new building and office suites on the 2nd floor.

-The new Batchelor Building adjoined the Batchelor Furniture and undertaking establishment on Pennsylvania Avenue.

-The new Batchelor Building was just completed earlier in Aug 1930 (a few days before the post office relocated in it. It was a two-storey structure, made of limestone, front trimmed with antique marble. The post office and a large storeroom comprise the first floor while several modern suites make up the second floor..........occupied by Dr. Harry T. Ellsworth (Dentist), Robert E. McCreary and John Prather (attorneys), Dr. John A. Riedel (Optometrist), and Miss Ann Grater (Beauty specialist).

Postmasters in this location were: Weinman again 1934-1935, George Lay 1935-1940, Frank Zinke, Jr. 1940 to at least 1963.

Apr 1961 – lot adjacent to the former George Washington School was determined as the site for the new post office building to be constructed. A local builder would construct the building and then lease it to the Post Office Department. This was done so taxes could still be collected on parcel since it wouldn't be owned by the government.

Apr 28, 1963 – New Post Office building was dedicated at 1015 Pennsylvania Avenue. It originally was beside the George Washington School building at that time. (The school was torn down and made into the current fountain/park area.)

Aug 1998 through Feb 1999 – discussion was to build a new U.S. Postal Service Office on property owned by the Monaca Volunteer Fire Department No. 1 ----- Pacific Avenue (across from Monaca Bowling Lanes).

- o The only building on the property in 1999 was garage owned by the fire department where emergency equipment was stored.
- o The fire department decided not to sell the land.

Fun Fact: *It is a rare sighting to currently find a mail box; they were at one time plentifully located throughout all areas of Beaver County and other communities.*

The post offices in this area no longer use these boxes and have removed almost every single one of them. The Monaca Post Office has two of these mail boxes set up at the front of the post office building for off hour mail drop offs. If you have never seen one up close, stop by and have a look. Also, in the rear of the Monaca Post Office, there are two slightly modified versions of them that the post office has set up for convenient drive up drop off of mail.

At front of the post office

At rear of the post office

Condensed list of post masters and post office locations:

Clement Baeltz, appointed postmaster Dec 6, 1856. He most likely received and mailed from
his home or the Sanitarium.
Anthony Knapper, appointed postmaster Feb 16, 1858 until 1877 – he lived at 111 Fourth Street
George Bechtel, appointed postmaster May 16, 1877 until 1881 – the Bechtels had moved into the
house located at 111 Fourth Street.
Bucheit Building on 703 Indiana Avenue - Michael J. Bucheit, appointed postmaster 1881-1888.
George Bechtel was postmaster again 1888-1892 and it was at 111 Fourth Street again.
Bucheit was postmaster again 1892-1893 and the post office was located at 813 Pennsylvania Avenue.
Kirk House – 1893-1897 – at 216 Sixth Street.
Agnes Mullen was post master in 1897 and the post office was at Fifth and Sixth Streets.
John H. Glasser – 1897-1906 – the post office was at 715 Pennsylvania Avenue.
John H. married Vinnie J.; they resided on Indiana Avenue.
Vesta A. Baker was Asst. Postmaster 1902/03.
David Kaye was appointed post master in Jul 1906.
Ida M. Kaye was appointed in Sep 1907.
Lenore Jolly Pipes was appointed post master in Dec 1913.
George W. Weinman, appointed in Oct 1916.
Frank T. Dindinger – was appointed in 1922-1934.
George W. Weinman – 1934.
George E. Lay was acting postmaster and appointed postmaster Apr 6, 1935. He died in 1940.
Frank H. Zinke was postmaster for 25 years – 1940–1965.
Walter Cronin – was acting post master 1965-1968.
Edward T. Anderson was appointed post master in Jul 1981.

Former bank to the left   Fountain plaza to the right
1963 to present U.S. Post Office building

W. P. A. (Works Progress Administration

aka   Work Projects Administration)

Street construction and

Monaca Water Works building

W. P. A.   -   Works Progress Administration
aka
Work Projects Administration

All of the following were in conjunction with the New Deal agency
- started by an executive order signed by President Franklin D Roosevelt May 6, 1933.
- was one of many Great Depression relief programs created under the auspices of the Emergency Relief Appropriations Act signed by Roosevelt in Apr 1933.
- American New Deal agency employing millions of unemployed people to carry out public works projects.
- between 1935 and 1943 the W.P.A. provided almost eight and a half million jobs to Americans who would have otherwise been on relief rolls.

1933 – 1934 – C.W.A. = Civil Works Administration.
1933 – 1938 – F.E.R.A. = Federal Emergency Relief Administration.
1935 – 1939 – W.P.A. = Works Progress Administration.
    The above 3 agencies were reorganized and effective Jul 1, 1939 the FWA (Federal Works Agency was established.   Their objective – Provided jobs to unemployed works on public projects sponsored by federal, state, or local agencies; and on defense and war related projects; and to unemployed youth through National Youth Administration (NYA) projects.   The FWA was abolished Dec 4, 1942, effective Jun 30, 1943.

W.P.A.= Works Progress Administration – renamed in 1939 as the Work Projects Administration.

In addition to doing physical work, the W.P.A. also had workers who sewed clothing and bed
    sheets to be used by the downtrodden.   Library books were delivered on horseback
    to rural outposts.   Slums were cleared, sick persons were helped, toys were repaired,
    and there was even electricity provided to those who had never seen an electric light.
    There was probably nothing they could not do.

The main accomplishment of the W.P.A. was that they provided dignity to Americans who were
    already relying on or would have had to begin groveling for a handout.

1933 – W.P.A. project enlarged the 1889 wharf or boat landing in the river. It would have been along
    the river bank to one side of the Monaca pump house.
    It was sometimes called the "hog back."
    Permission to construct a wharf along the Monaca river shore line was secured from the War
    Department which granted a maximum length of 1600 feet.   When completed, the wharf
    was 800 feet long and the river wall was 21 feet high, the terrace wall was 14 feet high,
    and the wharf proper was over 60 feet wide.
    It was constructed of approximately 7000 perch of cut stone.

1935 to 1937 – W.P.A. project was in the area above the Monaca Water Works.
    Two old houses with the included land were purchased. The houses were razed to permit the
    straightening of Atlantic Avenue and Eighth Street. In the middle of the street near this
    section a fountain surrounded by a circular wall of cut stone was built, along the sidewalk
    on the river side of the street a neat stone wall was constructed, atop the terrace a lily
    pond with a fountain in the center was erected and a band stand and grotto with
    retaining walls of cut and dressed stone were placed and arranged in an artistic effect.

1936 – The W.P.A. refaced the Monaca Water Works building. It was built in 1895 of brick at 599 Atlantic Avenue.
    The W.P.A. refaced the building with cut stone that was quarried in the borough.   The building then and
    now resembles a castle.   The W.P.A. also raised water pumps inside the building.

The retaining wall and all the stone work from the Water Works building up to and including that on Sixth Street
were done by the W.P.A. and its workers.

They placed marker stones on the Pump House and the Retaining wall that read "W.P.A. 1940."

The W.P.A. did not limit their work to just Monaca and its area; they did many projects in the area from Coraopolis to Midland. But that's another story and information for other publications. I will give them due credit at this time by quoting and copying the following information I found.

From 1935 to 1943, Works Progress Administration workers built:
- 650,000 miles of roads
- 125,000 civilian and military buildings
- 78,000 bridges
- 800 airports (built, improved or enlarged)
- 700 miles of airport runway

Workers also were responsible for:
- 900 million hot lunches served to school children
- 225,000 musical concerts presented to 150 million people
- 1,500 nursery schools operated
- 475,000 artworks 276 books and
  701 pamphlets created

W.P.A. street construction

1936-37 – W.P.A. project – two old houses were razed to permit the straightening of Atlantic Avenue at Sixth Street. Removal of these buildings altered the layout of the streets and made room for the previously described circular wall of cut stone built along the sidewalk on the river side, as well as the lily pond with a fountain in the center.

    These pictures show how the area looked prior to the 1936/37 W.P.A. project razing 2 houses and then after adding the circular cut stone structure that once had a fountain enclosed within it.

water works   1900 view of Sixth Street and Atlantic Avenue

*The building on the bottom/center with smoke stack (10) is former Water Works building. Where the stream of smoke ends is the where Atlantic Avenue was straightened and is the location of the circular stone structure now standing.

water works   More recent picture of same area

The area of this circular stone structure was often referred to as Five Points by local residents.

.....A P.W.A. grant in 1933 (which was the first P.W.A. project in Pennsylvania) let the Borough extend service to the Fourth and Fifth wards and built a booster station pipe system.

.....The W.P.A. workers built Allaire Park (now Antoline Park).

.....The W.P.A. worked closely with the C.C.C. (Civilian Conservation Corps) which was another New Deal agency.

.....The W.P.A. approved the Monaca project, for construction of a retaining wall on Fourteenth Street hill. It employed 40 men for 40 months. Work began shortly after Feb 1, 1937.

.....Between 1934 and 1937, the Monaca School District received special monies from grants amounting to approximately $73,700 from the W.P.A. towards making improvements to their schools

.....There was money spent through W.P.A. grants for repairs to the athletic field, plotting of all school grounds, and a complete inventory of all school properties.

.....In 1937, W.P.A. projects that were beginning were the grading of the Marshall road athletic field, adding a regular size football field and several tennis courts. There was a project to repair sewer lines in the athletic field, too.

A retaining wall around the Third Ward School building, made out of rough cut stone, 22 inches high and one foot wide with a rough top course. The wall was necessary to keep the sand from washing out onto the street and sidewalk, as well as adding to the appearance of the building and playground. The wall was completed late Aug 1937.

.....In Oct 1939, the Monaca School Board contacted the W.P.A. for improvements to be made at the high school field following a fire that destroyed the grandstand.

.....1940 – the W.P.A. project was nearing completion of their projects, including the new stone facing being added along with adding the 2nd storey on to the pump house.

The pointed object in the middle of the picture came from the old Monaca-Rochester Bridge.
When the bridge was torn down, both Rochester and Monaca received these objects from the peaks of the old bridge.

There was also a retaining wall constructed along the 14th Street Hill road in the 1930s. This wall is still standing today.

MONACA WAR EFFORTS

Roll of Honor
Tank Farm – Potter Township

War Efforts

Monaca residents and the surrounding communities were all involved in all war efforts over the years. I found many statements and articles about war bonds and/or the rationing programs; every American man, woman, and child was affected in one way or another with WWI and WWII. Everyone was urged to participate in the war efforts and local newspapers and publications seemed to be the major form of spreading the word and providing the information to the general public. For anyone who does not know about the rationing programs, here is a shortened version of them, as well as some examples of the advertising and actual rationing materials. From all articles and information found, Monaca, Center, and Potter residents did everything they could to support the war efforts. They participated in the Rationing programs, the War Bond programs, and even the Victory Gardens.

Rationing programs

WWI

In WWI, the United States' allies in Europe were facing starvation. Their farmlands had been turned into battlefields, or the farmers were participating in the war. Herbert Hoover was appointed head of the U.S. Food Administration by President Woodrow Wilson to form a voluntary program for Americans to support as a war effort. It involved managing a wartime supply, conservation, distribution, and transportation of food. There were posters found everywhere encouraging citizens to conserve their usage and consumption of wheat, fats, meat, and sugar. They were asked not to waste groceries and to eat more fresh fruits and vegetables since they were too hard to transport overseas. There was advertising of "meatless Tuesdays" and "wheatless Wednesdays" to also encourage Americans to curtail their eating habits so more could be shipped to the solders.

There were canning demonstrations at local Grange buildings and recipes published and distributed that had substitutions for the limited provisions. All the conservation and support that the American citizens provided allowed the food shipments to Europe to be doubled within a year.

WWII

Not long after America entered into WWII, the U.S. government found that voluntary conservation was not as effective as it was in WWI. Food shortages began almost immediately with the economy shifting to war production almost overnight. The U.S. government made the decision to ration certain essential items and on Jan 30, 1942, the Emergency Price Control Act granted the Office of Price Administration (OPA) approval to set price limits and ration food to discourage hoarding. They also felt that this would be the fair way for equal distribution of the scarce items. What did this mean for the American citizens? It meant that even if you could afford more, you could not simply walk into a store and buy sugar, butter, meat, and other items in whatever quantity or whenever you wanted to. Nor could you pull in to a gasoline station and just fill up your car whenever you wanted to. The government only allowed you to purchase a small amount of the items they labelled as being rationed.

By the spring of 1942, there were restrictions on imported foods and transportation of goods was curtailed due to the shortage of rubber tires. With this food rationing system in place, Americans could not purchase sugar without government issued food coupons. In Nov 1942 vouchers for coffee were introduced and by Mar 1943 meats, cheese, fats, canned fished, canned milk, silk, nylon, shoes, and other processed foods were added to the rationed list. Every American citizen was entitled to the war ration books. Once an application was made, you would receive a book containing stamps that could be used to buy restricted items. Each rationed item was given an amount of points based on its availability. You could use 48 "blue points" to buy canned, bottled, or dried foods and 64 "red points" to buy meat, fish, and dairy items each month (that is IF the items were in stock at the market). Shoes, household appliances, and many other items were among rationed goods. The OPA would accept the ration book applications and then issue ration books. Each book contained stamps that could be torn out in order to purchase food and other supplies.

"Types of rationing included:

    UNIFORM COUPON RATIONING (sugar is an example) provided equal shares of a single commodity to all consumers;

    POINT RATIONING provided equivalent shares of commodities by coupons issued for points which could be spent for any combination of items in the group (processed foods, meats, fats, cheese);

    DIFFERENTIAL COUPON RATIONING provided shares of a single product according to varying needs (gasoline, fuel oil); and

    CERTIFICATE RATIONING allowed individuals products only after an application demonstrated need (tires, cars, stoves, typewriters)."

*Major purchases such as automobiles, bicycles, and kitchen appliances required special certificates and proof of need.
*The government and military needed so many typewriters for communications, thus the need for their rationing.

There were four different series of war ration books that were issued over the periods of 1942 and 1943. The government had a fifth book prepared and ready, but none were needed, nor issued. Every member of a family, including children, was eligible to apply for a ration book.

Book One was issued five months after the U.S. entered the WWII in 1942.

    When this book was issued, the registrar would ask you, or the person who applied for your book, how much sugar you owned on that date. If you had any sugar, you were allowed to keep it, but stamps representing this quantity were torn from your group (except for a small amount which you were allowed to keep without losing any stamps). If your War Ration Book One was issued to you on application by a member of your family, the number of stamps torn from the books of the family was based on the amount of sugar owned by the family, and was divided as equally as possible among all the books issued to that family.

Book Two series was issued in Jan 1943.

    Instructions with this book stated "This book is the property of the United States Government. It is unlawful to sell or give it to any other person or to use it or permit anyone else to use it, except to obtain rationed goods for the person to whom it was issued. Persons who violate Rationing Regulations are subject to $10,000 fine or imprisonment, or both."

Book Three series was issued in Oct 1943.

Book Four series was issued toward the end of 1943.

On the application, at the bottom was the following:

READ BEFORE SIGNING
In accepting this book, I recognize that it remains the property of the United States Government. I will use it only in the manner and for the purposes authorized by the Office of Price Administration.

Most of the ration restrictions didn't end until Aug 1945; the restrictions and rationing on processed foods and other items like gasoline and fuel oil were removed, but the rationing of sugar was in place in some parts of the country until 1947. Sugar was the first item to be rationed since Japan caused our nation's supply of sugar to quickly be reduced by more than a third.

Along with the rationing books, citizens were asked to turn in old tires, raincoats, gloves, garden hoses, and rubber shoes and boots for recycling. To save rubber, Americans were also asked to cut back on their driving, to save gas by driving slower, and to share rides whenever possible. Gasoline was rationed nationwide in Dec 1942. Anything using metal was rationed and Americans were urged to turn in scrap metal for recycling. Women were urged to save waste fat and greases and turn them into the butchers who would pay for the fat and then sell it to rendering plants so it could be processed into explosives. Paper was needed for packing weapons and equipment to be shipped overseas, so scrap and used paper was also collected. With this tight rationing system, it didn't take long for misuse to crop up. The "black market" developed all over the country with forged ration stamps and stolen items that were illegally resold. Rationing ended when supplies were sufficient to meet demand. It has been recorded that by the end of WWII, there were over a hundred million of each of the ration books printed.

A condensed list of rationed items during WWII.

Rationed Items	Rationing Duration
Tires	January 1942 to December 1945
Cars	February 1942 to October 1945
Bicycles	July 1942 to September 1945
Gasoline	May 1942 to August 1945
Fuel Oil & Kerosene	October 1942 to August 1945
Solid Fuels	September 1943 to August 1945
Stoves	December 1942 to August 1945
Rubber Footwear	October 1942 to September 1945
Shoes	February 1943 to October 1945
Sugar	May 1942 to 1947
Coffee	November 1942 to July 1943
Processed Foods	March 1943 to August 1945
Meats, canned fish	March 1943 to November 1945
Cheese, canned milk, fats	March 1943 to November 1945
Typewriters	March 1942 to April 1944

*** *** *** *** ***

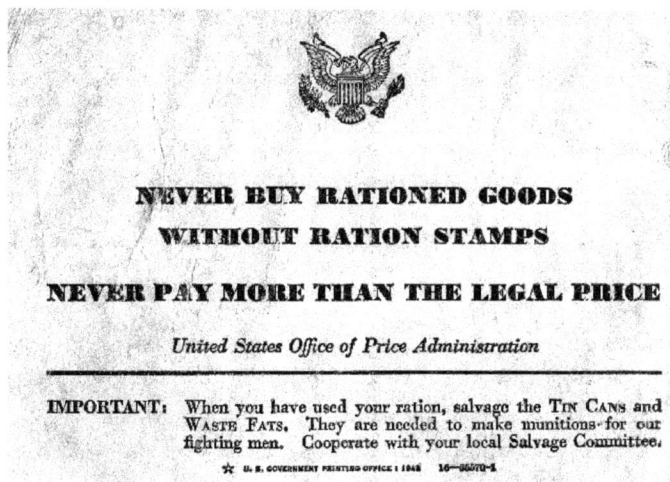

**NEVER BUY RATIONED GOODS
WITHOUT RATION STAMPS**

NEVER PAY MORE THAN THE LEGAL PRICE

United States Office of Price Administration

IMPORTANT: When you have used your ration, salvage the Tin Cans and Waste Fats. They are needed to make munitions for our fighting men. Cooperate with your local Salvage Committee.

☆ U. S. GOVERNMENT PRINTING OFFICE : 1945 16—35070-1

*** *** *** *** ***

HOW TO USE YOUR WAR RATION BOOK

IMPORTANT.—Before the stamps of the War Ration Book may be used, the person for whom it was issued must sign it as indicated in the book. The name of a person under 18 years of age may be signed either by such person or by his father, mother, or guardian.

For future reference, make and keep a record of the serial number of your book and the number of your issuing Ration Board, as indicated in your book.

Your first War Ration Book has been issued to you, originally containing 28 War Ration Stamps. Other books may be issued at later dates. The following instructions apply to your first book and will apply to any later books, unless otherwise ordered by the Office of Price Administration. In order to obtain a later book, the first book must be turned in. You should preserve War Ration Books with the greatest possible care.

1. From time to time the Office of Price Administration may issue Orders rationing certain products. After the dates indicated by such Orders, these products can be purchased only through the use of War Ration Books containing valid War Ration Stamps.

2. The Orders of the Office of Price Administration will designate the stamps to be used for the purchase of a particular rationed product, the period during which each of these stamps may be used, and the amounts which may be bought with each stamp.

3. Stamps become valid for use only when and as directed by the Orders of the Office of Price Administration.

4. Unless otherwise announced, the Ration Week is from Saturday midnight to the following Saturday midnight.
16—26640-1

5. War Ration Stamps may be used in any retail store in the United States.

6. War Ration Stamps may be used only by or for the person named and described in the War Ration Book.

7. Every person must see that his War Ration Book is kept in a safe place and properly used. Parents are responsible for the safekeeping and use of their children's War Ration Books.

8. When you buy any rationed product, the proper stamp must be detached in the presence of the storekeeper, his employee, or the person making delivery on his behalf. If a stamp is torn out of the War Ration Book in any other way than above indicated, it becomes void. If a stamp is partly torn or mutilated and more than one-half of it remains in the book, it is valid. Otherwise it becomes void.

9. If your War Ration Book is lost, destroyed, stolen, or mutilated, you should report that fact to the local Ration Board.

10. If you enter a hospital, or other institution, and expect to be there for more than 10 days, you must turn your War Ration Book over to the person in charge. It will be returned to you upon your request when you leave.

11. When a person dies, his War Ration Book must be returned to the local Ration Board, in accordance with the Regulations.

12. If you have any complaints, questions, or difficulties regarding your War Ration Book, consult your local Ration Board.

NOTE

The first stamps in War Ration Book One will be used for the purchase of sugar. When this book was issued, the registrar asked you, or the person who applied for your book, how much sugar you owned on that date. If you had any sugar, you were allowed to keep it, but stamps representing this quantity were torn from your book (except for a small amount which you were allowed to keep without losing any stamps). If your War Ration Book One was issued to you on application by a member of your family, the number of stamps torn from the books of the family was based on the amount of sugar owned by the family, and was divided as equally as possible among all these books.

EDU.075 ML

From Book One packet

UNITED STATES
OF AMERICA
War Ration Book One

WARNING

1 Punishments ranging as high as *Ten Years' Imprisonment or $10,000 Fine, or Both*, may be imposed under United States Statutes for violations thereof arising out of infractions of Rationing Orders and Regulations.

2 This book must not be transferred. It must be held and used only by or on behalf of the person to whom it has been issued, and anyone presenting it thereby represents to the Office of Price Administration, an agency of the United States Government, that it is being so held and so used. For any misuse of this book it may be taken from the holder by the Office of Price Administration.

3 In the event either of the departure from the United States of the person to whom this book is issued, or his or her death, the book must be surrendered in accordance with the Regulations.

4 Any person finding a lost book must deliver it promptly to the nearest Ration Board.

No. 22844 -190

OFFICE OF PRICE ADMINISTRATION

From Book Two

INSTRUCTIONS

1 This book is valuable. Do not lose it.

2 Each stamp authorizes you to purchase rationed goods in the quantities and at the times designated by the Office of Price Administration. Without the stamps you will be unable to purchase those goods.

3 Detailed instructions concerning the use of the book and the stamps will be issued from time to time. Watch for these instructions so that you will know how to use your book and stamps.

4 Do not tear out stamps except at the time of purchase and in the presence of the storekeeper, his employee, or a person authorized by him to make delivery.

5 Do not throw this book away when all of the stamps have been used, or when the time for their use has expired. You may be required to present this book when you apply for subsequent books.

Rationing is a vital part of your country's war effort. This book is your Government's guarantee of your fair share of goods made scarce by war, to which the stamps contained herein will be assigned as the need arises.

Any attempt to violate the rules is an effort to deny someone his share and will create hardship and discontent.

Such action, like treason, helps the enemy.

Give your whole support to rationing and thereby conserve our vital goods. Be guided by the rule:

"*If you don't need it, DON'T BUY IT.*"

☆ U. S. GOVERNMENT PRINTING OFFICE: 1942   16—20855-1

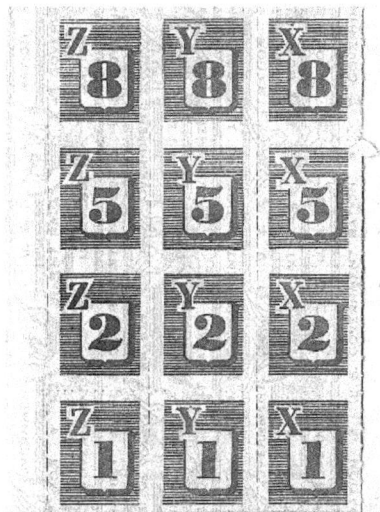

From Book Three

From Book Four

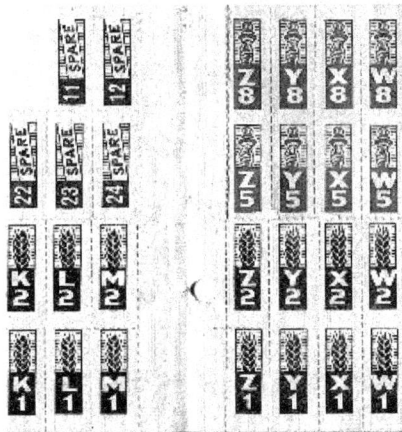

Points

Each cut of meat was assigned a point value per pound, based not on price or quality, but on scarcity. These point values varied throughout the war depending on supply and demand. "Variety meats" such as kidney, liver, brain, and tongue had little use for the military, so their point values were low. On May 3, 1944, thanks to a good supply, all meats except steak and choice cuts of beef were removed from rationing—temporarily.

*** *** *** *** ***

Ration coins (introduced in 1944) allowed retailers to give change back for food bought with ration stamps.

Ration Dates

MEATS, FATS, CHEESES
Red stamps P, Q and R in Ration Book 3 valid through July 31.

FRUITS AND VEGETABLES
Blue N. P. and Q stamps valid through Aug. 7 for the purchase of canned and frozen fruits, vegetables and soups. Blue R, S and T stamps will become valid Aug. 1.

COFFEE
Stamp 22 in Book 1 good for one pound through Aug. 11.

SUGAR
Coupon 13 in Book 1 good for five pounds through Aug. 15. Stamps 15 and 16 valid for five pounds each for use in home canning.

SHOES
Stamp 18 in Book 1 valid for one pair through Oct. 31.

GASOLINE
No. 7 coupons in new "A" books good for four gallons each.

FUEL OIL
No. 5 coupons valid for 11 gallons through Sept. 30. Period 1 coupons in new rations good for 10 gallons each through Jan. 3. 1-unit tickets good for 10 gallons; 5-unit tickets good for 50 gallons.

*** *** *** *** ***

The booklets or sheet with the "Mileage Ration" and "Fuel Oil Ration Coupons" had the following instructions, as well as a small form to be filled in by the dealer:

UNITED STATES OF AMERICA ★ ★ OFFICE OF PRICE ADMINISTRATION
MILEAGE RATION IDENTIFICATION FOLDER
B   C   (T)   E-R

IMPORTANT INSTRUCTIONS—1. This ration cannot be used for any purpose other than that which it was applied for and issued.
2. The type and serial numbers of coupons in this folder must be the same as those shown on the front cover.
3. Within five days after discontinuance of the use for which this ration was issued, this folder and all unused coupons must be returned to the War Price and Rationing Board.
4. "B," "C," or "T" coupons can be used only for gasoline transferred into the fuel tank of the vehicle, or a vehicle of the fleet, described on the front cover unless proper approval by a War Price and Rationing Board for bulk transfer is shown.
5. "B," "C," "E," or "R" rations must be returned to the War Price and Rationing Board within five days after any renewal of the ration becomes valid.
6. "T" rations must be returned to your District ODT Office within five days after the expiration date shown on the folder.
7. "E" and "R" coupons can be used only for obtaining gasoline for non-highway equipment and uses, and not for registered or commercial vehicles.
8. "B," "C," and "T" ration holders. You must surrender this folder and all unused coupons to your War Price and Rationing Board before selling your vehicle. The purchaser will not be issued a gasoline ration unless he presents the receipt which you receive at time of surrender.   16—37784-1

Fuel Oil Ration Coupons

"Dealers in fuel oil or their representatives are hereby authorized to deliver fuel oil to the above person or his agent for use at the above address, and are required to detach from this sheet coupons having a gallonage value equal to the quantity of oil delivered, in accordance with the rules and regulations of the Office of Price Administration in effect at the time of such delivery. At the time of delivery, the dealer or his agent must fill in the delivery record below."

*** *** *** *** ***

Feb. 7, 1944

SPECIAL NOTE:

Token program begins Feb. 27. One-point red tokens will be given in change for Red Stamps and one-point Blue Tokens for Blue Stamps. Stamps will be worth 10 points each. Tear Stamps out across Ration Book instead of up and down. Following Stamps become valid Feb. 27:

MEATS AND FATS

Red Stamps A8, B8 and C8 (Book Four) good for 10 points each, Feb. 27 through Mar. 20.

PROCESSED FOODS

Blue Stamps A8, B8, C8, D8 (Book Four) good for 10 points each, Feb. 27 through May 20. Following Stamps remain at present point values.

PROCESSED FOODS

Green Stamps G, H and J (Book Four) good Jan. 1 through Feb. 20.

Green Stamps K, L and M (Book Four) good Feb. 1 through Mar. 20.

MEATS AND FATS

Brown Stamps V (Book Three) good Jan. 23 through Feb. 26.

Brown Stamps W good Jan. 30 through Feb. 26.

Brown Stamps X good Feb. 6 through Feb. 26.

Brown Stamps Y good Feb. 13 through Mar. 20.

Brown Stamps Z good Feb. 20 through Mar 20.

SUGAR

Stamp No. 30 (Book Four) good for five pounds Jan. 16 through Mar. 31.

SHOES

Stamp No. 18 (Book One) good for one pair indefinitely. Airplane Stamp No. 1 (Book Three) good for one pair indefinitely.

FUEL OIL

Period No. 2 coupons good for ten gallons per unit through Feb. 7.

Period No. 3 coupons good for ten gallons per unit through Mar. 13.

Period No. 4 coupons and Period No. 5 coupons good for ten gallons per unit Feb. 8 through Sept. 30.

GASOLINE

No. 10 coupons in A book good for three gallons each Jan. 22 through Mar. 21.

B2 and C2 supplemental ration coupons good for five gallons each B1 and C1 coupons remain good for two gallons each. All coupons

Instructions with this listing stated:

Tear stamps out across Ration Book instead of up and down.
Sugar: Stamp No. 30 (Book Four) good for five pounds Jan 16 through Mar 31.
Fuel Oil: Period No. 2 coupons good for ten gallons per unit through Mar. 13.
Shoes: Airplane Stamp No. 1 (Book Three) good for one pair indefinitely.

***   ***   ***   ***   ***

1943 Sears, Roebuck and Co. catalog assured Americans that they could buy rationed shoes from Sears by mail. "*Simply detach War Ration Stamp No. 17 from your War Ration Book No. 1 (sugar and coffee book) and pin it to your order.*"

Even though the War Ration book states "void if detached." Under the shoe rationing order, the government permitted holders of War Rationing Book No. 1 to tear out War Ration Stamp No. 17 in order to attach it to orders when buying rationed shoes by mail.

Yes, You Can Buy Rationed Shoes from Sears by Mail

Simply detach War Ration Stamp No. 17 from your War Ration Book No. 1 (sugar and coffee book) and pin it to your order.

NO RATION COUPON IS NEEDED FOR THESE:
Soft and hard-soled house slippers, infants' soft-soled shoes, and rubber footwear such as arctics, gaiters, work, dress and toe rubbers.

Question: Can I buy Rationed Shoes by mail?
Answer: Yes.

Question: How?
Answer: Tear out War Ration Stamp No. 17 from your War Ration Book No. 1 (sugar and coffee book). Pin it to your order and send order in the regular way.

Question: Am I allowed to tear War Ration Stamp No. 17 out of War Ration Book No. 1?
Answer: Yes. Even though the War Ration Book states "void if detached." Under the shoe rationing order, the government permits holders of War Rationing Book No. 1 to tear out War Ration Stamp No. 17 in order to attach it to your order when buying rationed shoes by mail.

Question: Must I send money as well as War Ration Stamp?
Answer: Of course War Ration Stamp No. 17 merely permits you to buy shoes under the Rationing order. Handle all other details of your mail order in the usual way.

Question: If you cannot fill my order, will I get back my War Ration Stamp?
Answer: Yes, your War Ration Stamp and your money will be returned to you.

Question: Do I need to send in a War Ration Stamp on an even exchange?
Answer: No.

Question: Is War Ration Stamp No. 17 transferable?
Answer: Yes, among members of the same household. For example, mothers and fathers can use their War Ration Stamps to provide extra shoes for their children.

Question: Should I send in my complete War Ration Book with my mail order?
Answer: No. Send in War Ration Stamp No. 17 only when ordering shoes.

Question: How long may I use War Ration Stamp No. 17 in ordering shoes?
Answer: Until June 15th, 1943

Question: What happens after June 15, 1943?
Answer: The government will issue instructions as to the proper War Ration Stamp to use after that date. You will be advised through the newspapers and by radio

Question: What if I do not have a War Ration Book No. 1?
Answer: Apply to your local War Price and Rationing board.

Question: What if I have used all my No. 17 War Ration Stamps?
Answer: Apply to your local War Price and Rationing board for a shoe purchase certificate. Attach this certificate to your mail order.

HOW TO SHOP WITH WAR RATION BOOK TWO

... to Buy Canned, Bottled and Frozen Fruits and Vegetables; Dried Fruits, Juices and all Canned Soups

YOUR POINT ALLOWANCE MUST LAST FOR THE FULL RATION PERIOD

Plan How Many Points You Will Use Each Time Before You Shop

BUY EARLY IN THE WEEK   **BUY EARLY IN THE DAY**

SQUARE MEALS on SHORT RATIONS

WITH 337 WARTIME RECIPES

25¢

Americans!
SHARE THE MEAT
as a wartime necessity

To meet the needs of our armed forces and fighting allies, a Government order limits the amount of meat delivered to stores and restaurants.

To share the supply fairly, all civilians are asked to limit their consumption of beef, veal, lamb, mutton and pork to 2½ lbs. per person per week.

YOUR FAIR WEEKLY SHARE

Men, women and children over 12 yrs. old	**2½** Pounds per week
Children 6 to 12 yrs. old	**1½** Pounds per week
Children under 6 yrs. old	**¾** Pound per week

You can add these foods to your share: liver, sweetbreads, kidneys, brains and other variety meats; also poultry and fish.

HELP WIN THE WAR!
Keep within your share

FOODS PROCUREMENT COMMITTEE
War Production Board

Claude R. Wickard
Chairman

WAR RATION
BOOK ONE
(SUGAR)

☆

BUY WAR BONDS
AND STAMPS WITH
YOUR SAVINGS IN SUGAR

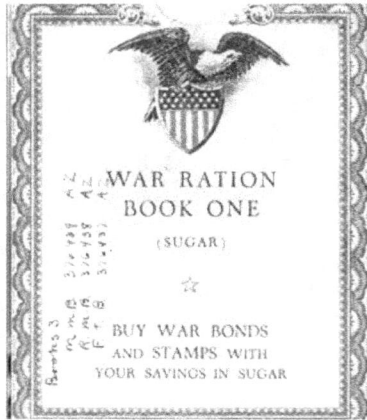

A May 1942 article was of interest since there was sugar and gasoline rationing going on.

Plans Complete For Sugar Registration In Monaca Next Week

Gasoline Rationing Registration Also Scheduled In Southside Town This Month

All persons residing in Monaca, regardless of age, must use a sugar ration stamp after May 4 in order to get sugar. It is necessary, therefore, that each person be registered and receive "War Ration Book One" during the following registration period:

May 4, 1 to 5 and 6 to 9 p. m. All persons whose last names begin with A to L, inclusive (if convenient).

May 5, 1 to 5 and 6 to 9—All persons whose last names begin with M to Z, inclusive (if convenient).

May 6 and 7—4 to 5 and 6 to 9—All residents of the First Ward are to register at the First Ward school; all residents of the Second Ward register at the Junior high school; all residents of the Third Ward register at the Third Ward school; all residents of the Fourth Ward register at the Fourth Ward school; all residents of the Fifth Ward register at the Marshall road school.

It is necessary for every individual who is not a member of the family to register in person. It is permissible for one adult person in each family to register for the entire immediate family. He should have the following information regarding each member to assist the registrar: Name, height, weight, age, color of hair, color of eyes, amount of sugar on hand.

GAS REGISTRATION

On May 13, 14 and 15, all car owners in Monaca must register for gasoline, and the following school buildings will be used for registration sites:

Marshall road school for residents of the Fourth and Fifth wards, 4 to 9 p. m. daily; Junior high school for residents of the First, Second and Third Wards, 4 to 9 p. m. daily.

Registrants must have owner's cards. Cards will be issued in three colors: White, 7 units; Blue, 11 units; Red, 15 units. Each consumer will receive a Basic (white) ration card or be required to file application for special (red and blue) card to fit his needs. The cards will last through June.

Monaca during the wars

Revolutionary War.............1775-1783
Anthony Baker – buried in the Baker Cemetery, 21st Street, Monaca

War of 1812..........1812-1815

Mexican War 1845-1848
John M. Srodes (Shrodes)

Civil War..........1861-1865
John M. Srodes (Shrodes)

Spanish American War 1898
William H. Hughes   Charles McCarthy   Lewis Weigle   H. S. Malone   David Mitchell

World War I...... - the First World War or the Great War – Jul 28, 1914 until Nov 11, 1918.
Died in war – Corp. Edward J. Scharchern, Privates Earl Hanshew and Sarafino Meichiorre, Corp Thomas McElwee, Private George A. Winkle.
Wounded – Sergeant Ralph Clarke, Sergeant William Murray, Private Andrew Kurtz, Private Robert Hunter.
Drs. James R Gormley, A.S. McKinley, and M.M. Mackall left their practices and entered the medical units.
Robert E McCreary, John Hanlon, Ralph Houser, Sarah Halleran, Molly McCarthy, and Caroline Ramer enlisted and served as nurses overseas.

World War II..........Jul 7, 1937/Sep 1, 1939 – Aug 14, 1945

Korean War........Jun 25, 1950 – Jul 27, 1953

Golf War .... 1990 – 1991

Iraq War ....2003 - 2011

Monaca residents were just as patriotic and supportive during all the military conflicts of the nations as all other American citizens.   To do their part in support of the war, many entertainment establishments would make admissions through war bond purchases only.   There were rallies and residents were encouraged to attend and purchase Defense Bonds /war bonds and stamps.   Savings and loan associations were authorized to act as agents in the distribution of Defense Bonds.   Citizens were encouraged to postpone spending and refrain from the buying of goods which demanded materials and labor from all businesses who should be concentrating on supporting the war effort.   Church services encouraged members of congregations to donate blood which would be used in saving the lives of thousands of wounded service men.

A few examples .....
Aug 1942 - The Roxy Theatre was the location of a program "Billion Dollar Month" which promoted the purchasing of bonds and stamps.   It was stated that a substantial amount was pledged in war bonds and stamps by those in attendance.

Jun 1944 - The Monaca American Legion Auxiliary aided in selling War Bonds.   The Auxiliary purchased a $100 bond and were looking for pledges and donation to the cause.

———————

In 1942, Monaca had a War Transportation Committee. They met with the war plants in the district to discuss workers transportation.   There was a growing problem of transportation facilities diminishing due to the drastic rubber shortage and lack of new equipment. Within the War Transportation Committee was a Traffic Committee that investigated the possibility of installing a passenger ferry to haul workers from Beaver and Vanport to the St. Joseph Lead Company plant and the new synthetic rubber plant.   By using a ferry system, it would eliminate a daily roundtrip now being done by a large volume of workers.

100% War Industry
NEEDS MEN and WOMEN

Also Boys 16 and 17 years of age who
can secure Work Permits.

PITTSBURGH TUBE CO.

Apply at Plant Office, Monaca, Pa., or U. S. Employment Office, Rochester, Pa.

U.S.E.S. Statement of Availability is required.

Aug 1944

ALL DAYLIGHT WORK FOR MEN AND WOMEN
WE WILL DEFINITELY EMPLOY WOMEN
AFTER THE WAR IS TOTALLY WON

**MEN AND WOMEN NEEDED FOR LABORING,
OPERATORS OF PIPE CUTTING MACHINES AND
TAPPING MACHINE OPERATORS**

Regular Work Week — 48 hours — 5½ days

GOOD WAGES — PIECE WORK — BONUS

PITTSBURGH SCREW and BOLT CORP.
COLONA DIVISION, MONACA

Apply U. S. E. S. or our office   Statement of
availability required.

May 1945

Other familiar advertising included with numerous want ads for employment were for boys 16 and 17 years old since the men were no longer as available being off and fighting in the war.   Women were definitely encouraged and did step in for the men.   Women were important in filling in where the shortfall of male workers applied. Many women were considered as "doing a man's work" as this picture below portraits.   Many ads from various companies and plants would have basically the same statements on their want ads in the employment section of local newspapers...............

WANTED
MEN and WOMEN

To Work on Army and Navy Ordnance Materiel, No
Experience Required.

**ALSO BOYS 16 AND 17 WHO ARE ABLE TO
PROCURE WORKING CERTIFICATES**

Women, here's your opportunity to help your husband,
brother, sweetheart, or friend in the service and make excellent wages while doing so!

We also need the following experi-----
Electricians, Lathe Operator-

APPLY --

Dec 3, 1943 – The United States Sanitary Manufacturing Company of Monaca and stock were sold
to The Richmond Radiator Company of Uniontown – a subsidiary of the Reynolds Metals
Company.   Although it was not disclosed the amount of the sale, Richmond paid cash for
the US Sanitary company which had an outstanding capitalization of $739,000.   The United
States Sanitary Manuf. Co. had more than 13 acres, four acres under roof, employed 600 to
700, produced cast iron enamel ware. Under a war directive, they had to discontinue normal
manufacturing in Jun 1942 and devoted, where possible, to war work only.

*** *** *** *** ***

A key "war plant"...........

The Koppers Company in Kobuta, Potter Township was built during World War II for the manufacturing of synthetic rubber. It was built by the government in 1943 at a cost of $61 million.   Koppers was still operating the plant on lease as they did during the war.   There is a complete listing for Koppers in the Mills Section of this book.
*see Mills and   Specific Area sections for pictures and much more information on Koppers Company and the community they built at the plant.

*** *** *** *** ***

Beaver County's First Total Blackout during WW II   -   Jun, 1942

It was 9:15 pm as sirens, factory whistles, and church bells signaled the start of the first total blackout in the history of Beaver County.   It was an eerie sight to see street lamps rapidly going out, section by section, town by town.   Then it seemed like an intense hush also settled over the entire area, as if all signs of life just ceased. The Beaver and Ohio valley turned from a bustling group of communities to a vast black mass.   There was only the light of the moon illuminating an occasional roof top.

There was total cooperation with not even a match flared in the darkness. No light, except that in plants engaged in war production, was visible. Lights were faintly visible at war plants in Monaca, but Conway Yard was in almost complete darkness.   A light did blaze at the site of Koppers, the new synthetic rubber plant.   A completely blacked-out passenger train sped across the Beaver-Monaca bridge.   There was a dull, red glow above the J & L plant, lights twinkled at the Colona river-rail terminal, and a towboat pilot making a landing briefly swept the shore with a searchlight. All of a sudden, the sirens began again, sounding the "all clear" signal. Section by section, town by town, area by area, the street lights came back on.   Automobile headlamps could be seen starting to move along streets and highways again.   Beaver County's first total blackout was over.

During the blackout, Monaca practiced simulated fires with the fire departments responding. There was a simulated injury case where a man lay down in the street near Eleventh Street and was given first aid treatment and prepared to be taken to the hospital.   A guard on the Rochester-Monaca bridge reportedly stopped a car and demanded to see credentials from the occupants. One of the occupants reportedly held up a machine gun and said to the guard "How will this do?" The two occupants of the car were U.S. Army officers, it was said, who were observing the result of the blackout in the county.   Monaca reported a successful blackout in the borough that evening with 100% cooperation from the citizens, persons passing through town, and businesses.   No violations of the blackout rules were reported.

*** *** *** *** ***

Memorials
There were many different groups formed to aid soldiers and the families of the soldiers in the war.
One local group was the Prisoner of War committee that worked with the Prisoner of War Program of the International Red Cross.   This group worked untiringly in the prison camps and distributed standard food packages and assisted with medical supplies and recreational equipment. In Jul 1944, the local Chairman was Mrs. Elsie Tate of Center Township (my grandmother).   They assisted the families of the boys held as prisoners (one was my father) with interpretation regarding regulations and with personal packages. The 1944 War Fund, Chairman, Robert E McCreary, Monaca, collected and distributed the funds for the Red Cross. With committees and funds as these, it saved duplications and confusions and permitted other groups and/or individuals with information regarding actual needs at the military posts and requests made by commanding officers.

1953

Monaca originally erected the Monaca Roll of Honor for WWII veterans on Pennsylvania Avenue in 1943.   It was built by the Monaca High School shop class.   As a Monaca resident entered the service, his name was added to the honor roll.   The honor roll was well kept with landscaping and scrubs surrounding the monument; the borough and veterans' organization doing the maintenance of the roll.   There were stone benches erected and a flag pole placed in the front.

The building on the left side of the picture was the Klingseisen Bakery. It was torn down and replaced by the new National Bank of Monaca building, now (2016) owned by Japanese restaurant.

In 1962, to make room for the Monaca Post Office, the honor roll was moved to Fourth Street and Pennsylvania Avenue. Today (2015), the Monaca Roll of Honor is located on the triangular lot between Fifth and Sixth Streets.

Sep 11, 1941 - Federal Works Agency chose a site in the Fourth Ward (Monaca Heights) for a 100-unit Defense Housing project.

Ads from war times......

Help Wanted—Male

"The War Manpower Commission has ruled that all males in this area may be hired solely upon referral of the United States Employment Service or designated agencies."

Help Wanted—Female

"The War Manpower Commission has ruled that all women in this area now employed in essential activity may be hired only by other essential employers and must have a Statement of Availability."

. 1944

MONACA NEWS

Garden Plots Will Be Available For Housing Project

Victory garden plots have been assured residents of Stephen Phillips Homes by housing authorities, if enough interest is shown in the proposed project. An early response is essential that the authorities can make arrangements in procuring the land.

May 1943

For Sale

FOR SALE: Six chick brooders, 100 capacity; lawn seed, Milorganite for the lawn, lime, onion sets, onion plants, loose garden seed, Victory Garden fertilizer, one cart, bay horse 7 years old, one English saddle and bridle. Jim Tweedy at the Feed Store. Phone Beaver 3040.   4 12-18 inc

Apr 1945

Oct 1943

Nov 1943

Nov 1944 ads in newspaper....

A 1943 notice in the local paper.............

WASTE PAPER will help win the War...

SAVE

and a return to PEACE ON EARTH

Residents were also told to save all their peach and apricot pits. They were collected in barrels in various locations throughout town and were given to the government who used the pits to make a war gas. (1914-1918 – WW I)

MONACA HAS WAR RECORD

Town Early Puts Up First Of It's Gold Stars—More Than 100 In Service

Monaca had its share of war misfortunes, but as a patriotic town of Beaver county it qualified for honors along with the rest. Aside from participating splendidly in all the war causes to help the United States win early the conflict, Monaca sent into the service of their country more than 100 of her best known sons. They fought a good fight and some of them did not return. Monaca early placed its first gold star on its service flag.

During the winter a movement was started to secure an Honor Roll to be set in a prominent place in the borough, the municipal building location being the chosen site. The Honor Roll was secured, and the names have been placed.

Monaca lost three men in war, besides one who died at Camp Sherman, Ohio. These were:

Joseph Engle.
Earl Hanshew.
Edward Schachern.

George Winkle, died at Camp Sherman, O., from disease.

Several were wounded or gassed, but there is only an incomplete record of them, so that they cannot be mentioned separately. There is also an incomplete record thus far of the men who arose to officers' places. However, among the list were: Capt. J. R. Gormley, medical corps; First Lieut. D. S. McKinley, medical corps; First Lieut. M. M. Mackall, medical corps; First Lieut. M. F. Schenk, medical corps, and First Lieut. Hubert Wagner, dental corps, in France.

Following is the list of names on the Honor Roll:

Joseph Adams, Harold Allen, Albert Anderson.

James Brobeck, Richard Blume, George Busang, David Busang, Max Barnett, William Barnett, Albert Brewer.

Wade Corne, Albert Clark, Ralph Clark, Lee Cain, John Cronin, Odell Carver.

John Dixon.

William Eberhardt, Ferdinand Eder, Joseph Engle, Richard Elstner.

Gordon Faust, Emmet Frank, Walter Folland, Michael Fleischer.

John Glasser, Glenn Glasser, George Griffen, Dr. J. R. Gormley, Fred Glasser.

Oscar Hage, Robert Hood, Mark Hill, Dalbert Henry, Raymond Hunter, Robert Hunter, Edson M. Hays, James D. Hicks, McKinley H. Henry, Joseph Hartman, Earl Hanshew, John Harrison, William Heckerman.

Elmer Johnston.

Brutus Kommel, George Kelly Oliver Kanshat, Howard R. Koehler, John L. Keefe, Thos. Keefe, William Kroen, Edward C. Koehler.

Otto Lewellyn, Thomas Liston.

Andy Mikulwo, James Moorehouse, William Moorehouse, Carl Mattauch, William Miller, Paul Miller, Ewing Markey, William Murray, Roy Miller, Dr. D. S. McKinley, Dr. M. M. Mackall, Robert Myers, James Myers, George Myers, William S. McKenzie.

Joseph Nick.

Zacharias Potter, John B. Potter, Ira Price, LeRoy Potter.

Christopher Ramer.

Frank Sephton, William Schwartz, Clair Sowash, Fred Sommers, William Skoog, Gust Stjernquist, Dave Sinclair, John Ross Sproull, Dr. M. F. Schenk, William Sullivan, John Sullivan, Herbert Creed Smith, George William Smith, Fred Schmidt, Merle Schachern, Edward Schachern.

Harold A. Taylor.

George Winkle, William Winkle, Dr. Hubert Wagner, William Walton, Robert Weinman.

Otto Zigerelle, James Zigerelle.

World War I Service Men

The Beaver County History Research and Landmark Foundation was fortunate enough to have received a copy of the book *Beaver Valley Towns in the World War*. This book listed residents from the following towns who served during WW I: Beaver Falls, New Brighton, Rochester, Beaver, Monaca, Freedom, Conway, Ambridge, Woodlawn, Other Nearby Places.

On Page 2 of the book there is no date of publication, author, publishing company, etc. It simply stated:

"Compilers' Note

We present here with "Beaver Valley Towns in the World War."

This work is to commemorate the part of local towns in the winning of the Great War, and we trust it will meet with the approval of all who may review its pages

Authentic war records, such as appear in this book, will form the most valuable data concerning the history of the days of 1917 and 1918. the canvass was made by an experienced force of representatives and no expense was spared to make the work as complete and accurate as possible. Whatever may be lacking comes not from want of honest endeavor on our part.

No attempt has been made to glorify one name at the expense of another. By design, all have been treated as nearly as possible in the same way, a fact that may possibly be appreciated more sincerely by the service men themselves than by any others. We trust that this history will be loved by children in the days to come because it records fathers and brothers, uncles or cousins who gave their services to our country in the time of need.

We extend our sincere thanks to the citizens of the communities, represented in this work who have shown their appreciation of the work by their patronage, also to those who so courteously assisted our representatives in collecting the information.

We offer our book believing it serves a useful purpose. We trust it will be received in the same spirit in which it was compiled.

WAR HISTORY SOCIETY.
        Publishers"

Unfortunately I do not know of any similar publication for all those from Korea, WW II, Vietnam, or any other wars or conflicts or I would have absolutely included them in this section also. Having at least this information, I felt it important to included it in this section of my book.

Please note - Even though the following few pages include the names of the service men of Monaca, Monaca Heights, and Colona, not all the names listed were exclusively from the Monaca Borough since these particular pages also include the names of service men from Georgetown, Hookstown, and Ohioville. I have reproduced the pages as they were originally published with all names included.

I am absolutely certain you will agree that this was an effort of love and respect for the War History Society to accumulate all this information and publish it to share and honor these service men.

CHAPTER V

The following records are those of the service men of Monaca, Monaca Heights, Colona, Georgetown, Hookstown and Ohioville

ADAMS, JOSEPH A.—Born December 28, 1898. Son of Mr. Joseph Adams. Entered service April, 1917. Assigned to Columbus Barracks, Fort Wayne, Detroit and Camp Merritt. Attached to Medical Department. Went overseas in March, 1918. Returned in May, 1919. Honorably discharged June, 1919.

ALEXANDER, GEORGE McKINLEY—Born August 20, 1895. Son of Mr. William Alexander. Entered service in the United States Navy March, 1915. Assigned to Newport, R. I. Attached to U. S. S. Delaware. Saw service in France and England. December 1, 1919, still in service at Scotland.

ALLISON, HOMER M.—Born May 5, 1893. Son of Henry and Ada Allison of Georgetown, Pa. Entered service October 5, 1917. Assigned to Camp Sherman, Camp Mills, Camp Merritt and Camp Dix. Attached to Supply Company, 323rd Field Artillery, 83rd Division. Saw service at Grand Montagne, Argonne Forest. Honorably discharged May 27, 1919.

BARNETT, MAX H.—Born January 1889. Son of Mr. Morris Barnett. Entered service April 2, 1918. Assigned to Camp Lee. Attached to Company A, 319th Infantry, 80th Division. Went overseas May 17, 1918. Saw service at Meuse-Argonne. Wounded. Honorably discharged June 9, 1919, with the rank of Sergeant.

BARNETT, WILLIAM—Born March 1, 1891. Son of Mr. Morris Barnett. Entered the service April 2, 1918. Assigned to Camp Lee and Newport News. Attached to Company D, 315th Machine Gun Battalion, 80th Division. Honorably discharged November 29, 1918.

BEAL, ERNEST D.—Born April 4, 1894. Son of Levi S. and Eva B. Beal, of Hookstown, Pa. Entered service June 26, 1918. Assigned to Camp Sherman and Camp Dix. Attached to Headquarters Company, 333rd Field Artillery, 79th Division. Went overseas September, 1918. Returned May 28, 1919. Honorably discharged June 4, 1919.

BEESON, HERBERT HAMPTON—Born August 12, 1892. Son of Mrs. Eva Hampton Beeson, of Cleveland, O. Assigned to Camp Hancock. Attached to Quartermaster Motor Transport Corps. Went overseas September 28, 1918. Returned February, 1919. Honorably discharged February 18, 1919, with rank of Second Lieutenant.

BEHARKA, JOHN—Born February 6, 1896. Son of Eva Beharka of Monaca. Entered the service October 7, 1917. Assigned to Camp Sherman, Camp Forrest and Camp Gordon. Attached to Company B, 17th Infantry. Honorably discharged January 22, 1919.

BELL, WILLIAM R.—Born October 18, 1888. Son of Mrs. J. A. Scott of Woodlawn, Pa. Entered service February 5, 1918. Assigned to Camp Sherman. Attached to Company F, 332nd Infantry, 83rd Division. Left for overseas June 8, 1918. Saw service in France and Italy. Returned April 14, 1919. Honorably discharged April 24, 1919.

BRANNON, JAMES CHARLES — Born October 21, 1900. Son of Mr. David Brannon of Monaca. Entered service April, 1919, in the United States Navy. Assigned to Newport, R. I. Attached to U. S. S. San Francisco. December 1, 1919, still in service.

BRECKENRIDGE, CLEMENS EHRENFELD—Born March 17, 1897. Son of Mr. and Mrs. William Breckenridge of Monaca. Entered service August 15, 1918. Assigned to University of Pittsburgh, Camp Jackson and Camp Meade. Attached to Battery E, 11th Field Artillery. Honorably discharged on January 6, 1919.

BROBECK, JAMES M.—Born February 28, 1890. Son of Mr. David Brobeck of Monaca. Entered the service February, 1917. Assigned to Camp Sherman and Camp Merritt. Attached to Central Record Office. Honorably discharged in June, 1919, holding the rank of Sergeant.

BROOKS, GEORGE—Born May 14, 1893. Entered the service April 25, 1918. Assigned to Camp Sherman, Camp Mills and Camp Upton. Attached to Company C, 308th Ammunition Train, 83rd Division. Left for overseas June 13, 1918. Saw service West of Meuse. Grand Montagne and East of the Meuse. Returned home April 27, 1919. Honorably discharged May 14, 1919.

BRYAN, WALLACE—Born May 10, 1882. Son of Robert M. and Belle S. Bryan of Hookstown, Pa. Entered the service June 23, 1917. Attached to Company G, 4th Infantry, 3rd Division. Participated in the battles at Marne Offensive, Chateau Thierry, St. Mihiel, Argonne and Verdun. Wounded. Honorably discharged.

BURNS, RALPH L.—Son of Mr. and Mrs. W. R. Burns of Colona, Pa. Entered the service September 18, 1917. Assigned to Camp Sherman. Attached to 304th Quartermaster Corps. Honorably discharged May 14, 1919.

BURNS, WILLIAM L.—Son of Mr. and Mrs. W. R. Burns, of Colona, Pa. Entered the service December 13, 1917. Assigned to Camp Sherman. Attached to Headquarters Company, 323rd Light Field Artillery, 32nd Division. Went overseas June 10, 1918. Saw service at Argonne, Grand Montagne and Meuse. Honorably discharged from the service May 27, 1919.

BUSANG, DAVID ALLEN—Born December 23, 1898. Son of Mr. Frank Busang. Entered service in July, 1917. Assigned to Gettysburg, Camp Greene, Camp Johnson and Newport News. Attached to Quartermaster Corps. Went overseas September, 1918. Returned July, 1919. Honorably discharged July, 1919, with rank of Corporal.

BUSANG, GEORGE WALTER — Born June 30, 1894. Son of Mr. William J. Busang of Cleveland, O. Entered the service April, 1918. Assigned to Camp Lee. Attached to Company A, 319th Infantry, 80th Division. Went overseas in May, 1918. Saw service at St. Mihiel and Meuse-Argonne. Wounded in action. Honorably discharged in June, 1919.

CLARKE, JAMES ALBERT — Born March 10, 1897. Son of Mr. and Mrs. James E. Clarke of Monaca. Entered service May, 1918. Assigned to Columbus Barracks and Camp Lee. Attached to Officers' Training School. Honorably discharged December, 1918.

CLARKE, RALPH GRAHAM—Born June 13, 1894. Son of Mr. and Mrs. James Clarke, Monaca, Pa. Entered service September 26, 1917. Assigned to Gettysburg, Camp Green and Camp Merritt. Attached to Company I, 60th Infantry, 3rd Division. Went overseas April 14, 1918. Wounded in the Argonne. Honorably discharged February 14, 1919, with rank of Sergeant.

CLOUGHLEY, ROBERT J.—Born September 1, 1899. Son of Robert and Mary Cloughley of Colona, Pa. Entered service May 6, 1918. Assigned to Fort Rodman. Attached to Battery E, 73rd Artillery. Went overseas September 25, 1918. Returned December 23, 1918. Honorably discharged December 30, 1918.

COENE, WADE M.—Born October 1, 1895. Son of Mr. Julius Coene of Monaca, Pa. Entered the service July, 1917. Assigned to Columbus, O., Kelly Field, Dayton and Wilbur Wright Field. Attached to Aviation. Honorably discharged March, 1919, holding the rank of Second Lieutenant.

COLLIGAN, JOHN J.—Born November 26, 1892. Son of James and Theresa Colligan, of Ironton, O. Entered service October 18, 1917. Assigned to Camp Hicks. Attached to 148th Aero Squadron. Went overseas February 26, 1918. Saw service at Somme. Returned March 24, 1919. Honorably discharged April 3, 1919.

CORNELIUS, FRANK H.—Born on July 4, 1898. Son of Mr. Vincent Cornelius of Monaca. Entered the service October, 1918. Assigned to University of Pittsburgh. Attached to Motor Transport, S. A. T. C. Honorably discharged December 10, 1918.

CREDE, LLOYD S.—Born May 5, 1893. Son of B. B. W. and Emma Crede of New Brighton, Pa Entered service November 21, 1917. Assigned to Princeton, N. J., Houston, Texas, San Leon, Texas. Attached to 96th Aero Squadron. Went overseas September 13, 1918. Returned February 6, 1919. Honorably discharged February 8, 1919, with rank of Second Lieutenant.

CURTIS, HARRISON—Born January 13, 1890. Son of Mrs. Harriet Curtis, of Monaca, Pa. Entered service April, 1918. Assigned to Camp Sherman, Camp Upton and Camp Dix. Attached to Company F, 802nd Pioneer Infantry. Went overseas August, 1918. Saw service at Verdun and Argonne Forest. Wounded. Honorably discharged April 15, 1919.

DALZELL, CLINTON, GEORGE — Born May 2, 1900. Son of Mr. William Dalzell, of Monaca. Entered service October 1, 1918. Assigned to University of Pittsburgh. Attached to S. A. T. C. Honorably discharged December 14, 1918.

DAVIS, EARL B.—Born December 17, 1892. Son of Mr. Frank Davis, Monaca, Pa. Entered service August 29, 1918. Assigned to Camp Lee and Camp Dix. Attached to 54th Guard Company, A. S. C. Went overseas October 14, 1918. Returned July 13, 1919. Honorably discharged July 18, 1919.

DELP, RONALD OTTO — Born March 22, 1896. Son of Mr. Turl Delp of Monaca. Entered service February 5, 1918. Assigned to Camp Sherman, Newark, N. J., and Camp Dix. Attached to Company G, 332nd Infantry. Honorably discharged May 14, 1919.

DINDINGER, FRANKLIN T.—Born February 13, 1890. Son of Mrs. Elizabeth Dindinger of Wampum, Pa. Entered the service August, 1918. Assigned to Fort Benjamin Harrison. Attached to Company A, 138th Engineers. Honorably discharged from the service December 18, 1918, with rank of Sergeant.

EBERHARDT, WILLIAM F.—Born January 9, 1894. Son of Mr. and Mrs. George Eberhardt, of Monaca, Pa. Entered the service December 14, 1917. Assigned to Camp Sherman. Attached to Company C, 158th Depot Brigade. Honorably discharged from the service December 10, 1918, with rank of Sergeant.

ELSTNER, RICHARD A.—Born on January 24, 1897. Son of Mr. and Mrs. Richard Elstner, Monaca, Pa. Entered the service August 29, 1918. Assigned to Camp Lee. Attached to Quartermaster Corps, Utilities Branch. Honorably discharged February 15, 1919, with rank of Sergeant.

ERB, GEORGE F.—Born May 13, 1891. Son of C. and Elizabeth Erb, of Monaca. Entered the service December 14, 1917. Assigned to Camps Sherman, Mills and Dix. Attached to Battery B, 323rd Field Artillery, 32nd Division. Went overseas June 10, 1918. Saw service at Meuse-Argonne and other battles. Honorably discharged May 27, 1919.

FANACCIA, JOSEPH—Born February, 1894. Son of Mr. and Mrs. Angelo Fanaccia, of Italy. Entered service February 6, 1918. Assigned to Camp Sherman and Camp Dix. Attached to 166th Ammunition Train, 41st Division. Went overseas March, 1918. Returned February, 1919. Honorably discharged March 4, 1919.

FAUST, GORDON LEE—Born June 23, 1893. Son of Mr. Phillip Faust, of Monaca. Entered service June 5, 1917. Assigned to Oakmont, Pittsburgh. Attached to Company F, 15th Engineers. Went overseas July 9, 1917. Saw service at St. Mihiel and Meuse-Argonne. Honorably discharged May 15, 1919 with rank of Corporal.

FAUST, HENRY LAIS—Born September, 1899. Son of Mr. Phillip Faust, of Monaca. Entered the service October 2, 1918. Assigned to Plattsburg, Pa. Attached to S. A. T. C. Honorably discharged December 23, 1918.

FINN, ROBERT—Born December 23, 1895. Son of Mr. Henry Finn, of Monaca, Pa. Entered the service May, 1917. Assigned to Camp Hancock. Attached to Company A, 18th Infantry. Honorably discharged November, 1918.

FLEISCHER, MICHAEL E. — Born March, 1897. Son of Mrs. Katherine Fleischer, of Monaca. Entered the service June 27, 1917. Assigned to Camp Hancock and Camp Dix. Attached to Headquarters Company, 108th Machine Gun Battalion. Went overseas May 3, 1918. In active service. Returned May 16, 1919. Honorably discharged May 26, 1919, with rank of Wagoner.

FOLLAND, WILLIAM B.—Born on June 1, 1890. Son of Mrs. Margaret Folland, of Monaca. Entered the service August, 1918. Assigned to Camp Lee and Camp Dix. Attached to Company A, 705th Regiment, 51st Guard. Left for overseas October, 1918. Returned July, 1919. Honorably discharged July, 1919.

GLASSER, JOHN—Born 1898. Son of Mr. Harry C. Glasser, of Monaca, Pa. Entered the service in July, 1917. Assigned to Kelly Field, Dayton, and Wilbur Wright Field. Went overseas in the Summer of 1918. Returned April, 1919. Honorably discharged in the Spring of 1919.

GOSS, GEORGE—Born April 29, 1900. Son of Mr. John Goss, of Monaca, Pa. Entered the service April 29, 1918. Assigned to Columbus, Ohio. Attached to Field Artillery. December 1, 1919, still in service.

HANSHEW, EARL—Born June 9, 1895. Son of Mr. W. A. Hanshew, of Monaca, Pa. Entered the service July, 1917. Assigned to Camp Hancock, Camp Upton and Schenley Park, Pittsburgh. Attached to Company A, 111th Infantry, 28th Division. Went overseas May, 1918. Wounded in action and died August 12, 1919. Buried in France.

HASLETT, ELLSWORTH—Born on July 4, 1899. Son of Mr. John Haslett, of Monaca, Pa. Entered service August 3, 1917. Assigned to Camp Sheridan and Camp Sherman. Attached to Company B, 135th Machine Gun Battalion. Went overseas June 15, 1918. Saw active service. Returned March 15, 1919. Honorably discharged April 9, 1919 with rank of Corporal.

HASLETT, ROBERT—Born November, 1894. Son of Mr. John Haslett, of Monaca. Entered service August 3, 1917. Assigned to Camp Sheridan and Camp Sherman. Attached to Company B, 135th Machine Gun Battalion. Went overseas June 15, 1918. Saw active service. Honorably discharged on April 9, 1919.

HAYS, EDSON M.—Born September 1, 1895. Son of Mr. and Mrs. F. M. Hays of Monaca. Entered the service December 5, 1917. Assigned to Columbus Barracks. Attached to Medical Corps. Honorably discharged June 27, 1919, with rank of Corporal.

HAZLETT, JAMES ROY—Born January 10, 1896. Son of Mr. James Roy Hazlett, Sr., of Monaca. Entered the service May, 1917. Assigned to Camp Humphreys and Camp Mills. Attached to Company N, 21st Engineers. Went overseas November, 1917. Returned July, 1919. Honorably discharged July, 1919.

HECKERMAN, WILLIAM H.—Born October 1, 1889. Son of William J. and Louisa Heckerman, Monaca, Pa. Entered the service April 1, 1918. Assigned to Camp Lee. Attached to Company 8, 2nd Battalion, 155th Depot Brigade. Honorably discharged February 21, 1919, with rank of Sergeant.

HENRY, DALBERT R.—Born October 28, 1896. Son of Mr. James Henry, Monaca. Entered the service September, 1918. Assigned to Camp Forrest. Attached to Company L, Engineers. Honorably discharged in February, 1919.

HICKS, JAMES D.—Born October 21, 1888. Son of Mrs. Anna G. Hicks of Monaca. Entered service, April, 1917. Assigned to Camp Lee. Attached to 32nd Company, 8th Training Battalion. Honorably discharged December 16, 1918, with rank of Sergeant.

HILL, MARK—Born Feb. 27, 1896. Son of Mr. Mary Hill, of Monaca. Entered service September 5, 1917. Assigned to Camp Sherman and Camp Mills. Attached to Battery F, 323rd Field Artillery, 32nd Division. Went overseas June 10, 1918. Saw service at Meuse-Argonne and other battles. Returned May 13, 1919. Honorably discharged May 26, 1919.

HOOD, JOSEPH B.—Born August 15, 1897. Son of Mr. William Hood of Monaca. Entered service August, 1918. Assigned to University of Pittsburgh. Attached to S. A. T. C. Honorably discharged December 15, 1918, with rank of Corporal.

HOUSER, RALPH DAVID—Born May 11, 1895. Son of Harry and Elizabeth Houser of Colona, Pa. Entered service February 5, 1918. Assigned to Camp Sherman. Attached to Battery C, 323rd Light Field Artillery, 32nd Division. Went overseas June 10, 1918. Saw service at Argonne, Grand Montagne and East of Meuse. Honorably discharged May 27, 1919, with rank of Corporal.

HUNTER, ROBERT F.—Born July 22, 1895. Son of Mr. and Mrs. James E. Hunter of Monaca. Entered service February 6, 1918. Assigned to Camp Sherman and Camp Merritt. Attached to Company F, 125th Infantry, 32nd Division. Went overseas March, 1918. Saw service at Alsace, Chateau Thierry, Meuse-Argonne. Wounded. Honorably discharged May 25, 1919.

JOHNSON, ELMER E.—Born September, 1897. Son of Mr. John H. Johnson of Monaca, Entered the service July, 1917. Assigned to Fort Benjamin Harrison and Camp Sherman. Attached to Field Hospital No. 15, 2nd Division. Went overseas December, 1918. Saw service at Aisne Sector, Chateau Thierry, Marne and St. Mihiel. Honorably discharged August 14, 1919.

JOHNSTON, MILO G.—Born August 17, 1897. Son of Mr. and Mrs. Alexander Johnston, of Monaca. Entered service June 7, 1918. Assigned to Camp Greenleaf. Attached to Base Hospital No. 55, Medical Corps. Went overseas on August 30, 1918. Gassed in action. Honorably discharged June 12, 1919.

KELLY, GEORGE THOMAS—Born January 1, 1899. Son of Mrs. Margaret A. Kelly of Monaca. Entered service Spring of 1917. Assigned to Pittsburgh, Pa., and Camp Hancock. Attached to Company A, 109th Infantry. Went overseas September 8, 1918. Saw service at St. Mihiel, Meuse-Argonne and Vesle. Honorably discharged May 16, 1919.

KINDELL, NOLON M.—Born 1895. Son of Mr. William M. Kindell, of Bradford, O. Entered the service May, 1917, in the United States Navy. Assigned to Newport, Pensacola and Fort Worth. Attached to Naval Aviation. Went overseas Spring of 1918. Returned Spring of 1919. Honorably discharged in August, 1919, with rank of Lieutenant.

KOEHLER, EDWARD C.—Born on February 21, 1898. Son of Mr. Paulus E. Koehler, of Monaca. Entered service Spring of 1917. Assigned to Camp Taylor. Attached to Officers' Training School. Honorably discharged June, 1919, with rank of Second Lieutenant.

KOEHLER, HOWARD R.—Born on May 31, 1889. Son of Mr. Paulus E. Koehler of Monaca. Entered service Spring of 1917. Assigned to Camp Sherman and Camp Mills. Attached to Company F, 323rd Field Artillery, 32nd Division. Went overseas June 10, 1918. Saw service at Meuse-Argonne. Honorably discharged May 27, 1919, with rank of Sergeant.

KOPCAK, JOSEPH—Son of Mr. Stephen Kopcak, of Monaca. Entered service January, 1919. Assigned to Washington, D. C., and Hawaiian Islands. Attached to Cavalry. November 29, 1919, still in the service.

LAIS, GEORGE JAMES—Born May 5, 1898. Son of Mr. and Mrs. George H. Lais, of Monaca. Entered the United States Navy October 1, 1918. Assigned to Pitt University. Attached to Naval Reserves. Released from service but subject to call.

LAIS, ROLLO V.—Born September 19, 1896. Son of Mr. and Mrs. George H. Lais, Monaca, Pa. Entered service June 30, 1918. Assigned to Naval Training Station, Cleveland. Attached to Naval Reserve. Released from service, but subject to call.

LAUGHLIN, ROBERT P.—Born in March, 1896. Son of James and Rose Laughlin, of Georgetown, Pa. Entered the service December, 1917. Assigned to Camp Sherman. Attached to Battery B, 323rd Field Artillery. Honorably discharged April 28, 1918.

LOTZ, CHESTER—Born January 9, 1895. Son of Mr. Nickolos Lotz, Rochester. Entered the service in September, 1917. Assigned to Camps Sherman, Mills and Dix. Attached to Battery E, 323rd Light Field Artillery, 32nd Division. Went overseas in June, 1918. Participated in several battles. Returned May, 1919. Honorably discharged May 28, 1919.

LAUGHLIN, HOMER—Born November 28, 1892. Son of Mr. R. L. Laughlin, of Georgetown. Entered service July 27, 1918. Assigned to Camp Lee, Newport News, Camp Mills and Camp Dix. Attached to Company L, 61st Infantry, 51st Division. Went overseas September 15, 1918. In the battle of Meuse-Argonne. Returned July 19, 1919. Honorably discharged July 26, 1919.

LISTON, THOMAS GEORGE—Born April 7, 1896. Son of Mr. and Mrs. M. M. Liston, of Monaca. Entered service October 7, 1917. Assigned to Camp Sherman. Attached to Battery F, 323rd Field Artillery, 32nd Division. Went overseas June 10, 1918. Participated in battles at Argonne, Grand Montague, Marne. Honorably discharged May 27, 1919.

McCARTHY, MOLLY A.—Born on March 22, 1884. Entered service March 1, 1917. Assigned to Belview Hospital, N. Y. Attached to Belview Unit. Went overseas in March, 1917. Honorably discharged June, 1919.

McCLURG, MILO J.—Born August 22, 1887. Son of J. R. and Martha McClurg, of Monaca. Entered service September 4, 1918. Assigned to Camp Forrest. Attached to Second Provisional Regimental Company. Honorably discharged December 20, 1918.

McCREARY, JOHN CHARLES—Born January 29, 1899. Son of Mr. and Mrs. T. W. McCreary, of Monaca. Entered service September, 1918. Assigned to Allegheny College, Meadville, Pa. Attached to S. A. T. C. Honorably discharged December, 1918.

McCREARY, ROBERT EMMETT—Born August 24, 1898. Son of Mr. and Mrs. T. W. McCreary, of Monaca. Entered service August 30, 1918, in the United States Navy. Assigned to Cleveland, Chicago and Palm Bay. Attached to Navy. Released May 10, 1919, subject to call.

McELWEE, JOHN—Born April 23, 1891. Son of Mrs. Hanna McElwee of Ireland. Entered the service November 17, 1917. Assigned to Camp Hamilton, Canada. Attached to 58th Canadian Infantry Battalion. Went overseas January, 1918. Participated in several battles. Honorbly discharged March 23, 1919.

McELWEE, THOMAS—Son of Mr. and Mrs. James McElwee, of Monaca, Pa. Entered service August 17, 1917. Assigned to Syracuse, N. Y., and Camp Greene. Attached to Company M, 38th Infantry. Participated in the battles of the Meuse-Argonne. Died from wounds received in action October 10, 1918. Buried in France.

MACKALL, GAIL—Born May 12, 1896. Son of Mrs. Harriet Mackall of Georgetown. Entered the service February 21, 1918. Assigned to Camp Travis, Camp Merritt. Attached to Company N, 19th Engineers. Went overseas April 22, 1918. Saw service at Chateau Thierry. Honorably discharged in May, 1919.

MACKALL, JOHN EDWARD—Born August 7, 1887. Son of Mrs. Jennie B. Mackall, of Georgetown. Entered service December 13, 1917. Assigned to Camp Sherman, Fort Niagara, Newport News and Camp Dix. Attached to Company B, 45th Battalion. Honorably discharged January 21, 1919.

MARKEY, EWING H.—Born in 1893. Son of Mr. James Markey, of Monaca. Entered service April 1, 1918. Assigned to Camps Lee, Dix and Sherman. Attached to Company E, 319 Infantry, 80th Division. Went overseas May 18, 1918. Saw service at St. Mihiel and Meuse Argonne. Honorably discharged June 12, 1919.

MATTAUCH, CARL—Born January 17, 1889. Son of Mrs. Annie Mattauch, of Australia. Entered the service April 1, 1918. Assigned to Camps Lee, Dix and Sherman. Attached to Company E, 319th Infantry, 80th Division. Went overseas May 18, 1918. Saw service at the Meuse-Argonne and St. Mihiel. Honorably discharged June 12, 1919.

MIKSCH, CARLTON ARNOLD—Born October 11, 1899. Son of Mr. and Mrs. Miksch, of Monaca. Entered the service October 23, 1918. Assigned to Allegheny College, Meadville, Pa. Attached to Company A, S. A. T. C. Honorably discharged December 11, 1918.

MIKSCH, HARRY NORTHWOOD—Born November 11, 1897. Son of Mr. and Mrs. Carl Miksch, of Monaca, Pa. Entered the service October 23, 1918. Assigned to Allegheny College, Meadville, Pa. Attached to Company A, S. A. T. C. Honorably discharged December 11, 1918.

MILLER, JAMES A. JR.—Born January 20, 1899. Son of Mr. and Mrs. James A. Miller, of Monaca. Entered service September, 1918. Assigned to University of Pittsburgh. Attached to S. A. T. C. Honorably discharged December, 1918, with rank of Corporal.

MILLER, PAUL JAMES—Born September 26, 1892. Son of Mr. and Mrs. J. A. Miller, of Monaca. Entered service February 6, 1918. Assigned to Camp Sherman. Attached to 20th Engineers. Went overseas March 27, 1918. Returned on June 1, 1919. Honorably discharged June 12, 1919.

MILLER, ROY M.—Born July 28, 1894. Son of Mr. and Mrs. Fred Miller, of Monaca. Entered service September 18, 1917. Assigned to Camp Sherman and Camp Dix. Attached to Headquarters Company, 323rd Field Artillery. Left for overseas June 10, 1918. Saw service at Meuse-Argonne, Montagne. Honorably discharged May 27, 1919, with rank of Corporal.

MILLER, WILLIAM J.—Born September 6, 1894. Son of Mr. and Mrs. J. A. Miller, of Monaca. Entered service September 6, 1917. Assigned to Camp Sherman. Attached to Battery C, 323rd Light Field Artillery, 32nd Division. Went overseas June 10, 1918. Saw service at Argonne, Grand Montague, East of Meuse. Honorably dischrged May 27, 1919, with the rank of Sergeant.

MOOREHOUSE, JAMES H.—Born July 7, 1893. Son of Mr. and Mrs. J. W. Moorehouse, of Monaca. Entered service January 15, 1918. Assigned to Army Field Clerk. Went overseas February 8, 1918. Awarded citation from General Pershing. Honorably discharged September 19, 1919.

MURPHY, PATRICK—Born June 30, 1891. Entered service July, 1918. Assigned to Camp Merritt and Camp Gordon. Attached to General Pershing Guards. Went overseas August, 1918. Returned June, 1919. Honorably discharged June, 1919.

MURPHY, WILLIAM—Born April 13, 1895. Entered service September, 1918. Assigned to Camp Humphreys. Attached to Engineers. Honorably discharged December, 1918.

MYERS, ROBERT—Born March 4, 1892. Son of James and Alice Myers of Monaca. Entered service July 11, 1917. Assigned to Gettysburg and Camp Greene. Attached to Company C, 7th Infantry, 3rd Division. Went overseas April 6, 1918. Participated in several battles. Honorably discharged on August 27, 1918.

MYERS, GEORGE WALTER—Born August 1, 1889. Son of James and Alice Myers of Monaca. Assigned to Camp Sherman. Attached to Headquarters Company, 112th Infantry, 28th Division. Went overseas May, 1918. Saw service at Meuse-Argonne, Chateu Thierry and St. Mihiel. Returned May, 1919. Honorably discharged May 12, 1919.

MYERS, JAMES W.—Born March 15, 1887. Son of James and Alice Myers of Monaca. Entered service September 19, 1917. Assigned to Camp Sherman, Waco, Texas, and Camp Upton. Attached to Battery F, 323rd Light Field Artillery, 32nd Division. Went overseas May 7, 1918. Saw service at St. Die. Honorably discharged August 8, 1919.

NELSON, HAROLD M.—Born February 27, 1895. Son of Frank E. and Maud E. Nelson, Hookstown, Pa. Entered the service December 11, 1917. Assigned to Columbus Barracks, Kelly Field and Hempstead, L. I. Attached to 258th Aero Squadron. Went overseas May 2, 1918. Returned May, 1919. Honorably discharged May 12, 1919, with rank of Sergeant.

NICKLE, CHARLES LEROY—Born October 6, 1894. Son of Henry S. and Lorena M. Nickle, Hookstown, Pa. Entered the service April 25, 1918. Assigned to Camp Sherman and Camp Mills. Attached to Company B, 112th Infantry, 28th Division. Went overseas June, 1918. Participated in the battles at St. Mihiel, Verdun and Argonne Forest. Killed in action. Buried in American Cemetery at Exermont, France.

ORR, SAMUEL J.—Born January 13, 1897. Son of Mrs. J. A. Scott, of Colona, Pa. Entered service on August 17, 1917. Assigned to Columbus Barracks. Attached to 102nd Aero Squadron. Went overseas on November 23, 1917. Saw service in England and France. Honorably discharged in May, 1919.

POTTER, JOHN B.—Born December 29, 1894. Son of Mr. John P. Potter, of Monaca. Entered service October 7, 1917. Assigned to Camps Sherman, Mills and Dix. Attached to Company F, 323rd Field Artillery, 32nd Division. Went overseas June, 1918. Saw service at Meuse-Argonne, Grand Montague. Returned May 13, 1919. Honorably discharged May 27, 1919, with rank of Sergeant.

POTTER, ZACHARY F.—Born July 15, 1892. Son of Mr. John P. Potter of Monaca. Entered service on October 3, 1917. Assigned to Camp Sherman and Camp Mills. Attached to Battery E, 323rd Field Artillery, 32nd Division. Went overseas June 10, 1918. Saw service at Meuse-Argonne and other battles. Honorably discharged on May 27, 1919, with rank of Saddler.

PROVENCE, DAVID L.—Born December 1, 1889. Entered service in January, 1917. Assigned to Camp Sherman and Camp Lee. Attached to Company E, 323rd Artillery, 32nd Division. Went overseas June 10, 1919. Saw service at Meuse-Argonne and Chateau Thierry. Honorably discharged May 29, 1919, with rank of Corporal.

REINEHR, ALBERT—Son of Andrew Reinehr, of Monaca, Pa. Entered service June, 1918. Assigned to Camps Merritt and Sherman. Attached to Company H, 332nd Infantry, 83rd Division. Participated in several engagements in Italy. Honorably discharged April, 1919.

SCHACHERN, LELAND J.—Born March 1, 1900. Son of Joseph Schachern of Monaca, Pa. Entered service October 1, 1918. Attached to Company A, S. A. T. C., at Allegheny College, Meadville, Pa. Honorably discharged December 13, 1918.

SCHATZINGER, EDWARD J.—Born October 7, 1887. Son of John and Mary Schatzinger, of Colona, Pa. Entered service April 2, 1918. Assigned to Camp Lee. Attached to Company F, 319th Infantry, 80th Division. Went overseas May 18, 1918. Saw service at Meuse-Argonne, and St. Mihiel. Honorably discharged June 12, 1919.

SCHATZINGER, JOSEPH J.—Born September 13, 1887. Son of John and Mary Schatzinger, of Colona, Pa. Entered service September 22, 1917. Assigned to Camp Sherman. Attached to Company C, 26th Infantry, 1st Division. Went overseas June 28, 1918. Saw service at St. Mihiel, Meuse-Argonne and Sarzerais. Honorably discharged September 24, 1919, holding rank of Corporal.

SCHUPAY, STEVEN JACOB—Born July 18, 1897. Son of Mrs. John Schupay of Monaca, Pa. Entered service September 21, 1918. Assigned to Camp Greenleaf and Camp Upton. Attached to Base Hospital No. 110. Went overseas November 12, 1918. Honorably discharged July 10, 1919.

SCHMIDT, FRED W.—Born April 27, 1897. Son of Mrs. M. Kirchner of Monaca, Pa. Entered service September 5, 1918. Assigned to Camp Lee. Attached to Quartermaster Corps, U. S. Army. Honorably discharged May 14, 1919, holding rank of Corporal.

SCHWARTZ, WILLIAM ROSS—Born January 22, 1891. Son of Mrs. F. R. Schwartz of Monaca, Pa. Entered service September 5, 1917. Assigned to Camp Sherman. Attached to Battery C, 323rd Light Field Artillery. Went overseas on June 10, 1918. Saw service at Argonne Sector, Grande Montague. Honorably discharged May 27, 1919, holding rank of Sergeant.

SEPHTON, FRANK—Born August 7, 1887. Son of John T. Sephton of Monaca, Pa. Entered service April 1, 1918. Assigned to Camps Lee and Sherman. Attached to Company G, 320th Infantry, 80th Division. Went overseas May 18, 1918. Saw service at Meuse-Argonne and St. Mihiel. Awarded Victory Medal. Honorably discharged June 9, 1919.

SERGEANT, CHARLES E.—Born April 19, 1889. Son of Harry and Matilda Sergeant, of Colona, Pa. Entered service February 6, 1918. Assigned to Camp Sherman. Attached to Company G, 332nd Infantry. Went overseas June 8, 1918. Saw service at Vittoio Venteo, Tagliamento River, Pont della Delizia and on the Italian front. Honorably discharged April 24, 1919.

SERGEANT, KENNETH J.—Born June 15, 1896. Son of Harry and Matilda Sergeant, of Colona, Pa. Entered service September 6, 1918. Assigned to Camp Greenleaf. Attached to Medical Department. Honorably discharged March 3, 1919.

SHEMONE, JOSEPH CHARLES—Born March 1, 1897. Son of Mrs. Anna Shemone of Monaca, Pa. Entered service September 4, 1918. Assigned to Camp Forrest and Camp Sherman. Attached to Company B, 124th Engineers. Honorably discharged December, 1918.

SIMMONS, LAWRENCE F.—Born December 10, 1897. Son of John and Anna Simmons of Colona, Pa. Entered service August 17, 1917. Assigned to Columbus Barracks and San Antonio, Texas. Went overseas November 23, 1917. Served in England and France. Honorably discharged May 1, 1919, holding rank of Corporal.

SKOOG, WILLIAM F.—Born May 5, 1895. Son of Mrs. L. F. Skoog, of Monaca, Pa. Entered service December 14, 1917. Assigned to Camp Sherman. Attached to Battery B, 323rd Artillery. Honorably discharged January 23, 1918.

SOMMERS, FREDERICK FRANK—Born April 13, 1895. Son of Mrs. Frederick Sommers, of Monaca, Pa. Entered service October 7, 1917. Assigned to Camp Sherman. Attached to Battery F, 323rd Field Artillery, 32nd Division. Went overseas June 10, 1918. Saw service at Meuse-Argonne. Honorably discharged May 27, 1919.

SOWASH, CLARE R.—Born January 17, 1898. Son of Charles B. Sowash of Monaca, Pa. Entered service July 21, 1917. Assigned to Camp Greene. Attached to Company A, 58th Infantry, 4th Division. Went overseas May 7, 1918. Saw service at Meuse-Argonne, Champagne and Aisne. Honorably discharged August 2, 1919.

STEINER, THEODORE ARNOLD—Born May 20, 1900. Son of E. B. and Florence M. Steiner. Entered service October 1, 1918. Assigned to Thiel College. Attached to S. A. T. C. Honorably discharged December 11, 1918.

STJERNQUIST, CARL F.—Born August 1, 1889. Son of Mrs. Josephine Stjernquist, of Monaca, Pa. Entered service April, 1917. Assigned to Camp Upton. Attached to 106th Infantry. Honorably discharged March, 1919.

STJERNQUIST, GUST E.—Born May 12, 1895. Son of Mrs. Josephine Stjernquist, of Monaca, Pa. Entered service October 5, 1917. Assigned to Camp Sherman. Attached to Battery F, 323rd Light Field Artillery. Went overseas on June 10, 1919. Saw service at Argonne St. Mihiel, Grande Montague and Meuse. Honorably discharged May 27, 1919.

SWEARINGEN, CHARLES R.—Born November 12, 1892. Son of Jackson and Lillian B. Swearingen, of Georgetown, Pa. Entered the service October 2, 1917. Assigned to Camp Funston, Camp Kearney, Camp Mills and Camp Merritt. Attached to Headquarters Company, 160th Infantry, 40th Division. Went overseas August 8, 1918. Gassed. Honorably discharged July 10, 1919, with rank of Corporal.

TAYLOR, HAROLD A.—Born November 7, 1897. Son of Herby J. Taylor, of Monaca, Pa. Entered service November, 1918. Assigned to Paris Island, S. C. Attached to U. S. S. M. C. Honorably discharged April, 1919.

TINPANO, ANGELO—Born April 13, 1891. Son of Fernando Tinpano, of Monaca, Pa. Entered the service December 13, 1917. Assigned to Camp Sherman. Attached to Company B, 323rd Light Field Artillery, 32nd Division. Honorably discharged October 29, 1918.

TODD, FRANCIS O.—Born January 16, 1887. Entered the service July 29, 1918. Assigned to Camps Merritt and Dix. Attached to Quartermaster's Corps. Honorably discharged February 3, 1919.

TODD, THOMAS D.—Born November 18, 1889. Entered service February 4, 1918. Assigned to Camp Sherman. Attached to Company G, 332nd Infantry, 83rd Division. Honorably discharged March 13, 1919.

TRUMPETER, WILLIAM CLIFTON—Born November 26, 1898. Son of Mr. and Mrs. W. M. Trumpeter, of Monaca, Pa. Entered service October 2, 1918. Assigned to Carnegie Tech. Attached to S. A. T. C. Honorably discharged December 17, 1918.

TURNECK, RALPH J.—Born March 17, 1896. Entered service May 23, 1917. Attached to Company D, 5th Engineers, 5th Division. Went overseas July 9, 1917. Saw service at Chateau Thierry, Verdun, Soissons and Belleau Woods. Returned May, 1919. Honorably discharged May 14, 1919, with the rank of Sergeant.

WEIGHEL, WALKER JENNINGS—Born March 7, 1897. Son of Henry Weighel, of Monaca, Pa. Entered service September, 1918. Assigned to Great Lakes. Attached to Naval Reserve. Honorably discharged January, 1919.

WEINMAN, ROBERT B.—Born January 29, 1894. Son of Mr. and Mrs. George Weinman of Monaca, Pa. Entered service September 1918. Assigned to Washington, D. C. Attached to Medical Department. Honorably discharged June, 1919.

WINKLE, GEORGE A.—Born August 23, 1895. Son of George W. Winkle of Monaca, Pa. Entered service September 5, 1917. Assigned to Camp Sherman. Attached to Battery F, 323rd Light Field Artillery, 32nd Division. Died, April 21, 1918, at Camp Sherman, Ohio.

WOODFIELD, CHARLES — Born April 20, 1892. Son of James and Louisa S. Woodfield of Colona, Pa. Entered service September 18, 1917. Assigned to Camp Sherman. Attached to Battery F, 323rd Field Artillery. Went overseas June 10, 1918. Saw service at Argonne, Bois-de-Grande. Honorably discharged May 27, 1919, with rank of Corporal.

WRIGHT, WILLIAM ROY—Born July 2, 1895. Son of Charles S. and Julia V. Wright. Entered the service September 19, 1918. Assigned to Camps Sherman, Mills and Dix. Attached to Supply Company, 323rd Artillery, 83rd Division. Went overseas June 10, 1918. Saw service at Meuse-Argonne. Slightly gassed. Honorably discharged July 15, 1919.

ZIGERELLI, JAMES—Born April, 1896. Son of Mr. Joseph Zigerelli, of Monaca. Entered service in January, 1918. Assigned to Camp Sherman and Camp Dix. Attached to Company M, 16th Infantry. Went overseas April, 1918. Was wounded in action twice. Honorably discharged October, 1919.

ZIGERELLI, JOHN F.—Born January 29, 1897. Son of Mr. Frank Zigerelli, of Monaca. Entered the service September 4, 1918. Assigned to Camp Forrest and Camp Sherman. Attached to Engineers. Honorably discharged December 20, 1918.

ZIGERELLI, OTTO—Born July 4, 1891. Son of Mr. Joseph Zigerelli, of Monaca. Entered the service September, 1917. Assigned to Camp Sherman and Camp Dix. Attached to Company F, 323rd Field Artillery, 32nd Division. Honorably discharged December, 1918.

ZINKE, FRANK H.—Born August 24, 1899. Son of Mr. and Mrs. Frank Zinke, of Monaca, Pa. Entered the service in September, 1918. Assigned to Geneva College. Attached to S. A. T. C. Honorably discharged December, 1918.

War Bonds

WAR NEEDS MONEY!

. will cost money to defeat Japan. Your government calls on YOU to help NOW.

"Buy Defense Bonds and Stamps today. Buy them every day, if you can. But buy them on a regular basis.

"Bonds cost as little as $18.75, Stamps come as low as 10 cents. Defense Bonds and Stamps can be bought at all banks and post offices, and Stamps can also be purchased at retail stores and from your newspaper carrier boy.

"This newspaper urges all Americans to support your government with your dollars."

Apr 1945

It doesn't take any spade work to cultivate this kind of Victory Garden!

All it takes is common sense.

If you plant a War Bond that costs you $37.50 you get a yield of $50.00. The wisest financiers will tell you there's no better investment in the world. An investment free from every kind of risk—every future disaster! An investment that offers you, in the uncertain years to come, tangible security guaranteed by the United States Government.

Rich or poor—you cannot afford to ignore the rich return your country offers for the loan of your money, or the wisdom of this, the shrewdest investment you can make!

Buy Bonds now when your country needs your dollars to help win the war.

And once your money is safe and sound in War Bonds—don't be tempted to cash them in. Wait for the golden harvest you're entitled to—wait till they're fully matured!

Keep Faith with our Fighters—buy War Bonds for keeps!

*** *** *** *** ***

Tank Farm – Potter Township

Ships, aircraft, and other military equipment required (and still do today) massive amounts of fuel. In their preparation for the war in 1942, the U.S. Government established strategic fuel facilities near key locations and ports; one was the Monaca Tank Farm project located in Potter Township on Mowry Road. The government felt these facilities were needed to hide and protect the storage of aviation fuel from possible air attacks by the enemy. This "tank farm" was classified a secret project with the government making the decision to build the massive tank farm on the 305-acre plot of land. This acreage was going to hold over 10-million gallons of high-octane aviation fuel in six huge underground tanks. This was such a secretive operation that the local residents were sworn to secrecy. The acreage was disguised as a farm and contained what appeared to be a farmhouse and two large barns, along with a few pieces of farm equipment strategically placed. The farmhouse was a change and generator house and the barns were used for ethyl blending. Pump houses were also erected and skillfully disguised as residential homes of the area.

Throughout the years that the property was actively being used, the locals took their sworn secrecy seriously and would ward off any trespassers or curious persons and actually kept quite tight lipped about the actual usage of the property. By the mid 1960s it was no longer a secret project and the folk lore began to spread. Along with the many tales of mystery and fabrications of why this property had a chain link fencing around it and what it was really being used for, bits and pieces of the truth also began to emerge. About 1965 to 1975, a Sunday ride would almost always include a drive by the property to see if there was any activity at all on the property or if you could spot anything but one of the barns and a small building.

Along with the tanks, there was also an estimated 8 miles of pipeline which led from the tank farm to a barge area and railroad car and truck loading area. The pump houses would aide in the moving of the fuel as needed. The fake farm was constructed by trucking in the needed steel components to build the storage tanks; each was riveted together on-site. Once the tanks were all completed, the area was filled in with dirt to cover and hide them, making them officially known as underground storage tanks (UST). As the tanks were being completed, the supposed farm buildings and miscellaneous houses were erected. The tanks themselves were no longer being used after 1963, yet they still remained in place along with all the piping, all buried underground.

The actual ownership of the property changed hands over the years. From 1941 to 1963 the Air Force owned the property, then 1964 to 1984 – St. Joe Mineral, then 1985 to 2004 – Horsehead Industries. With a Chapter 11 bankruptcy proceeding, Horsehead Industries abandoned the tank farm and Potter Township became the owners. Under the Formerly Used Defense Site (FUDS) program, the U.S. Army Corps of Engineers Baltimore District began the process of assessing and finding a solution to the properties. Many studies and assessments were done over the years to evaluate the environmental impact of the entire site. Explosive Ordnance Technologies, Inc (EOTI) was awarded the project portion of it all; this was awarded through the US Army Engineering Support Center Huntsville Worldwide Remediation Services (WERS) contract.

The remediation project was started, as was the chore to expose and remove the underground piping and tanks; all to be properly taken apart for off-site recycling.

Photos from Milestone s BCHR&LF

This is a photo of one of the underground hi-octane aircraft fuel tanks (a 1.74-million-gallon tank) being removed by the US Army Corp. of Engineers. The Air Force Petroleum, Oil and Lubricant Facility was located along Mowry Road in Potter Township, Monaca during WWII. These underground tanks on the fuel tank farm were removed in 2012.

*** *** *** *** ***

Phoenix Glass Company — WW I and WW II

The Phoenix Glass Company was one of the valley concerns which operated full capacity during the entire period of the war on "essential work". During the period of WW I the Monaca plant engaged in the production of glassware for the United States government. Phoenix turned out a volume little known by even the citizens of Monaca, and had the distinct ion of operating full, with the approval of the government, during the entire period of the war. In 1919, there was a large article in the newspaper....

PHOENIX GLASS CO.
AIDS THE COUNTRY
IN ITS WAR CRISIS

The article stated that Phoenix Glass Company operated at full capacity on essential work during the entire period of the war. The company made glassware for the United States Government, and the product they were making was so important that the plant had work done on both night and day shifts. The average monthly production of the various types being used by the U.S. Government in various departments, together with glassware of national importance, averaged approximately 83 %, reports made monthly to the government.

There were approximately 700 people employed during the period of the war. The great demand for the work at this plant, as with so many other businesses, required a change in employment to meet the demand. The work that had previously been done by exclusively male employees had to now be done without men or boys who were either drafted or had enlisted. Girls and women were given employment that had previously been done by the men and boys; and the majority of the jobs, the girls and women did the work equally as efficient as the men had. The records of Beaver County show the employees of Phoenix Glass Company as being of a very patriotic spirit. They made generous subscriptions to the various benevolent funds for war purposes. Of those were included First, Second, Third, and Fourth Liberty Loans, the latter showing a 100 per cent contribution. The plant also had a 100 per cent record in connection with the Fifth Victory Loan.

Jan, 1943, Monaca Council voted to adopt a resolution contributing to the war effort – to make all street car rails and other metallic track materials immediately available for war use by War Materials Inc, agent for the Metals Reserve Company which remove the rails and replace the streets in the borough in consideration of the sum of $1. Council also decided all cars parked on streets of the borough which were out of running condition and evidently disabled for the duration of the war would be removed from the streets at the owner's expense.

*** *** *** *** ***
*** *** ***

WWII

There were many individuals from Monaca and surrounding areas that served for their country during WWII. Unfortunately, many became prisoners of war or gave the ultimate sacrifice - their lives. I found records of all WWII service persons who were killed or missing from Beaver County, but there was no indication what specific town or area of each person listed. The listing was very, very lengthy, and I made the choice to not include the information.

I am going to mention one former Monaca resident in particular because it is popularly cited that he was one of the first to be killed during WWII and his plane was also one the first US aircrafts to be destroyed (on the ground). Louis Gustav Moslener, Jr. was a 1935 graduate of Monaca High School. He was born in 1918, the son of Louis Gustav and Blanch (Mechem) Moslener of Twelfth Street, Monaca. He joined the Air Corp in May 1940. Following training school, Lieutenant Louis G. Moslener, Jr. became a navigation officer for the U.S. Army Air Corps and a crew member on a B-24A #40-2371. They were part of the 88th reconnaissance Squadron, arriving at Hickam Field, Hawaii on December 5, 1941. They were said to be in the process of completing final preparations for a secret project to photograph Japanese military bases in the Marshall and Caroline Islands; their plane was still at the air force field on the morning of Dec 7, 1941 due to some problems with installing machine guns. Moslener and his crew were at the hanger preparing to do a short check flight before leaving on their assignment when the Japanese attack. It was written that Moslener and another crew member were killed by shrapnel when the second bomb dropped hit the corner of the hanger; this bomb also did the damage to the fuselage of their plane. Four other crew members were wounded. The Pittsburgh Press reported on Dec 10, 1941 that including Lieutenant Moslener's death, it "brought to six the total number of victims thus far announced in Western Pennsylvania."

Below is a picture of Louis G. Moslener, Jr. as it appeared in the newspaper when his death was announced. The second is a photograph of the damaged plane; this photograph was contributed by Greg Campbell who has done extensive research.

```
***   ***   ***   ***   ***
      ***   ***   ***
```

LOCKS and DAMS

The Davis Lock and Dam

Glenfield / Emsworth Dam

Glen Osborne Lock and Dam

Legionville Lock and Dam – No. 4

United States Lock and Dam No. 5

United States Lock and Dam No. 6 – Beaver/Merrill Dam

Montgomery Island Dam

LOCKS and DAMS

I did not plan on including any information on locks and dams with this book, but while researching and reading information for my discussion of the swimming areas, bridges, ferries, wharf, and other areas associated with the connections to the Ohio River, locks and dams definitely came into play.   Although you will not find an in-depth discussion or history of dams and locks in the Monaca area, I have included some information that I found while doing my research.

In investigating the dams of the Monaca area – three names always seemed to surface.....Senator Matthew Stanley Quay, Captain John F. Dravo, and Honorable (Congressman) C. C. Townsend ---- all three were advocates for making the Ohio River a national waterway, they promoted river improvements, and were involved in the conception of the dams and locks, not to mention seeing the water of the Ohio being cleaned and restored.

Sadly, my original discovery of the lock and dam near Monaca was the repeated mention of the lives that were lost to drowning in the river; the majority of these were younger children who ventured into unwelcoming waters to do boating, swimming or fishing.   Most of the deaths I discovered occurred while youngsters were swimming at the site of the United States Lock and Dam No. 5.   This area was not a place that children were encouraged to go to and swim, rather it was the opposite of that – they were greatly discouraged; but with the waters being a bit deeper at the site of the dam, it was intriguing to the children of the area.

In lieu of one of the published recent drownings of a young teenager, the paper had an article in their late summer 1928 edition that stated in the opinion of river men, this lock (No. 5) was one of the most dangerous places along the river.   They said unless the perils of swimming there were pointed out to the children by parents and others, more lives would be lost in the future.   Each lock and dam had tool and maintenance sheds along with a guard house; US Lock and Dam No. 5's buildings were located on the opposite side of the dam and near Freedom.   The article went on to explain how upsetting it was for the employees of the dam being forced to watch helplessly while the broad Ohio would claim yet another victim far over on the Monaca shore.   Parents of all lower Beaver Valley towns were urgently requested by the government men to forbid their sons (and all children) to swim in the deep, treacherously swift water above the bear traps* of any lock and dam and to point out to the children the risks they take if they would go to these areas to swim.

In doing just a little more research to determine where exactly the lock and dam No. 5 was located, I found the following information and decided to share it all just for general purpose since some of the dams would have also affected the levels of water in the Monaca area.

   *Bear traps is a name given to a type of dam device used in various dam constructions.

*** *** *** *** ***

The locks and dams along the Ohio River within the Monaca area were built to help create pools and increase the depth of the river.   Because the Ohio River had a history of becoming too shallow almost every summer, making navigation impossible, Congress passed the River and Harbor Act of 1875.   By 1881, Congress recommended constructing locks and dams on the Ohio River to maintain a 6 foot depth.   The dams were constructed of wooden wickets that were raised to hold back water during times when the water levels were low and would be dropped to the river bottom during periods of high water.   By 1905, Congress had approved increasing the depths of pools on the Ohio River to 9 foot.

Lock tenders and their families lived on-site at the lock and dam complexes on the Ohio River, therefore, each site had a well-constructed and nice sized lock tender house built at each site.   The first to be built was the Davis Island Dam (No. 1). It was completed and opened in 1889 with a large celebration since it was the first in the area.   Davis Island is situated on the Pittsburgh end of Neville Island.   Coming down the Ohio toward Monaca, there was Lock and Dam No. 2 at Glenfield (Emsworth); No. 3 was the Glen Osborne, near Sewickley; No. 4 was the Legionville, near Logstown (Ambridge); No. 5 spanned the Ohio near Freedom to Monaca; No. 6 was the Beaver/Merrill Dam (near Vanport).   The erecting of locks and dams 7, 8, 9, etc. continued on down the Ohio within the same time frame as all I just mentioned.

Davis Island Lock and Dam - No. 1

Located near Emsworth / Bellevue.

Work on the lock began Aug 19, 1878 and was completed about 7 years later, opening on
Oct 7, 1885. A wicket dam, composed of wooden bulkheads hinged on the river bottom with
bulkheads lowered when the river flow was high.

As of 1985, the American Society of Civil Engineers Board of Direction designated Davis Island
Lock and Dam on the Ohio River as a national historic civil engineering landmark.
At the time, it was the world's first lock gates and the widest lock chamber ever built; it was the
largest moveable dam built in the 19th century. It was removed in 1922 and replaced with the
Emsworth dam.

Views of the Davis Lock and Dam

c 1904

All that remains of the Davis Island Lock and Dam (2014).

Glenfield / Emsworth Dam – No. 2

Located near Emsworth and Bellevue.

The Emsworth dam was considered to have replaced the Davis Lock and Dam.

The contract for Glenfield was dated Dec 7, 1897; work commenced in Apr 1898.

The Emsworth Locks and Dam is located less than a mile downstream from the Davis Lock and Dam site.   It was constructed and replaced the Davis Lock and Dam after it was dismantled in 1922.

Construction on the Emsworth replaced the original and work began in 1919 and continued until 1922 with it opening in Sep 1921.   This dam was converted to a gated structure between 1935 and 1938 to accommodate larger, more modern barges.

1922 view of Glenfield /Emsworth Dam

Emsworth Dam - 2014 – main channel dam and locks and the back-channel dam (top of photo)

Glen Osborne Lock and Dam - No. 3

Located in the Sewickley area; approximately 1 mile above Coraopolis.
The contract was dated Dec 7, 1897; work commenced in Mar 1899.
Began operation in 1908, razed in 1930; replaced by Dashields Dam.

This original wicket lock and dam was replaced by the Dashields Lock and Dam which was constructed from 1927 to 1929, opening in Aug 1929. It is the only fixed crest type dam still in service on the Ohio River and maintains the pool from Glenwillard, PA upriver to the Emsworth Locks and Dam.

The Dashields Dam received its name from David Shields, a member of a prominent local family and longtime postmaster of Old Sewickley Bottom in the 1800s.

Legionville Lock and Dam - No. 4

Located between the former Northern Lights Shopping Center and Old Economy.
This was the fourth movable dam constructed on the Ohio River.
It was started in Apr 1898 and completed in Feb 1908.
Contained bear traps (a term associated with the type of dam that was built).
Most of original infrastructure of this lock and dam was demolished by the U.S. Army Corps of
        Engineers in 1936 due to the damages that occurred during the Great Flood of 1936.
The remaining structures on the eastern shore of the Ohio River were determined to pose no
        interference with river traffic, so they were left intact. The lock gates remained intact
        temporarily, but were later removed.
The Montgomery Lock and Dam, opening Jun 1936, contributed to the decision of not repairing,
        but removing Lock and Dam No. 4.
Much of the ground of the abandoned lock and dam site was disturbed with the CONRAIL
        railroad lines and construction of Rte. 65. There were still the lock tender's buildings and a
        powerhouse that remained partially intact but they were being severely vandalized. The property
        was owned by the River Salvage Company who decided to bulldoze the remaining buildings for
        liability reasons since displaced individuals were continuing to use and vandalize them.

Fun fact: In 1898-1900. the 5.731 acres of land for this Lock and Dam was owned by
Land of the Union Company (the Harmony Society).

East bank of Ohio River along Rte. 65 – all that remains of Legionville Lock and Dam No. 4

United States Lock and Dam - No. 5

Located just below Freedom and by the upper end of Monaca.

The contract was dated Dec 7, 1897; work commenced in Mar 1899.

There are two pictures – one of the dam crossing the Ohio River, and one of a tug boat, the Harmony being swept over the dam. The captain tried to maneuver the boat over the dam
during some flooding when the dam was not operating in Sep 1911.

This is photo of the #5 Dam that spanned the Ohio River between Monaca and Freedom, PA.

Towboat *Harmony* damaged on bear trap No. 5 Dam.

United States Lock and Dam – No. 6 – Beaver/Merrill Dam
    Located in Industry – near Vanport.
    Wickets, bear traps, and outside lock wall at Lock #6 were removed as soon as the Montgomery
        Island dam was finished.
    Work was started on this dam Jun 1892 and the dam was completed approx. 10 years later.
    It received its name from Col. Merrill who was in charge of government operations at that time
        Merrill Dam was gone by Aug 1936.

Merrill Lock and Dam No. 6

Lock and Dam buildings prior to becoming a restaurant

Then came the Montgomery Island Dam…….

The Montgomery Island Dam was dedicated on Aug 29, 1936.

Can be seen over the hillside, to your right, as you go up the hill into Potter Township
after passing over Raccoon Creek on the Potter Township bridge.

It replaced/eliminated United States Lock and Dams No. 4, No. 5, and No. 6.

Oct 1929 - Plans for a permanent dam were developed.

With the completion of a permanent dam at Emsworth prior to Oct 1929, this meant an open
pool of water would be available from Emsworth to the Montgomery Dam.

This dam is considered a "roller crest dam"/"roller top" dam on the Ohio – 31 miles below
Pittsburgh at Montgomery Island.

It was bid to be 1,380 feet, equipped with 10 roller gates (each 100 feet long and 16 feet high).
With piling, gates and service bridge it would be 1,500 feet long.

The Montgomery Island Dam is located on the Ohio, near Vanport on one side of the river, near
the mouth of Raccoon Creek on the other side of the river.

The caption of this pictures stated "New Montgomery Dam is monument to man's conquest of elements."

Picture from the opening ceremonies of the Montgomery Dam in 1936

All of the information on these locks and dams was included to give a bit of the background and tie into to the importance of how business and industry was increased and improved for Monaca along the Ohio River. Each lock and dam increased the depth and created pools for larger boats and barges to navigate along the Ohio. Lastly, they also contributed to the recreational boating side of the Monaca area of the Ohio River, all lending to the vision of and developing of the Monaca Riverfront Park.

*** *** *** *** ***

*** *** ***

BOAT BUSINESSES

Flat boats

Ferry boats and landings

Monaca – Rochester Ferry

Davis Brothers' Ferry

Lashell's Ferry

Miller's Ferry

Logstown Run Ferry

Logan's Ferry

West Economy Ferry

Fallston Ferry

Vanport Ferry

Roger's Ferry

Smith's Ferry / Georgetown Ferry / Dawson's Ferry

Cook's Ferry / Shippingport-Midland Ferry

Stoops Ferry

Midland Ferry Company

Boat Businesses

Many locations in Beaver County were popular places for the building of boats in the 1800s.   There were three popular styles of flat bottom boats built then - keel-boats, cotton boats, and canal boats.   A keel-boat had a prow (the part of the bow above the waterline) at both ends in order that the boat could go in either direction without having to be turned; most were between one hundred ten feet to one hundred twenty-five feet long and were finished with a cargo box.   A cotton boat was very similar in style to a keel-boat but was smaller in size; usually not over one hundred ten feet long.   A cotton boat was made to transport cotton out of small streams and onto the Mississippi.   The canal boats were long narrow boats that were used on the canals.

Many publications state that Phillips & Graham had their boat building business located in Phillipsburg prior to moving to Freedom in 1832.   There were many others in the area that prospered in the boat building business in the Beaver County area also.   John Boles was the first to start the boat building industry in Beaver County. In the 1820s, John settled between Rochester and New Brighton, establishing the boat yard Bolesville.   Hartman Whisler, who had been one of his employees, became Boles's partner; all of Boles's shares were sold to Whisler a few years after the partnership was formed and the business continued to prosper.

There were a few different types of boats that were built in the 1800s but with the levels of water in most of the local rivers being quite low, especially in the warmer weather and dry seasons, one type was the most commonly built in and around Beaver County – the flat boat.

In James Patterson's sketch of Beaver County, he states that "the first steamboat used for carrying passengers to run from Beaver to Pittsburg, by John Dickey and others."   The steamboat he wrote about only passed through the locks of the canal entering the Ohio once.   It was such a tight fit and took too long of a time that the steamboat was only used below the locks from then on; with this limited location of that steamboat being unproductive, it was sold to go on down the river.   Patterson also mentions the steamboats *Beaver*, *Fallston*, and *Newcastle* were put into successful operation.

With Monaca being a "river town," you will always find references and discussions about the Ohio River connected one way or another to Monaca.   With these discussions, you will also repeatedly hear about how the depth of the water varied and how important the water level was to residents and businesses.

There were times when the angry waters of a flooding condition threatened many people and/or their properties and other times when the low water level posed problems of a whole different matter.

1881-River traffic was halted when the Ohio River reached its lowest level on record, 1 foot, 9 inches.

Little Beaver Historical Society   Monaca Rochester bridge –
This picture shows a shallow stage of the Ohio River....look how much of the shore is exposed from the normal high water mark.   The right side of the picture is on the Monaca side of the river.

During the periods of very low water levels on the Ohio, the steamboats and other boats could have possibly still made it up or down using the very middle of the river if all they were doing was passing through.   If ships had cargo to be delivered, it would have to be carried to the wharf area or close to the normal shore line, wading through the water from the boats across the exposed river bed and onto the shoreline or wharf area.   For people who wanted to board or disembark a steamer or other larger boat, this would have been an exhausting venture also.   Passengers boarding or arriving in Monaca would have most likely had to do some wading and definitely walking over and through the sandy, gravely, dirt ground of the former river bed that was then exposed due to low water levels.   Those who did not come from a river town or area that greatly centered around the waterway for support, business, and transportation just did not appreciate what low water level could mean.

Monaca Wharf / Boat Landing

1889 – council approved constructing a wharf or boat landing in the river opposite the
pump house of the Monaca Water Works.   It was sometimes called the "Hog back."   This landing was used extensively by all river packets when receiving or delivering freight shipped by water.   Residents could board excursion and passenger steamers from the wharf, too.

1933 – early W.P.A. project enlarged this wharf.
Completed wharf was 800 feet long, the river wall is 21 feet high, and the wharf proper was over 60 feet wide.

> Friday, May 25, was set as the date for the annual school picnic, to be held at Rock Springs Park, Chester, W. Va., on the steamer Washington Under a guarantee the boat will be docked at the Monaca wharf, Thursday evening, May 24, at midnight. The board encountered some difficulty last year the boat arriving several hours late at the Monaca wharf.   1935

See W.P.A. section and Monaca Wharf / Boat Landing section for more detailed information on the wharf.

*** *** *** *** ***

Flat boats –

Pictured is a cropped image of an Alfred Waud engraving showing persons traveling down a river by flatboat in the late 1800s.

Flat boats were propelled by sweeps which were what the men were called that controlled the giant oars.

These boats were all very good when going down stream, but it required men of iron muscle and gigantic frame to propel them back up the stream.

The flatboat men were rugged men. They were hard-working, hard-drinking, hard-fighting men that most river towns dreaded to see stop.

There were hundreds of these "rough men" who not only handled the sweeps and steering oars on the rafts and keelboats. They also spent their monies in the local taverns which were known to line the river fronts. Gambling and drinking soon became quite the universal pastimes of these men when they were not aboard ships working. Of course with gambling and drinking there was usually quite a bit of disagreement that led to fighting. Keel boatmen and flat boatmen were just natural enemies, and the "meetings" between them were usually preludes to quite the show of opposing forces.

There was quite a bit of time that both keelboats and flatboats were used on the waterways; keelboats essentially did replace the flatboats. The advantage of keelboats was their ability to make a return trip, often times being pulled by steamboats. Georgetown was in many respects a typical river town. Captain Adam Poe of Georgetown, PA, wrote in his book about keel boating and how many of the local farmers had the strength to make good "polers." (A "poler" was one of several men who would be lined up along the side of the boat beginning from the front of the boat. Each man placed one end of a long pole on the river bottom, the other in his armpit and would then they slowly walk along the catwalk of the ship toward the back of the boat while pushing backward against the river bottom. This would force the keelboat upstream.) The keelboats eventually went the way of the flatboats when the technologically superior steamboat was developed.

> *Fun Fact:* There were many folklore songs written about the river men and one had some lines in it that would describe how these men thought of themselves and why they were more of a "scrapping lot":
> Oh, my name is Mike Fink, I'm a keelboat poler
> I'm a Salt River roarer and I eat live coals
> I'm a half-alligator and I ride tornaders
> And I can out-feather, out-jump, out-hop, out-skip
> Throw down and lick any man on the river

*** *** *** *** ***

Ferry boats

As much of the area became settled and pioneers were developing communities, towns, and areas, it was necessary to have connections and access to all the areas. This led to the building and improvements of roads. Engineers found no better way to create, develop, and build these roads than to follow trails of the Indians. These trails proved to be the best for traveling and the shortest distance between many locations. Since many of the Indian trails were used, the settlers found that these trails were the most appropriate places to upgrade and make into roads. As these trails were gradually becoming roads, those that lead to the rivers were of the next concern for settlers.

After the roads began to develop, the need to cross water ways was next on the list so that many roads and areas could also be connected. This led to the use of rafts for that purpose; these rafts developed into ferries. Henry Volhardt was the operator of the first canoe or ferry boat for pedestrians between Phillipsburg and Beaver. Cruder rafts were made to carry more people and supplies across rivers, thus forming the first ferries. These ferries piled between Phillipsburg (Monaca) and Rochester for many years until the steam ferry was developed, along with the construction of the first suspension bridge between Rochester and Monaca in 1896. The first ferry in Phillipsburg between Rochester and Phillipsburg was established in 1833 by the New Philadelphia Society called the *Messenger*. This ferry was in service until about 1847, maybe a bit longer. It was eventually replaced by the *W. C. Gray* and the *Mary C. Campbell* (see pictures further).

Hard to believe that during the summers of the 1800s and into the earlier 1900s, the Ohio River would run only about 1 foot deep between Pittsburgh and Cincinnati. During periods of more drought-like conditions and especially in the winters, boat traffic would be put to a halt, but people could easily cross the very shallow or frozen water. Before the Montgomery Dam was built in the 1930s, the Ohio River usually ran at least 14 feet lower than it currently does*. People always found it necessary to cross the Ohio River; just had the need to get to the other side. *It is quite hard to even guess with all the current dredging that occurs on the Ohio River in this area, exactly how deep the river actually is in many areas.

Even though the ferry was a flat-bottomed boat, it would be grounded until the winter's ice melted and the spring rains raised the water levels. Dredging of the Ohio River changed the depth of the middle of the river. Though the current depth of the Ohio River might only be 10 to 12 feet closer to the banks of the river most of the time, the middle of the river can run about 60 feet deep. The Ohio River was <u>once</u> known for its blue water and for being able to see the bottom in many of the places up and down the river.

Phillipsburg was no different than other parts of the county and country in beginning to use ferries. Henry Volhardt's ferry was not used for anything by transporting persons; it began as a canoe that traveled between Monaca and Beaver. Henry lived in the area between the current Alloy plant and the water works plant, along the river; this was the area of his ferry business also. The *Messenger* plied between Philipsburg and Rochester for many years; located between the current water works plant and the Monaca-Rochester bridge. The *Messenger* was succeeded by a steam ferry.

Ferries began to come into play up and down the Ohio. You could find a ferry business from Sewickley to Coraopolis, Moon Township and Ambridge to the South Heights, Rochester and Beaver to Monaca, Vanport to Bellowsville (which was near the Center/Potter line on what was Koppers, St. Joseph Lead, and/or Horsehead Industries properties). There were two ferries in Industry; one went to Shippingport prior to the Shippingport Bridge opening in 1964, and the other ferry was located in another defunct area, Safe Harbor, (which is now a boat mooring across the Ohio where Wolfe's Run empties into the Ohio and is now Shippingport).

Outside Industry, Rte. 68, there was Smith's Ferry in Georgetown. Anyone familiar with local history should know of the story of Meriwether Lewis who had a noted voyage 200 years ago with his leaky boat which landed in Georgetown. There is still a road down to the bank of the river at the end of Market Street in Georgetown that leads to the former ferry stop. Smith's Ferry began to operate before the Civil War.

When one of the ferries would be out of commission due to weather, low waters, or whatever, it meant that everyone had to walk, go by horseback, or wagon to their destinations. It would be a 22 mile drive to the Chester-West Virginia bridge, then to East Liverpool-Ohio, and back to Pennsylvania. There were many weather related events, as the extremely high water in the 1930s, that put many small bridges underwater and ferries out of commission.

For the most part, ferries were very safe; but like all other modes of transport, there were accidents. The Georgetown ferry landing is an example. There was a fatal accident late at night. While the ferry was closed for the day in the late 1940s, a car sped onto the flat boat. The car snapped both chains stretched across the entrance ramp, traveled straight across the deck of the ferry, and again snapped the chains on the exit ramp at the other end, plunging into deeper water since the river was running high at the time. It was not until the river level dropped that the top of the car was discovered with two couples found dead in the submerged car. Another deadly accident occurred in 1963 when there was one of the worse fogs in the area. A towboat with 11 empty barges wrecked head-on into the Shippingport Ferry boat. The ferry was completely full with 8 cars and thirteen passengers. When the crash occurred, some people panicked; one jumped onto an empty barge and one jumped into the river. The Crucible worker from Pittsburgh who jumped into the river unfortunately died.

Many ferries were just a form of updated rafts; most built to accommodate carrying horses and buggies. They would ride/sit right at water level and hand rails were simple strung cables that kept people and vehicles from pitching overboard. There was a ramp type lip that would drop down and turn into a landing, loading, or exit ramp. The cost was on an average 35 cents a car or a nickel for people on foot. Once the horse and buggy began to fade out, a typical ferry could hold up to eight cars.

The ferry man (aided by whoever may be willing to help) would guide the ferry boat across the river by pulling, hand over hand, on the cable. These types of ferry boats were called cable ferry, chain ferry, swing ferry. The cable would be made of either heavy rope or steel chains and eventually were replaced with more durable wire cable. Before the bridges totally eliminated the use of ferry boats, there were engines that propelled the ferry boats across the waters. There were gas powered "pushers" or "yachts" attached to the sides of the ferries. These would have a swivel type device on them so the ferry could travel in either direction without having to be turned around. Passengers could travel in the "pusher" or "yacht" area, but it was more common to see them just standing on the decks. Once the gas-powered engines were being used, ferries would often take people from as far as Georgetown, up the Ohio to Pittsburgh on a daily basis for work. These commutes were quite time consuming since it would normally take about 10 minutes just to make a crossing of the river. Yet using the roadways and/or accessing an appropriate bridge could be even more time consuming.

Most ferries ran from 6 am until 6 pm on what they called "slow time" (standard time) and from 6 am until 8 pm on "fast time" (daylight saving time). A typical load for a ferry each day would be about 100 cars.

Once the Pennsylvania and Lake Erie Railroad came to Monaca, it did indeed bring in new factories, more residents, and diverse businesses; but it also proved the ferry businesses to have outlived their lives and usefulness. The opportunity to sit and watch a ferry cruise across the river, the excitement and wonder on the face of a person traveling on a ferry for the first time, the livelihood of many ferry owners all joined the ranks of becoming but a memory.

The next several pages will give some descriptions of more local ferries, and if available to me, I also included pictures of many of these ferries.

John Rainbow (Rambo?) is listed in the 1841 Directory with his occupation as *Ferryman*. No location or name of the ferryboat, nor whether it traveled across the Ohio River specifically to Beaver and/or Rochester. He may not have had his own business, but instead been employed by Mr. Volhardt or even worked on or ran one of the shifts of the *Messenger* -? -.

———

The Borough-Bee
    I found one (1) statement making claim to *The Borough-Bee* being the ferryboat that made communications between Rochester and Phillipsburg before the bridge was constructed. I found no further information to give a time frame or to verify this statement.

———

Monaca – Rochester Ferry

The ferry launching site was along the river shore by the former and current site of the Monaca Water Works.

> 1833 - ferryboat *Messenger* was the first vehicular ferry that traveled between Monaca and Rochester. The *Messenger* was established by the New Philadelphia Society. It was succeeded by a steam ferry.
>
> 1862 - the *W.C. Gray* was also a ferryboat that traveled between Monaca and Rochester. It was rebuilt and named the *Mary C. Campbell*.

courtesy BCHR&LF

Messenger - The first Monaca-Rochester ferry boat – sitting along the Ohio River bank at the shoreline in Monaca.

The *Mary Campbell* ferry boat plying the Ohio River at Monaca.

The view in this picture of the *Mary C. Campbell* is looking toward the Monaca shore – the pointer is indicating the building at the top of the hill to the right – this was the old Shrodes / Point Breeze Hotel (now razed); the water works building would be to the right of the picture .

Other ferries that existed over the span of time before being basically put out of business by the construction of railroad bridges, as well as multiple pedestrian, vehicular, and street car bridges were:

Unknown name - There was a ferry between Fort McIntosh in Beaver and the southern shore, but by 1788 this ferry no longer existed.   It may have been the.......

Lawrence's Ferry
This ferry landing was opposite Beaver Town (now Beaver).

Niblow's Ferry
This ferry was located somewhere in the vicinity of where the Monaca P & LE RR bridge reaches the shoreline in Monaca. It was opposite the former Harmony warehouse, Beaver.

Miller's Ferry
This ferry was at the foot of Main Street; it would go from Haysville (by Neville Island) to the bottom of Main Street in Coraopolis.   George Miller, owner, would also rent out boats prior to the 1920s.

Logstown Run Ferry
As New Sheffield grew, there was a Pittsburgh to Beaver stage coach line.   Sheffield Road was built to get to this ferry at Logstown Run.

Logan's Ferry

Fallston Ferry
This ferry crossed the Beaver River.   Use of this ferry was eventually replaced by the Sharon Bridge.

Little Beaver Historical Society   A full view of the *Fallston Ferry* crossing the Beaver River.

Fallston Ferry on the Beaver River at Sharon (Bridgewater)   This was a "cable ferry."
I have enlarged a portion of the picture to show the actual cable. You can easily see the cable and a few of the men are working to pull the ferry across the river.

West Economy Ferry   Was located where the (2016) Aliquippa- Ambridge bridge stands.
This ferry was used by many New Sheffield residences traveling from New Sheffield to Scottsville, to Longvue Avenue, and then down a steep Economy Road (which was used until Rte. 51 became four lanes), and then down to this ferry location.

Davis Brothers' Ferry   In the Ambridge and South Heights area.
It carried workers from Ambridge to West Economy, near South Heights. The Ambridge Bridge was built in 1927 at Ethel's Landing near South Heights post office (prior to 1905).   The *Davis Ferry* crossed near the current bridge location.

Lashell's Ferry   This ferry was located near the current Sewickley Bridge (2016).   It went from Sewickley at Chestnut Street to Coraopolis (before the Sewickley Bridge in 1911).

Midland Ferry Company   This company and Ferry were dated from Oct 1905.   The establishment was started for the maintenance of the ferry.   The ferry navigated over the Ohio River near the foot of McCoy Street in the town of Midland, Ohio Township, PA.   It went to a point opposite the south side of the river, near the end of Hookstown Road in Green Township.   The ferry site was about 2 miles from the Smith Ferry and Georgetown ferry, and was also about 2 miles from Cooks Ferry.   It was also about nine miles from the nearest bridge which was the P&LE railroad bridge in Monaca / Beaver, about ten miles from the Monaca/Rochester bridge, and six miles from the bridge in East Liverpool, Ohio.

Vanport Ferry   This ferry ran between Ferry Street in Vanport and Bellowsville (Potter Township).   It was operated from at least 1807 to a bit beyond 1915.   This ferry was an example of an underwater cable ferry.   This type of cable was said to keep a ferry steady for its crossings.   Though it became a gasoline powered ferry, it was known for its forge. The actual crossing of this ferry over the river would have been almost exactly where the current (2016) Vanport Expressway Bridge now spans the Ohio River.   F. Cuming wrote *Sketches of a Tour to the Western Country* and in this writing, he alludes to the Vanport ferry as he saw it and was describing the Ohio River in 1807– "A ferry two miles below Beaver is a handsome situation, beyond which the banks are high on both sides, and the river does not exceed one hundred and fifty yards wide."

Vanport ferry – 1915   courtesy BCHR&LF

This map shows the location of the ferry landing that was located between Vanport and the former area called Bellowsville (Potter Township).

Roger's Ferry
This ferry was located in Industry, PA.   This Ferry crossed the Ohio River in the area just below Potter Township, a bit past the current Montgomery Dam.

Little Beaver Historical Society

Smith's Ferry   aka   Georgetown Ferry   aka   Dawson's Ferry
The earliest documented report describing a ferry was in 1794 when the troops from Burgettstown
        crossed the river on *Dawson's Ferry* and marched along the Tuscarawas.
There was a steamboat landing known as Rock Port which was located about a quarter mile above Smith's
        Ferry area.
Jesse Smith purchased the ferry boat from Benjamin Dawson in 1817.
There was a stagecoach line that traveled from Pittsburgh through Georgetown with mail and
        passengers. It would cross the Ohio River by ferry at Smiths' Ferry to get to Cleveland.
There was a toll bridge erected about a mile from the mouth of the Little Beaver in summer/fall
        of 1809 on the road leading from Washington County to New Lisbon, Ohio.
Ohioville is located on the Ohio River near the southwestern corner of Ohio township.
It is across the river from Georgetown.   The two were connected by a ferry that was in operation since
        about 1804.   Smith's Ferry was a means of communications between the southern and
        northern portions of the county.   The ferry was run by Thomas Smith and is mentioned in a road
        petition in Dec 1799.   Thomas Smith came from Maryland about 1790 with his family.   He was
        one of the first settlers at Georgetown and Smith's Ferry community was named from this family.

Benjamin Dawson owned the ferry sometime prior to and during 1817; it was bought again by Jesse
        Smith. Jessie died in May 1818 and his sons Jesse and Thomas ran the ferry after their father's
        death.   The ferry did cease operations in 1949 after a gruesome accident involving the ferry. Even
        without the horrible accident, the lack of use/business and the building of more bridges caused its
        closing and it ceased operation after more than 150 years of service.

Little Beaver Historical Society -   Photo by Nate Thomas

Photos from the Pittsburgh Sun-Telegraph newspaper

SCENE OF TRAGEDY . . . This is the Georgetown Ferry where police believe an auto drove onto the boat and in- to the water. Two West Virginia couples were found drowned in the auto when it was pulled out yesterday.

Additional Smith Ferry information: Before the dam of the area was built and the water levels were raised, in Smiths Ferry, PA, there were Indian carvings in the rocks along the bank of the river. These are now submerged with the depth of the river being increased.

INDIAN ROCKS, Smiths Ferry, Pa.

1908 postcard

Cook's Ferry aka Shippingport-Midland Ferry

Went from Industry to Shippingport.   It was started in 1858 by George W Cook.

In Apr 1964, the equipment of the ferry company was impounded by the US Court, Pittsburgh. The owners of the ferry were named defendants in a case stemming from the death of two men in Oct 1963 when the ferry boat struck a towboat owned by the Consolidation Coal Co, Pittsburgh.   In 1963 and 64, more than 400 motorists still patronized the ferry daily, or they would have had to drive to East Liverpool, Ohio, and Chester W.VA, or drive to Rochester or Monaca to cross the river on a bridge.   The owners had to post bond and obtain property and liability insurance which presented a problem since there were not many ferries still in operation at that time.

The Shippingport Bridge, built in 1964, probably is what really sealed the fate of this business.

Little Beaver Historical Society   Cook's Ferry– late 50s/early 60s

Stoops Ferry   Stoops Ferry was located at Narrows Run Road north of the Sewickley Bridge.
Went from University Blvd, Moon Township. It was used more by farmers bringing all their
goods to market or by residents who would go for picnics and hiking outside the area.
There's a Stoops Ferry Road there which was also referred to as Shousetown and Stoops Ferry Road.
Stoops Ferry was named after William Stoops, the 19th century riverboat captain.

Looking west toward the Sewickley Bridge

Stoops Ferry station – looking from the Sewickley bridge

Unidentified Ferry Boat crossing the Ohio River - 1907

***   ***   ***   ***   ***
***   ***   ***

STEAMBOATS

Phillipsburg boat yards

Area boat yards

Details on local steam boats

New Orleans

Enterprise

Washington

The Homer Smith renamed The Greater Pittsburgh

Tom Reese

The Jim Wood

Exporter

Arabia

Cape Giradeau / Gordon C. Greene / Sarah Lee / River Queen

Great Republic

The Queen City

John A. Wood

Joseph B. Williams

The American Queen

The Delta Queen

Costanzo

People and personnel associated with the river business

Steamboats

There were probably more than 11,000 paddlewheel steamboats traveling the rivers in America prior to the Civil War. Some of these boats were like floating mansions and had wonderful trimmings and luxurious inside furnishings. Most people associate a steamboat with Mark Twain, Dixieland celebrations, or money hungry-card playing gamblers.   Whatever your idea and memory of a steamboat may be, they are an important part of the American history.   Only the Delta Queen Steamboat Company is still active in operating a fleet of overnight passenger steamboats, with those being on the Mississippi River system.

Steamboats that once were quite numerous on the rivers each had their own distinguishing characteristics. Pilots and river men could easily identify a boat by them.   They would know if it was a side-wheel or stern wheel – whether it was large or small – what kind of trimmings were on the smoke stacks – what type of markings were on the pilot house – was there a "Texas" or no "Texas" (the Texas was a structure or section of a steamboat that included the pilothouse and the crew's quarters). One of the most important characteristics of a steamboat was the sound of the bell or whistle. (See more on bells and whistles at the end of this section.)

Very large cargoes were taken down river by steamboats; steamboats were also popular for towing the dismantled hulls of old boats. This was the beginning of the "tow" of current days.

> *Fun Fact: Currently people today say a tow boat is moving barges up or down a river. A barge is never "towed" -- it is "pushed," so instead of calling the boats that are moving barges up and down the rivers "tow boats," they should correctly be called "push boats." Of course we all know that will never be changed.*

Most of the pictures included in this section were called packet boats since they were steamboats that ferried passengers to specific destinations and back again.   Steamboats were so accurate in their departure and arrival times that they were even contracted to carry the mail.   There were large side-wheel packets that were popular for their speed, maneuverability, ability to haul large numbers of people and cargo, and were preferred for longer, regularly scheduled daily runs.   The other style of steamer was on the smaller side and called stern wheel packets. These were used for shorter routes; sometimes used for longer runs when the river levels were too low for the larger "side wheel" packets.

Once they were introduced, it was a more common site to see steamboats regularly passing under the Monaca bridges and traveling the Ohio River as seen in this early 1900s photograph.

Little Beaver Historical Society

A steamboat passing under the 1st Rochester/Monaca Suspension bridge which was built 1896 (bridge was replaced in 1930).

Although I am not writing this book about steamboats, I thought I would share snippets of information as they were found; this does not apply merely to this section and steamboats, but being rather applied and evident throughout the entire book. However, in this section, without doing additional and extensive researching, I do not even try to make claim to having a complete list of steamboats of the area, boat yards, or other information. What I have included is an extremely shortened version on multiple miscellaneous informational steamboat related topics.

This quote from The Western Pennsylvania Historical Magazine, Vol. 47, Oct 1964, Number 4, very eloquently describes what residents of Monaca and the surrounding river towns would have experienced during the steamboat era:

".... the memories of George Shiras, Sr., who beginning in 1837 with the purchase of his downriver farm near the present Baden, in Beaver County, had heard "the hoarse whistles of packet steamers straining for speed on the river; the cries of boatmen ; the rumble of farm wagons along the valley road," and had seen "the procession of towboats pulling heavily laden barges of coal ; the timber rafts piled high with logs from forests on the hillsides of the Allegheny and Monongahela ;the keelboats and flatboats loaded with cargoes of every description, riding the current down to faraway New Orleans ; the little stern-wheel steam tubs thrashing and panting against the stream, inching their way up to Pittsburgh, and at night, the glow of steamboat furnaces .... the showers of sparks .... the lonely lanterns of small craft creeping between the black hills." This rather colorful language doubtless reflects quite well the mood of many observers in what was a period of considerable romance."

I will share with you that historical research has compiled a list of one hundred and sixty-six steam boats were built in Beaver County. They were built at one of these boatyards: George Baker-Phillipsburg/Monaca; Phillips and Graham-Phillipsburg/Monaca; Phillips and Graham...then Phillips and Betz-Freedom; Charles Graham-Industry; McFail and Thomas Rogers –Industry; Baker, Hall and Co. –Freedom; Freedom Boat Building Society; Midland Barge Company; John Graham and G. W. Rogers –Freedom; A & G Coffin-Freedom; R. Moffett and G. W. Rogers; George Hall; Eakin & Co.; S. W. Rogers. Details on these companies and which boats they all made may be found in a book *Built in Beaver County and What Happened to Them*.

> *Fun facts:* Freedom was a leader in steamboat construction with 108 steamboats built there.
> Shousetown Boatyard (Glenwillard) built their first steamboat in 1829, the Kentuckian.
> The last steamship they built was the Great Republic in 1867. They produced more than 112
> steamboats in its time of business. Peter Shouse was the owner.
>
> The small area on the very top of a steamer was reserved for the more affluent passengers.
> Since they used hog posts to raise or keep a steamship from sagging in the middle since it was
> so flat, it was considered "living high on the hog" to be in this cabin area on top of a steamer – thus
> the phrase "living high on the hog" coming to mean doing well.

Two of the only boat building business in the 1800s that I found mentioned as once being in Phillipsburg before moving and establishing their businesses in the Freedom, PA area were:

Phillips and Graham   and   George Baker

> *Fun Fact:* Boats without sails or oars were definitely a surprise to all who witnessed them for
> the first time; they caused such a great sensation all along their travels. The first steamboats
> were especially amazing to the slaves and the Indians who had no idea what they were. It is
> said that the first steamboat that was seen on Lake Michigan by the Indians was called "Walk
> in the Water" because they actually believed it when someone jokingly told them it was drawn by
> a team of trained sturgeons.

———

Phillipsburg boat yards:

Built by Phillips & Graham at Phillipsburg:
    Unknown years – *Paul Jones, Red Rover*
    In 1825 – *General Wayne, Liberatore, Paul Jones*
    In 1826 – *Pocahontas, Florida, Columbus, Echo*
    In 1827 - *Essex, La Grange, Pittsburgh and Wheeling Packet, Yazoo*
    In 1828 – *Missouri*
    In 1829 – *Cora*
    In 1830 – *New Jersey, Gleaner, Peruvian, Boston, Hermit, Louisville, Carrollton*
    In 1831 – *Winnebago, Antelope, Michigan, Mowhawk, Transport*
Built by George Baker, Phillipsburg: *Narragansett, Pawnee*

Other local boat yards.........
Many of the steam boats that regularly passed by and even did business in Monaca but were not built in Monaca:

Built by Phillips and Graham on the west side of the Ohio River, 3 miles above Beaver:
    In 1822 – *Pennsylvania, Rambler*   In 1823 – *Eclipse, President*
    In 1824 – *Lafayette, Gen Brown, Wm. Penn**   In 1825 – *Bolivar*
    In - ?? - *Louisville, Madison, St. Charles, Shawnee, Hibermian, Rienzi, General Pratt, New Castle**
        *The *New Castle* was a smaller sternwheeler of 40 tons – and her sister ship...........
        the *Fallston*.   Both ships plied the Pittsburgh-Beaver trades which connected with canal boats.
        *The *William Penn* is said to have carried the Harmonites from their second settlement in New
        Harmony, Indiana, to their third home, and finally to Economy.

Built by Stephen Phillips & Co. at Freedom:
    1832 – *Fame, Return, Chester, Missourian, Boonslick*
    1833 – *William Penn, Majestic, Galenian*
    1834 – *Potosi, New Castle, Ivanhoe, Mogul, Siam, St. Charles*
    1835 – *Detroit, Dewbuke, Selma, Madison, Alton, United States*
    1836 – *Palmyra, Troy, Boonville, Rienzi, Louisville, St. Louis*
    1837 – *Arial,* two steamboats on the stocks

Built by Graham & Rodgers 3 miles above Beaver:
    In 1828 – *Potomic, Phoenix, Talma, Huron*

> *Fun fact: By the 1830s, when Stephen Stone built a hotel in Bridgewater at the confluences of the Beaver and Ohio Rivers, Beaver Point had also become the site of boat-building and a stopping-point for riverboats.*

Built in Bridgewater:
    The *Michigan*, commanded by Captain Brice Boies;   the *Lake Erie, No.12*, Captain John Gordon;   the *Fallston*, Captain John Dickey;   the *Beaver*, Captain James Murray and also Captain Charles Stone.
        The *Beaver*, ran daily between Beaver and Pittsburgh, leaving Beaver at 8 am, arriving at Pittsburgh by 12:30, left Pittsburgh at 3 o'clock and arrived at Beaver 5:30 pm.   One of the other 4 ships above also made regular runs between Beaver and Pittsburgh.

Built by John Graham at Bridgewater – *Belfast, Wabash Valley, Fallston (see above)*

Built by George Baker & Co, Freedom - *Pilot*

Built by Freedom Boat Building Society: *Majestic, Missourian, Pirate, General Pratt, Lake Erie, Laura, Winchester (in 1851), Major Darien (in 1852), Miner, Washington, Jane Franklin*

Built in Freedom - *Atlas*

Built by _?_ - *New Lisbon, Wellsville, Massillon, Liberty, Shanon*
    All made frequent runs to & from Pittsburgh, Beaver and Wellsville, Wheeling-O, Brownsville

Built by G. W. Rogers (Freedom) - *Rose of Sharon*

    (John Graham and George W. Rogers formed a co-partnership firm Graham & Rogers)

Built by McFail and Thomas Rogers, Industry - *Financier, America*

Built by Joseph Hall company - *Newcastle*

Built by Jacob Poe company - *Yorktown*

Built at Christler's Landing - *Bedford*

Built by Midland Barge Company - *Cincinnati*

Built by _?_ - *Sunshine* – 1910   (made excursions from Monaca)

1826 - *Albian* - 50-ton packet launched at Brownsville, PA, and entered the Pittsburgh–Louisville trade.
    She was the first steamboat to make a run upward on the Allegheny River to Kittanning.

1828 – *William D. Duncan* – 110-ton packet

1830 – *Allegheny* – 64 passenger and 25-ton packet – a double stern wheeler - left Pittsburgh on
    May 14, 1830 and arrived in New Orleans on May 21st.

Built in Shousetown by Peter Shouse company: *Kentuckian* (was the first one built in 1829), *Nile, Baltimore, Talisman, Red Rover, Kensington, Huntsman, Gondola, Mohican,* **Enterprise***, Georgian, Mobile, Scout, Baltic, Chief Justice Marshall, Juniatta, Chancellor, Columbus, Ohian, Hunter, Huntress, Canton,* **Arabian***, Algonquin, Eloisa, Termont, Havanna, Columbian, Chamois, Buffalo*; and in 1866/67, the last steamboat built at Shousetown was *the* **Great Republic.**
        *Bold print indicates there is a picture and/or specifics on this boat included in this section.

        Once again, not specifically on Monaca, here is another direct quote that provides quite a bit of information of steam boating on the Ohio – it came from the section on Bridgewater from *History of Beaver County Pennsylvania and its Centennial Celebration*, by: Rev. Joseph H. Bausman, A. M. Knickerbocker Press New York, 1904:

"The land lying west of the mouth of the Big Beaver and running down to the Ohio River, known in early times as Beaver Point* and later as Stone's Point* was bought as early as 1803 by the Harmony Society. They built here a warehouse for storing goods received and shipped by river. This they sold before their removal from Butler County west to Indiana. It was used for the same purpose as late as 1840. On this point a number of town lots were sold by Stephen Stone, Oct 18, 1831, and he also sold lots on the island which formerly existed a short distance below the present dam and bridge, but which has been entirely obliterated by the floods. At this point in early times a good deal of boat building was done. In his sketch of Beaver County, James Patterson says:

Upon the locks of the canal entering the Ohio was built the first steamboat used for carrying passengers to run from Beaver to Pittsburg, by John Dickey and others, of a size which they calculated would pass through these locks. It did pass through once, but was found to be too tight a fit, consuming too much time in the transit. She ran for a time below the locks, but it was found that she was too small for that trade, so she was sold to go down the river. The steamboats *Beaver, Fallston and New Castle* were quickly built and put in successful operation, landing for a time at that place and also at Rochester, where large warehouses were erected to accommodate the trade. Stone's Point* was a stopping place for the steamboats passing up and down the river, and a place of resort for the citizens of Beaver and Bridgewater, where they assembled to hear the news from Pittsburg and other points, or to see the eminent persons who not infrequently traveled up and down the Ohio when it was a main route of transportation from the East to the West. A large hotel was built at the Point by Mr. Stone, which was much frequented in the days of steam boating.   Some of the packets of about the year 1840 were the *Michigan*, commanded by Captain Brice Boies; *Lake Erie, No.12*, Captain John Gordon; *Fallston*, Captain John Dickey; and the *Beaver,* Captain James Murray. Two packets left daily for Pittsburg when the stage of water permitted.................."

*Beaver Point aka Stone Point was at the confluence of the Beaver and Ohio Rivers, Bridgewater.

***   ***   ***   ***   ***

With Freedom just across the river from parts of Monaca, many of the steamboats that were built in Freedom were a common sight.   Phillips and Graham / Phillips & Betz boat building businesses were succeeded by Abel Coffin Company.   Charles Graham & Company (Chas. Graham, Robert McCaskey, and Thomas G. Kerr) succeeded Abel's business; then becoming McCaskey & Kerr.   McCaskey & Kerr's company were in business for thirty-eight years until Robert McCaskey died, but it was agreed that the business continue under the same name.   If I were doing a history on Freedom, I'd continue with the many companies that succeeded, but instead I'll end with the statement that many steamboats and steam engines were produced in Freedom with the result being many steamboats that served or frequented the Monaca area.

c. 1890 - steamboats at docks in Freedom, PA

Unidentified steam boats

courtesy BCHR&LF

Two sternwheelers waiting to move their barges along the Ohio shoreline in Monaca.

Steam boat at Lock No. 5 which crossed the Ohio between Monaca and Freedom.

*** *** *** *** ***

Although not of news directly related to Monaca, Center or Potter, I felt while on the subject of steamboats that this one bit of information was worth including and sharing. Bear in mind, the original steamboat, *New Orleans*, passed by Monaca in 1811 (see specifics on that steamboat)..........

There was a grand celebration in Pittsburgh in 1911 during their centennial activities. Forty-seven different packet boats came to Pittsburgh and lined up, side by side, along the Monongahela River wharf. They came to honor the launching of a replica of the *New Orleans*. The *New Orleans* was going to repeat the same journey as was made back in 1811 (which meant it would be passing by Monaca again in 1911). It must have been such a wonderful scene to see all these wonderful steamboats lined up to honor another steam boat being launched and making a repeat of the original's maiden journey.

This 1911 postcard only shows about one third of the forty-seven steamships that were lined up for the event.

*** *** *** *** ***

Details on some local Steam Boats known to frequent Monaca

New Orleans   Oct 20 of 1811 was the date the first steamboat started down the Ohio River from Pittsburgh. This steamboat was the *New Orleans*, captained by Nicholas J. Roosevelt (brother of Theodore Roosevelt's great grandfather).   It took 9 days to reach New Orleans.   Its draft (the minimum depth of water a ship can safely navigate) was too deep for her to be regularly used on the Ohio River, so the boat was then used on the Mississippi which proved to have deep enough water.   The *New Orleans* sank in Jul of 1814 when it struck a submerged tree snag.

It is said that residents of Monaca, Rochester, and Beaver cheered as this boat passed by on the Ohio River in 1811.   During the 1911 centennial celebration in Pittsburgh, a replica of the *New Orleans* was launched and was to repeat the first original voyage down the Ohio River.   (See previously included mention of this.)

Washington   In 1816 the *Washington* steamboat was built at Wheeling, West Virginia, for Captain Shreve and four partners. She was a 150-foot-long, 400-ton stern wheeler with a shallow hull.   The boilers were placed on the main deck.   She also had twin smokestacks and a pilot house.   The design of the *Washington* permitted the minimum draft necessary to clear the shallow bottom of the Ohio River.   The *Washington* was one of the steamers that made several excursions from Monaca.

USA 25 — Washington 1816

Commemorative stamp issued in 1989

Enterprise   1814 – The fourth steamboat on the local rivers was the *Enterprise*, built by Daniel French at Brownsville (Pittsburgh), PA for The Monongahela and Ohio Steam Boat Co.   She was the first steamboat to conduct regular commerce on the Ohio River; transporting freight and/or passengers. Israel Gregg was the captain, with this position going to Captain Henry M. Shreve.   She also transported munitions to New Orleans from Pittsburgh for Andrew Jackson's army to use during the Battle of New Orleans.   The *Enterprise* had many "firsts" – it was also the first steamboat to make a return trip from New Orleans to Louisville.   Captain Shreve piloted her on many voyages down the Ohio.

Fun Fact: Popular folklore tells of Captain Shreve as the person who cut his cabin up into small rooms and then named them after the current states in the union, there-fore the name they are now called around the world – staterooms.   Another popular story tells how Nicholas Roosevelt built the luxurious steamboat George Washington in the 1830s containing 26 rooms. With there being 26 states in the union at that time, each of these rooms was given the name of a state – thus the current reference of ....staterooms.

The Homer Smith --   renamed............   The Greater Pittsburgh

1914 to 1931 - sternwheeler, wooden hull excursion boat

Image from post card

Built at the Howard Ship Yards and Dock Company in Port Fulton (now Jeffersonville), Indiana.

Homer Smith had a dance floor on the forward end of the main deck with staterooms behind. The Texas deck also held staterooms. In 1915, she ran excursions on the lower Ohio River in the Louisville area, and once tried the Louisville-Cincinnati trade. In 1916, she ran a Pittsburgh-New Orleans Mardi Gras trip and then an Easter Cruise, Pittsburgh-New Orleans. She became a regular excursion boat at Pittsburgh, with the cabins and staterooms being removed. *The Homer Smith* would winter in the mouth of the Kanawha and ran tramp excursions in the spring. She also was known for running day trips to Sewickley, Pennsylvania to Walnut Beach, a resort. She was sold to the Pittsburgh Amusement Company in 1928 and renamed *Greater Pittsburgh*.

Greater Pittsburgh steamer was well known for taking people to Rock Springs Park. In Jul 1930, many Monaca residents were among about 1,000 people who were passengers on this steamer; others went by street car or automobile with 200 in all from Monaca in attendance at the park that Jul day.

This steamboat burned and was destroyed in Apr 1931; the watchmen were jailed for arson in her burning.

* Note – the bent stack. Steamships did this to be able to fit under bridges.

Event Will Be Community Affair and Entire Valley Will Attend—Many Awards Will Be Given

A partial list of prizes to be given by the Monaca Board of Trade at their outing to Rock Springs Park on the steamer Greater Pittsburgh on Wednesday, July 9, reveals that some lucky persons are to be well repaid for attending. Among the most interesting of these prizes are a basket of groceries each to the tallest married couple on the boat (combined height), the shortest couple, and the couple with ** largest family. The prize **- boat also will be quit**- **he first prize will**

1930 article referencing Monaca and the *Greater Pittsburgh*

Tom Reese

The *Tom Reese* steamboat was built in Freedom in the late 1890s.

Photo courtesy the Beaver County Historical Research and Landmarks Foundation
c. 1898 view of the *Tom Reese* docked in Freedom, PA

Senator   Originally built in 1883 in St. Louis, MO.   This steamboat went by *Diamond Jo* and was rebuilt in 1892, 1903, and in 1917; owned by Streckfus Line. She was rebuilt once again and made into an excursion boat. She was rebuilt one last time in 1939 as the *Senator*.   She retired from excursion service in 1942 and was abandoned near St. Louis in 1953.   This excursion steamer, *Senator*, was also used for transporting residents to Rock Springs Park in the early 1940s.

This is an ad that was in the newspaper for the Beaver school picnic, it is included just to show how the steamboats were used for transportation.   There were many of these ads each time a specific area such as Beaver, Monaca, Freedom, etc. had one of their school or community picnics. This sample is NOT for Monaca, but it was the most legible since the other ads that were for Monaca did not copy well and were too blurry to read.   With the *Senator* being the steamboat most often used for these excursions, I just wanted to share at least one sample. (This was in a The Daily Times May 1940 edition.)

> *Fun fact: Steamboat racing was a very common event with the river men for many years, more or less "bragging rites." Although the general public considered these events very exciting and entertaining, with many bets being placed, these races were also considered extremely dangerous events and multiple times ended with explosions, extreme damage to the boats or complete loss of a boat, and even physical injuries, including some fatalities. Throwing caution to the wind, these races were taken very seriously by the captains and crews of the ships with the only concern being labeled the winner. To be victorious, this meant having the power of the boiling steam engine and to those who would stoke it higher and higher, closing the safety valves to ensure the fastest time. With titles on the line, many dangerous maneuvers were taken such as loading lard into the engines to make them burn hotter.   Creating so much power in the engines and the non-release of steam from the boilers created the perfect set up for violent explosions; with explosions, comes the likelihood of fires. Steamboats being constructed of wood, meant an explosion made them veritable firetraps. In 1852 government regulations were imposed on steamboat boilers which cut down on the number and desire for such races, but they were still held whenever possible.*

The Jim Wood and the Exporter

The *Jim Wood* and *Exporter* were two steamers built in Freedom, PA. They were part of a coal fleet and were both paddle wheel boats.

COAL FLEET IN NO. 3 POOL, FREEDOM, PA.

_ 1913

Arabia

She was constructed at a boatyard in Brownsville in 1853 by John Pringle's Boat Yards. The *Arabia* was a power side wheel steamboat. Although she did transport some passengers, she was basically a cargo ship. This steamboat was found buried 45 feet under in a cornfield in Kansas City. The *Arabia* sank in 1956 on the Missouri River after hitting a snag (sunken tree); it was carrying 220 tons of cargo that day. Among the cargo were many, many guns which were to be used in the battle of states approving or disapproving slavery (this movement was called "Bleeding Kansas"); also, there were two prefab homes as part of the cargo. When it sank, there were no human casualties, but the body of a mule that had been tied to some machinery was found when they excavated the ship.

*visit the Heinz History Center for display and more information on the *Arabia*

John A. Wood

 The *John A. Wood* was a stern wheel packet, built in 1887 in Harmar, Ohio.   She had a three-chime whistle that came from George Strecker, a mechanically-minded farmer from West Virginia. She traveled the Ohio River, Mississippi River and St. Croix River. The *John A. Wood* sank in Louisiana in Mar, 1916.   She was originally used her first year to carry John Robinson's famous circus on tour.   She was sold to Mississippi River Amusement Company where she was used for excursions.   The *John A. Wood* passed by Monaca several times on different ventures while on her circus tours.

Launched as **Cape Giradeau** – then became………..
> **Gordon C. Greene** (passenger/freight Pittsburgh – Cincinnati 1935-47) – then….
> **Sarah Lee** (floating hotel – 1952)– then……
> **River Queen** (floating restaurant/night club)

1923 to 1967 – Stern wheel paddle -This ship made many trips to Ohio with Monaca residents aboard.
The Howard Ship Yards & Dock Company in Indiana built this ship. She initially was used for carrying passengers and freight between Kentucky and Missouri.   In 1935, she was renamed the *Gordon C. Green* and was operated as a tourist boat on the Ohio River between Pittsburgh, PA and Cincinnati, Ohio.   There was an extra sun deck added in 1936 which also increased the number of passenger cabins. She was later converted from coal to oil fuel and by 1951 was withdrawn from service.   From 1952 to 1964 she was sold many times and was converted and served as a floating restaurant, a night club, a restaurant, and finally sold for the last time in 1964, moored in St. Louis as a bar and restaurant. She sank at her mooring on Dec 3, 1967, under the name *River Queen*.

The *Gordon C. Green* appeared in the famous movies "Steamboat around the Bend," "Gone With the Wind," and "The Kentuckean."

Former *Gordon C. Green*, in 1965 under the name *River Queen* as she is sinking while moored in N. Y. Dec 3 1967.

Great Republic

The *Great Republic* was put into service 1866.   She was renamed the *Grand Republic* in 1876.   This was many times referred to as "the finest ship afloat" in its time.   Unfortunately, the ship was considered a jinxed craft from the start.   This was the last steamboat built at Shousetown (in Glenwillard, PA).

There was a man killed while the hull was being launched in Nov 1866 – this was one of the worst possible omens for a ship.   She skidded across the Ohio and stuck in a mud bank, having to be pulled out by a towboat.

There were 54 staterooms; was elegant inside – ungainly outside.   She started her maiden trip with a construction lien of nearly $100,000; the cost to build was a total of $235,000.

The owners of her were bankrupt by the end of 1868 but they reorganized when only one bidder appeared at the sale.   Finally, in 1871, she was sold for $48,000.   In 1876 the ship was renamed the *Grand Republic*. Unfortunately, even with new owners and a new name, that didn't change her luck and she caught fire and was totally destroyed in 1877.

From a painting by Pittsburgh artist, William Coventry Wall

The pilot house of the *Great Republic* - Note the size of that steering wheel.

Main cabin ladies' salon in the palatial steamboat *Great Republic* shows luxury living.   Heating was by stove. Note the stovepipe in the center, and silver urn atop the table in the lower right.

The Queen City

The *Queen City* was launched the first of Jun in 1897 in Cincinnati. She was billed as "the finest steamer ever afloat on Western waters." She was a sternwheeler packet. The *Queen City* was first owned by the Pittsburgh and Cincinnati Packet Line and was an elaborate packet designed to attract a more affluent class of steamboat passengers. As far as steamboats go, she had an unusually long life operating up to 1933. She then became a wharf boat in Pittsburgh where she sank in 1940 and her remains burned in Feb 1941. Her roof bell was placed on the *Delta Queen*.

It is said this picture was taken by Captain Anthony "Tony" Meldahl who was her pilot from 1897 until 1909.

Aliquippa

The *Aliquippa* was a Vesta Coal Co. craft and she sank after striking a snag while maneuvering a large tow of coal. She overturned in 18 feet of water in the Ohio River near Aliquippa, PA, near the J & L Steel Corporation. There were 4 casualties when she turned completely upside down and sank in Aug 1928 including a chambermaid, a deck hand, and a watchman. Twenty others were rescued or swam ashore.

She was a steam sternwheeler that was used to push barges on the Ohio River; built in 1914.

American Queen

A statement was found saying this ship was the largest river steamboat ever built.   She is a six-deck recreation of a typical stern paddlewheel Mississippi riverboat built by McDermott Shipyard for the Delta Queen Steamboat Company and was built in 1994/95.   As of 2015, she was still in service.

Times photo by Sylvester Washington, Jr.

The *American Queen* passing by Monaca late in Jun 1995.

Delta Queen

Deckhands working on the Delta Queen's paddle wheel during a layover in Pittsburgh.   Oct 1986

The *Delta Queen* making an annual passage down the Ohio River past Monaca on its way to the Mississippi River.

It stopped operating as an overnight vessel after 2008 due to not being given exemption of the Congress's Safety of Life at Sea Act for wooden boats as they had in the past. There was a strong movement to "save the *Delta Queen*" and have it back on the rivers. A private company led by Louisiana business man bought the paddle-wheel vessel the first of 2015 and plan to return it to service in 2016. After the previously mentioned *Queen City* burned, her bell was placed on the *Delta Queen.*

view of the deck area on *Delta Queen*

Costanzo

1943 *Costanzo* (of Wheeling W. VA) on the Ohio by Monaca

Steam Boat Personnel

1869
Anthony Baker – river worker
George Bickerstaff – steamboat mate
Robert Biddle - boatman
August Biddle – ship carpenter
Joseph Brown – steamboat pilot
Joseph Brown – river pilot
Jacob Buhhat – boatman
Daniel Eckler – steamboat pilot and captain
Christian Fisher – boatman
Henry Fisher - boatman
Leonard Hahn – boatman
D A Jolley – steamboat mate
A. J. Jolly – boatman
Matthew Kettlewood – steamboat eng
John Laughlin – boatman
John Merriman – steamboat mate
James Ransom – steamboat captain
Oliver Red - boatman
John Shroadel – steamboat captain
William Stewart – steamboat mate
Hindman Stiles – steamboat engineer
Henry Volhardt - Ferryman
Morrison Hemphill – steamboat watchman

1876
Taylor Baker – steamboat mate
Jefferson Bickerstaff - river man
Joseph Brown – river man
Alonzo Ferguson – pilot
John Ferguson – pilot
Lafayette Graham – pilot
John Merriman – steamboat mate
James Miller – steamboat mate
William Stewart – steamboat mate
Henry Volhardt – Ferryman

1910
James Morris – captain – steam boat – Beaver Ave
    His son -   Charles Morris – pilot – steam boat
    His son -   Alfred Morris – pilot – steam boat

STEAM BOAT CAPTAINS AND OTHERS ASSOCIATED WITH THE STEAM BOAT BUSINESS BETWEEN 1850 AND 1900

All names below were obtained from census.

Years of census follow the occupation 1850 = 50, etc

Jacob and Mary Ift – ferryman 60
Jacob Rensing – ferryman - 60
William Shrodes – ferryman -50
William Volhardt– Ferryman 80
Henry Vollhardt – ferryman 70

Philip Baker – St Boat pilot – 60
Taylor Baker – river mate 70, 80
Zachariah Baker – Steam Boat Capt - 1900
Francis Beckhert – cabin boy – 60
Jefferson Bickerstaff – mate on steamboat 70, 80
Albert Biddle – river mate – 70
Isaac Bickerstaff – river laborer 70
Joseph Brown – river pilot 70, 80
David Brobeck- St Boat mate - 60
Joseph Brum-coal boat pilot - 60
Philip Brobeck – boatman - 50
Harrison Brobeck – boatman -50,60
Jacob Buhardt – boatman -50, 60

Benjamin D Clapper – boatman -50, 60
Jolly Dickerson – steam boat mate 60
John Ecker – river laborer - 70
Daniel Eckler-st boat pilot -60, 70

Martin Faut – ship carpenter -50
Alonzo Ferguson – St Boat pilot - 70
John Ferguson – Ohio Rvr Boat Pilot -50, 60, 70
Christian Fischer – boatman -50
- River man – 60
- River labor – 70
Christian Fosteer – river man - 60
Andrew Goetz-coal boatman – 60

Lafyette Graham – steam boat capt - 70
Walter Hays – St Boat Steward – 60
James Hemphill-river man – 60
Morrison Hemphill – river laborer 70
Hall Hogan – river laborer – 70

George Jenkins – steam boat captain - 80
Alphens Jolly-St Boat mate – 60
Andrew Jolly – river mate – 70
Dickson Jolly – river mate - 70
William Jordon – river hand - 60
James Jordon – coal boat pilot – 60

John Laughlin – boat stewart - 70
Caleb Maratta – boatman – 50
Frank Marcus – river laborer - 70
Alexander McKee – ship carpenter -50
John Merriman – boatman -50, 60
John Merriman, Jr – steam boat mate – 60, 70, 80
James Merriman – boatman -50, 60
Leonard Merryman-coal boat pilot - 60
Philip Metchan- river hand – 60
Godfrey Miller – Steam Boat Capt - 1900
George Morris – Steam boat engineer -50

James Ransom – steam boat capt - 70
Oliver Reed-coal boat pilot – 60, 70
Philip Roeck – boatman – 50

John Schnobel – ship carpenter – 80
William Schnobel – ship carpenter – 80
Milo Stewart – pilot – 80
William Stewart – riverman – 70, 80
John M Srodes – steam boat pilot -50
Hyman Stiles – steam boatman – 70
George Swager – boatman -50
George Young – boatman -50

*** *** *** *** ***

Once again, I go off the beaten path a bit and provide random general information.

Steamboat Bells, Whistles, and Calliopes

As I briefly mentioned previously, a captain and ship mates could easily identify a ship by the tone/pitch of a ships' bell and/or whistle.   For river men especially, this form of communication was vital.   A ship's bells were very important not only to other ships, but for communications on board ship also; a way of signaling departure, discharging passengers and a means to "bark" orders to the crew.   Engineers onboard would react according to which bell and the number of tolls the captain would sound.   On a stern wheel steamboat, a bell for stopping and starting was located on the engine room side of the ship; the backing bell was on the opposite side.   The number and/or combination of times each of these bells would be tolled would indicate the speed and direction the engineer would engage the ship's engines. Each bell had its own tone, some had and have a quite beautiful sound - some more musical - but each distinctively different to a seasoned river man.

Once steam whistles began to also be used, they were applied in landings or when two boats were meeting or passing each other.   A rule of the river seems to be that the boat going downstream on the river has "the choice of the river," but the ascending boat sounds the whistles first.   Ex – if two boats are coming upon each other, the ascending boat will blow one whistle – if the pilot on the descending boat has no problem with these two ships meeting up, then he will answer with one whistle; but if there is some problem, then the descending boat's pilot would answer with five short whistles, a short interval and then two whistles.   The ascending boat must answer with two whistles and then both boats bear to a little to their right.   The whistles on a boat were an important means of on board ship communication, too.   Even if no other boats are in sight, five short whistles mean a "call to quarters" for the crew.   Another example would be if a boat is at a landing, three taps of the bell meant the boat was almost ready to leave. River men and ships' crews totally relied on all these bells and whistles going off, each having specific meanings and unspoken instructions.   I like to think of the current phrase of something having "all the bells and whistles" meaning everything you need to do a job well, yet meaningless or extra to someone else.

Steam calliopes are musical instruments introduced and used on steamboats since the mid 1800s.   They were originally patented to be used in churches, but adapted quickly for circus use and steam boats.   A calliope can have between 25 to 67 whistles, but traditionally there are 32 on a steam calliope, the most commonly used type of instrument on a steam boat.   Calliope is a word that is pronounced two ways –circus personnel tend to say….call eye oh pee; river people tend to use …..*kal lie o pee*.   Circuses would often have their calliopes in a separate wagon and the player of the key board would add to the mystic of the circus being obscured from view.   All early calliopes had keyboards that directly produced the sound that came out of the pipes; as inventions were developed, these human players were often replaced with mechanical devises, much like a player piano. A steamboat's calliope could be heard for miles as the boats traveled up and down the rivers.   Since calliopes were found mainly on excursion boats which were much more ornate and decorated than other packets, people would quickly gather at the riverbanks or upper floors of buildings with a view of the river when the distant sound of an approaching calliope would be heard; all wanting to view the magnificent boats as they passed by playing their music.

While researching steam calliopes, I found one current steamboat, the *Natchez*, was christened in 1975 is using an exact copy of a steam calliope that was built over 100 years ago.   The *Natchez* does year-round, daily cruises out of New Orleans, traveling on the Mississippi.   Current organizations that track and report on steamboats still being used, state that there are only between 4 to 10 such calliopes still in use on riverboats.   What a shame that such a wonderful instrument, such a lighthearted mood setter, and musically mystic sound is among so, so many other things that are slowly dwindling from existence.

*** *** *** *** ***
*** *** ***

BRIDGES

Beaver River Bridge

Ohio River Bridges

East Rochester Bridge

Vanport / Expressway Bridge

Non- River Bridges

BRIDGES

General Information:

A **suspension bridge** is any type of bridge that makes significant use of tension rather than or in addition to compression. A suspension bridge usually has main cables (else ropes or chains), anchored at each end of the bridge. Any load applied to the bridge is transformed into a tension in these main cables.

A **cantilever bridge** is a bridge built using cantilevers, structures that project horizontally into space, supported on only one end. For small footbridges, the cantilevers may be simple beams; however, large cantilever bridges designed to handle road or rail traffic use trusses built from structural steel, or box girders built from prestressed concrete. The steel truss cantilever bridge was a major engineering breakthrough when first put into practice.

Bridge Plant
I found the following information in four different publications from 1902:

"The National Bridge Co. recently organized under the laws of New Jersey is preparing to build a large bridge plant on a site of 47 acres upon, which an option has been secured at Monaca, Pa. Bids for grading the property are already being received and the buildings of the new plant will cover about 14 acres. An office of the company has already been opened in the Fitzsimmons building, Pittsburgh, and E. M. Schofield, formerly manager of the Youngstown, O., plant of the American Bridge Co., is in charge."

Beaver River Bridge

The first bridge between Rochester and Bridgewater over the Beaver River was long before Rochester was incorporated.   It was a wooden, covered bridge completed in 1815. It was blown down in a severe windstorm in 1821. The next bridge to replace that covered bridge and was completed in 1826. It stood until the great flood in 1884; it was swept away.   Bridge #3 was erected in 1885 and was a toll bridge.   The toll was removed and it was taken over by Beaver County.   This same bridge was taken over in 1930 by the State of Pennsylvania.

Although these bridges were of no real help to the residents of Monaca unless they crossed the Ohio River by some form of boat, they were important to the valley.

Ohio River Bridges

One of the important Indian trails located in Beaver County once crossed the Ohio River near the mouth of the Beaver River.   This trail led north to Lake Erie, Canada, and the Northwest.   Trappers, traders, the army, and even immigrating settlers all found it necessary to cross a river or larger stream/creek at some point in their travels.

The first bridge to span the Ohio River from Monaca was between Monaca and Beaver. It was a wrought iron bridge constructed in 1878 to accommodate the railroad traffic.   This first RR bridge was considerably damaged in the 1884 flood.   With the extensive repair work that was needed and all of it not be completed until 1889, the P &LE railway considered this a second bridge because they reference it as being built in 1889 and not 1879.

This railroad bridge was replaced by a true second railroad bridge which was considered a gigantic engineering feat at the time it was erected in 1890.   The first bridge (1878/1889) was razed soon after the new cantilever bridge was completed in Jun 1910.
    *Also see RAILROAD section for much more information and pictures.

The information in this section is dedicated to the bridges used by pedestrians, vehicles, and streetcars.

Fun fact --- In 2015, local people associate and have nicknames for the bridges in the area…….. expressway bridge, railroad bridge, Bridgewater bridge, the toll bridge (East Rochester/Monaca), the Monaca-Rochester / Rochester-Monaca bridge, etc.

Well, even without motor vehicles, people in the late 1880s and early 1900s had their own bridge to reference with a nickname ……the Monaca-Beaver bridge (or depending where you lived, either just the Monaca bridge or just the Beaver Bridge). It was a bridge built for the railroad usage only.

Monaca was given even more access to the upper valley towns with the non-railroad 1895 suspension bridge being built for the general public to accommodate pedestrians, wagons/vehicles, and street cars. The Beaver Valley Traction Company extended its line from Rochester to Monaca across this suspension bridge. In the booklet that was distributed for one of the dedications for a new bridge, it was stated that there was a main Indian trail that crossed the Ohio River near the mouth of the Beaver River. Trappers, traders, and army men used to follow this Indian trail and it was also then used by settlers. In 1795 there are records of a French explorer stopping with a ferryman at the mouth of the Beaver River.

#1 --- 1895 Ohio River Bridge

Completed 1897.   Demolished – by the end of 1930.

The current Monaca-East Rochester bridge was not the first toll bridge for Monaca. The Ohio River Bridge in Monaca, as it was known from 1895 into the very early 1900s, was once a toll bridge. The county took over the bridge in 1905 and the toll was removed, making it the first free bridge over the entire Ohio River. William B. Thornburg, of Monaca, was one of the toll keepers on the Ohio River Bridge.

Fun Fact: The first passenger bridge to span the Ohio River between Pittsburgh and Wheeling, and the only highway bridge over the Ohio in Pennsylvania was this bridge between Monaca and Rochester; completed and opened for traffic on Jan 22, 1897.

Fun Fact: In 1901, President A. J. Jolly of the Ohio River Bridge Company had three men arrested when they crossed the bridge without paying their toll. They were riding in a spring wagon and claimed they were entitled to cross the bridge without paying more than the 15 cents toll as they were all employees of the same company and had a right to ride on the wagon. Isn't it interesting that in 1901 the toll on this bridge was 15 cents per person and yet in 1958 when the Monaca-East Rochester Bridge was constructed, the toll per vehicle (not person) was still only 15 cents. It appears that crossing the very first bridge in Monaca was much more expensive since 15 cents was quite a sum of money to an individual in 1895 to 1905.

Fun Fact : When this bridge was originally built, it was among the longest bridges in the country. It had a center span of 800 feet, which was only 10 feet shorter than the entire length of the great Niagara Suspension Bridge.

Ohio River Bridge from Rochester shoreline

This was the first bridge constructed over the Ohio River that was strictly to accommodate foot, wagon, and street car traffic and the first to span the Ohio River between Pittsburgh and Wheeling.   For many years, this was also the only highway bridge over the Ohio in Pennsylvania.

Another important fact about this bridge is that it carries two state highways, #51 and #18, and the main boulevard on the south bank of the Ohio from Pittsburgh to the Northwest.
This first bridge over the Ohio River was between Rochester and Monaca; it was a suspension bridge.
This 1895 Ohio River Bridge was located in Monaca and extended to the lower end of Brighton Avenue in Rochester.
In 1895 a charter was obtained for a toll bridge over the Ohio River connecting Rochester and Monaca.
The Beaver-Monaca P & LE railroad bridge was only 3,000 feet below the location of this new bridge.
This was a toll bridge until 1905 when it was taken over by the County.   It was taken over by the State of Pennsylvania in 1930. This first bridge was demolished in 1930.

There were first plans for a cantilever bridge, 2,200 feet long with a 700 foot channel span to accommodate foot, wagon, and street car traffic.   It would have cost $230,000. This amount was considerably more than the travel would have justified, so plans were tabled for a year.   The engineer began to redesign and to keep inside the fixed sum of $175,000.   He chose to change from a cantilever design bridge to a suspension bridge design.   With the plans being changed to a suspension bridge, it changed the channel span to be 800 feet.

During construction of this bridge, with the planking and laying of the rails almost completed, without the least bit of warning, the trestle gave way.   Though resting on piles, it is supposed that the trestle was weakened. The minor collapse caused the shore span to sag a bit more than 3 ½ feet below the horizontal and caused the towers to be pulled 9" out of plumb. The engineer had changed some of the design of the bridge from previous bridges and if this had not taken place, then the cables would have been resting on nests of rollers on top of the towers which would have caused the bridge to go into the river.   Thank goodness this did not occur because there were 40 workers on the bridge at the time of this mishap and they would have all been killed.

There was a terrible wind storm in the Beaver Valley Area on Apr 7, 1909. This wind storm was so severe that the County Commissioners issued a warning to persons using the bridge between Monaca and Rochester crossing the Ohio River due to the swaying of the bridge.   Persons insisting on crossing the bridge were told by the bridge keeper that they did so at their own risk.

There was a fire started on the bridge Aug 2, 1917, about 1400 feet from the Monaca end of the
    bridge.   The floor of the basically iron bridge was made of wood and it was suspected
    that a lit cigerette was the cause of the fire.   The flames burned a number of the floor
    planks and charred, but did not greatly damage the ties and stripping under the floor.   Both the
    Rochester and Monaca Volunteer Fire Departments were called. The distance from the Rochester
    side was too long for the firemen to get to the fire; the Monaca department had to send for extra
    hose before they could get water to the fire.

*Fun fact: They once kept barrels filled with water sporadically placed along
        the bridge to be used for all small fires that occurred on the bridge.
        With the flooring and sidewalks constructed of wooden planks and
        susceptible to frequent small fires from a carelessly thrown cigarette
        or cigar, it was important to have the water readily accessible.*

Additional views and pictures of the Ohio River Bridge 1895 – 1930:

Rochester view of the Monaca Rochester Bridge.   The Beaver River is about middle of picture.
Part of the Monaca-Beaver railroad bridge can be seen in the distance - upper left corner.
        Note – a trolley going over the bridge in this picture.

Looking from up on the hill in Rochester   -   The Monaca Rochester Bridge

Rochester side of the river, looking toward Monaca   (Note the style of car in the lower left.)

Fun fact: Nov 13, 1922
There was a parade when the Monaca football team won the county honors.
There was such a huge densely packed crowd of people who all marched onto
the entire length of the bridge.   This amount of humans marching across the
bridge made a much heavier total weight load than if the bridge had been filled
with loaded trucks.

This tremendous weight caused the suspension bridge to begin to sway. Luckily a
Rochester police officer, George Copeland, noticed the swaying and ordered the
people off the bridge.   His action is said to have averted a possible disaster.

Looking from Rochester toward Monaca

E. K Morse was the Chief Engineer of the Ohio River Bridge

1914 postcard with view of the Monaca Rochester suspension bridge – from the Monaca side looking toward Rochester.

Little Beaver Historical Society   1st Rochester/Monaca Suspension bridge built 1896 – replaced 1930

"The Ohio River Bridge" post card   Looking from Monaca to Rochester.

1889 – there was a group of men (Ohio River Bridge Company) who had surveys made by Leaf Brothers of Rochester for the construction of a suspension bridge across the Ohio River from the end of Phillips Street (now Ninth St) in Monaca connecting on the other side of the river at or near the end of New York Avenue, Rochester.   Due to the high cost of iron and steel at that time, it was too expensive and the plan was abandoned.

1894 – a new company was formed by local men to build the first Rochester-Monaca bridge – The Ohio River Bridge Company.

1896 – construction began on the first Monaca-Rochester Bridge.   Jutte and Co. provided the stone foundations, the anchorages, and the piers for the bridge.   The Penn Bridge Company did the iron work and built the bridge.

1897 – the bridge was opened for traffic.   Entire length of bridge was 2280 feet and its low water mark was 90 feet.   The channel span was 800 feet, which fell a little short of being the longest span in the U.S.A. – that honor went to the Niagara Falls bridge.

*In 1940, you could still see the dead end of the street car tracks in Rochester, marking the location of the end of the first 1895 bridge (at the end of Pleasant Street, Rochester, near Brighton Avenue).

#2 --- Monaca–Rochester Bridge   aka   Rochester-Monaca Bridge

Truss cantilever bridge - unusual three-tower cantilever bridge.
Opened Sep 1, 1930.   Closed 1982 – demolished 1984.

This second bridge was an unusual three tower cantiever bridge.   After the design was completed, bids were received and the contracts were awarded.......on Aug 22, 1928, to the Dravo Contracting Company;   on Jan 10, 1929, to the American Bridge Company for the steel superstructure; and the F. W. Scott Company was awarded two bids - on May 3, 1930, for the floor slabs and approach paving and on Jul 21, 1930, for pylons and parapet walls.   The total cost for the bridge was to be $1,087,500.

It was opened and dedicated on Sep 1, 1930, and was 2,162 feet long. The bridge opening on Sep 1, 1930, was a well attended celebration.   There were Monaca and Rochester officials and Beaver County officials present for the dedication and opening ceremonies --- there were ribbon cuttings ---- there were aerial maneuvers ---- there were parades on both sides of the river.   All the Monaca and Rochester residents were quite happy to celebrate the opening of this new bridge.

1937 view of bridge

BCHR&LF

In this picture you get to see the new 1930 bridge standing beside the old 1897 bridge before it was torn down. (Looking from Rochester toward Monaca.)   The new bridge was dedicated Sept 1, 1930; the old bridge was torn down within 90 days of this opening.

I apologize for the quality of this picture, but it is a view from Ninth Street in Monaca the day the new bridge was dedicated.

View is from Monaca side looking toward Rochester. Note all the buildings at the intersection of Atlantic Avenue and Ninth Street just before going onto the bridge. So many are no longer there (2016).

Another view of the three-tower cantilever bridge from the Rochester side of the river looking onto the Ohio River with Monaca across the river.

This bridge was closed down Jun 17, 1982, without much notice; there were structural deficiencies found. There had already been a 12 ton weight limit posted for the bridge since Feb, 1980, but the complete shut-down was a surprise. The 52 year old span showed that the steel in the bridge was abnormally brittle. There was an average of 18,300 cars that used this bridge daily. Traffic was detoured to the East Rochester-Monaca bridge. This detour caused the whole Monaca downtown area to turn into a giant bottleneck with traffic not moving sometimes for almost 45 minutes. Businesses in Monaca were preparing for the soon-to-come loss of income if the bridge was to remain closed for at least a two year period as planned.

The bridge was closed in Jun 1982 by PennDOT after an inspection found the steel had deteriorated.

photo by Pete Sabella

This is a picture of the 400 foot middle section of the Rochester-Monaca Bridge being lowered to a barge for disposal – Jun 1985. This bridge was torn down by the Century Steel Erectors of Pittsburgh.

This picture is the end section of the Rochester-Monaca Bridge being dismantled in Feb, 1986.

In Feb 1984, the Rochester-Monaca Bridge had been closed for 20 months and was about to be reduced to rubble very soon and was demolished in 1984.   PennDot had plans to build a new two lane structure using the existing piers for the new span. Residents were to add another year on to *the no bridge* situation just for the design work alone; with the construction contract being awarded in early 1985. It was finished and reopened mid Nov 1986, with firework display and an official dedication ceremony.

#3 -- Monaca–Rochester Bridge

Opened in 1986.   Dedication of the current continuous truss bridge was on Nov 25, 1986.

1986   Monaca Rochester Bridge looking from Atlantic Avenue, by the Monaca Water Works area toward Rochester.

Fun Fact: It is said that in 1988, the Rochester Manager Ed Piroli and Monaca Manager Tom Stoner made a bet signed with a handshake that gave the naming rights of the bridge to the winning football team of that year. With Monaca High School's merger into Central Valley High School, the 2009 game was the final game to determine naming rights. By winning the 2009 game, the bridge will be known as the Rochester–Monaca Bridge through the end of the school year. After that, it will be called the Rochester–Monaca Bridge on the Rochester side, and the Monaca-Rochester Bridge on the Monaca side.

East Rochester-Monaca Bridge   aka   Toll Bridge

Prior to the completion of the East Rochester-Monaca Bridge, the current Monaca-Rochester Bridge had about 25,000 vehicles crossing it daily.   During rush hours there would be a delay of as much as one hour to get across and a wait of a half-hour during other periods of any given day.

In 1958, this bridge was the first toll bridge within the confines of Pennsylvania in many years.   It had become customary to think of bridges across the Ohio River in Pennsylvania in terms of free transportation, so why a toll bridge in the county which had two "free bridges" in a 25 mile length of the river?   The answer would be that the county commissioners of Beaver recognized the demand for another bridge to handle the traffic across the river, but there wasn't enough money to erect a bridge and no promise for an all-state financed bridge.   The state took on the cost to build the approaches to the new bridge and the county had to make a loan to the bridge authority to construct the bridge itself and also would have to assume all other expenses of operation and maintenance of the bridge.

Therefore it was necessary for a toll of 15 cents to be assessed per car and up to 60 cents for vehicles with five or more axles, with monies going toward the loans and bonds.   The bond issue amounted to $2,875,000.   The tolls turned out to generate between $160,000 and $180,000 in gross revenue annually.   With the bridge costing $4.8 million to build, the county still owed about $2,665,000 in bond issues.   The toll bridge was completed in Feb 1960.   Dravo Corporation built the sub-structure and American Bridge Division of US Steel built the superstructure. The last toll bridge in Western Pennsylvania was turned over to the state and became free to motorists in 1973. The only other toll bridges remaining in Pennsylvania in 1973 were at the eastern border of the state and across the Delaware River; about a dozen of them.

The bridge was closed Sep 27, 1973, for extensive repairs, including removing the toll booths.   It was reopened Nov 28, 1973 – toll free.

Once again, the valley suffered when this bridge was closed for about a month for PennDOT to make repairs to the bridge – replacement of deck, structural work and painting.   It closed in Oct 1991 and was completed early 1993.

1969   BCHR&LF

Expressway Bridge

It was first stated in 1958 that a freeway would be constructed.   With this freeway, a bridge would have to cross over the Ohio River at Vanport.   This all would be part of a connecting road to link the Penn-Lincoln Parkway and Greater Pittsburgh Airport with the proposed Keystone Shortway.   It was considered to be beneficial to a large segment of the state in contrast to the localized appeal of past bridges over the Ohio River. The firm of Michael Baker, Jr. assisted in the plans during the 1950s including the Beaver Valley Expressway.

View from Center Township looking down the Ohio toward Midland – Vanport would be on the right.

Non River Bridges

This would have been the Twenty-first Street crossing mentioned in many articles. Prior to the overpass or viaduct being built over the railroad tracks below, it was originally just a crossing similar to the Fourteenth Street location with vehicles and people crossing directly over the railroad tracks.   There were many mentions of mishaps and accidents occurring at this location along the railroad tracks, so there were alterations made for the roadway to connect with this viaduct and all was raised up and over the tracks.

Little Beaver Historical Society

Looking NW   - from Beaver Avenue down into the end of Monaca - 1938

On the top of this bridge, you can make out "*Fort Pitt Bridge Works.*"   Fort Pitt Bridge Works constructed the bridge and they are laying the tracks for the street car in this picture.   Not only would raising this roadway up and over the railroad tracks eliminate many of the accidents, it was also built so the street car tracks could be laid and not interfere, nor cross directly on the railroad tracks.   The mill you see in the background through the bridge was Pittsburgh Tube.

This bridge was torn down in 2014 and was replaced with an open overpass/viaduct at the same site.

*** *** *** *** ***
*** *** ***

Western Union Telegraph Company

American Express Company

Railroad Depots/Stations and Companies

Sixth Street Station

Freight Station

Colona Depot/Station

Monaca Passenger Depot/Station

Railroad Companies

Monaca-Beaver Railroad Bridges

TELEGRAPH and TELEPHONE COMPANIES

AMERICAN EXPRESS COMPANY

The C. D. & P Telegraph and Telephone Company – Pennsylvania Avenue
1898

Federal Telephone Company - Ninth Street
1901, 1902, 1903
>   Opened its office late Apr 1901.
>   Was located opposite the Hotel Monaca.

Western Union Telegraph Company – P & L E Station
1898, 1902, 1903
>   James M. Davis was the Manager in at least 1898.

American Express Company – Sixth Street
1892, 1893, 1902, 1903, 1912
>   The American Express Co. moved its main office to Monaca on Mar 15, 1912.   Monaca became
>   the distributing center of the American Express Company for the entire lower Beaver
>   Valley.
>   The former office in Beaver was closed and that agent was transferred to Youngstown.
>   American Express was previously located in Beaver.   All of the companies'
>   business was transacted from the Monaca office. The Beaver express wagon was
>   transferred to Monaca where in the forenoon it   was used to service Monaca; in the
>   afternoon, it made distributions through Rochester, Freedom and Beaver. Two extra
>   clerks were scheduled to be hired in connection with this transfer.
>   David G. Hood was the P&LE RR and American Express agent in 1892 and 1893; Chas. Houston was
>   also referenced as an *Agent.*

This building was used by the American Express Company; constructed in 1911.

Little Beaver Historical Society

Sign hanging in front says "*American Express Co.*"

2016

View is from Pacific Avenue, looking toward the railroad tracks. The former Monaca Depot/Station sits just to the left of this former American Express Depot.

2016

*** *** *** *** ***
*** *** ***

RAILROAD DEPOTS / STATIONS

Many quick and lasting changes occurred from the 1822 beginning of Phillipsburg (Monaca) especially when the Pittsburgh & Lake Erie Railroad laid their tracks in 1877. The great center of population to the south now had access and could be easily connected to many communities. The erection of the Monaca Beaver Railroad bridge over the Ohio River increased the need to erect railroad stations/ depots.

A bit of history on the P & L E Railroad Company:

The P & L E Railroad Company was organized under the general laws of the State of Pennsylvania on May 11, 1875, when a prominent Pittsburgh businessman, William McCreery, chartered the new system. McCreery resigned his position as president after 2 years. There had been little progress to show in 1877; not a single rail had yet to be laid. The railroad eventually began construction after 1877 and by 1879 had its main line from the Monongahela River north, then parallel to the Ohio River, through Monaca, PA, to Beaver, PA, on north along the Beaver River to New Castle, PA, then along the Mahoning River, crossing into Ohio just below Lowellsville, finally to reach Haselton, Ohio, which is the Western end of the railroad. Although the railroad was never more than 100 miles in length at its largest, it became quite famous because of the great amount of tonnage it transported and moved; becoming known as the "Little Giant."

The P & LE Railroad Company's controlling interest was owned by many others, with full control handed to Conrail in 1993 who slowly integrated the railroad into its system. CSX Transportation renamed the system Three Rivers Transportation and still operates the P & L E's former main line today.

Even though Monaca was formerly known as Phillipsburg, a form of railroad ticket that was issued in Dec 1880 was printed to cover the years 1879-1883 inclusive. These tickets had both Phillipsburg and Monaca (with Monaca, the latter being shown as the next stop/station to the south). It was the tradition of the rail road companies to use Indian names for cities and other places of interest. It is said this is where the name Monacatootha originated. Tradition also seems to be that the railroad is also credited with the name now being *Monaca* because it was a shortened version of Monacatootha they printed on tickets and schedules since the whole name would not fit. The name Monaca was adopted Sep 20, 1892, making it the official name of Phillipsburg from then on.

Sixth Street Station

Built in 1879 – opened Feb 1879.   This was the first station in Phillipsburg.

Elijah Stewart was the first agent operator.

The first station at this site was destroyed by fire in 1888 and a new passenger station was erected.

There was also a freight office at this location & it was converted into a ladies' waiting room.

When the station was built, there was a gents' waiting room on one end of the building and the ladies' waiting room on the opposite side.   The need for a freight storage area was needed, so the ladies' waiting room area was converted.   When the new freight station at seventeenth street was opened, this allowed for this station to be converted back to its original intended state of having waiting rooms on each end.

When the new depot at Fourteenth Street was finished, this station was closed (1910).

The building was to be razed since they wanted to straighten out the tracks and eliminate a big curve – B U T instead – in Nov 1910, Prof. Fred Bechtel purchased the old Pittsburg and Lake Erie passenger depot (located on Sixth Street).   It had been abandoned for several weeks since the new depot was opened at Fourteenth and Pacific Avenue. He had the Sixth Street Station placed on his property (now 416 Sixth Street – near the Siebenberger's Hall) about ½ block from where it was built.

o   Prof. Bechtel had the old depot moved to be remodeled and be a permanent headquarters for the German Beneficial Union of Monaca.

It is still standing today – on Sixth Street and used as a model train museum.

Sixth Street Station when it was located along the tracks at the end of Sixth Street prior to 1910.

2014   courtesy BCHR&LF

A view of the former Sixth Street depot building as it appears nowadays at the site it was moved to in 1910.

New Freight Station – Sixteenth Street

Frame building -   Construction started in 1897 and completed in 1898.

It was built to accommodate the large increase in shipments; the Sixth Street Station was too small to handle all the passengers, freight express business, and shipments being sent.
   o   When this freight station was opened, the old freight office at the Sixth Street station was then converted back to a ladies' waiting room.

In a report of the Board of Directors to the stockholders of the P&LERR at the end of 1907, there was a statement that said "A new station has been built at Colona for accommodation of business in the Monaca-Colona district."   There was no other explanation as to if was recently built, how old it was, its exact location, etc.   Was there an additional depot built or were they referencing the one that was completed about 10 years prior?   Numerous mentions of the Sixteenth Street freight station stated it as "the Colona Station" so it is difficult to sort this all out.   The fact that there was indeed at least one freight station on Sixteenth Street and it was referenced as "the Colona Station" is the only proof positive I can state at this time.

Later in 1907, the freight and ticket agencies were separated, meaning there were separate positions for the Freight Agents and Ticket Agents until again the two positions were consolidated in Dec 1930; the one position had jurisdiction over both offices.

It was still in use and referenced as "the Colona Station, Monaca" in Jul 20, 1931.
This freight station was on the south side of Pennsylvania Avenue; torn down early in 1990s.

Freight Station – Sixteenth Street

Colona Depot -   corner of Twenty-First Street and Beaver Avenue
Built in 1903.
    Built on site of the old Baldwin property, about 10 yards south east of the Opalite Tile Works
Work began on the foundation in Jun 1903 and was almost completely done by Jul 9, 1903.
- o   They hit a spring and had to dig 3 feet deeper to get a good foundation.
- o   The tile floor was started the end of Sep 1903.
- o   Cost was about $25,000.

The building was a brick and concrete structure.
It was moved to the Fourteenth Station location in May 1910.
- o   The move started on May 3 and was expected to be done by May 14, 1910.
- o   May 1910 - it was a difficult job, but the Kress House Moving Company did an excellent job.
- o   As of May 20, 1910, it had about another 100 feet to be moved to be placed on the new foundation.

The station had the word "COLONA" in the exterior masonry.

This a photo of the depot in the process of being moved to its new site at the corner of Fourteenth Street and Pacific Avenue.

Monaca Passenger Depot / Station – corner of Fourteenth Street / Pacific Avenue

Monday, Jan 31, 1910 – Monaca Council granted the P & LE railroad permission to move the passenger station from Colona to property purchased at Fourteenth Street/Pacific Avenue.

This move of the Passenger Depot to Fourteenth Street was done to consolidate and create a more centrally located depot.   This meant moving the Colona depot, which was .6 of a mile south (the one by Opalite) and closing the Sixth Street Station which was .4 miles north.   The move was completed and it was opened to the public on Tuesday, Nov 1, 1910.

There was a concrete cellar and the subways put in prior to the station being in use.

It had northward and southward station platforms, umbrella sheds, and passenger and baggage subway features. Although some of the features were new and this station was new to the location/site, it was not new since it was the former Colona station.

1969 the building was purchased by Monaca-Center Masons and is used as their lodge.

1970 the P & LE RR station became the lodge for Monaca-Center Lodge No. 791 Free and Accepted Masons and is still standing (2015).

P. & L. E. Station, Monaca Pa.

1912 postcard of the P & L E RR station

The passenger and baggage tunnel was just to the right of the stairs.

Note the covered waiting areas along the tracks and stairs leading to and from the tracks in both pictures.

1953

The next few pictures are current views (2016) of the former Monaca Passenger Depot.

It was formerly the Colona Passenger RR Depot and moved to sit at this Fourteenth Street and Pacific Avenue lot becoming the main, centrally located Monaca Station.

It has been closed prior to 1969. In 1969 it was purchased by the Center-Monaca Masonic Lodge No. 791 and converted into their current Lodge.

2016

View from the corner of Fourteenth Street and Pacific Avenue, looking toward the railroad tracks.

2016

View looking toward Pacific Avenue from where Fourteenth Street crosses over the railroad tracks.

This view is of the portion of the former depot that faces the railroad tracks.
Fourteenth Street is to the right/far side of the building.

View is from Fourteenth Street, the railroad tracks are on the left,
Pacific Avenue is to the right of the picture.
Also pictured is the former American Express Depot.

*** *** *** *** ***
*** *** ***

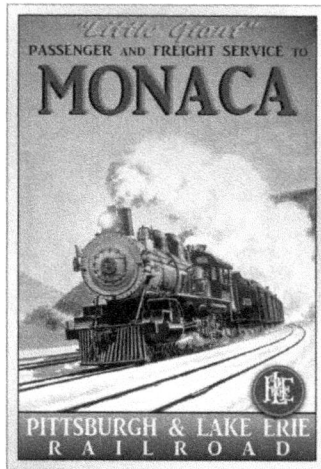

"Little Giant"
PASSENGER AND FREIGHT SERVICE TO
MONACA
PITTSBURGH & LAKE ERIE
RAILROAD

RAILROAD COMPANIES

There were two railroads people spoke of in 1903 -- the Cumberland and Pennsylvania Railroad /C & P RR   and the Pittsburgh and Lake Erie Railroad / P & LE RR.   Of these two, it appears that Monaca was closely connected with the P & LE RR since it passed through the town and there were stations/depots with official freight and passenger stops.

Pittsburgh and Lake Erie Railroad / P & LE RR

The railroad tracks in Monaca were laid by the Pittsburgh and Lake Erie Railroad – P & LE RR
    The P & LE railroad of Pittsburgh is 137 years old in 2016.

This is a picture of the *Little Steamer* Engine No. 1.

It was inaugurated into service in 1879 when it left Beaver Falls, PA, for Pittsburgh, passing through Monaca on its maiden trip.

This is a picture of the sleek diesel of 1954 on the P & LE.
It was known as the big freight carrier - *Steel King.*

P & L E RR passenger train.

CSX Transportation– 1 Industrial Park Road, Monaca – railroad/train
Services many companies including Colona Transfer Terminal.

CSX engines and trains pass through Monaca on a daily basis.

CSX train passing through the RR crossing in Monaca PA.

***   ***   ***   ***   ***
***   ***   ***

MONACA-BEAVER RAILROAD BRIDGES

Courtesy Beaver County Genealogy Center

This is a picture of what was left of the original Monaca-Beaver P & LE railroad bridge after the flood in 1884 destroyed it, along with 3 other local bridges.   This photo is looking from the Beaver side of the river toward Monaca. Note the men standing on the tracks in the lower left of the photo, no doubt evaluating and inspecting the damage.   (This same photo appears in Weather section of this book.)

This was a wrought iron bridge built in 1878.   It was the first railroad bridge from Monaca to Beaver and the P & LE railroad referenced the repaired/replacement bridge as the second with the now standing (2015) railroad bridge being considered the third bridge between Beaver and Monaca.

Photo from Transactions of the American Society of Civil Engineers

1890 single track bridge that replaced the wrought iron bridge built in 1878, it was torn down after the new bridge was completed in 1910.

The new 1910 double track cantilever railroad bridge

Note: Beside the smaller, 2nd bridge, you can still see the original piers of the first bridge.

Little Beaver Historical Society   Another view of old train bridge (2nd old bridge) and new train bridge.

New Ohio River Bridge
Looking North - 3,24, 10.
S.E.Y.

Removing Old Ohio River Bridge
Beaver-Monaca Jan. 4th 1911 S.E.Y.

Little Beaver Historical Society   The removal of 1890 Monaca-Beaver railroad bridge
Print in bottom right corner – "Removing Old Ohio River Bridge   Beaver-Monaca   Jan 4, 1911 S.E.V."

The current Monaca-Beaver railroad bridge was significant due to its length and heavy cantilever truss.   The official length of the bridge is 1,709 feet consisting of two spans, a southern cantilever through truss of 769 feet and 320-foot anchor arms; and a northern camel back through truss of 370 feet.   The bridge was constructed from both sides of the river simultaneously, and when it met in the center after two years, the two sides were less than 1/4 inch apart.

Construction on the massive cantilever railroad bridge was started in Mar 1908 and completed in May 1910. It is one of the most famous bridges in America. It is classified as a pin-connected cantilever through truss with suspended span and a pin connected subdivided camelback through truss.

The bridge is distinct in that rather than selecting an alternate proposal, the P & LE railroad proceeded with its original plan in Jul 1907 to erect the cantilever bridge over the Ohio River even though its similarity to a bridge that proved defective had been planned to cross the St. Lawrence River. The Quebec bridge was being built and collapsed Aug 29, 1907 during construction. This disaster caused similar projects to be cancelled. Even though the disaster of the infamous Quebec bridge had ceased to be a news item, the engineering press kept updated to the progress of the Monaca-Beaver Bridge project.

Photo from Transactions of the American Society of Civil Engineers

The above image shows the erection of the traveler. A traveler was used to erect the Pennsylvania truss span as well as the anchor arms of the cantilever. These, tall, box-like crane structures had multiple hooks that could be used to erect the bridge. Travelers were commonly used in the construction of earlier cantilever truss bridges like the Beaver – Monaca Bridge.

Construction of the truss span of the bridge.

Erecting Cantilever arm with creeper traveler.

The McClintic-Marshall Construction Co. of Pittsburgh built the Monaca-Beaver railroad bridge. Construction of this bridge is said to have broken new ground in bridge assembly and included a number of innovative structural details, along with the erection procedures formulated by Albert Lucius, the consulting engineer from New York, and Paul L. Wolfel, the chief engineer of McClintic-Marshall Construction Co. The project's success was due to the P & LE Assistant Chief Engineer, A. R. Raymer maintaining strict quality control along with precise specifications, design checks, materials testing, and meticulous review.

Monaca side of the Beaver-Monaca P & L E railroad

Considering the oblique angle and pier protection, the main span was required to be 769 feet long. This length was beyond the capabilities of any simple truss design, but was within the range of a cantilever. A cantilever uses structural flow over the piers to dole out loads to adjoining spans called anchor arms.

Putting in place the pin supporting diagonal member.
A pin is held in place by two cables or ropes.   A crane suspends a large ramming
device which workers pull back and manually drive a pin into place.

This new bridge built in 1908 actually replaced a single track bridge which was built to span the Ohio River at the river mile 26.7.   The old structure was a single track bridge built in 1890, replacing a wrought iron bridge at the same location.   The wrought iron bridge was built in 1878 by the Philadelphia Bridge Works.   The new cantilever bridge was built 300 feet upstream from the old bridge.   The relocation of the bridge required permission from the U.S. War Department since they had jurisdiction over navigable waterways.   Permission was contingent upon the railroad constructing the bridge to provide a 700 feet clear channel for shipping.

Can you believe..........................The bridge was constructed from both sides of the river simultaneously, and when it met in the center after two years, the two sides were less than 1/4 inch apart.   This photo shows the completion of the suspended span.

The bridge measures:

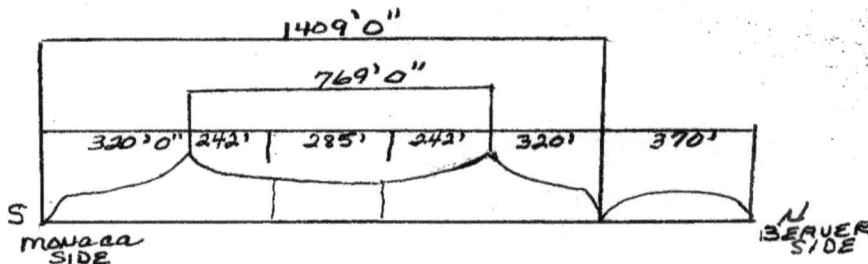

MISCELLANEOUS RAILROAD INFORMATION

I was told that from almost the beginning of the railroad bridge being built in Monaca and for many years, there were armed guards placed at the ends of this bridge.   They said there were labor problems at the period in time it was built and some threats were made about bombing the bridge, so they positioned the guards as a precaution.   About the time period of WWII, the guards were said to have been quietly removed.

Little Beaver Historical Society   Special train – first to cross Monaca Beaver train bridge
Print in the lower left corner states "Vice Pres. Special – Beaver   First Train over New Ohio River Bridge
May 14, 1910 - Vandivort"   Look at the clothing/fashion styles; these people are dressed in their "best."

Monaca old timers who grew up with mostly hearing river and riverboat conversations soon had the topics switched to river, riverboat and railroad tales.   On one side of Monaca, residents could easily sit and get lost in watching river activities or just absorbing the steady and calming flow of the Ohio River.   On the other side of town, away from the river people could hear the haunting sound of approaching trains or watch a passing train enjoy the clickety clack as it passed over the well laid tracks.   All this within a few blocks and in walking distance of each other!   You can even get the best of both worlds if you position yourself by the water works pump house.   Both the river and the trains can be viewed from the park area.

Riding and shipping via the railroads was known as a quite safe means of travel.   There were very view reports of accidents; yet they did periodically occur.   The photo below is of one of those accidents.   It occurred just outside Monaca, in the Colona area.

Little Beaver Historical Society

Little Beaver Historical Society   laying rails 1937 Monaca Colonial Steel in background

View of the construction taking place on Pennsylvania Avenue – arch 1903   Little Beaver Historical Society
Print in lower left corner – "Pennsylvania Avenue Arch   Oct 6, 1908   Monaca PA "

The Daily Times – Sep 9, 1908
The P & L E RR award the contract for the building of the concrete arch under the new bridge between Monaca Borough and Moon Twp. to McKelvy & Hinds, general contractors of Pittsburgh who began work at once.
Print in lower left – "Pennsylvania Avenue Arch   Oct 19, 1908   Monaca PA "

***   ***   ***   ***   ***
***   ***   ***

Cabooses

Anyone born prior to the 1970s and living near or having to cross over any railroad tracks most likely has seen a train passing by. Those who have been driving since before the mid 1950s and had to cross any railroad tracks will definitely relate to the following......

As a train passes by a crossing area on a roadway, the length of a train could cause the wait to seem endless. People in the vehicles who may be in a hurry to be able to cross over the tracks would find the seemingly endless passing of the train cars quite frustrating; the sight of the end of the train is most welcoming. Anyone who has been doing this routine for many years will recall a different mindset. In the past, for all young children waiting in the cars, the end of the train meant that they finally got to catch a glimpse of the train's caboose.

Ah, yes, the caboose. When was the last time you remember seeing a caboose pass by at the end of a train?

> *Fun fact: The word caboose is said to come from the Dutch word kambuis which means cabin house or ship's galley. Cabooses have also been known to be called cabin cars, way cars, and even other such nicknames as hacks, monkey cages, and crummies. Over the years, the term caboose has come to mean the rear, back end, back side of things.*

I wanted to take time to give tribute here to the railroad caboose because as a child waving to the men in a caboose was a treat in itself not to mention cabooses are just another piece of Americana that is rapidly slipping into the past. Part of my family tree has one family alone with over 150 years of railroad employees including engineers and conductors, so the stories of trains, tracks, and cabooses are endearing to me. Since about the 1960s until today that wonderful small box car has been replaced, like so many other things, with technology. Freight trains now have what is called *the end of train device.* This computerized device is a portable steel box that resembles and is approximately the size of a suitcase. It attaches to the back of the train's last car and railroad companies will tell you that it performs all the functions needed, only cheaper and better than when cabooses were used. Technology and *the end of train device* also eliminated the load of former paperwork, so conductors no longer need the area in the caboose for a workspace.

American railroads began to first use cabooses about 1850. The first cabooses were more like a rolling hut; they steadily grew in their size and in their usage; most cabooses were only used on freight trains. They were more of a plain box car until 1895 when they were being constructed with a cupola located in the center or one end of the car for the conductor to be able to watch the length of the train for problems, such as fires or dragging equipment. The cupola consisted of one to two seats for the conductor(s) to perform his duties while viewing the whole length of the train. Some cabooses featured bay type windows on the sides. The caboose evolved into becoming a conductor's office where he could do his paperwork, as well as a place where railroad crews could work, cook, eat, and even sleep. It would be fair to call a caboose a rolling office and living quarters, the headquarters of the train. They were usually equipped with a desk, restroom, water supply, stove, heater, bed and even an icebox. And, of course, all sorts of supplies from oil cans to red signal flags, lanterns and extra lantern fuel.

In the later 1800s and early 1900s, applying the brakes was done manually and required turning a wheel located on each car. The brakemen would climb to the top of the train via a ladder and walk along the roof of the cars to access the brake wheel for each of the cars. Later, trains became equipped with an air-brake system and there was still at least one brakeman aboard all trains. One of his duties was to walk the length of his train to check air hoses making sure they were properly connected from car to car. When he finished his inspection and had reached the end of the train, he would use a tooting horn or swing a lantern that signaled to the conductor "all systems were a go." The brakeman would then climb aboard the caboose as the conductor started the train rolling down the track.

Although many of the unions and crews tried to keep the cabooses from becoming extinct, by the late 1970s it was obvious the fate of the caboose was grim. The railroad companies even won over the fact that some states were developing laws requiring the use of cabooses on freight trains. The companies wanted to eliminate the caboose and used the fact of it draining them financially and with the new technology available, the caboose was an unnecessary expense, as was the manpower that accompanied them. The railroad companies flatly stated they saw no reason to drag a caboose around any longer.

Like the caboose, brakemen are no longer a norm on the freight trains since *the end of train device* now also monitors air brake pressure and reports to the engineer its findings. This device will also provide information to the engineer as to how fast the train is moving which translates to the engineer exactly how taut or slack it is between each of the cars. Thanks to this new "device", the railroad freight crew has been reduced from four or five men to usually just the engineer and the conductor. With only two persons needed on any given freight train, the need for an area/car for the crew was also eliminated.

1925-26 caboose built in McKees Rocks, PA at P&LE shop – cuploa on top.

Example of bay windows on the side.

Typical views of inside a caboose.

views from inside of cupola areas   end-of-train device

As with so many other things that have been lost to time and change - the typewriter, vinyl records, much of the American landscaping, wonderful architectural, historical buildings – the caboose unfortunately is added to the list; being visualized in memories and imaginations only.

*** *** *** *** ***
*** *** ***

Street Cars

Motor Coaches

STREET CARS

Street cars became a very popular means of transportation for many of the residents of Monaca.   Prior to the affordability of automobiles, the use of ferryboats and later trains were the only means for the people to travel from Monaca to Rochester, Beaver, New Brighton, Beaver Falls, etc. Walking was another popular means for people to get from one end of town to the other; the street cars gave help with this activity once the tracks were laid throughout the town.

It was a happy day in Monaca when the street cars laid tracks across the Monaca- Rochester bridge.   This practically eliminated passenger usage of the once popular ferryboats.   Of course the bridge concept itself was responsible for the drastic decline in the need for the ferryboats, but the trolley and street cars gave more freedom from having to mount a horse or go through the routine of hitching a horse to a buggy or wagon and going across the river or to the other end of town.

There were two companies that had tracks laid through Monaca - Coraopolis and Monaca Street Railway Company and Beaver Valley Traction Company.   There were separate lines for each of the companies so power could be supplied appropriately.   Monaca Council approved an ordinance in Aug 1901 granting the Coraopolis and Monaca Electric Street Railway Company the right to operate a street railway on certain streets and highways.   There were specific stipulations included in the ordinance.   There were 17 separate stipulations; a few samples of these are: not more than two squares of streets to be torn up at the same time during the construction of the railway; the company was to give good and efficient service to its patrons; to construct and maintain, repair, all electric appliances, motors, apparatus, fixtures, etc.; that paving within the rails be done immediately upon the construction of the said railway; and if the railway was not completed and in operation at the time specified then Monaca would be paid the sum of $10 for each and every day thereafter until the railway was completed and in operation.

The first street car passed over to Monaca from Rochester on the evening of Jun 23, 1901.   The car ran very slowly over the bridge and partly over the company's line up Pennsylvania Avenue.   Even though the street car had accessibility to run cars to Monaca as of this date, there was NOT a steady use of the street cars as of that date because of a contract with the bridge company that stated additional lateral braces to the bridge had to be in place before any cars were to run over the bridge again.   The car that did cross the bridge on that Jun evening was left sitting on Pennsylvania Avenue where it surely attracted considerable attention.

As mentioned above, there were two companies that serviced Monaca during the same time period.   On Aug 30, 1930, the Beaver Valley Traction Company began to lay and maintain a single track railway for its electric railroad. It ran cars between the Morado Park area of Beaver Falls and Leetsdale, Rochester and Vanport Township, and Rochester and Monaca.   There were transfer points at Conway's Corner – at Brighton Avenue, Rochester – at Pleasant Street, Rochester.   Street cars were also operated on Riverside Drive in Bridgewater between Bridge Street and the once Sharon Bridge which spanned the Beaver River at Junction Park (close to the site of the new Veteran's Bridge, 2015).

Many street car and trolley rails seemed to just end – not leading to any destination - this was on purpose. You see when a trolley/street car hit the end of the route, the driver would simply move from the north end of the trolley to the south end and start the return trip on the track.   Some street cars had turnarounds, like the one in Leetsdale, but most found it more efficient to have the driver change position rather than the car itself.   It cost 5 cents to ride the trolley / street car from Monaca to Rochester in 1903.

There were street cars on Monaca Heights as early as 1903. The Monaca Heights Railway Company did grading of the street preparing to lay the tracks.   It stated that the cars would be running by the middle of Jul, 1903.   At the same time, the roadways were prepared and a new street car line was laid to run through the Welch Plan.
As early as 1932, there was serious consideration for abandonment of the use of trolley/street cars since there was a steady decrease in revenues for the traction companies due to the number of private automobiles.   Slowly, but surely, the street cars and trolleys were eliminated and replaced with the usage of motor coaches and buses for public transportation.

The Traction Co. was notified in Sep 1935 to discontinue their street car services in Rochester. It appears this did not settle well with the company because they had the following ad in the local paper.

The last trolley car rode through Monaca on Sep 19, 1935. Though not utilized any longer, trolley tracks remained on Ninth Street and Pennsylvania Avenue well into the 1950s.

from Milestones/BCHR&LF – photo courtesy Ruth and Bernd Mrusek
1919 Beaver Valley Traction Company car

Beaver Valley Traction Company

Eventually there were various companies that operated streetcars in Beaver County at one time; they merged and became the Pittsburgh Railways Co. – later becoming the Beaver Valley Traction Co. The main office of this company, along with the powerhouse and car barns, were located at Junction Park in Rochester Township, where the Beaver Valley Motor Coach Company office eventually was located.

Ninth Street and Pennsylvania Avenue.
Monaca, Pa.

View on this post cart is of Ninth Street coming from the bridge to the intersection at Pennsylvania Avenue. Carey's on the left – Citizen's Nat'l Bank in back ground (on Ninth Street).

Rochester Transit Corporation

Photo by Shelden S. King   Rochester Transit Corporation car

Monaca Heights Street Railway Company
1903, 1905

Grading was completed and all was made ready to lay the tracks in 1903; the cars were to be up and running by mid July. James H. Welch (of Welch Fire Brick) petitioned Monaca Borough for a street railway franchise to start the Monaca Heights Street Railway Company in 1903. James H. Welch was the President, W. G. Moffett was the Secretary, and Fred Bechtel was the Treasurer. They were incorporated in 1903. James H. would have had an interest in this company being developed because he owned extensive acreage and had a Welch Plan of homes in Monaca Heights. This company was far from a giant success, but I did find it listed in various reports in 1903, 1904, 1905.

*** *** *** *** ***
*** *** ***

MOTOR COACHES

There were several different motor coach companies with offices in Monaca throughout the years.

J. H. Mitchell put a notice in The Beaver Times in Mar 1903..... "To the general public. I have equipped myself for the draying and transferring business. Your Patronage solicited."   The date indicates he would have most likely been using some type of "horse powered" equipment in his business.

___

Mitchell Bus Company – one side of /part of building at 812 Pennsylvania Avenue
> beside the original and former Kemmer's Hardware Store and Tin shop

1930s, 1940s
> Owner and operator was James Mitchell of Monaca.
>> David Mitchell (James' father) was the owner of his own lumber company in Beaver Falls, but was living in Monaca in 1920. In 1930 David had the occupation of *a dealer in the motor truck business* in Monaca.
> This was a newly established bus line that ran between Monaca and the plant of the St. Joseph Lead Company in Potter Township (listed as Josephtown as it was known at that time).
> A bus ran from Pennsylvania Avenue and Ninth Street and made nine trips daily between Monaca and Josephtown; also making 13 trips daily between Monaca and Monaca Heights and Colona Heights.
> There was only one bus in operation in Dec 1930, but Mr. Mitchell expected to place another bus in operation after Jan 1, 1931, operating between Monaca and Colona.

___

Red Star Transit Company had an office and garage at 1500 Pennsylvania Avenue.
> In business in 1949, 1956

___

Oliver C. Moffitt was the owner of a bus line in 1920.   There was no indication as to the name of the company, the type or number of buses, or if it was even in Monaca proper, etc.

___

Early charges of bus rides were 10 cents for a "one-zone" ride and 5 cents for each additional zone.

___

On Dec 22, 1942 there was a terrible landslide along the roadway on Constitution Boulevard between Aliquippa and Ambridge.   The slide entrapped a Motor Coach bus and there were 22 of 25 people killed on board the Motor Coach Co. bus.

___

In 1939 there were two major coach companies servicing the Monaca area - The Rochester Motor Coach Company and the Beaver Valley Motor Coach Company.   They were not the only companies running coaches and buses, but probably the biggest companies.

___

Rochester Motor Coach Co. – in 1942 their address was 609 Pennsylvania Avenue
in 1956 their address was 1730 Pennsylvania Avenue.   Passenger Service and Charter service.

ROCHESTER MOTOR COACH COMPANY

SAFETY STEEL COACHES ARE . . . SAFE . . . COMFORTABLE . . . ECONOMICAL

2013 view of former building at 1730 Pennsylvania Avenue.
This building was razed in 2016.

ROCHESTER MOTOR COACH COMPANY TAKES EVERY PRECAUTION FOR
SAFETY & SANITARY MEASURES! EACH SEAT COVERED WITH A
FRESH TOWEL FOR EACH TRIP!

OPERATING A FLEET OF
NEW 29 AND 37 PASSENGER
LUXURY COACHES.

Phone SPruce 5-0844
for Rates for Tours

FOR SCHOOLS, PICNICS, CAMPS,
CLUBS, CONVENTIONS, THEATRICAL
AND ORCHESTRA TRIPS & TOURS.

THE BEST SERVICE ANYWHERE, ANY TIME!
INSURED LICENSED DRIVERS HAVE BUILT OUR FIFTEEN SUCCESSFUL YEARS!

SIGHT
SEEING
TOURS

ROCHESTER MOTOR COACH CO.
1730 Pennsylvania Ave., Monaca, Pa.
Telephone SPruce 5-0844

TRANSPORTING
PEOPLE TO & FROM
INSTITUTIONS;
EMERGENCY CREWS
TO & FROM
BREAKDOWNS, ETC.

"Rain or Snow, Hail or Blow, Rochester Buses Always Go."

Beaver Valley Motor Coach Company

They had their offices and parking area at Junction Park stretch, New Brighton, PA.

Beaver Valley Motor Coach Company Buses

Will Begin A

Detour Through Monaca & Aliquippa

on the First Run Monday Morning, April 5th

When Route 88 is closed between Freedom and Conway. The detour will be the same route used last year when the road was closed between Freedom and Baden. No traffic will be permitted between Fourteenth street, Freedom, and Tenth street, Conway. Buses will carry passengers to Conway by way of Monaca, Aliquippa and Ambridge. Beaver Valley Motor Coach buses will not be permitted to pick up or discharge passengers between Colona in Monaca and Eleventh street, Ambridge. Passengers picked up at or before a bus reaches Colona will be discharged at Ambridge or beyond, however, and the same will be true on the return route.

1948

*** *** *** *** ***
*** *** ***

CHURCHES

St Peter's German Lutheran Church
Luther Church of the Redeemer
First Presbyterian Church of Phillipsburg
First Presbyterian Church of Monaca
Slovak Lutheran
Emmanuel Baptist Church
McGuire Chapel
Methodist Episcopal Church of Phillipsburg
Monaca United Methodist Church
New Beginnings Church of the Nazarene
Free Methodist Church
Free Methodist Church of Sylvan Crest
Monacrest Free Methodist Church
Colona United Presbyterian Church
Calvary Baptist Church
Emmanuel Gospel and Tract Mission
St. John the Baptist Catholic Church

Other area churches
Mill Creek Church
St. Frances Cabrini Catholic Church
North Branch Presbyterian Church
Bunker Hill Community Church
Church of Jesus Christ of Latter Day Saints
Jehovah's Witnesses Kingdom Hall
The Vankirk Lutheran Church
Faith Lutheran
Open Door Baptist Church
Trinity Evangelical Free Church

"Spirituality is difficult to gauge because of the nature of the available evidence."   I believe the real church is, of course, the body of believers and their beliefs.   Being raised a Christian, I also believe that though physically and financially there was labor, toiling, and sacrificing put in each building, every house of worship, and the growth of congregations are indeed part of history. When all is said and done, is the true work done by us?

As in all areas, having houses of worship has been and still is a very important part of Monaca, Center and Potter. Readers will find some of the more important facts for each of the different places of worship listed in this section, with much more detailed information being omitted or greatly condensed.   This is not meant to diminish any importance or to in any way indicate pastors, organizations, or notable individuals did not contribute considerably to any given sector.

A directory from 1898 listed the following:

Presbyterian – Rev. J. T. Hackett

German Lutheran – Rev. Lemcke

St. John's Roman Catholic – Rev. C. J. Hughes

Methodist Episcopal – Rev. Pascoe

English Lutheran – Rev. C. L. Holloway

St Peter's German Evangelical Lutheran Church - Pennsylvania Avenue and Sixth Street

ST. PETER'S EVANGELICAL LUTHERAN CHURCH CONSTRUCTED 1832 BY SEPARATISTS FROM THE HARMONY SOCIETY, UNDER THE LEADERSHIP OF COUNT MAXIMILIAN DE LEON, ORGANIZED AS NEW PHILADELPHIA SOCIETY. 1840-FIRST SCHOOL BUILT. 1850-FIRST PIPE ORGAN IN BEAVER COUNTY.
BEAVER COUNTY HISTORICAL RESEARCH & LANDMARKS FOUNDATION

2015

Oldest church in Monaca...first substantial stone church in Beaver County and believed to
    be the oldest standing church in Beaver County.
Mar 1832 – designed by Count Maximilian de Leon and for years he also did the preaching
Organized in 1934.
As of 1937, the church had 336 members and a confirmed membership was 256.
Church bell in the tower was the first in Beaver Valley. The first church bell was dedicated on
    Oct 31, 1832. It was a 322 pound bell bought by John Gallagher of Pittsburgh for
    $130.75; installed in the cupola of the church and used for at least 52 years.
        Two new bells were bought in 1882 from A Fulton's Son and Company of Pittsburgh.   The two new
        larger bells were used until Nov 1930; this is when the original and famous cupola had to be razed
        due to structural safety issues.   Late 1940s – a new belfry was build and the Schulmerich Carilonic
        Bell System was installed.
Mar 1832 - First called *New Philadelphia Congregation.* The building of the church was
    completed in the same year. It was the first substantial stone church in Beaver County.
After Aug 10, 1833, the congregation was re-organized and the work of the church kept up
    by the remaining members of the former society.
Rev. H. Daubert of Pittsburgh preached there until 1835.

1835 to Mar 1, 1859 – Rev. Edward Ferdinand Winter was the regular pastor.
    He founded eleven congregations during the half century he preached.
        St. John's Church (known as Burry's Church) near Zelienople was one of these
        congregations.   During his pastorate at Phillipsburg, his parish consisted of 5
        churches. In addition to his pastoral duties, he found time to cultivate his other
        many talents including scholar, accomplished artist, and musician. He also organized
        a public school system and remained under the supervision of the church until 1884.

The congregation purchased the ground property of the church, the school lot, and buildings
and cemetery lot from the former New Philadelphia Society.

In 1849, the second re-organization of the congregation took place. The official
name of the church was given as the *United Evangelical Protestant Church of
St. Peter at Phillipsburg.* The trustees of the new congregation were Dr. Edward Acker, Anthony
Knapper, and Jacob Schaefer.

St. Peter's church was the first in Beaver County to have church bells and a pipe organ.

The organ was built by the organ builder, Johannes Mueller of Zelienople, in 1850 for $240.
It was installed the same year. This organ was used for all services until 1929 when
a new two manual pipe organ was installed by the congregation.

This church conducted their own day school since there was no public school system and had
two school buildings opposite the church. These buildings were sold to the borough in
1882 and 1900 and the property was given to the community for a public park area.

1876 – church was remodeled, vestibule added, new stained glass windows, pews were installed.

Apr 2, 1877, the congregation secured a new charter, retaining its former name.
1930 another amendment of the charter was approved.

Through all the charters, since 1865, the church was commonly known as
St. Peter's German Lutheran Church. Services were still being held as of 1990.

Fact: Many of the Siebenbürgen (Transylvania) Saxons joined when they immigrated.

St. Peters German Lutheran Church   Little Beaver Historical Society
This picture would be prior to Nov 1930 since the building still has the original
steeple / bell tower structure.

BCHR&LF

This photograph of the church building was taken after Nov 1930 since the
original steeple / bell tower was razed at that time.

English Lutheran Church - Washington Avenue and Ninth Street   aka
Lutheran Church of the Redeemer – 813-819 Washington Avenue

Around 1849, The Rev. Dr. William Passavant, a Lutheran and tireless missionary, came to
America. With the help of Rev. Henry Reck, pastor of Grace Lutheran Church, in
Rochester, he tried to establish an English speaking Lutheran church here, in 1865.
The English speaking church fell apart, but it was revived in 1879 by Rev. Passavant
and in May, 1882, a temporary organization was made with 20 adult members.

Organized Nov 28, 1868 – used the English language.
This church was organized by Prof H. E. Jacobs of Thiel College which created the need for a
Lutheran church using the English language.

First few years of services were held in the St Peter's German Church until 1890.

When Thiel College moved to Greensburg in 1871, the young congregation declined drastically.

1882 – congregation was reorganized.

Jul 1, 1887 – permanent organization, constitution adopted charter received Aug 30, 1889.

1888 - 2 lots on Washington Avenue, toward Ninth Street, were purchased and on Sep 2, 1888 –
the corner stone was laid for the brick church building.

Mar 17, 1889 – first service was held in the uncompleted church.

1937 – the church had been modernized.
o   had membership of 476 members.

Spring of 1959 - the property was expanded eastward, a new parsonage was built, and a pipe
organ was purchased.

1965 work began to reshape the old church area into an educational unit and make a new
sanctuary.
o   Aug 21, 1966 the first service in the new sanctuary was held.

Redeemer Lutheran Church

Slovak Lutheran

This church was used by the Slovak Lutherans under the name *Dr. Martin Luther Slovak Congregation.* Organized in 1934 and held services in the German Lutheran Church.

Emmanuel Baptist Church – corner of Twelfth Street and Virginia Avenue – 1200 Virginia Avenue
Started by immigrants from Czechoslovakia.
Rev. H. C. Gleiss spoke both German and English (German was the 2nd strong language
of almost all Czechs and Slovaks who came to Monaca).
Rev. Gleiss and the church belonged to the Pittsburgh Baptist Association.
1903 – first organized as a Slovak Mission on Monaca Heights.
Mr. Slabey of Monaca Heights built a 2 storey brick house on the hillside in Monaca Heights and
made the front room very large to accommodate/serve for meetings of the Slovak Baptist
group. This room became too small so in 1904 plans to build a church building were made.
James H. Welch, a Baptist owner of a brickyard (where most of the Slovaks worked) donated two
lots on Monaca Heights near the reservoir. The local Slovak immigrants gave as much
as they could afford and there was a drive for donations from the whole community, with
gifts ranging from 20 cents up to $10. Between 1904 and 1909, there was a total of
$200.35 collected, which in those days was a goodly sum. Welch's two lots were on
Marshall Road.
Feb 1905 the church was completed and dedicated and officially organized Nov 8, 1910
as the Emmanuel Slovak Baptist Church.
Due to congregational growth, the building on Marshall Road was sold and……..
1914 – a new building was erected on the corner of Twelfth Street and Virginia Avenue;
dedicated Feb 1914.
1940 – services were now conducted in English; prior to this date they were in the Slovak
language.
The first minister in 1910, Rev. Henry Ibser.

Colona United Presbyterian Church

Organized in the old Thomas Jackson homestead in 1902 with Rev. H. L. Hood.
The building was dedicated in 1903.
1938 – the church building was sold by order of the Presbytery and congregational relations were
dissolved.

First Presbyterian Church of Phillipsburg – 1029 Pennsylvania Avenue (in 1912
- close to corner of Pennsylvania Avenue and Eleventh Street)

The congregation first used the Chapel of the Orphans' Home, then the Methodist church.
Then the place of worship was in the ARK, a frame building that was once one
of the first schools in the borough and originally located on the triangle lot at Fifth and Sixth streets
(where a band stand was built – veteran memorial now on lot/2015).
The Ark building was moved and situated closer to Ninth Street, on one of the lots to the right of the
borough building and then used by the Presbyterian Church.

Though often it is mentioned that William G. Taylor served the First Presbyterian Church, he was technically not a pastor of the church, but should receive credit for helping form the congregation. The main religion of Phillipsburg in the 1830s and 1840s was Lutheran with the majority of the families in town being German; there were only 3 Presbyterian families in Phillipsburg at that time. Rev. Taylor regularly preached in the orphans' school chapel for over 10 years and gradually, a Presbyterian congregation began to grow. He remained in the area even after the fire at the orphans' school and obtained supply of ministers to the congregation and found places for them to meet. By 1885, there was the need for a permanent place of worship.

The First Presbyterian Church of Phillipsburg was founded Apr 16, 1885 and incorporated.
Oct 28, 1886 ----- Nov 22, 1886 - Charter was granted; twenty-three members were in the congregation at this time.
This building was a new wood frame church built at 1029 Pennsylvania Avenue and services were held there until the fall of 1931 when it was torn down for the construction of the George Washington School building. The land for the new church building at 1301 Indiana Avenue, was purchased by the Ladies' Aid.

BCHR&LF
This picture was taken when the church was at 1029 Pennsylvania Avenue.

Jun 1924 – the charter was amended and the name changed to.........

First Presbyterian Church of Monaca – 1301 Indiana Avenue
>May 3, 1931 – corner stone was laid for new building at the corner of Indiana Avenue and
>>Thirteenth Street.
>The final service to be held in the church building on Pennsylvania Avenue was on Oct 11,
>>1931.   Pending the completion of the first floor of the new building on Indiana Avenue,
>>services were held in the high school auditorium.
>Dedicated the new brick building on Dec 20, 1931.
>>Although the new building was not completed, by Dec 1931 it was occupied.
>>In 1937, there were approximately 740 members and Rev. Clarence W. Kerr was pastor.
>>This current structure is of brick, has 10 large stained glass windows, and a pipe organ.

Picture is from the churches' website   2015

McGuire Chapel – Chapel Road, Center Township
>1857 - Was organized as a Methodist Society and met in the Davis School on Chapel Road.
>Corban Prophates donated two acres of land and the church building was completed early 1859.
>McGuire Chapel was a Methodist Episcopal Church and was named after the first pastor.
>Mar 1866, McGuire Chapel was dropped from the circuit of churches and attached to
>>the Monaca Methodist Church in Phillipsburg.
>There were still activities and festivals held at the McGuire Chapel in 1908.
>The building was eventually torn down after many years and the lumber used to build a near
>>by home.   The McGuire Cemetery remains on Chapel Road.
Many of the members of McGuire Chapel were residents in Phillipsburg and organized a Sunday
School, erecting a building in 1865.

From this Chapel and congregation, the Monaca Methodist Church began……..

Monaca United Methodist Church   aka
                    Methodist Episcopal Church of Phillipsburg - 813 Indiana Avenue
                              (still called Methodist Episcopal at least into the 1930s if not longer)

      1866 - Property purchased, the frame church was erected and dedicated.
      The members of McGuire Chapel organized a Sunday School and this became part of this
           church in 1865/66.
      1899 – the lot adjoining the church was purchased and a parsonage was constructed.
      1902 – the church was removed from a circuit with other Methodist churches and no longer
           had a shared minister, but had a full-time pastor of its own.
      1908 plans were made for erecting a new church......the old church was moved to the rear
           and incorporated into the new structure.   Rev. Daniel L. Marsh was pastor in 1909.
      1937 – Rev. Ross Hunt was pastor and there was a membership of 285.

    1939 – the name changed to...........

Monaca Methodist Church - currently called **Monaca United Methodist Church** – 813 Indiana Avenue
      There was a fire at the church, it burned down and parish helped rebuild it.
      2014 -The current church expanded and was adding a multipurpose community center.

Monaca Free Methodist Church

BCHR&LF

The above building served as the parsonage and church in 1909 prior to the current church building being erected.

Methodist Episcopal Church

Church of the Nazarene   aka   **New Beginnings Church of the Nazarene**

- 899 Jackson Avenue – Colona / Monaca Heights
–corner of Jackson Street and Ridge Road

Sep 5, 1943 - Started with a tent meeting at the corner of Ridge Road and Blaine Road in Colona
Heights.   The first pastor was Rev. Donald Brickley.
Oct 17, 1943 was the first service in the newly purchased old Presby. church building at
corner of Ridge Road and Jackson Avenue.   Services were still being held in the church.

Free Methodist Church – corner of Elm Street and Wagner Street - Fourth Ward
In the winter of 1903 there was a series of revival meetings held at the house John Rambo.
These led to the organizing of a Free Methodist church in January 1904 with twelve charter
members.   Rev. D. G. Shirer was the first pastor of the congregation.   They purchased a
site on Elm Street in the Fourth Ward of Monaca Heights and erected a church.
Organized in Jan 1904.

Free Methodist Church of Sylvan Crest   aka   Sylvan Crest Free Methodist Church
- Sylvan Crest, Center Township
Established in 1943; the interested residents built a basement and met in it until the church
building was completed in 1956.   Rev. Donald Rosenbaum was the first pastor.
The former church building was sold after the merger and was converted into a private home.

The two churches above merged/joined in 1971 and became...............

Monacrest Free Methodist Church – corner of Elmira and Walnut St., Monaca Heights (995 Elmira Street)
1972 this building was dedicated.   1987 the fellowship hall and more parking were added.

St. John the Baptist Catholic Church - first located at 1409 Pennsylvania Avenue – then to the corner of Fifteenth Street and Pennsylvania Avenue (1499 Pennsylvania Avenue or 1501 Virginia Avenue)

Lot was purchased in Dec 1886. Founded and work began on church in autumn of 1888 – finished in 1889.   They laid the cornerstone of the first church in 1889.

It was "a mission" until 1905, with the pulpit filled by pastors of other places.

Rev. Father Leo Stengel was the first pastor. The first church building served the congregation until 1913.

1903 congregation purchased a lot at Fifteenth and Virginia Avenue with intention of erecting a parish house. This was never done.

Jan 1906 the church became its own parish and the pastor lived in a rented house which in 1909 was purchased as parish rectory.

1908 – 5 lots were purchased on the corner of Fifteenth Street and Virginia Avenue to build a Catholic school. This building had a swimming pool in the basement – it was called St. John's Lyceum.

Courtesy BCHR&LF

This is the first St. John church; built in the fall of 1888 at 1409 Pennsylvania Avenue.   This first St. John Church building was sold to the Polish National Alliance Group and was moved to Pacific Avenue in the mid 1940s and was used as the PNA meeting hall.

The parish Lyceum, built in 1910, was to be used for various entertainments and had a gymnasium. This Lyceum was converted into a church and dedicated Aug 3, 1913.   The second church also became too small.

This is the second church; formerly the Lyceum and in May 1913, it was converted to the church building.

By May 1930, plans for a new church were being developed.   A cornerstone for a larger church was laid May 4, 1930 and new church was dedicated May 30, 1932.   This new, larger structure is the current church – 2016.

This church building was constructed of Kentucky limestone.   Rev. Fr. John L. Canova was the pastor of the church in 1937, coming to Monaca in Oct 1922.

The cornerstone was laid on May 4, 1930 for the third and current church.   This church structure was dedicated on May 30, 1932.

St. John The Baptist Catholic School and MSGR Farri Hall (Monsignor Emilio Farri) – Virginia Avenue
        Established in 1951/52 and blessed on Apr 12, 1953.
                -       1957 a new convent was constructed (had been at corner of Virginia Avenue
                        and Fifteenth Street).
                -       The school was staffed by the Sisters of Divine Providence from 1951 through the 1990s, then
                        was totally staffed by lay teachers and personnel from the area.
                -       1960 a new wing was built and named MSGR Farri Hall.   It contained a
                        Gymnasium, bowling alley, and 4 classrooms.
        Jun 30, 2014 – the school (Kindergarten thru grade 8) was closed.
        Preschool for children ages 3 and 4 remains opened and operational and the remainder of the
                school building is used for CCD School of Religion, houses the parish offices, the parish
                St. Vincent de Paul Society, and as a Parish Center (as of 2014).

Parish School

Calvary Baptist Church – corner of McClellan Street and Wayne Avenue – 999 McClelland Street
        Organized in Jun 1953 but ground was not broken for building until Mar 1954 and was
        completed in the summer of 1957 with services still held in the basement until the first one in the
        auditorium on Sep 11, 1960.   During construction of the church in 1953/54, services were held
        in the Fourth Ward Fire Hall.   The first pastor of this church was Rev. William Koltovich.

Emmanuel Gospel and Tract Mission – Marshall Road
>Began by meeting in a garage of Mr. & Mrs. Tony Parona on Marshall Road in Aug 1938
>>under Pastor Cecil E. Jones, a Christian layman.
>Apr 1939 a permanent building was built on the Parona property.
>The church was an independent and unorganized branch of the Christian and Missionary
>>Alliance.

Other Local Churches Serving Monaca Residents

Mill Creek Church – South Side of Beaver County - 5005 Rte. 151, Service Church Road, Hookstown, PA
1784 to Present   Mill Creek was once said to be the oldest of any denomination in Beaver County,
>but it was discovered that the Service Church was operating at least by 1779, so now many find
>a better statement to be "Mill Creek Presbyterian Church is among the oldest living congregations in
>Beaver County."

———

Church of Jesus Christ of Latter Day Saints (Mormon) – 114 Church Drive, Center Twp.
>Mormon missionaries served in this area for many years.
>Building was erected in 1968/71; the chapel was added 1978.

———

Jehovah's Witnesses Kingdom Hall – 108 Spruce Drive, Center Township
>Building was erected by volunteers in 3 days in Oct 1988; dedicated in 1989.

———

St. Frances Cabrini Catholic Church – 115 Trinity Drive, Center Township
>Parish was founded in 1961 and church was formerly dedicated Jul 19, 1964.

———

Bunker Hill Community Church – Pleasant Drive, Center Township
>Originally held meetings in former Bunker Hill School – non-denominational church.
>Started as a Sunday School in the V. F. W. hall in 1942.
>The Bunker Hill Community Church was organized June 6, 1951; chartered in 1955.

———

Mt. Carmel Church -   Although this church building is now located in Sheffield, Aliquippa, brick remains of two of the earlier church's structures have been detected adjacent to the Mt. Carmel Cemetery further up Brodhead Road in Center Township. The congregation for this church has been dated from 1800 and many history books state it was then known as White Oak Flats. The name White Oak Flats was changed to Mt. Carmel.   There is no exact date as to when the old church building(s) that once was off Brodhead Road by the current Mt. Carmel cemetery was razed or removed.   A new church building was erected, received a few remodeling events, and still stands on the lot at the intersection of Brodhead Road, Kennedy Blvd., and Mill Street in Sheffield.   Mt Carmel was the parent church of North Branch United Presbyterian Church in Center Township.

———

North Branch Presbyterian Church – former Moon Township, now Center Township
>It was started in 1833 as a branch of Mt. Carmel U.P. Church, New Sheffield (Mt. Carmel was
>>first known as the White Oak Flats Church).
>Original services were held in the house and/or barn of Daniel Weigle.

———

Van Kirk Mission   aka   The Van Kirk Lutheran Church – 106 Van Kirk Road, Center Twp.
Mar 10, 1929 – mission was started in the Van Kirk School House as a Sunday school.
The school house was moved to nearby church property and remodeled into the church.
A new building was erected in 1970.

_____

Open Door Baptist Church - 118 Community College Drive – Center Township
Held services in 1969 in the former Meiter's Garage and old tavern.   Church building completed in 1981.   The Open Door Baptist Church sold the building in 1992.

_____

Trinity Evangelical Free Church – 118 Community College Drive – Center Township
Currently the Centerpoint Community Church

_____

Faith Lutheran Church – 100 Center Grange Road, Center Township
Established in 1953. Meeting first in the Center Grange Hall building. The first service was held in the new church building on July 20, 1958.

_____

Christian House Chapel /Southern Baptist Council / University Baptist Church
This church was started in Apr 28, 1991.   It was located in the area by the Montgomery Dam; then moved into Raccoon Township in 1991 to the former Mount Pleasant Presbyterian Church site.

I have no dates to include, but the University Baptist Church (Southern Baptist Council) temporarily used the former office supply building in Center Township along Brodhead Road (a short distance from Lucci Plaza).

*** *** *** *** ***
*** *** ***

CEMETERIES

Baker Cemetery aka Baldwin Cemetery

**Monaca German Lutheran Cemetery   aka
St. Peter's Church Cemetery**

St. John the Baptist Parish Cemetery

Beaver County Poor Home Cemetery

Fairview Cemetery   aka   McLaughlin Cemetery

Union Cemetery

McGuire Chapel Cemetery

North Branch Cemetery

Beaver County Memorial Cemetery

Cemeteries

Residents of Monaca, beginning in the very early years to the present, are known to be buried in any one of the numerous cemeteries known to be in the immediate Monaca, Center, and Potter areas. I have included information on several of these cemeteries, including the two located in Monaca.

Baker aka Baldwin Monaca Cemetery
Monaca German Lutheran Cemetery aka St. Peter's Evangelical Lutheran
Beaver County Poor Home Cemetery
Fairview Cemetery   aka   McLaughlin Cemetery
Union Cemetery
McGuire Chapel Cemetery
St. John's Catholic Cemetery
North Branch Cemetery
Vankirk Cemetery   aka   McCullough Cemetery

There were many smaller and more personal cemeteries in the Center and Potter Township areas.
I have not included information on these since many were considered family burials grounds, but with the connection between these two areas to the families in Monaca, I wanted to include at least their names and locations for anyone interested in the genealogical aspect.

Moon/Center Township
Baker Cemetery   aka   Figley Farm Cemetery
Beaver County Memorial Park Cemetery
Braden/Potter Cemetery
Douds Cemetery
Fath Farm Burial – on Elkhorn Road
Kozar's Burial
Laubscher Farm Burial – on Chapel Road
Mt. Carmel Cemetery
Otto Farm Burial – Temple Road
Smega Farm Burial – Elkhorn Road
St. Joseph's Cemetery
Weigel Private Cemetery

Potter Township
Braden/Potter Cemetery
Stone Cemetery
Weaton Cemetery

Baker Cemetery   aka   Baldwin Cemetery - located within Monaca Borough
Located on portion of the original Baker lands and afterwards sold to the Baldwins.
One hundred yards south of Twenty-First Street (between the overhead pass of Beaver Street and the private entrance of the Colonial Steel Company).
In 1901/02, the property on and around this cemetery was purchased for the building of a railroad spur to service the local factories. The Baldwin family members, being the current owners of the property, petitioned and were granted an injunction for the area of the cemetery to remain undisturbed. This cemetery has remained in its original condition since that time and is accessible to the public.
1799 - Anthony Baker received his patent to this property. He set aside this plot for the private burying ground; there are approximately 50 graves including Anthony Baker, Revolutionary War soldier.

Almost all the first two or three generations of this Baker family are buried in this cemetery, including Anthony Baker himself.   Many other soldiers and family members are also buried here.   Other names found include Shrodes, Alcorn, Holsinger, and Rambo.

BCHR&LF

Monaca German Lutheran Cemetery   aka   St. Peter's Church Cemetery
Located at the lower end of Monaca; at the entrance to Monaca from Rte. 18.
This cemetery once belonged to St. Peter's Evangelical Lutheran Church of Monaca, but in Jul 1944, the St. Peter's Church transferred the church cemetery, commonly known then as "the old Monaca Cemetery" to the Borough of Monaca.   The borough accepted the transfer and promised to preserve the cemetery as an historic landmark of the community and to keep the same in a dignified and clean condition.
There are at least 288 interments in this cemetery.
Most of the church members were from Germany, so many of the graves are in German
Geboren = born   Gestorben = died   Hefrau von = wife of

Some very early burials (many of these were infants and children):

Johannes Bonnet-d. Mar 1837
Catharina Dimiotti-d Feb 1779
Louise Gerhardt b Mar 1830-d Dec 1839
Christine Wiegand Goetz b Mar 1811-d Nov 1839
Samuel Keiff-d Nov 1839
John C Langendoerfer b Nov 1838-d Nov 1838
Trephma Reif b 1834-d 1839
Unk Schmidt b Jul 1812-d Apr 1835
Aug. Streit b Oct 1835-d 1836
Maria M Thorwarth b May 1838-d Feb 1839
Maria (Forstner) Zoll b 1768-d Nov 1835
Elisabeth M (Rehmann) Wolfer b May 1768-d Jul 1836

Jacob Diem b Feb 1839-d Jul 1839
Salome Erb b Jan 1825-d 1838
Karl Hostavson b 1796-d 1832
Johannes Jaeger b Oct 1838-d Jul 1839
Benjamin Knapper b Mar 1836-d Nov 1837
Caroline Mueller b Aug 1837-d Mar 1838
Augustus Schmidt b Jul 1744-d ukn
Johan Friedrich Sippel b Mar 1803-d Aug 1837
Jorinda Strohecker-d Nov 1839
Frederich Trompeter b Jan 1939-d Jul 1839
Sophia Vorstner(Forstner) b Oct 1835-d Aug 1837

Beaver County Poor Home Cemetery – Potter Township

The cemetery that was located on the property of the Poor Home no longer exists. There have been references and mention of over 300 bodies being interred on this property.

Unfortunately, there are no records of more than a few of the burials that did occur at the Home. There were 11 residents of the Poor Home buried in the Beaver County Memorial Park Cemetery on Baker Road in Center Township.

Jonas Potts and his wife Mary Heckathorn Potts were originally buried on Phillis Island, on the Ohio River (the Shippingport/Georgetown area). They were later reinterred in the Beaver County Poor Home Cemetery. James died at a very advanced age in 1814; his wife died about 1812/1813.

The former Poor Home property was not accessible to the public once it became private property of the ZCA plant. Today this former property is totally unrecognizable with all the land moving that has occurred due to the Shell company. Did all these gravesites also meet with industrial construction and/or land moving equipment over the years or more recently, or were they reinterred elsewhere? I have no further information to answer those questions.

Fairview Cemetery – Center Township

This cemetery is now within the Union Cemetery property. It is the circle portion at the very top of the hill. It has numerous WWI veterans buried there.

Mr. Schlosser owned the Fairview Cemetery. The road to this cemetery began on Marshall Road, just opposite a barn, and extended to the top of the hill. A small part of the road was still used by the owners of a garage across from the Mateer's car sales.

In a November 1933 article, I found information on this Monaca Cemetery. The article alluded to this being a cemetery in Monaca, but then went on to provide this information:

Monaca Cemetery, in Center Township, formerly Moon Township....

On the north by Marshall Road Extension.....

On the east by lands of Frederick Dockter & now or formerly of William Temple heirs.....

On the west by the Union Cemetery...   Total - containing 10 acres and 71 perches......

In my researching, I found numerous mention of veterans of WWI that were said to be buried in the Fairview Cemetery; from visiting other gravesites in the Union Cemetery, I can verify that there are numerous veterans that are indeed buried there in this portion of the cemetery.

This is now called the *Fairview Section* of the Union Cemetery.

Union Cemetery – Center Township

Located on corner of Brodhead and Chapel Road

It is listed among one of the oldest and most historic cemeteries in Beaver County since there are many war veterans and distinguished community leaders buried in the cemetery. The original property of this cemetery was purchased from George Dockter in 1890 and consisted of 35 to 40 acres. It was originally started by Edward Kaye and Herman Speyerer, later owned by the Bachelor Brothers until the early 2000s; and today is under other ownership.

Fairview Cemetery was the original cemetery and became incorporated into the Union Cemetery.

Until more recently, there was a stone and metal fencing that enclosed a gold fish pond and lily pond. This was originally built under a beautiful weeping willow tree. The tree has long since been removed and with all the stone border and railing around the pond removed, the pond has a very natural look to it.

The Union Cemetery office was located at 1020 Pennsylvania Avenue in 1956.

McGuire Chapel Cemetery – Center Township
> Located on Chapel Road; a short distance from intersection of Chapel & Center Grange Roads
> > heading toward Monaca
> It was established at the time of the McGuire Chapel in 1859. The chapel building sat along the
> > same area of the road as the cemetery location and was built in 1858/59 on 2 acres of a
> > grove donated by Corban Prophater, then of Moon Township which became Center
> > Township. The name came from the first pastor Latchall McGuire.

St. John the Baptist Parish Cemetery –   Center Township
> Located on Chapel Road; a short distance from the corner of Brodhead and Chapel Road; just
> > past the Monaca Turn Verein parking lot.
> The cemetery consists of 11 acres. An above ground columbarium was added in the 2000s.
> > There are more than 600 burials in this cemetery.

North Branch Cemetery – Center Township
> Located beside the church on North Branch Road which is off Brodhead Road.   The church
> > and cemetery are visible from the intersection of Routes 18 and 51.
> This is considered to be first used beginning when the church was built in 1833.   It indeed is a
> > very old cemetery and was closed off to any additional lots being sold in about 2002.
> Some of the names of family members buried in this cemetery include: Alcorn, Badders, Bailey,
> > Baker, Barto, Bickerstaff, Black, Blair, Bruce, Campbell, Cochran, Davis, Douds, Dunn,
> > Engle, Figley, Grinder, Hicks, Huffmyer, Irwin, Johnston, Jordan, Landis, Manor,
> > McCullough, McDonald, Meaner, Minor, Raw, Shroads, Smith, Stewart, Todd, Weigel,
> > White, Winkle, Zimmerly.
> A few of the oldest burials I found on record were Samuel Baily - d Dec 1826; William Shroads – d Feb
> 1842; Nancy Jane Shroads - b Jan 1847 d Apr 1847, Brown Irwin - d Dec 1849;
> > Susannah Bickerstaff – d Aug 1847

Van Kirk Cemetery   aka   McCullough Cemetery -   Center Township
> Located in the woods at the end of Van Kirk Road which is off Monaca Road.
> The 1876 atlas shows Andy McCullough owned 47 acres, Jas. McCullough owned 48 acres, and
> > Wm. Van Kirk owned 28 acres – all surrounding the area of the cemetery.
> There are only about 16 stones still visible. From these stones, it is evident that this cemetery
> > existed at least by the 1830s.   There are even records that indicate there were burials
> > here prior to 1785.   The earliest stone still visible is of Catharine Winkler who died
> > 10/3/1837 aged 73 years.   A few others indicate John Winkler died 12/30/1848, aged
> > 98 years; Elizabeth Hicks, daughter of William and Abigail, was born 10/4/1836 and died
> > 2/20/1851.
> The American Legion of Monaca used to maintain this cemetery; current caregivers are unknown.
> > More recently, it was terribly overgrown.
> Names of family members known to be buried in this cemetery are Van Kirk, McCullough, Black,
> > Carson, Cassiday, Craig, Ewing, Graham, Hicks, Huffmyer, McCullough, Red, Winkler.

*** *** *** *** ***
*** *** ***

FINANCIAL INSTITUTES

Phillipsburg Building and Loan Association of Beaver County

Monaca Federal Savings and Loan Association

Colony Federal Savings and Loan Association

Colony First Federal Savings and Loan Association

Colony Savings Federal Savings Bank   aka   Colony Savings Bank F.S.B.

Mortgage Lending Solutions

The Citizen's National Bank of Monaca

The Monaca National Bank

The First National Bank of Monaca

The National Bank of Beaver County

Century National Bank

Sky Bank

Huntington

CAMMAR Building and Loan Association

FINANCIAL INSTITUTIONS

Prior to 1837, establishing a banking or financial institution in the U.S. was most often a quite complicated process as every bank needed to obtain a charter from the legislature of the state in which it was being founded. The number of available franchises in the states was limited. In 1836, the Congress closed the public institution known as the Second Bank of the United States; it was a public financial institute with more than two dozen branches across the United States.   This closing prompted the need for new banking institutions for lending, investing, accepting deposits, and issuing monies. New York state was the first to pass the free banking statute in 1838; Michigan was next; and by 1860 there were about eighteen more states that had enforced laws for some sort of variant of the free banking law first formed by New York. This was the beginning of banks, savings and loans, credit unions, and financial institutes in general, even in small communities such as Phillipsburg and Monaca.

Phillipsburg Building and Loan Association of Beaver County

1889 to 1937
> Sep 30, 1889 – first financial institute in the area.
> Felix Lay was its first president.
> Did not have its own bank building.
> > o   Met at lodge room in 498 Pennsylvania Avenue, then a local barber shop.
> Money was ferried across the Ohio to Rochester for safe keeping until 1901.
> > o   They held meetings and had their offices in the Monaca National Bank building starting about 1903 at 829 Pennsylvania Avenue.

> It was approved on May 5, 1933 to have the name changed and was officially submitted to the Department of State of the Commonwealth of PA on Aug 7, 1937.....................

Monaca Federal Savings and Loan Association
1937 to 1971
> They began with having offices at 1308 Pennsylvania Avenue.
> In 1939, moved to 1299 Pennsylvania Avenue (corner of Thirteenth Street/Pennsylvania Avenue).
> The building is still standing (2016) – on the opposite corner from former Taormina's market.
> In 1954 they did extensive exterior and interior remodeling project.
> > o   Loan office facilities were moved to the 2nd floor.
> > > ▪   1959 opened branch office in Aliquippa Shopping Center.
> > > ▪   1963 opened another branch office in West Hills Shopping Center.
> As of 1971 (span of 82 years) – there had only been 5 presidents – Felix Lay, Martin W. Carey, Paul Mattach, Alex Bucsko, and then John W. Figley.

> Changed its name in Sep 14, 1971 to.................

Colony Federal Savings and Loan Association – the Monaca office remained at 1299 Pennsylvania Ave
1971 to 1982
> In 1981 they purchased the former site of the Exxon Gas Station on the corner of Ninth Street and Pennsylvania Avenue.
> They remodeled the gas station and installed drive up windows; the office at 1299 Pennsylvania Avenue was closed once the new location was open for business.
> Jan 1984, they moved their home office to 139 Golfview Drive, Center Twp.; also had offices in Aliquippa, West Hills, and Moon Township (Allegheny County).

> They merged with First Federal of Erie early in 1982 and again changed the name...........

Colony First Federal Savings and Loan Association
1982 to 1990

After using this renovated gas station as their bank building, with the Phoenix Glass plant's growth and the revitalization of Monaca, Colony Savings used a portion of the property the bank was sitting on and along with the lot beside them that was the theatre, and they made the decision to construct a new building in 1983. The former renovated service station building was torn down and a new building was erected on the corner of Ninth Street and Pennsylvania Avenue – 900 Pennsylvania Avenue. This new structure was a 12-sided brick colonial building. (See pictures further.)

The home office of this merged institute had been in Erie since 1982 and it was moved to north Pittsburgh. The building in Monaca had only been one of its branch offices in Beaver County.

In a 1984 ad, it stated 900 Pennsylvania Avenue was the address in Monaca; they were also still at branch offices at 139 Golfview Drive-Center Township, 2111 Main Street-Aliquippa, and 846 Beaver Grade Road-Coraopolis.

By May 1990 once again the name was changed to..............

Colony Federal Savings Bank   aka   Colony Savings Bank F.S.B.
1990,

They were in business through 1990 at 900 Pennsylvania Avenue.

When they closed their doors of business, the building was then purchased by Mortgage Lending Solutions.

INSURED

Phillipsburg Building & Loan Association
of Monaca, Pa.

**SAFETY
of Your
INVESTMENT**
in this Association
**I N S U R E D
1 0 0 %
up to
$5,000**

BY THE
FEDERAL SAVINGS
&
LOAN INSURANCE
CORPORATION
Washington, D. C.

An agency of the
U. S. Government

Serving the interests of the home owners of this County we are naturally proud of the construction of the new annex to the Municipal Building the construction of the extension to the Municipal Water System, and the building of streets and sewers.

Truly, Monaca is a real place to live. We will be glad to share your problems in the matter of the purchase of a home that will suit your income.

Now in our new and modern home—
1308 PENNSYLVANIA AVENUE

OFFICERS

PAUL MATTAUCH, President   JOSEPH HERMANN, Secretary
ALEX BUCSKO, Vice President   J. RENWICK GORMLEY, Treasurer
CLERKS—STEVE LEITSCHAFT, GERALDINE WEIGEL.

DIRECTORS

PAUL MATTAUCH   R. H. MARKEY   JOSEPH HERMANN
ALEX BUCSKO   L. I. LeGOULLON   W. R. LEIGH
HOWARD S. SHANKS

SOLICITOR – D. R. HARTFORD

1940s

At 1299 Pennsylvania Avenue.

1954

Then the building had a face lift........

Monaca Federal Savings and Loan Association – 1299 Pennsylvania Avenue

from 1956 ad

MONACA FEDERAL SAVINGS
AND LOAN ASSOCIATION
1299 PENNSYLVANIA AVENUE
MONACA, PENNSYLVANIA
DIAL:
SPruce 5-0330

This is a picture of the old gas station building that was converted into the Colony First Federal Savings and Loan Association building before they erected the new 12-sided building on the site.

Colony Federal's new building in Monaca is 12-sided.   Times photo by Pete Sabella   1983

For the genealogy buffs......
The Monaca National Bank's first Board of Directors was:
George Lay, Martin Carey, Harry C. Glasser, Charles Houston, James R. Gormley, Henry J. Eckert, and Robert L. Hood.
The first officers were: George Lay-President; James R. Gormley-Vice President; and Robert L. Hood was cashier.

Mortgage Lending Solutions – 900 Pennsylvania Avenue
2000, Current
Founded Jul 16, 2000.
Moved to this location from East End Avenue in Beaver Jul 1, 2003.

2014 view of the 12-sided building – now Mortgage Lending Solutions business.

The Citizen's National Bank of Monaca – 312 Ninth Street
1901 - 1937

> This bank had offices in the opera/theatre building, frequently noted as the Business Block building. The
> > building was adjacent to Hotel Monaca at the corner of Ninth Street and Washington Avenue.
>
> Jun 25, 1901 – charter was issued.
>
> The bank was located in the corner room of the "handsome new Opera House block"
> > on Ninth Street.
>
> The building had several businesses in it with access to them on Ninth Street. The American
> > Legion also had their post in the basement area of the Citizen's Nat'l Bank building.
> > - o Entrance to the basement stairs were to the side of hotel building, off Washington Avenue,
> >   between Koehler's property and the hotel.
>
> > *The first Board of Directors of this bank was:*
> > > *John T. Taylor, James H. Welch, John J. Allen, Henry C. Fry, Edward Kay,*
> > > *Christian Will, Frederick Bechtel, J. C. Martin, and A. M. Jolley.*
> > *The first officers were:*
> > > *John T. Taylor-President; John J. Allen-Vice President; and*
> > > *Thomas C. Fry was cashier*

Carey's Corner   Bank building   BCHR&LFF
> *A full view of the above post card is in the *Views of Monaca* section.

The Monaca National Bank
1901 to 2012/2013-?

> Apr 4, 1901 – charter was issued; organized May 2, 1901.
> > (Bausman's book states the charter was on Jul 1, 1901.)
>
> 1912 to 1922 the bank held business at 829 Pennsylvania Avenue; it then moved to 999 Pennsylvania
> > Avenue and Ninth Street. A new building was erected on the corner of Pennsylvania Avenue
> > and Tenth Street. The first floor was the banking room and director's room; the second floor
> > was office rooms and apartments.
> > - o George J. Harbison was awarded the contract for the new buff brick, stone trimmed, two
> >   storey building.
>
> In 1929 the bank installed a new clock that was electrically operated, chimed on the quarter
> > hour, the half hour, and the hour; it was brightly illuminated at night.
>
> There were apartments rented in this building in 1927, 1929, 1932 – called the Monaca Nat'l
> > Bank Building.

> > *When it opened in 1901: George Lay-President; James R. Gormley M.D.- Vice*
> > *President; Robert L. Hood-Cashier. Officers were: M. W. Carey, H. C. Glasser;*
> > *Henry J. Eckert, and Charles Houston.*

In Jan 1937, after the consolidation, the first officers elected of the First National Bank of Monaca were:

> *George W. Weinman-President; Alonzo S. Batchelor-Vice President; and Charles W. Weinman was cashier.   With the death of Mr. Weinman in Jan 1937, Alonzo S. Batchelor became President, F. A. LeGoullon and Dr. D. C. Moore were elected vice presidents.*

Jan 2, 1937 - The Citizens Nat'l   and   Monaca Nat'l consolidated and were named.............

First National Bank of Monaca at 999 Pennsylvania Avenue

The First National Bank of Monaca

After the consolidation, business was continued at 999 Pennsylvania Avenue.

Sep 1953 - Properties located at Pennsylvania Avenue and Tenth Street were purchased from Ms. Eleanor Fisher and others. These were located across Tenth Street from the then Monaca Nat'l bank building (999 Pennsylvania Avenue).   The properties combined had – 70 ft frontage – 149 ft deep.

Before the new bank building could be erected, they purchased properties and razed a two storey building at 315 Tenth Street (was Fishers' home in 1942), a one storey building at 1001 Pennsylvania Avenue (was Fisher's Store in Dec 1946), and the building at 1003 Pennsylvania Avenue (was Klingseisen Bakery for many years, then became Standard Refrigeration Sales & Service in Feb 1946.)   All this occurred by Apr 1954.

REQUEST FOR BIDS

The First National Bank of Monaca will accept sealed bids for the following:

1. Plymouth warm air gas furnace located at 315 Tenth Street, Monaca, Penna.

2. Winkler warm air oil furnace located at 1001 Pennsylvania Avenue, Monaca, Penna.

3. Suspension type natural gas heater with fan located at 1003 Pennsylvania Avenue, Monaca, Pennsylvania.

Removal of each unit from property not later than April 24, 1954. Bids accepted for individual units or group bid. Successful bidder to provide full coverage on Workman's Compensation and Public Liability Insurance.

TERMS: Payment in full on acceptance of bid. Right to reject any or all bids reserved
BIDS WILL BE RECEIVED FOR FOLLOWING PROPERTY.

1 Two story frame building located at 315 Tenth Street, Monaca, Pennsylvania.

2 One story frame building located at 1001 Pennsylvania Avenue, Monaca, Pennsylvania

One story building located at 1003 Pennsylvania Avenue, Monaca Pennsylvania.

Each bid to include removal of property from site, clearing property to foundation line, not later than May 15, 1954.

Bids accepted for individual units or group bid. Each bid to be accompanied by deposit of $100.00 or Certified Check as guarantee of fulfillment of terms of bid, or part payment on account. Successful bidder to provide full coverage Workman's Compensation and Public Liability Insurance

TERMS Cash or satisfactory credit on acceptance of bid. Right to reject any or all bids is reserved.

All bids on equipment and or buildings due 9 00 A M Saturday, April 10, 1954, at The First National Bank of Monaca, Pennsylvania. Inspection of equipment or buildings available on appointment at The First National Bank of Monaca, Monaca, Penna., during banking hours

The First National Bank of Monaca,

Monaca, Pennsylvania.

4 6-7-8

Apr 1954

Sep 1, 1974 – the First National Bank of Monaca became......

The National Bank of Beaver County - 1001-1003 Pennsylvania Avenue
1974 to 1983

Then ....

Century National Bank
Dec 9, 1985

They wanted to add on drive through lanes between bank and post office.

Then by 2002 it was............

Sky Bank

Then......

Huntington ▬ before it closed the Monaca Branch Offices Mar 9, 2012

Tenth Street   Post Office
1001-1003 Pennsylvania Avenue – now a restaurant business (as of 2015)

CAMMAR Building and Loan Association – 308-312 Ninth Street –then 1236 Pennsylvania Ave.
1901 to 2000

Organized Sept 14, 1901.   Began as a combination of Colonial and Allaire Land Companies and
was joined by the Moon Township Land Co.
Began by using the Citizen's National Bank until 1937, then moved their office to
1236 Pennsylvania Avenue.
CAMMAR stood for areas they served:
C-Colona A-Allaire M-Moon Twp. M-Monaca A–Aliquippa R-Rochester
In business in 1965 and up to Apr 2000.
May, 2000 - Due to state banking laws, CAMMAR was forced to make a choice – either obtain
Federal Deposit Insurance (FDIC), merge with another federally insured entity, or go out
of business.   Nov 1998, the state gave institutions 30 months to get federal insurance
or close.
o   CAMMAR made the choice to merge with Farmers Building and Loan in Rochester.
o   Farmers was founded in 1884, CAMMAR in 1901.
o   Farmers was already FDIC insured and the paperwork for CAMMAR to do the same was out of
the question.
This merger was completed very shortly after May 31, 2000.

***   ***   ***   ***   ***
***   ***   ***

MEDICAL

Pharmacies and Drug Stores

Doctors

Hospitals

Beaver County General Hospital
(aka   Rochester General Hospital)

Beaver County Home   aka County Poor Farm

Beaver County Tuberculosis Sanitarium

Water Cure Sanitarium

PHARMACIES & DRUG STORES

The inside of an early 1900 drugstore in Monaca.

There was no indication of exactly which pharmacy this was.

~

Citizen's Pharmacy – was located on Ninth Street in 1898 to 1903 – but not at the Bank Building.
    –moved into 310 Ninth Street (Citizen's Bank Building) in Apr 1903
1898 until after 1928
    Opened 1898 and was located along Ninth Street somewhere other than at 310 Ninth
        Street since that building was not erected until early 1900s.
    Was owned by George F., John and Francis Zitzman.
        George F. was listed as druggist and stationer in 1902/03 Directory.
            George lived on Washington Avenue in 1903.
    George moved the business to the storeroom at 310 Ninth Street (in the Citizen Bank Building)
        in Apr 1903.
    W. L. Treiber, optician, gave free eye examinations at Zitzman's pharmacy.
    George Zitzman began courses at the Pittsburg School of Pharmacy – Jan 1901.
        Geo. Zitzman sold a frame house on Pennsylvania Avenue (near Ninth Street) to Justice
            Merkle, who moved the house a short distance further west on Pennsylvania
            Avenue from its original location.   George intended to move his store building
            from Ninth Street to the lot where they removed the house and would add an
            additional storey to it.
        Mar 21, 1903 – The brick work of the new building erected on Pennsylvania Avenue by
            George Zitzman was completed. He did not move in though – instead he was
            renting it out (it was a millinery store in 1906/07 and again in 07/08).

    May 29, 1908 – Emmett M. Callaghan purchased this pharmacy from George Zitzman.

Citizen's Pharmacy became.........

Callaghan's Pharmacy - 310 Ninth Street until Apr 1963, then moved to....

1026 Pennsylvania Avenue

1928 to 1999

> May 29, 1908 – Emmett M. Callaghan purchased this pharmacy from George Zitzman.
>> Emmett and Anna were residing at 824 Atlantic Avenue in 1912.
>> E. M. didn't come to Monaca until 1903, not moving to town permanently until 1908 when he purchased the store from Zitzman BUT – see Penn Avenue Pharmacy because E. M. was there in 1905 – then going to Pittsburgh for about a year – then coming back to live in Monaca and purchasing Citizen's.   E. M. Callaghan graduated in pharmacy from the University of Maryland in 1892.
>
> Sep 1911 – ad states E. M. Callaghan was proprietor and owner of the Citizens Pharmacy.
>
> Feb 1925 – E. M. Callaghan was proprietor.
>
> Dec 1939 – E. P. (Gene) Callaghan, Emmett's son, began to work in his father's store at age 12 and took over the business after his father became ill.   Gene maintained the name Citizen's and stayed at 310 Ninth Street.

Apr 1, 1963 - business was moved to 1026 Pennsylvania Avenue when the Monaca Post Office moved out and into their new building across the street on Pennsylvania Avenue. The Citizen's Pharmacy had been at 310 Ninth Street for 55 years prior to the move.

The front and interior were remodeled (this was at 1026 Pennsylvania Avenue).

A Junior partner was taken at this time – Louis Pupi (who had been working there since 1949).

The new store had a stainless steel framed glass front, black walnut paneled interior, plexiglass panels on ceiling over the lights. There were a few old cases from the original pharmacy, otherwise, all was new. Gene had a portrait of his father hanging on the paneled, curtain wall. The prescription department was at the rear of the store with upholstered chairs provided for waiting customers.

E. P. (Gene) Callaghan stepped down in Jul 1971 as pharmacist and proprietor of the Callaghan Pharmacy. Louis Pupi, who worked and was partners with Callaghan became full owner of the business. Gene's son did not pursue a career in pharmacy. Gene's brother, Max A. Callaghan, practiced dentistry in Monaca from 1927 until he retired in May 1970. Gene and his wife lived in Center Township.

In a newspaper article, Gene reminisced extending credit to many customers and recollected that not many paid back the debt after the depression years, yet they remained faithful customers. He made a guess and estimated that he "produced just what the doctor ordered" about 500,000 times. He also remembered how 90 percent of prescriptions were compounded by hand; today the manufacturers make almost everything. His inventory before closing consisted of 15,000 different drugs and he mentioned that to be an efficient pharmacy, you had to "carry all of them."

Jun 1, 1971 – Louis Pupi became the sole proprietor due to an illness of Gene Callaghan. Louis Pupi and his sister Roberta Dusold operated the Callaghan's Pharmacy at 1026 Pennsylvania Avenue.

In 1994 this was the sole drug store in Monaca.

In Feb 1997, they were celebrating being a part of a business with 100 years of quality services to the Beaver Valley. Louis Pupi was still the owner of the pharmacy since 1971.

The Pharmacy closed Mar 31, 1999 when Louis Pupil made the choice to retire.

Jul 1971
E. P. Callaghan filling his last prescription.

Apr 1999   photo by Pete Sabella
Louis Pupil taking down Emmett's picture.

1956 at 310 Ninth Street

1990 ad

1950 ad

People's Drug Store – Ninth Street
1900
> H. F. Mitchell of Pittsburgh – manager in 1900.
> This was a new building in 1900.

———

Penn Avenue Pharmacy – 1301 Pennsylvania Avenue
1902, 1903 Feb-1904, 1919
> David A. Berry was proprietor in 1902/03.
>> D. Berry and family lived at same address as the pharmacy, but moved
>> elsewhere in Apr 1904.
>
> Fred O. Harley was manager of pharmacy in 1903 when he resigned and moved to Bellevue.
> E. M. Callaghan was then the manager of the pharmacy and tendered his resignation late
>   Oct 1906.   He went to Pittsburgh for about a year, then returned back to Monaca in 1908
>   and purchased the Citizen's Pharmacy from Mr. Zitzman.
> Ira C. Hoffman succeeded him; he was formerly conducting a drug store in Westmoreland
>   County.
> Dr. Ira C. Hoffman (physician and druggist), was the proprietor from 1906 until 1919.
>> 1912 – Ira C. Hoffman was owner; lived at the same location as pharmacy.
>> John Hoover, Dr. Hoffman's brother-in-law, was a clerk here in 1908.
>> They also served ice cream, soda and root beer.
>
> Dr. Hoffman sold the business to devote his full time to the practice of medicine.
> Jul 1919 - the business was sold to George T. Rowse (of Homestead) – brother to Beaver
>   druggist, Edwin S. Rowse.

became ......

Rowse's Drug store –1301 Pennsylvania Avenue (1299 Pennsylvania Avenue in 1931)
1919, 1921, 1928, 1931
> George T. Rowse - owner.

STOPS YOUR COLD BEFORE IT TAKES 'A' HOLD!'

LEM-BALSAM Quickly Relieves the Most Severe Coughs and Colds. Pleasant to Take and Contains No Narcotics.

Sold and Recommended by
Rowses' Drug Store, Beaver and Monaca
Central Drug Store Monaca
and all leading druggists

Get a 65c Bottle Today

May 1921

———

Kistner Drug Store – 1299 Pennsylvania Avenue
1930s, 1943
> Carl Kistner was the owner.
> W. A. Rowse was involved in this drug store – he became the primary listing on the tax lists 1931
> > to 1943; I only found a young William Rowse, druggist, living in Beaver during this period (his
> > father was Edwin who was also a druggist in his own store).
> Business was out of this building by 1939 because the savings and loan moved in here in 1939.
> > I have nothing further on the location between 1939 and 1943.

_____

National Cut-Rate Drug – 1106 Pennsylvania Avenue
1930, 1936, 1940, 1956
> Opened in 1930.
> Advertised free delivery.

_____

The Only Drug Store – at corner of Sixth Street and Pennsylvania Avenue
> > -then moved to the Keystone Building (in late 1903)- 1014 Pennsylvania Avenue
1892, 1893, 1901, 1907, 1916, 1917
> Opened in 1892.
> Windham Sparling, Manager/druggist and David Kaye, Jr., proprietor in 1898, 1902/03 to 1905.
> > Windham lived on Sixth Street in 1902/03; then was living in Ingram, PA by the end of 1916.
> > > W. Sparling was manager/druggist until 1905.
> > > When they moved it to the Keystone block building, there was a new soda fountain
> > > installed.
> > > Mar 26, 1904 – Windham opened his new ice cream parlor in the rear of this drug store.
> > > o   The parlor was finished in mahogany with furniture to match and could accommodate 28
> > >   people. The walls were painted and bear scenes of the four seasons -- spring, summer,
> > >   autumn and winter.
> > > o   In 1892/1893 Mr. Sparling was known for being a dealer in watches, clocks, and jewelry, too.
> David Kaye, Jr. was a clerk in the store in 1902/03, then graduated from Dept. of Pharmacy of
> > Western Univ. of PA in Pittsburgh.
> Mr. David Kaye, Sr. died in 1907; his son David, Jr. was a member of the Kaye-Levis firm, took
> > charge and continued the business until May 1916. David Kaye, Sr.'s son, Walter
> > D. Kaye, Jr. devoted his time to the store after his father passed away in 1907.
> Oct 1907, Walter purchased the stock and fixtures of the drug store from his father's estate
> > keeping the name of the drug store and keeping it in the Keystone building location.   Then he
> > went into partnership with Vincent H Levis who conducted a Rexall drug store in
> > Rochester.   They opened a new store in Rochester (Kay-Levis Pharmacy) and still
> > conducted the Only Drug Store in Monaca.
> David Kay, Jr. and family lived on Washington Avenue –David was also a foreman at Phoenix Glass.
> Walter Kaye, Jr. was partners with Vincent H. Levis in Kaye-Levis and they continued the
> > business until Jan 1917 when..........

William Pfaff, Beaver Falls bought The Only Drug Store and took charge of the store on Jan 16, 1917.

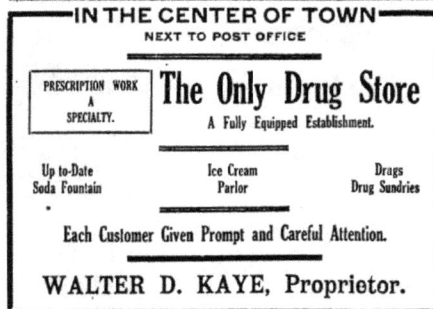

```
┌─IN THE CENTER OF TOWN─┐
       NEXT TO POST OFFICE

 ┌──────────────┐ The Only Drug Store
 │ PRESCRIPTION WORK │
 │      A       │  A Fully Equipped Establishment.
 │   SPECIALTY.  │
 └──────────────┘

   Up to-Date        Ice Cream          Drugs
  Soda Fountain        Parlor        Drug Sundries

   Each Customer Given Prompt and Careful Attention.

   WALTER D. KAYE, Proprietor.
```
1904

_____

Central Drug Store – Pennsylvania Avenue
1910, 1921, 1922

May 1921

_____

Bender's Pharmacy – 1106 Pennsylvania Avenue
1949, 1993

> Opened Feb 1949 by Howard T. Bender.   They also had a soda fountain area in the store.
> Closed - Nov 6, 1993 after 42 years of business – was being operated by Howard's son, Dan.
> - o   Revco acquired Benders Pharmacy in Nov, 1993.
> - o   There were notices and ads stating that all the prescriptions, files, and records
>   from Benders were transferred to the Revco Drug Store that opened at the Wal-Mart
>   Shopping Center Plaza in Center Township. Dan Bender was going to be among the
>   pharmacists working in Revco.
>
> Howard and his son Dan had a few reasons for closing their store.   One was the chain stores
> and insurances requiring people to fill their prescriptions in these types of stores.
> Another reason was that the owner of the building was forcing them out so he could
> permit the adjacently located Chris' Trattoria restaurant to expand.

Howard Bender and his son Dan in 1993.

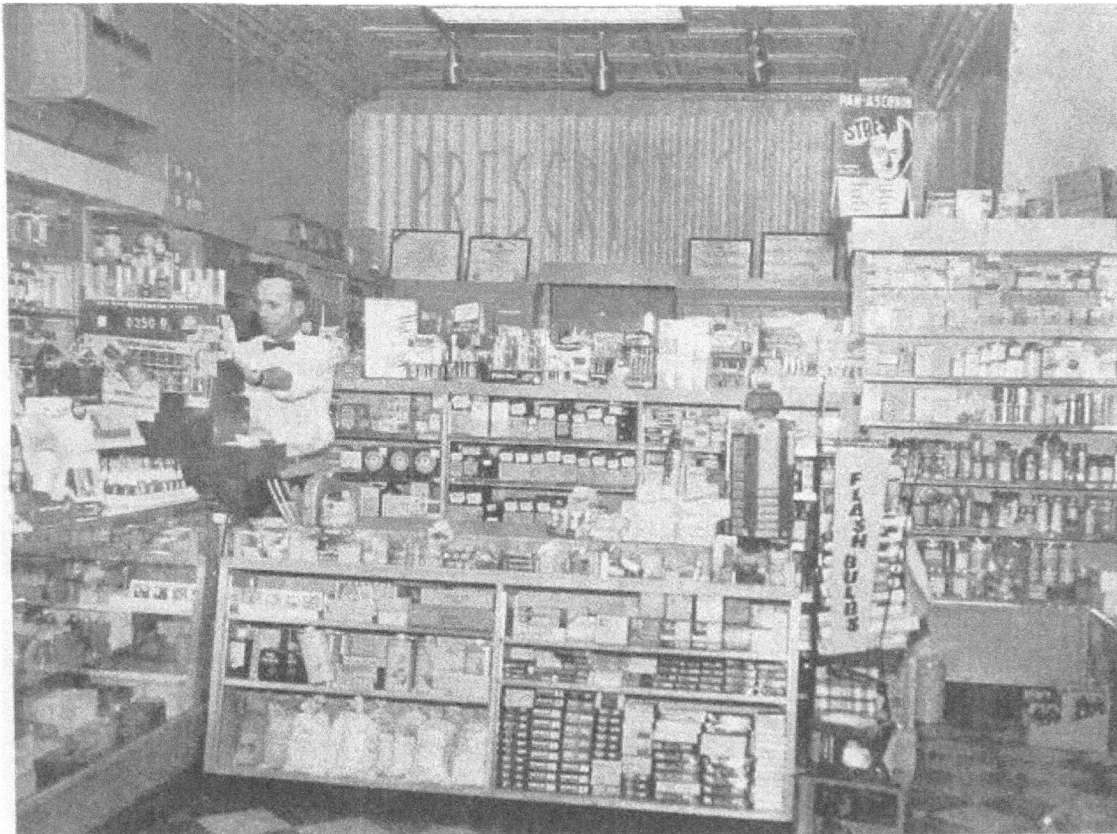

1956 - Howard T Bender, B. Sc. working in his store at 1106 Pennsylvania Avenue.

———————

Watson Drug Store – 1412 Pennsylvania Avenue in 1927, then 1426 Pennsylvania Avenue (1928, 1930)
1925, 1928, 1930, 1931, 1943
      Opened for business in Jun 1925.
      Herbert T. Watson, R. P. owner.
        Had a soda fountain with Tech Ice Cream.   Tech ice cream was advertised..... "The Kind
        That Smiles Right Back at You."   They sold Brick Ice Cream, too.
      This pharmacy was located where Celeste Tavern was in 2000s.

1931

for **Thanksgiving**
Mary Lincoln Candies

THANKSGIVING is the greatest feast day of
the year. Complete the feast with Mary
Lincoln Candies
One and Two Pound Boxes
Specially Wrapped   70¢ Pound

WATSON'S DRUG STORE
1426 Pennsylvania Avenue, Monaca.
Phone 9044 Roch. 9177 Roch.   Night Calls 1748-M Roch.

1930 /31

_____

CVS Pharmacy – 850 Pennsylvania Avenue
2007   Opened Jan 1, 2007.

_____

Hoffman's Center Pharmacy – had the business in downtown Monaca, then........
            – moved to 1495 Brodhead Road, Center Square Shopping Center (next to Loblaw's)
1908, 1917, 1963, 1980
        Opened _?__.
            Opened at Center Township location early October, 1962; Spiro Nellas was pharmacist.
        Closed __?__.
        Handled Rexall products.
    John Hoover was a clerk in the store; he was Ira's Hoffman's brother-in-law but had to quit his
        job since he was moving to Hooversville, PA, permanently as of Jun 1908.

$ DoLLAR DAY

THE REXALL DRUG STORE
Has Prepared For Its Patrons

A Dollar Day Surprise

And invites you to come to our store
on Thursday (Dollar Day) and look
over the bargains prepared for you.

LOOK FOR OUR WINDOW DISPLAY

HOFFMAN
Drug Store

—THE REXALL STORE—

MONACA PA.

1917

AT OUR *Rexall* DRUG STORE
HOFFMAN'S
CENTER PHARMACY, INC.
Center Square Shopping Center, 1495 Brodhead Road
Monaca — Next To Loblaw's — Phone 775-5700
AMPLE FREE PARKING

1963

Pete's Apothecary - 1026 Pennsylvania Avenue
1998, 2000, 2005, 2006
>Opened in Nov 1999.   Owned by Pete and Terri Antinopoulos.
>Were capable of making a gel or a cream form of a medication for those unable to take a
>>product by mouth.   They also customized veterinary medications.
>Had another store in New Brighton on Third Avenue.
>FBI raided both businesses on Sep 28, 2005.   The newspaper account of this incident stated
>>FBI people removed numerous cardboard boxes and plastic storage containers from the
>>drug store and adjoining building in New Brighton.   I could not find any follow up
>>articles to exonerate anyone or prove anyone's wrong doing.
>The Monaca store stopped filling prescriptions at this location in 2006.   Customers could drop off
>>their scripts, but they would be filled in New Brighton and returned to this store for pick
>>up or delivered to the customer's home.
>In Dec 2006, Pete planned on turning the front of the store into a coffee and dessert shop and
>>was going to call it Terri's Sweet Shop Café for his wife.

*** *** *** *** ***
*** *** ***

DOCTORS

In the 1800s and early 1900s, there were many different names given to a diagnosis of some of the illnesses.   I have listed a few of these; see if you know what the **definition of these** illness/conditions were.   (See the descriptions at the end of this section.)

Ill from brain fever (1904)	Bealed jaw	Dyspepsia
Grippe / Grip	Piles	
Quinsy	Imbibe / Imbibed / Imbibing	
Dropsy	Consumption	

*** *** *** *** ***

The physicians that served the people of Monaca (and surrounding areas) were very well educated and trained in their profession.   They provided medical services for everything from common colds to badly injured limbs.   I am sure the Monaca residents were quite satisfied with the services they provided.

Rudolph Wier – physician
1850   He started his practice in his twenties; born c1826.

_____

Gottleib Esenwine- physician
1850   Gottleib was from Germany; born c1807.

_____

Dr. Edward Acker – Physician
1841, 1848, 1850

Dr. Acker was born and raised in Monaca; first practicing physician on the south side of the Ohio River. In 1848 he purchased several of the buildings owned by the New Philadelphia Society and established a sanitarium known as Water Cure.

His holdings went to Dr. Clement Baeltz, who conducted the sanitarium for a few years, then sold the buildings to Mr. Cimotti who opened a hotel and summer resort. These same buildings eventually became Soldiers' Orphan School before the main building burned.
Dr. Acker died at age 68 in 1853.

*See Prominent People section for complete story on Christina Acker, one remarkable and strong woman.

———

Dr. Malvern Mackall – corner of Ninth Street and Pennsylvania Avenue
1920s, 1930s, 1950s

He taught school at the Alcorn one room school house in the 1920's before taking his medical training. He was born in c1885; he didn't always live in Monaca.
His memoirs and medical equipment were donated to the Beaver Area Heritage Foundation; it mentions he was a lifelong physician.

———

Dr. Craig Temple – 515 Atlantic Avenue
1880, 1885, 1900

Served as a physician in Monaca a little before 1880 until 1900.
Dr. Temple and family were living in Alliance, Ohio, by 1900.

Temple Family – 515 Atlantic Avenue - c1887   Photo courtesy Richard Temple
Dr. James Craig Temple b 1851 is standing in front of the horse.
Standing in the gate is Anna Hinkle Temple, wife of Dr. J.C. Temple, son Archibald R., daughter Edith, and Mary Hinkle, sister of Anna. Dr. Archibald Bryon Temple, brother of Dr. J.C.

———

Dr. John J. Allen – physician – corner of Washington Avenue and Eighth Street - 804 Washington Ave
1892, 1893, 1900, 1910, 1920, 1930

On 1898 directory his practice was listed at Pennsylvania Avenue.

He owned and rented out a small house on Eighth Street that sat behind their home.

They owned several buildings in Monaca, one was a home on lower Atlantic Avenue known
as Five Points.

John was born in Ireland in 1859. His wife's name was (Jeannette) Nettie M. Armstrong, they
lived at same address as his office.   They had children: Harold, Janet, Isabel,
and also took in orphan children.

In 1920, they had a servant living with them.

In 1930, at age 71, he was still listed as a physician.   They were still living in their home
as of Dec 1930, but I could not find anything on either Dr. or Mrs. Allen after that date.
It became the American Legion's home in 1931 and was sold in 1953 when the Legion
constructed a new building.

The quite large and once elegant 2 ½ storey building is still standing (2015) and used for
apartments.

Dr. Allen's former home in 2015.   This is the side of the home facing Eighth Street.

c1930

John Venn – Physician
1876

_____

Dr. Frederick Hum (of Beaver) – first floor of the Wm. Figley building – Ninth Street
1901
     Dr. Hum resided in Beaver but had an office located in Monaca.

_____

Dr. H. C. Hum – Ninth Street
1902, 1903
     In 1902/03, he lived in Beaver Falls.

_____

Dr. Theron L. Blackledge – Physician - Ninth Street (in 1910) – in New Brighton by 1912
1902, 1912
     By 1910, Dr. Blackledge was no longer located in Monaca, he still had patients he would tend to
          here though.
     Dr. and Mrs. (Anna M.) Blackledge lived in furnished rooms of the same building as his office prior to
          1910 before moving to a beautiful home in New Brighton.
          In 1910 they had a servant and a hostler (looked after horses).

_____

Dr. John Fife –
1902, 1903
     He married Rachel A., was a widower by 1902/03 and living with Rev. J. T. Hackett.

_____

Dr. James. R. Gormley – general physician – 1008 Pennsylvania Avenue -910 Pennsylvania Avenue
1890, 1900, 1902, 1903, 1908, 1913, 1930s
     He first had his office in two adjoining houses on Ninth Street in Mar 1900; by 1902/03,
          his office was on the first floor.
     He was born in 1867; married Lydia __ . They lived in same location as his office.
          The house was razed and property turned into a parking lot for the borough.
     He was the president of the Monaca National Bank, in 1934 and re-elected in 1935,
          served as vice president since it organized in 1901.
     The family moved to Dutch Ridge Road in the early 1930s.
     His brother, Dr. Fred Gormley also practiced in Monaca.

Dr. James R Gormley

_____

Dr. Fred T. Gormley – general physician – Pennsylvania Avenue
1902, 1903, 1912
     Dr. Fred and Dr. James Gormley were brothers.
     He married Myrtle A____, they lived at same address as his office.
     By 1912, only James was still in Monaca.

_____

Dr. John A. Mitchell – 910 Pennsylvania Avenue
1934, 1956, 1972

He started his business in Monaca on Aug 23, 1934; in the same location as former Dr. J.
Gormley.

He held his practice and office in Monaca.   The house was razed when the area was needed
for a parking lot in 1961.

In 1930, he was living in Mt Lebanon with his wife's parents and his father-in-law was
an undertaker/mortician.

In 1940 they had a maid living with them in Center Township.

Dr. Mitchell was honored at a dinner at the PNA Club in Feb 1972 for his services to Monaca with
many persons of the Monaca community in attendance.

———————

Dr. E. L. Perri - 193 Ninth Street (between Atlantic Avenue and Indiana Avenue)
1923, 1930,

He built a new brick dwelling on Ninth Street in 1926 with plasterers working in Aug 1926
(possibly 193 Ninth Street).

Following an automobile accident, he did not practice for several months.

Dr. Ernest Perri died while at his summer cottage at Ocean City, NJ on Jul 9, 1939.

He was noted as a stomach specialist and moved to Monaca in about 1923.

———————

Dr. Robert A. Marquis – 914 Atlantic Avenue
1938, 1940

Filled in when Dr. Perri was out of town in 1938.

In 1930, Dr. Marquis was a pharmacist with his own drug store in Beaver. He finished his
education and became a physician by 1938.

———————

Dr. Darious C. Moore – physician and surgeon – 315 Thirteenth Street
1904, 1910, 1912, 1928

He filled in for Dr. Allen for 3 weeks in 1906 while Dr. Allen and family were out of town.

Dr. Moore then set up a practice in Monaca shortly after 1906.

1910 and 1920 Darious and Nelle lived on Thirteenth Street; they were living in the same building
as his office; they moved to Beaver in 1928.

While still living in Monaca, Dr. Moore once served the office of Coroner of Beaver County,
served on the board of the Citizens National Bank, then on the Board of Directors
and vice president of the National Bank of Monaca.

———————

Dr. Howard F. Mitchell – 1008 Pennsylvania Avenue
1956

———————

Dr. Samuel Tomasi –
1940

He was lodger at 1013 Indiana Avenue in 1940.

———————

Dr. David Patrick –
1940   He lived at 1100 Washington Avenue in 1940.

———————

Dr. William G. Milliron – 834 Pennsylvania Avenue
1956

BCHR&LF

Dr. Milliron's office and home –on the right, with the dormer and bushes

The First Ward School building was to the right of his home/office.　(A picture with a continuous street view of this section of Pennsylvania Avenue may be seen in Street Views section.)

_____

Dr. Thomas W. McCreary III – lived at 1317 Thirteenth Street / 1301 Virginia Avenue
1930, 1940, 1962, 1970
> As a lifelong resident of Monaca, even without a practice actually in Monaca, I felt it
>> fitting to include him in this section.
> He started his career in 1929 in a pathology laboratory at Rochester Hospital.
> He had a clinic named after him– the *Thomas W. McCreary Clinical Pathological Hospital.*
> He retired from the pathology practice in Dec 1970.
> A Monaca native and longtime friends and neighbor with Dr. John Mitchell.
> Thomas was born in Monaca Sept 1900.

_____

Dr. John H. Trumpeter – physician
1930, 1940, 1950s
> Lived at 935 Atlantic Avenue, moved to his parents' home on 1299 Indiana Avenue in 1930.
>> John was a widower with children in 1930.　His father had died by 1940, his mother was
>> still living with them and he was remarried.
> They moved to Beaver prior to 1959.　John died unexpectedly in Aug 1959.
> I believe that John always had his obstetrics practice in Beaver, but was born in and a native of
>> Monaca.

_____

Dr. John A. Riedel, Optometrist – 1026 Pennsylvania Avenue
(2nd floor of Batchelor building, beside Batchelor Furniture store)
1920s
> He was living in Allegheny County by Apr of 1930.

_____

Dr. James I. Armstrong – 1400 Pennsylvania Avenue (on the corner of Fourteenth Street and Pennsylvania Avenue) (current location of the CoGo's service station)
1920s, 1934, 1940, 1960s

      James was boarding in a hotel on New York Avenue in Rochester in 1920; listed as a physician; also listed as married, but there was no wife with him.

      1930 – James and his wife were living in Monaca with their children.   They had one servant living with them, too.

      1934 – They were a very generous couple and took in children; they received custody of three of those young children who were already living with them in 1930.

      When the property on Pennsylvania Avenue was sold for a service station to be erected, rather than raze their beautiful home, it was moved one block back to where it still stands (2016) at the corner of Fourteenth Street and Pacific Avenue – right along the railroad tracks, on the opposite corner to the former railroad depot/now Masonic Lodge.

photo courtesya friend, originally from Hank Bechtel
Home when located on Pennsylvania Avenue

2013
Home now located on Pacific Avenue

———

W. L. Treiber, Optician
1901, 1902, 1906

      Dr. William Louis Treiber would do free eye examines at Zitzman's Pharmacy and every Wednesday at The Only Drug Store.   William lived in Beaver and had his main office there; coming to Monaca was strictly to provide the free service.

———

John Monyak, M.D. – Ninth Street (between the bridge and Washington Avenue) / 924 Atlantic Avenue
1978, 2010s

———

Javad Jamshidt, M.D. – Ninth Street
1978

———

E. W. Schmuck, M.D. – beside or in 915 Pennsylvania Avenue (Schmuck's Shoes)
1978

———

Chung Lew, M.D. – 1414 Pennsylvania Avenue
1978

———

Gregg S. Zernich, D.O. – 1598 Virginia Avenue
at least 1990

———

Dr. Michael Sisk, D.C. – 432 Indiana Avenue - 200 Ninth Street (corner of Ninth Street and Indiana Avenue)
1989 - current
> Opened business in 1989.

————

Rock Chiropractic Center – 1712 Pennsylvania Avenue
1994, 1995

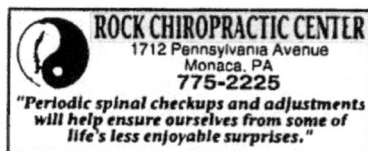

ROCK CHIROPRACTIC CENTER
1712 Pennsylvania Avenue
Monaca, PA
775-2225
"Periodic spinal checkups and adjustments will help ensure ourselves from some of life's less enjoyable surprises."

————

Dr. Andrew S. McKinley – 1212 Pennsylvania Avenue in 1912
> -in 1956, he was at 1403 Pennsylvania Avenue

1912, 1956
> He was the s/o John and Elizabeth McKinley; born in 1881.
> Dr. McKinley came to and lived in Monaca in 1908.

————

Dr. H. S. Malone – (1920, 1930) 1110 Pennsylvania Avenue – (1940) 935 Atlantic Avenue
1930, 1940, 1958
> Dr. Herbert "Bert" Searight Malone was a native of Rochester, but owned and operated a
> jewelry store and practiced optometry in Monaca for many years.   He sold the jewelry
> business; it became McNees Jewelers.   He continued to practice optometry.
> He retired in 1958 and died at his retirement home in Florida in Feb 1972.
> Dr. Malone was a former Monaca School Board member and member of several Monaca
> organizations.

————

Dr. Vincent Troia – 1712 Pennsylvania Avenue – currently at 1100 Pennsylvania Avenue
1996, current
> Dr. Troia graduated from Monaca High School.
> > His sister, Linda Troia, is the office manager and his mother Mrs. Terzina Troia is the
> > receptionist.

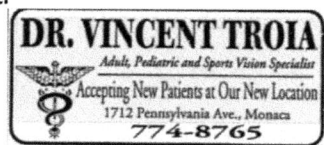

DR. VINCENT TROIA
Adult, Pediatric and Sports Vision Specialist
Accepting New Patients at Our New Location
1712 Pennsylvania Ave., Monaca
774-8765

1996

————

Dr. G. Robt. Campbell – 212 Ninth Street
1956

————

Dr. N. A. Hetzler – 1100 Washington Avenue
1956

————

Dr. John H. Shugert – 199 Ninth Street
1956

————

Dr. Jos. H. Weigel – 914 Atlantic Avenue
1956

————

Dr. Norman A. Hetzler – unknown location
1949

_____

Dr. C. W. Hetzler – Dentist - 1098 Pennsylvania Avenue
1956, 1978

_____

Dr. Ira H. Todd – Dentist - In the Keystone Building on Pennsylvania Avenue; also on 2nd floor of John
                Anderson's 2 storey office building – beside H. Simpson, Sr.'s music store –
                1298 Pennsylvania Avenue.
1901, 1903, 1920, 1930
        Dr. Todd was living in New Sheffield in 1900.
        After he married in 1905, they were living in an apartment in the Keystone Building on
            Pennsylvania Ave, then owning a home Atlantic Avenue.

_____

David A. Lurlano, D.D.S., Family Dentist – 212 Ninth Street
2015

_____

Dr. Harry T. Ellsworth – Dentist - Pennsylvania Avenue (2nd floor of Batchelor building, beside Batchelor
1928, 1930   Furniture store)

_____

Dr. Ray E. Reppert – dentist – 905/907 Pennsylvania Avenue and in Keystone Building (1978)
1956, 1976, 1988
        He was the owner of the building for the new Dairy Queen going in at the corner of Ninth Street
            and Pennsylvania Avenue in 1974.
        He was the school's dentist and would do the examinations along with the physical
            examinations by Dr. Sheets for grades 3 through 10 – both costing $2.50 per exam (1976).
        Dr. and Mrs. Reppert lived in Beaver.

_____

Dr. Hanna – dentist – unknown location
1927
        Dr. Hanna and his family left Monaca in Aug 1927; he was going to serve as intern at
            the Bellevue Hospital in New York City, specializing in oral surgery.
        He sold his office equipment to Dr. Callaghan.

_____

Dr. M. A. Callaghan – dentist – 899 Pennsylvania Avenue - 2nd floor/above Krall's Men and Boys' Wear store
1927, 1956, 1963   (the old bank's building)
        He was the s/o Mr. and Mrs. Emmett Callaghan
        Dr. Maximilian Allen Callaghan opened his office in the Monaca National Bank Building
            the first of Aug 1927.   Dr. and Mrs. Callaghan moved from an apartment on
            Pennsylvania Avenue to an apartment in the Monaca National Bank building in Mar
            1929.   By 1937, they were living in a very nice home in Mona Manor, Center Township.

_____

Carl F. Jernberg – Dentist - 298 Ninth Street
1940, 1956   Dr. Jerberg died in 1979 at age 78.

_____

Dr. Barrett Sakol – Dentist - Ninth Street
1978, 1982,

———————

Dr. Robert L. Rumbaugh, III – Dentist – 1012 Pennsylvania Avenue
1989

———————

David Iurlano, D.D.S. – 212 Ninth Street – dentist
2010s

———————

Michael F. Dragonjac, D.M.D. – 1598 Virginia Avenue
1986, 1990, 1998
          General dentistry.   Was at 300 Marshall Road in 1998.

***   ***   ***   ***   ***
***   ***   ***

HOSPITALS

Beaver County General Hospital   aka   Rochester General Hospital

Rochester General Hospital,
Rochester, Pa.

1913 photograph of the hospital   Courtesy the BCHR & LF
The photo was originally submitted by Fritz Blasche.   Two popular forms of transportation in 1913 are also illustrated in this photograph – Dr. Shugert's automobile and Dr. Cloak's horse and buggy.

The former Beaver County General Hospital was located in Rochester. It was founded in 1899 and was a semi-private hospital / institution and the name was changed to Rochester General Hospital very shortly after it opened. The original Board of Directors: Drs. Allen, Gormley, Shugert, Armstrong, Scroggs, Baker, Boal, Wickham, and Ague; several of these doctors being associated with and/or based in Monaca.

The original building was destroyed on Mar 11, 1901, by a fire. In 1902, the hospital was turned over to its board of directors. A modern building was then constructed with monies from a state appropriation and an equal amount being raised. In 1922, there was an annex built to the building. This hospital was regarded by the Pennsylvania Hospital Association as one of the leading and best-equipped hospitals in the state at that time.

With the large growth in industry during the WWII era, there was a serious shortage of space in the hospital, so a 48-bed addition was completed in 1943 along with a complete lab and an X-ray department. In 1972, the Rochester General Hospital became a unit of the Medical Center of Beaver County. The hospital ceased to exist and was converted into, and now serves as the Rochester Manor and Villa (Retirement Community) at 174 Virginia Avenue, Rochester, PA

Water Cure Sanitarium

Dr. Edward Acker bought several large buildings built in approximately 1833 and owned by the New Philadelphia Society. In 1848 he established the Water Cure Sanitarium. Dr. Acker established it as a type of health spa where he used hydropathy (treatment through the use of water) to heal different ailments. The sanitarium was credited with being the first such hospital in Beaver County. It flourished under his management. Water-cure physicians were quite out spoken and constantly criticized "allopaths" (forms of alternative medicine), or for doctors who were treating their patients with drugs, potions, lotions, and herbs. It has been published that in 1852, the hydropaths were probably more correct than not since there was very little knowledge available about most diseases, let alone the supposed cures. Drug treatments were basically based on old Indian remedies, what were often said to spur from old wives' tales, and/or pure deviousness. Over time, the discovery, advancement, and proof of the germ theory for diseases, along with reliable pharmaceuticals as treatments, became more popular and most of the beliefs in alternative medicines such as water-cure have fairly disappeared. Even though hydropathy did offer a few more minor benefits for the body when matched to modern medicine, (although short lived), it was definitely a part of Phillipsburg's and Beaver County's history. The strain on his not very strong body, along with his dedication to his work resulted in his premature death. Dr. Edward Acker died in 1953 at age 44. His 2nd wife, Christina did not have an easy life. There is a complete write up on Dr. and Christina Acker under Prominent People category. The continuation of his work was suspended for some time until Dr. Baeltz came into the picture.

When Dr. Baeltz took over the sanitarium, under his management it was more of a resort than a healing sanitarium or hospital. A man named Cimotti then purchased the buildings and opened a hotel and summer resort which was in operation in the earlier 1860s. These same buildings were then purchased by Rev. William G. Taylor in Dec 1865 who had taken on the challenge of organizing and being in charge of the Soldiers' Orphan School. (There is more on this school under the Schools category.)

Water Cure – 1860 Census only listed Dr. Baeltz and his family with a few of the hired help, no
      other residents were included on the census except Edward Winter, age 11 and Levina
      Moretz, age 13.
          Dr. Clemenz Belz – professor & physician; Emelia – wife, Rosa 11, Sarah 7, Emilia 4
            Charity Baker, 19 – domestic   *Martha Rambo, 21 – domestic*
            Helena Miller, 26 – domestic   *Joseph Speice, 30 – laborer*

There is a historical marker near the site of the former Water Cure Sanitarium buildings. It was placed at the intersection of Fourth Avenue and Pennsylvania Avenue.

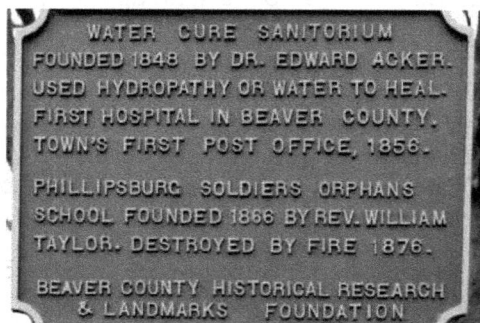

The Water Cure Sanitarium in Phillipsburg was not the only one in the country. In New York, there was *The Water-Cure Journal* published. The journal was mainly full of endorsements from people who felt they were cured/healed by the treatment of water. It also went into details on new practices of medicine and theory.

Within an 1852 publication of the journal was an ad for Phillipsburg's establishment.

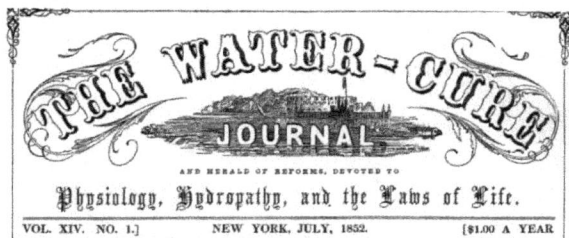

Letterhead of journal

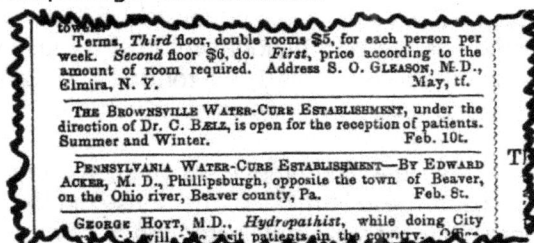

excerpt of ad in the journal

Both of these were from 1979 publication of Milestone of BCHR&LF

*** *** *** *** ***

c1921

Beaver County Home   aka   County Poor Farm

Although the Beaver County Home and Hospital (aka County Poor Farm) was located in Potter Township, it was generally associated with Monaca and Center also because of the close proximity and the connection of roadways from the Home to those areas.   In 1831, 31 years after Beaver County was founded, there was a meeting at the courthouse to discuss providing a home for the poor.

Prior to the Beaver County Supervisors presenting the voters with the request to build a larger County Home, a smaller, less formal Home was put into use.   This first of other buildings was a small one storey frame structure. In 1842 it was reported the poor-house was located on the south side of the Ohio River, about 2 ½ miles below Beaver; this description places the first poor-house building on the very same location and property as the larger poor-farm/house that has received so much history written of it.   This first "poor-house" was under the management of Mr. and Mrs. Shrodes, and then under the management of Mr. and Mrs. Stephen Minor who received $500 a year from the county for their services; with a board of directors supervising the house. Mr. Minor supervised 140 rods (equals 770 yards) of board fencing being put up by the "inmates" who did this in exchange for a small quantity of tobacco.   Mrs. Minor would make pies and cook for everyone; she was assisted often by Mrs. Shrodes, the wife of the former manager.

BCHR&LF

1842 view of the first County Home – address was Bellowsville, Beaver County, PA

Building of a larger Home was presented to the voters for them to express their will regarding the establishment of such an institution. The votes in 1831 showed 1,533 were for the institution and 2,336 were against it. Another vote in 1841 also proved to be a majority vote not to build the home. In 1851, the county home was put to the voters again, this time the vote was 1,855 for and 1,738 against. An official building for the care of the Beaver County poor, disabled, and infirm was erected in 1853.

Inmates reported very clean and first-class conditions; there was an average of 25 males and 25 females who resided at the home. These inmates of the house did the farming and much of the maintenance of the home. Growing of crops was quite successful with tons of hay, bushels of potatoes and wheat, along with acres of corn and pumpkins. There was also livestock, usually 3 horses, 10 cows, 1 bull, and 29 hogs.

The Poor House/Home was first established to accommodate poor and indigent persons, but over the course of its existence, it also gave refuge to the elderly, the infirm, the sick, and occasionally to the insane.
- It was a functioning institute until the last residents moved to new building (now Friendship Ridge) Apr 1959.
- Court-House debate voted down building the institute in 1831 and again in 1841; finally was approved by a narrow margin in 1851.
- the county bought a 138-acre farm for $6,900 from George Stone where the first structure was erected.
- originally built to house persons who had no one else to take care of them – were elderly, infirm, poor, blind, crippled, unwanted.....it was considered a "black mark" if you ended up in the poor house because it meant you could not take care for yourself.
- located in what was called Moon Township in the 1850s, now Potter Township (on the property of Zinc Corp. of America, the former St. Joe Mineral property) adjacent to current Center Twp.
- it sat ½ mile from the main road, along the bank of the Ohio River, directly across from the Merrill Locks (No. 6 – Industry, PA).
This hospital was described as one of the most modern and complete of its kind in the state.

1859 - the original building was replaced in 1859 by another one-storey frame building on same site.
1868 - due to the increase and demand to enlarge the much needed home, the county added on to that building with a two storey brick complex. They replaced the two older structures at a cost of $18,000; it was completed in 1870.
   - due to the low location of the site by the Ohio River, the almshouse property experienced frequent flooding; Feb 7, 1884 had water rise 7 feet above the ground level.
1884 - the poor farm could accommodate 100 paupers.
1913 - a new facility was being built to replace the aged structures, on the same property, but in a location which would not flood – this facility was completed in 1916.
   This new facility had a central building with two storey wings on either side; the central building sported a large pillared portico/porch. This facility added an additional 100 beds, superintendent's residents, a morgue, and various farm outbuildings, as well as several jail cells.
1937 – under supervision of James L. Blair; Mrs. Blair in charge of all office work and looked after the welfare and comfort of the women.
   There were 219 residents in 1937 – 186 men and 33 women.
   Within the home, there was a fully equipped hospital with two trained nurses on duty regularly.
   The W.P.A. project in 1937 was repairing two porches and a passageway between the laundry and the main dormitory.
1940 – the demand for more room continued to increase - a large 100 bed hospital was added/completed as a rear wing to the building – it was exactly as long as a football field.
   - the extensively remodeled home in the 1940s unfortunately bore no resemblance to the home pictured; after the improvements and it was then known as the Beaver County Home and Hospital.

The 1940 remodeling and updated added other features...............
    -it had 9'x12' jail cells in the basement that housed unruly residents from time to time.
        The cells were removed in the summer of 2014 when demolition was being done –they were stored/placed behind Potter Township municipal building to be available for display at the Potter Family Reunion events.
    - had a modern laundry in the basement as well as an auditorium.
    - when remodeled in 1940, it featured a chapel, pharmacy, two solariums, and rooms with outside exposure, along with living quarters for a medical staff of 12 persons.
    - still consisted of the building and a working farm complete with a dairy herd, sheep, pigs, chickens.
    - residents were called "inmates" and all able-bodied inmates had to work on the grounds to earn their keep.

1948 – Jan 1 – William H. Bickerstaff was superintendent of the county home; he was appointed by the commissioners.
1950s – the poor house turned its focus more toward the old and infirm rather than the poor and insane of old.
1952 - all food used in the home was still being grown there.
    - gigantic gardens and everything was canned for the winter.
    - still had cows, pigs, fresh milk, butter, buttermilk and eggs, hundreds of chickens; butchering was done in the fall and there was a smokehouse.
1956 – to alleviate overcrowding, infirm residents were moved to a former Beaver County Tuberculosis Sanitarium in Center Twp. (now Penn State Beaver Campus).
1959 –Apr - about 220 residents still living in this facility were moved into the new center that the county built (Beaver Valley Geriatric Center, now named Friendship Ridge).

As of 1955, the property was sold to St Joseph Lead Co. for $750,000 for plant expansion. St. Joe leased the property to the county for $1 a year until the new structure in Brighton Township was completed. As of 2003, the former poor farm buildings and the old hospital wing served as Zinc Corporation's company corporate offices; becoming the property of Horsehead Corp.

View of the Beaver County Almshouse in the c1870s

Fun fact: The North Branch Church was closed beginning in Jul 1961 through the fall of 1962 so the educational wing of the building could be completed as well as renovations to the sanctuary area. During this closing, church services were held in the Poor House. This location was used since the Poor House had been abandoned in 1959.

Rear of the Poor Home before being razed

Front of the Poor Home before being razed

Photo courtesy Richard "Bud" Temple
View of the former Beaver County Home from across the river in 1916.

c. 1939/1940 aerial view.   Date determined since this photo includes the newer addition
that was added on the rear of the structure.   Note – the front of the building (with the
giant pillars) is facing the Ohio River.

*** *** *** *** ***

Beaver County Tuberculosis Sanitarium – Center Township

The Beaver County Sanitarium was opened for the care of tuberculosis patients. It was located in Moon/Center Township, and like the Beaver County Home, it also was generally associated with Monaca.   It was many times referred to as the Monaca Sanitarium.   Also, as stated with the County Home, this sanitarium was listed as one of the outstanding public institutions in Beaver County.

Opened Feb 14, 1923 -   closed Jul, 1957
The first patient was omitted on Feb 14, 1924 – a Belgian refugee of French origin who had
been a prisoner in the first World War.

An Ayrshire dairy farm – Brodhead Road (where the TB Sanitarium was located and is now Penn State) was owned and operated by Dr. Turnbull, a prominent Pittsburgh doctor. He built a 14-room structure and planned to use it for his patients. His plans never developed and the property became owned by the Carnegie National Bank.

A few years later, the property was divided and sold. H. T. Grimmell, a real estate agent in Monaca, purchased 54 of the acres. He used a portion of this acreage and built a home for himself; then sold off the other portion of that property – all being known as *Mona Manor.* Sidney Huffmyer purchased the remaining portion of Dr. Turnbull's property and turned the 14-room building into his home.

The sanitarium was built on the piece of property that included 40 acres and large frame building owned by Sidney Huffmyer.

50 beds were expanded to 60 bed capacity, with a waiting list of sometimes 30 or more.

There were originally sun porches and chart rooms in the building, but they were converted to expand the number of beds as was a stone cottage. The grounds were planted and seeded and became a wonderful show place.

Primary physicians were Drs. Fred and Ruth (Walker) Wilson; while they were the physicians, they had 3,475 patients admitted and cared for. Dr. Fred Wilson developed active tuberculosis in 1918 after the flu epidemic that year. He went to a sanitarium in New York; when he returned home, he realized the need for such care in Beaver County and was responsible for taking the steps to have the Beaver County TB Sanitarium built.

Building contained a kitchen and dining rooms on the first floor – there were quarters for the nurses and maids on the second and third floors – X-ray room – a laboratory.

Most of the produce was grown in the sanitarium gardens with the help of patients; it raised its own chickens and pigs and always had supply of eggs.

Old sanitarium and the land around it were donated to Penn State by Beaver County Commissioners. The building became the administration building for Penn State University – Beaver Campus from 1965 until 2004 when the Ross Administration Building opened.

The last of all the original buildings of the sanitarium were razed as of 2016.

*** *** *** *** ***

Old time cures.................

1909 – "The old fashioned way of dosing a weak stomach, or stimulating the Heart or Kidneys is all wrong. Dr. Shoop first pointed out this error. This is why his prescription—Dr. Shoop's Restorative—is directed entirely to the cause of these ailments, the weak inside or controlling nerves." "It isn't so difficult," says Dr. Shoop, "to strengthen a weak stomach, Heart or Kidneys, if one goes at it correctly." "Each inside organ has its controlling or inside nerve. When those nerves fail then those organs must surely falter. These vital truths are leading druggists everywhere to dispense and recommend Dr. Shoop's Restorative. Test it a few days, and see. Improvements will promptly and surely follow. Sold by F. H. Mayo, Beaver; Walter D. Kay, Monaca."

Also from 1909.......Foley's Honey and Tar was advertised – "a safe-guard against serious results from spring colds, which inflame the lungs and develop into pneumonia. Avoid counterfeits by insisting upon having the genuine Foley's Honey and Tar, which contains no harmful drugs."

*** *** *** *** ***

Answers to the medical conditions at the beginning of this section:

Ill from brain fever (1904)   Brain fever was used to describe the medical condition for the inflammation of part of the brain, the condition also caused a fever.   This was usually a life-threatening illness caused by a severe emotional upset.   Some other conditions that would have caused "brain fever" are: Encephalitis – caused by a viral infection; Meningitis – the inflammation of the membranes that cover the brain and spinal cord; Cerebritis – inflammation of the cerebrum; Scarlet fever - symptoms can include paranoia and hallucinations.

Grippe / Grip   This was the old fashion term attached to the condition commonly called "influenza" nowadays. It is a viral disease.

Quinsy   Associated with tonsillitis.   It occurs when an abscess forms between one of the tonsils and the wall of the throat.   It is a bacterial infection.

Dropsy   The old fashioned, less technical term, for edema – an excess of watery fluid collecting in the cavities or tissues of the body.

Consumption   This was the term often used for the various forms of tuberculosis, a condition brought on by the tubercle bacillus bacteria.   Often times, pneumonia conditions were associated with consumptions.

Dyspepsia   This was often the name given to a common condition and described a group of symptoms from what is nowadays known as reflux or hiatal hernia, heartburn, belching, etc.   It covered more of a group of symptoms than just one of the specific conditions.

Bealed jaw   This was generally caused by a cold settling on a decayed tooth.

Piles   Hemorrhoids

Imbibe/ Imbibed/ Imbibing   Drinking or consuming too much.   In one word.........drunk.
"They had imbibed far too many beers."

How'd you do..........would you have been a good physician and family doctor in 1800 and early 1900?

*** *** *** *** ***
*** *** ***

UNIONS

MILLS and INDUSTRY

UNIONS

Beginning in the early 1700s, working people in Pennsylvania led American labor's efforts to form unions, federations, benevolent organizations, and workers' cooperatives. The desire of workers to have improved working conditions and the assurance of their families being taken care of was the start to secure rights for ensuring safety and decent working conditions. Unions were the herculean forces of many difficult struggles. Work stoppages in North America go back into the colonial times. Philadelphia printers were the first to demand a minimum wage of $6 per week, staging the first documented strike for higher wages in 1786. From this beginning, Pennsylvania workers have continued to seek protection of their jobs and benefits through unions.

Workers soon found that more often than not the state and federal courts would uphold employers' rights to manage their workers. This only fueled the workers who were trying to unionize but meeting with companies who felt empowered to resist. From the 1860s to the 1970s it is documented that militias and troops were being employed during some of the more violent confrontations, as well as local police following and harassing labor organizers. Even with this resistance, Pennsylvania workers still formed some of the largest and strongest unions in the country. There were many union groups during the years of Phillipsburg and Monaca. Not all of these had a local hall in Monaca. If information was found on a union, it is listed below. Know that this is only a sampling of all that were actually available to the work forces of Monaca.

American Flint Glass Workers' Union – Local No 36
1907
> One place stated they used to hold meetings at 1232 Virginia Avenue.
> They were also referenced with the AFL (American Federation of Labor, which became
> associated with the CIO – Congress of Industrial Organization).

United Steelworkers of America – Local Union 1261 – Monaca PA
> Located at 1428 Pennsylvania Avenue in 1956.
> Had their Monaca Union Hall at 1317 Pennsylvania Avenue in 1970.

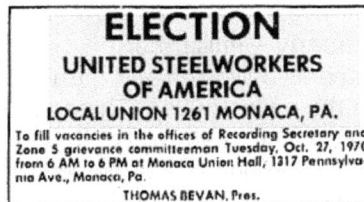

> ## ELECTION
> **UNITED STEELWORKERS OF AMERICA**
> **LOCAL UNION 1261 MONACA, PA.**
> To fill vacancies in the offices of Recording Secretary and Zone 5 grievance committeeman Tuesday, Oct. 27, 1970 from 6 AM to 6 PM at Monaca Union Hall, 1317 Pennsylvania Ave., Monaca, Pa.
> THOMAS BEVAN, Pres.

1970

Oil, Chemical and Atomic Workers Int'l Union – Local 874 -1299 Pennsylvania Avenue
> A strike was averted in 1969 at the Sinclair Koppers Co. plant.

Plumbers and Steamfitters Local Union 115 – 186 Wagner Road

The teachers in Pennsylvania had their own union through PSEA.

Did you know.......
In 1941, the government defense work had a lease agreement with the Superior Steel Products Company, made by the Defense Plant Corporation for construction of a plant for annealing alloy steel bars. The DPC estimated that $75,000 would be spent for land and buildings and $150,000 for machinery and equipment would be spent. The Monaca Borough approved an ordinance providing for the vacating of a portion of the sidewalk in Beaver Avenue to make room for the expansion of the plant.

MILLS and INDUSTRY

As stated in the Borough category, Monaca very recently was working with Beaver County to explore the adoption of a new riverfront redevelopment district zoning overlay for its riverfront lands. The ability to create a new mixed-usage zone in this area would provide complete public access along the river's edge with a potential trail connection such as the proposed Ohio River South Shore Trail (ORSST). It would have a significant economic impact on Monaca and would also represent a major shift in riverfront land use along this stretch of the Ohio River. The major identified Brownfields* parcels in the project area include:

>   The Moore Industrial Property – all adjacent to the Monaca-East Rochester Bridge
>   This was originally part of the Colona Steel Mill; riverfront site; has 80+ year steel mill
>   buildings on it; private developers have shown interest in redeveloping the site for
>   community and/or hotel complex usage with river frontage.
>   The Colona Transfer Property – part of the Colona Steel Mill; now used on a small scale for industrial
>   activities and warehousing; contains large industrial buildings along the riverfront.
>   The Beaver County Corporation for Economic Development (BCED) Property – a large industrial
>   building; part of the Pittsburgh Tube Company Steel Mill; being used as multi-tenant facility
>   McClymonds Coal Transfer – is a river to truck bulk coal transfer facility; planned on closing by 2014.

*"A brownfield is a property, the expansion, redevelopment, or reuse of which may be complicated by the presence or potential presence of a hazardous substance, pollutant, or contaminant. It is estimated that there are more than 450,000 brownfields in the U.S. Cleaning up and reinvesting in these properties increases local tax bases, facilitates job growth, utilizes existing infrastructure, takes development pressures off of undeveloped, open land, and both improves and protects the environment."

After all the years of doing researching and genealogy, the location of the Woolen Mill in Phillipsburg is still a mystery. No one seems to be able to pin down a location of this building, just the fact that it did exist and was the first mill in Phillipsburg.   The same drawing of this mill is displayed repeatedly, so I found no reason not to include it one more time for any readers who may have escaped seeing it.

German Manufacturing Company – Phillipsburg
>   This company was listed as a Woolen Mill. It was said to be the first factory in Phillipsburg,
>   beginning business in the early 1800s.   There are some listings that state the buildings from this
>   company were sold in the late 1840s to Dr. E Acker who used them as part of the Water Cure
>   Sanatorium; and those same buildings later became the Soldiers Orphans School.   This would
>   place the location of this company in the area of the current site of the water treatment plant on
>   Pennsylvania Avenue Extension.

In 1841, a directory of the men and their businesses listed Jacob Koenig as the only brick maker in Phillipsburg on this directory.   I have no location or other information on his business.

A large article published in The Daily Times in 1911 listed the following ten manufacturing plants credited with being in Monaca at that time:

American Glass Specialty Company
Colona Manufacturing Company - Pennsylvania Avenue (1912)
Monaca Roller Mills
Monolith Steel Company
Opalite Tile Works
Phoenix Glass Company (having three factories)
Pittsburgh Tool Steel Wire Company
Pittsburgh Tube Company
United States Sanitary Manufacturing Company
Welch Bright Brick Company

In 1954, Monaca was credited with having 13 industries in the Monaca area:

Beaver Valley Alloy Foundry Company
Colonial Steel Division of the Vanadium Alloy Steel Company
Interstate Amiesite Company
Koppers Company-Potter Township
Penn Monaca Steel Company
Phoenix Glass Company
Pittsburgh Screw and Bolt Corporation
Pittsburgh Tool Steel Wire Company
Pittsburgh Tube Company
Richmond Radiator Company
St. Joseph Lead Company
Superior Drawn Steel Company
W. A. Laidlaw Wire Company

*** *** *** *** ***

In February 1970, there was an Apprentice Information Center at 1136 Pennsylvania Avenue. Interested young men between 18 and 28 years of age could complete applications to enter apprenticeship training to become journeymen operating engineers.

*** *** *** *** ***

Beaver County had numerous businesses (over a hundred) that engaged in the mining of clay and the manufacturing of brick, as well as other products made from clay.   These businesses were in existence from the early 1800s until about 2006. The last operating brick yard was in Darlington and it closed in 2006 with the plant being sold in 2009 to an auto salvage company.   Monaca had several mining operations and brick yards throughout the years.   After reviewing a few of the publications printed by different brick associations, I found from just a mention of a business to much more information on another; regardless, I have included all I found within this section.   The brick yards would have used kilns in their production of their products.   I did not find any photos of the mines, kilns, or brick yards in Monaca, but wanted to include some information to give the readers an idea of what brick making would have entailed.

Can you imagine being HUNDREDS of feet in a mine digging out clay and /or coal?

The first in the process of making bricks was to mine the clay. This would have been such a hard occupation, not to mention it would have taken special men to want to go that deep into the earth to work.   There were many mines along the steep embankments of Monaca and Moon (Center) Township along the Ohio River.

The next process (2nd) ......Mined clay would have to go through a process before being made into bricks.   It was cut into smaller pieces to begin with, then would be broken up into even smaller pieces or a powdery form and mixed with a proper amount of water.   To thoroughly mix the clay and water, the process of tempering or pugging was done.   This meant it was kneaded --- in the earlier years this was the hardest process because it was done by hand (actually kneaded with the hands and feet).   By about the mid 1800s, someone invented horse-drawn pug mills to accomplish this task.

The 3rd process was called the moulding (older spelling of "molding").   If you see an ancestor on the census with his occupation being "moulder," this is what he would have been doing.   The brick moulder was the "key" to the operation and was usually the head of the team.   A moulder would stand at a moulding table from 12 to 14 hours a day and help his assistants make the quota of bricks for the day; this being sometimes up to 3500 or 5000 bricks a day.   They would take a "clot of clay," roll it and then "dash" it into a sanded mould; pressing it down with their hands and removing the excess clay with a flat stick that was soaked in water.   Talk about hard work!   The sand was used to keep the bricks from sticking to the mould. Eventually machines were invented to replace this process.

The 4th process was the drying.   In the very early days, all the moulded bricks were strategically stacked and then allowed to dry in the air and the sun for days.   They would then be restacked "under roof" or covered with straw to protect them and allow for further drying.   Again – eventually this process was refined and kilns were used for the drying process since it sped the process greatly.

The photo below shows some kilns but NOT from Monaca - from the Dando brickyard – Industry.

BCHR&LF

The final step was burning.   This is when the bricks were fired in the kilns.   Kilns would have first been fueled by wood and coal and had to have a specific temperature maintained in them for a proper firing.   Coal for the kilns was most likely not mined on site, but would be purchased elsewhere and delivered to the site of the brick yard. Coal fired kilns were eventually updated so gas would provide the heat.   Gas was a cleaner method for firing and gas was easier to regulate temperatures with, too.   (Many brick yards in the later years were closed down due to air pollution regulations.)   Bricks were placed inside a kiln for the firing process. The first day inside the kiln was called the "smoking day" and wet bricks would start to completely dry off before the main firing would begin. (Steam could be seen coming out of the kilns as the last of the water was evaporating out of the bricks – thus the "smoking day.")

So, there is a very condensed lesson on brick making.

Fun facts:
---Bricks achieve their color through the minerals in the fired clay; sometimes
   this color is through a coating that is applied before and after the firing process, thus
   providing a very durable color that never fades or diminishes.
---Bricks shrink during the manufacturing process.
---The method used to form a brick will impact its texture.
---Most bricks are used within 500 miles of a brick manufacturing plant.

The brick yards located in Monaca are not condensed together in this section, but will be found throughout the entire section.

*** *** ***

L. S. McKallip Brick Yard (Stewart Bros. and Troup)
He may have been a manager of the brick yard, or purchased it, keeping the name?

_____

Stewart Bros. and Troup Brick Yard - unknown address

_____

Abrams Paper Weight Company
Mid 1890s to c 1910s

The Abrams Paper Weight Co. was the successor to the Barnes & Abrams Co., which appears to have been for a time in Syracuse, NY and then Grapesville, PA. The Abrams Paper Weight Co. was located at first in Pittsburgh and later Monaca, PA (Holiner and Kammerman, 2002). As the company name implies, their main production was paperweights.

I did not find a sample with their Monaca stamp, but here is an example with their Pittsburgh one so the reader knows what to look for when viewing antiques.

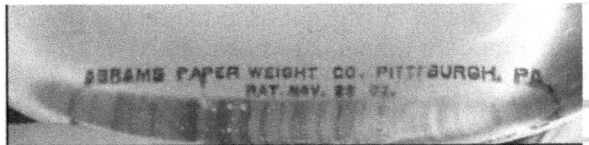

ABRAMS PAPER WEIGHT CO. PITTSBURGH PA
on an advertising paperweight.

_____

Eikins Glass Company – unknown location
1917

S. P. Eikins was also found in the sales dept. of the American Glass Decorating Co., Monaca in
   1917 – he severed his connections and went to work for Star Glass Co. at Star City in W. Va.

_____

Caldwell's 1876 map indicates two brick yards along the hillside above the Ohio River, at the very edge of the Monaca line, most likely more in Moon Township (became Center Township).

The particular area where both the Quay and Pendleton yards were indicated (along hillside below the current Sylvan Crest location) were noted for all the mining that went on along that hillside and entire area, so it must have been rich in clay and/or coal. Even James Welch and/or his company held all the rights to the mines adjacent and under Sylvan Crest for many years.

M.S. and Mary Eliz Quay Brick Yard – along the river just past the Monaca town's borderline (in the
gray area of Moon Township/Monaca boundaries). I could not find any official name of this brick
yard unless it was simply the Quay Brick Yards or it may have just been owned by the Quays -?-

Pendleton & Bros. Fire Brick Company - along the river – adjacent to Quay yard.
Records indicate they had a fire-brick works in Rochester, also. The company in Rochester was one of the earliest firms in Rochester, established in 1856. There is no date as to when they were in Moon Township, but it was prior to 1877 since they are noted on a map. Capt. Gilbert and Joseph R. Pendleton were the owners and made furnace linings, fire bricks, and tile.

_____

McNees and McKinney (French and Quay) – unknown address
This brick yard may have been connected to the "Mary Eliz. Quay Brick Yard" mentioned above.

_____

Park Bros.'s Brick Works   aka   Park Fire Clay Co.   – unknown address
1898, 1890, 1901, 1903
John Park also had large interests in the Pennsylvania Clay Co. of Rochester.
When John Park retired, he was succeeded by Wm. Bald of Sewickley.
John Martin was a foreman in 1901.
Had their head office in Rochester, PA. It appears the Park Bros. had several brick works; one was found in New Brighton. They also had a bricks work at Freedom; in 1894 there was an incendiary fire that resulted in a $40,000 loss (no insurance) and put fifty men out of work.
Two storey building, the bricks on the upper floor dried by the ascension of heat from the first floor.
The building in Monaca collapsed; fortunately there was no loss of life; but the loss of the green and partially dried bricks were a very big loss for the company.
At the time of the collapse, it was not ascertained if it would be rebuilt, but if so, it would be with a modern tunnel drier being erected.
The company manufactured fire clay and furnace brick.

_____

Glass Works – unknown address
1892, 1893
I found two men listed as foreman.........
Peter Bradley – Foreman.   David Kays – Foreman.

_____

Monongahela Fire Clay Co. – unknown address
1892, 1893, 1895
They were a paving brick plant. Their capacity was 30,000 bricks per day of either fire clay or shale. The company was up for sale in 1895 stating the owners were in other business.

_____

Monaca Lamp Company – Pennsylvania Avenue
1917

An article in Jul 1917 stated that Harry Schwendermann had sold his interest in the Monaca Lamp Company to Ralph E. Nippert of Beaver Falls.   Mr. Nippert was taking charge of the company and the Monaca headquarters was being transferred to Beaver Falls.

The article also stated that the Columbia Lamp Company had taken over the Gardner Bros. Lamp interests in the county; but it did not state specific location of either.

――――――

American Glass Specialty Company   aka   American Specialty Glass Co.
– along what was Fifteenth Street on Beaver Avenue side of the tracks
1900, 1902, 1906, 1912, 1925

Brick work was completed May 1903; iron roof was next to be done.
The company manufactured decorated and enameled glassware, fine cut, decorated and
enameled bottles.
Jas. Hogan, President (he lived in Pgh); Louis Kleyle, Secty. and Treas.; W. A. Miksch, Gen. Mngr.
Am. Glass Specialty Co. bought the Jeanette business when Louis E. Smith purchased other
interests.
Louis Kleyle was one of the founders of the Am. Specialty Glass Co.
Located in immediate vicinity of bottom of Fourteenth Street hill - beside Pgh Tool plant.
In May 1925, the huge fire at Mecklem Hardware caused some of the adjacent businesses to
suspend operations for the day. American Glass Specialty Co. was one of them due to
electric poles and wiring being charred.
In Sep 1903 they were listed as "National Glass Budget" under independent glass makers.
In 1940, the Pgh Tool Steel Wire Company purchased the adjoining property of the old Am. Glass
Specialty Co. – the buildings were still standing and all but two scheduled to be razed.

#9 in the drawing below (upper center) is indicated as the location of American Glass Specialty Company in 1900

W. A. MIKSCH.   CARL MIKSCH.
American Glass Specialty Company,
Manufacturers of
Decorated and Enameled Glassware. Indestructible
Labels. Enamel and Gold Lettering on Bar Goods
a Specialty.
Monaca,   -   -   Penn'a.

Miscellaneous newspaper article from early 1900s regarding the American Glass Specialty Co.

Secured a Wagon Load of Stolen Chinaware

Chief of Police John M. Shroads and Constable Frank M. Hays, of Monaca, went to the old Miksch property in Fourteenth street, Monaca, occupied as a Slav boarding house, yesterday afternoon, and secured a wagon load of imported china ware, new shoes and various kinds of goods stolen from time to time in Monaca, and vicinity, and stored away in the boarding house. Four boarders were arrested by the officers and taken to the lockup.

For some time Carl Miksch and Lewis Kieyle, proprietors of the American Glass Specialty Company at Monaca, have been missing ware from their factory and suspicioned the occupants of the boarding house, which is conducted by Joseph Radler. Mr. Miksch made information yesterday before Squire W. W. Morgan, and the officers went to the house, where they found all kinds of stolen articles, including much glass ware. Radler and one of the boarders managed to make their escape. The four men arrested were released last evening, as they are not the parties wanted by the police. Radler and the boarder who skipped with him are the two who are wanted.

The officers paid another visit to the boarding house after one o'clock this morning and discovered another large trunk packed and ready to be shipped to the old country. It was opened by the police and was found to contain imported china, which had been stolen from the American Glass Specialty works. The ware was all decorated and the contents of the trunk was valued at more than $100. The trunk was taken to the factory, where it will be held until Radler and his boarder are apprehended.

Penn Glass Company - Seventeenth Street in Monaca (Phillipsburg)
Prior to 1876
    This plant then became Dithridge Flint Glass Works in 1876/1877.

Dithridge Flint Glass Works – Seventeenth Street
1876, 1881
    As of 1876, Dithridge & Co. was operating two factories with two furnaces firing twenty pots.
        They took over the old Penn Glass Co. glassworks located on Seventeenth Street in Monaca (Phillipsburg).
    It appears there was a separate company called the Dithridge Glass Co. who bought the glassworks at that time.   Any connection between the Dithridge Glass Co. and Dithridge & Co. is unknown. The location of the glassworks and office differ, which indicates that they were different concerns.   It is possible that one of Edward Dithridge, Sr.'s sons branched out separately.
    It is certain that the glassworks, located at the foot of Seventeenth Street on the Southside, was operated by Dithridge Flint Glass Co. starting 1876/77. The year prior to their first listing was the Penn Glass Co. at that location.
        1876 – Penn Glass Co., foot of Seventeenth Street.
        1877-1878 – Dithridge Flint Glass Co., foot of Seventeenth Street.
        1879 - Dithridge Chimney Co. Limited, foot of Seventeenth Street.
        1880–1882 – Dithridge Chimney Co. Limited, foot of Seventeenth Street
    In 1881, Edward Dithridge became "connected" with the Phoenix Glass Co. of Phillipsburg when they leased the Dithridge & Co. glassworks located there (Monaca).   Edward managed the factory for them until 1883.   Dithdrige & Co. had constructed the Phillipsburg glassworks a short time prior to the Phoenix Glass Co.'s move there.
    They moved their business to New Brighton. Once this plant was up and running, they leased the Monaca factory to the Phoenix Glass Co. starting about 1881 and eventually closed around 1900.
    I did not find an advertisement with the Monaca address, but here is one with Pittsburgh.

DITHRIDGE CHIMNEY CO., LIMITED.
MANUFACTURERS OF THE ORIGINAL GENUINE
DITHRIDGE FLINT GLASS LAMP CHIMNEY.
OIL POLISHED ORIENT RADIATORS,
SILVERED GLASS REFLECTORS,
PITTSBURGH, PA.

1881

Pittsburgh Novelty Works– Pennsylvania Avenue (past Sixteenth Street)
1906, 1907
> Began business in 1906.
> Located in south Monaca – property adjoining Pgh Tube Co. (Twenty-First Street)
> > - by Pgh Tube Co. and Opalite Tile Works.

————

Deidrick Glass Company – (office at...) Pennsylvania Avenue - near Seventeenth Street.
1914, 1922
> Built their smaller factory in the summer of 1914.
> Manufacturer of glass and all kinds of glass ware.
> Marvin C. Wallover, Harry W. Deidrick- Beaver; Joseph S. Edwards-Rochester.
> In Dec 1915, the company erected a new wareroom.
> Hired 8 more men in Oct 1914 bringing total employees to about 50 as of that date.
> Their factory was leased to The Dayton Taxicab Co., Inc. in Nov 1923, so the glass company
> > must have closed by then.

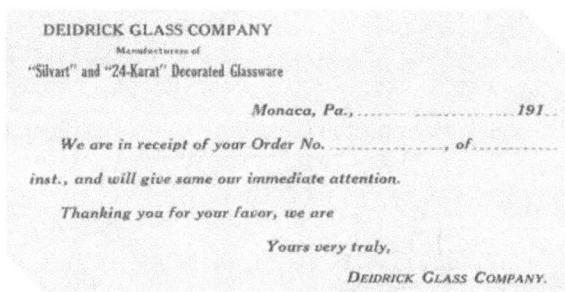

DEIDRICK GLASS COMPANY
Manufacturers of
"Silvart" and "24-Karat" Decorated Glassware

Monaca, Pa., ... 191..

We are in receipt of your Order No. ...., of ....

inst., and will give same our immediate attention.

Thanking you for your favor, we are

Yours very truly,

DEIDRICK GLASS COMPANY.

————

Penn Clay Co.   aka   Pennsylvania Clay Company
1880s, 1890s, 1900, 1905
> Located on other side of the railroad tracks – between Eleventh and Twelfth Streets,
> > (more toward Twelfth Street) and beyond where Metropolitan Glass Co. plant
> > was located (to the location of Railroad Street).
> The local offices were located in Rochester – Jerome Hill, Pres; W.W. Cunningham, S.M. (1895).
> > Also had factories at Conway and Fallston with General Offices in Pittsburgh.
> John Martin was foreman of the company since 1897.   Began work in a brick yard at age 13.
> > John Martin – b 1869; married Lillie Mennall; 2 children; he was a member of
> > the Woodmen of the World.
> Mr. W. W. Cunningham was treasurer of the company, then elected president and general manager
> > in 1905.
> The plant was controlled by Park Brothers of Rochester.
> They were manufacturers of vitrified fire clay paving brick; known as "No. 4" for exclusively
> > manufacturing paving brick.
> They could put out 25,000 finished bricks per day.
> Devoted to manufacturing paving brick exclusively.
> The yard was established many years prior to 1890s, but came into possession of Park Bros. in
> > 1895. It contained 40 acres of clay and a 12 ft vein sunk through a 72 ft shaft.
> The yard had excellent location being beside the P & LE RR.
> They employed over 35 men.
> > (See map printed with the Metropolitan Glass Company information.)

————

Metropolitan Glass Company - btw. Twelfth and Thirteenth Streets on other side of the RR tracks
1897, 1900s
> They were known for producing paperweights, but they also advertised the manufacture of bar
> and beer bottles, tumblers, soda bottles, and syrup cans.
>
> They etched and enameled glassware made by other companies.
>
> W. J. Patterson-President; J. C. Miller-Secretary (were the owners of this company -?).
>
> Plant was located between Twelfth and Thirteenth Streets – on other side of the tracks –
> somewhere at the end of where (2016) current Railroad Avenue ends.

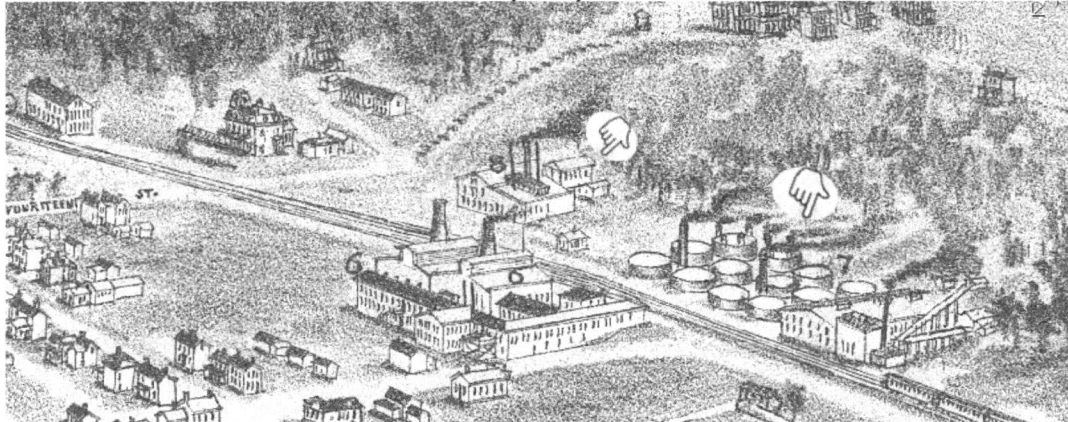

#8 is Metropolitan Glass Co.   #7 is Penn Clay Co.

W. J. Patterson, President.   J. C. Miller, Secretary.

METROPOLITAN GLASS COMPANY,
Manufacturers of

Indestructible Enameled Labels
Burned In On the Articles.

Bar Bottles, Beer Tumblers, Barber Bottles, Bitter Bottles; also Clay Steins for Breweries.
An advertisement cannot be removed from the glass or defaced in any manner.

Monaca,   -   -   Penn'a.   1900

Paperweight

Joseph Doyle & Son – Tenth Street and Washington Avenue
1881, 1882, 1883
> Joseph Doyle left Doyle & Co. and with his son William began a new business in Phillipsburg.
> They constructed a lamp chimney factory that opened in Jun 1881.
>
> They were listed as glass manufacturers ("Tableware") in Phillipsburg in 1882 as one of the two
> "large glassworks" located there (Polk & Co. 1882).   The company is said to have gone into
> receivership in the early 1880s and the works were subsequently leased by the Phoenix Glass
> Company of Phillipsburg (Monaca).   There were several attempts to sell the Phillipsburg factory
> in 1884, but the offered amounts were too low. Phoenix Glass Co. is said to have eventually
> bought the glassworks in the fall of 1885 BUT – there was an article that mentioned the Electrical
> Glass Appliance Co. briefly leased the "old Doyle & Co." glassworks in 1889. (This may have been
> mentioned this way since the original works was owned by Doyle and thus the credit for being
> the owner of building -?   Although Phoenix history does not show purchasing any Pgh factories within
> this time frame, it does state leasing the glassworks built by Joseph Doyle & Son in 1881.)

Laubscher brick yard – Chapel Road, Center Township
    Phillip Laubscher owner.
    He used red clay found in the township and started a family business.
    They made quality bricks that came for the kilns located on Chapel Road – what is bordering on
        what is now Edgewater Drive.
    Many of the homes in the area were built using these bricks.

———————

Opalite Tile Works – Pennsylvania Avenue - in the Fifteenth and Sixteenth Streets area
                  (by Colonial Steel, Sanitary Co., and Pgh Tube Co.)
1900, 1908, 1912, 1913, 1917, 1921
    Came to Monaca Jan 1900, built new plant, and began operations in Apr 1900.
    Engineering book stated it started Jul 1900.
        First officers were: Henry C. Fry-President; John A. Harper-Secretary and Treasurer;
        Walter McLintock-General Manager; H. J. Sage-Superintendent.
    Manufactured high class art tiles.
    Purchased 25 to 30 acres of the Ferguson farm in the East End of Monaca – from the South
        Monaca Station to the Ohio River.
    Purchased by a number of capitalists with H. C. Fry of Rochester Tumbler Co. as their leader.
    Late Jan 1900, S.S. Bennett, Rochester contractor began excavating the foundation and the P &
        LE railroad company began laying the new side-track.
    Jan 27, 1900, the Opalite Tile Company made a statement for those who had contracts for
        the erecting and equipping of their buildings.
    Finished the building in Jan 1900.
    There was a plant located in Greensburg and made high class art tiles. They moved and were
        open by Apr 1st, 1900.
    They produced opalite white sheet glass in widths up to 38 inches and lengths approaching 108
        inches. Sheet thickness ran from 3/16 to ¾ of an inch.
    James_?_ and his wife were given a proposal to make a wonderful deal with the Opalite Tile
        Company in late Jan 1900 - it was to sell their property to S. S. Childs of Pittsburgh for
        the site of the new works of Opalite Tile Company. The considered offer of the property
        was $14,162.50 – in 1900, that was quite a sum of money.
    President was H.C. Frye in 1902.
    Built a new office building in Nov 1903.
    South Side Trust Co. of Pittsburgh received all stocks of Opalite Tile Co. – May 1917.

OPALITE White GLASS.

Is used for Wainscoting; Table and Counter Tops; Store, Show Case and Counter Base, Shelves and various other purposes.

Opalite in stock sheets or cut to dimension.

Widths up to 30", lengths up to 108" and from 3/16 up to 1 inch thick.

THE OPALITE TILE CO.,
MONACA, PA.

The Jan 23, 1916, Pittsburgh Daily Post stated that the "Officials of the Opalite Tile Works, this place, today announced that commencing Monday, Jan 24, all employees will be given a 10 per cent increase in wages. More than 100 men are affected in the Opalite plant."   It didn't state what the wages were prior to the increase, so I have no idea how much 10% increase would have been.

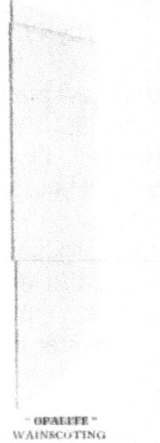

Portion of a page from a 1910 catalog publication by The Architectural Record Co.

Welch, Gloninger & Co. - Fire Brick manufacturers – unknown address
1881, 1893, 1898, 1903

> J. H. Welch and J. H. Gloninger owners.
> This company was an independent company; separate from James Welch's own company.
> It was also the predecessor of the Vanport Brick Company.

Welch, Gloninger & Maxwell Co. –unknown address
1892 - 1898

WELCH

Welch Fire Brick Company – on far side of the P & LE RR bridge where Atlantic Avenue ends in Monaca - sat almost exactly where the Alloy Company is now located (2016).
1878 to 1905

> Started in 1878; organized in 1880.   One of the first few big businesses in Monaca.
> James H. Welch, proprietor and general manager.
>> James came from England in 1867 and settled in Pittsburgh.
>> He owned a very nice home in Monaca which stood upon an elevation above the town and was called "Welchmont." It had an excellent view.   He also owned a 354 acre dairy farm in Borie Township. He owned quite a bit of real estate in the area and began to sell off portions for housing.
> He was recognized for years as one of the leading brick makers of Pittsburgh and Ohio Valley.
> James disposed of this company and sold it to the Welsh-Bright Fire Brick Co. in about 1905.
> His business started with square kilns; James made improvements and added modern appliances and eventually outclassed all others in the locality. In connection with the business was 135 acres of clay land, to which an incline leads by way of a side entry (all located under the area currently known as Sylvan Crest in Center Township). There were many

buildings – one 175 x 90 feet, another 3 storey building 112 x 60 feet, with dry
tunnels carrying 90,000 bricks which had a capacity of 25,000 bricks per day.   The
office of the business was located near the railroad and he had the general offices and
salesroom in Pittsburgh.   They employed 50 employees.
The company consisted of hand moulded and machine-made fire brick from clay found on the
property.   The factory had a feature no other fire brick works in the Ohio Valley had – a
continuous kiln employed for baking the ware; the results indicated it was quite
successful.
They furnished the brick to be used in the erection of the business block/opera house in Monaca
(known as the Citizen's Bank / Campbell Storage building).
Their buff brick was used in Madison Square Garden in New York City.
A new 5-mold soft-mud brick machine was installed in 1903/04.
This company was one of three companies in or near Pittsburgh that had "continuous kiln."
As of Nov 1902, James was installing a third plant in Monaca. It was described as being located on a
high elevation a short distance from the P & LE RR; not to be of very large capacity; was to
depend largely on local trade; used a gas engine, a Freese clay disintegrator, and 4 tunnel drier.
See more on James Welch in *Prominent People and Families* section.

James H. was said to have various enterprises and had accumulated quite a deal of property and business interests which he was disposing of as of 1905.   He had sold his property on Monaca Heights (Welch Plan) and it was subdivided and being sold as residential lots.   He also sold his home and all the land he owned on what is now known as Sylvan Crest, but retained the mines and all the resources (clay and coal), those were sold to the Welch-Bright Co.   (The clay that came from the mines was used in the making of the companies' bricks.) He sold his company to the Welch-Bright Co. which continued to own land and mine for resources.   The Welch-Bright Co. was still in business as of 1951; Clifford S. Marshall had been President, his son Clifford S. Marshall, II was current president in 1951 when he was killed in an auto accident on Ohio River Blvd.   He was report to have had started in the business in 1880 and his involvement in the business was with companies: Welch Bros.; Welch, Palmer & Maxwell; Welch, Gloninger & Co.; Welch Fire Brick Co. (1890-1905); Welch-Bright Co.

James had purchased a plant at Barking Station, PA (on the Allegheny River about 15 miles from Pittsburgh) which produced red shale bricks before the plant caught fire and burned. It then remained untouched until transferred/incorporated as the Victor Brick Co.; James H. became the chief advisor in the manufacturing department of the Victor Brick and Clay Company in Pittsburgh. He was also interested in the firm Welch, Gloninger & Maxwell near Cumberland, MD.   His name was attached to many of the brick companies over the years, but I found no other information connecting him personally to some of them.   His is however said to have been associated with being in the brick business starting in 1880 with the Welch Bros., again this is all the information I have on this company.

then ....

Welsh-Bright Fire Brick Co.   aka   Welch-Bright Co.
from 1905 to at least 1950s
James disposed of his first company and sold it to the Welsh-Bright Fire Brick Co. in about 1905.
He retained an interest in this new company, but withdrew from active management.
All of the rights to and the mines that appear to have been "under" the current Sylvan Crest were
retained by the company even though all the land "of" Sylvan Crest area was sold.
There was a terrible explosion at the works Feb 3, 1908.   George Fabish was killed, another
man was expected not to live and three others severely injured when a boiler exploded
causing $220,000 property damage.
A fire at the Beaver Valley Alloy Foundry Co. the first of Jul 1924 did not damage the Welch-
Bright company which adjoined the building of the Alloy Foundry – this information
provides proof of the location of the company's location.
An unexpected heavy snow fall of 40 to 48 inches on Nov 24, 1950 caused the roof of the
company to collapse.
This company made reports in the very early 1900s of making 25,000 bricks per day – fire brick.

By 1922, they made claim to 2,220,915 bricks and 1,291 tons of clay – the average wages paid through the company was $43,920.43.   They also were making terra cotta and fire clay products by 1920.

The pointer to the right indicates the Welch Bright would be the building below with smoke coming from stack.   The RR tracks run just below it.
The pointer to the left indicates the roadway on the left of the picture which would be the present day Pennsylvania Avenue Extension, through the RR tunnel and turns into Rte. 18.

Manufactured "W" fire brick, fire bricks of all kinds for mills, furnaces, locomotive tile, cupolas, and buff-building brick.   Their products were shipped all over the country.
The Welch-Bright Co. only used a "W" with a circle around it for their marking.

————

Monongahela Brick Works
I did not find out anything further on this except it was located in Monaca. It was put up for Sheriff's Sale in 1895 and P. C. Orr of Pittsburgh purchased the company.

————

Saw Mill of Baldwin & Baldwin – office was on Sixth Street
1902
> They had a saw mill near the water works/pump house; their office was located on Sixth Street and their stables were located on the corner of Virginia Avenue and Fifteenth Street.   They were known for being dealers in coal, stone, lime, sand, cement, brick, etc.   See an ad and ownership information in the Hardware Section.

————

Colona Division of Ampco-Pittsburgh Steel Co. plant   aka   Colona Thread Protector Division
                                                              aka   Colona Steel
1916, 1924, 1979, 1986
> They manufactured and reconditioned thread protectors for the oil industry – cold finished steel bars.   Closed in Dec 1986 by the parent company - Ampco-Pittsburgh Corp.
> At the time of closing, there were fewer than 20 people employed and no production for quite some time.   The Ampco-Pittsburgh Corp became known as Wyckoff Steel Inc.
> Wyckoff was sold Apr 29, 1987.

————

Interstate Amiesite Corp. – Blacktopping business - Twenty-First Street and 1901 Beaver Avenue
1939, 1954, 1965, 1976, 2013
> In May 1976, they were known for bituminous paving of driveways and roadways.
> In 1962, this corporation donated a heated trailer to the Recreation Assoc. for use by ice skaters.

Better Roads: our job

The New Interstate Amiesite Plant In Industry

Interstate Amiesite Corp.
IN MONACA SINCE 1939

_____

Colona Manufacturing Company – Pennsylvania Avenue
1908, 1916, 1924, 1929
> Began operations in 1908.
> Had want ad for *lathe hand / running milling machine* and another ad for *handy man to do odd
> jobs and rough carpentry work*.
> They made pipe, fittings, and valves.
> They advertised for first class machinist and several good laborers in 1918 and then in 1919 advertised
> for "good strong girls for machine operators".

Wanted—Handy man; one who can do sundry odd jobs and rough carpenter work. Colona Manufacturing Company, Monaca, Pa.	WANTED—At once, first-class machinist and several good laborers. Colona Manufacturing Co., Monaca, Pa. dec13-19inc.	HELP WANTED—FEMALE WANTED — AT ONCE, GOOD STRONG GIRLS FOR MACHINE OPERATORS;FORMER EMPLOYES GIVEN PREFERENCE. COLONA MFG. CO., MONACA. 6,3-9
1916	1918	1919

became known as.................

Pittsburgh Screw and Bolt Corporation plant – Moon Township/adjacent to Monaca -Pennsylvania Avenue
1929, 1953, 1954
> Feb 1929 – merged and consolidated with Colona Manufacturing Co.
> In 1940, it was located on Pennsylvania Avenue.

_____

Nichols Wire Co.   aka   Nichols Steel & Wire Company –
1923, 1937, 1941,
> Organized in the 1890s in Pittsburgh District – Pittsburgh Hanger Company and started
> operations in Rochester.
> Came to Monaca in 1923 -- three parcels of property were purchased in Monaca (one was
> Paulus Koehler's on Pennsylvania Avenue near Seventeenth Street.
> Nov 1925 occupied their first building.

1941 - property was purchased, reorganized, and incorporated to become ....

W. A. Laidlaw Wire Company of Pennsylvania

1941, 1956, 1979

Was reorganized Dec 7, 1941.

Closed by 1980.

In 1979/early 1980, the former Laidlaw Wire Co. building was used by Phoenix Glass Co. as a warehouse while they were rebuilding from the massive fire in their plant.

Laidlaw Wire Co. is above on the left of this picture. The RR depot is across the tracks and out of the picture on the right. This picture would have been taken while standing at the point where Fourteenth Street cross the tracks. Monaca would be to your right and to the left would be heading to Beaver Avenue and/or up to Monaca Heights.

Pittsburgh Tool Steel Wire Co. - Sixteenth Street and P & LE railroad line

(which would put it on Beaver Avenue -to right of bottom of Fourteenth Street Hill)

1902, 1955, 1966, 1991

Founded Apr 3, 1902.

Jul 1955 – merged with Vanadium-Alloys Steel Co. of Latrobe, PA.

Made improvements in 1962, 1963.

Became part of Teledyne Inc. of Century City, Calif. in 1966.

1969 ads stated "A Teledyne Co."

Was often called "the wire mill."

American Glass Specialty Co. had property right beside them; they purchased the property and planned to expand; to raze all but two of the older buildings for their use.

All the "wire mill" buildings were razed in 2016.

Former Pittsburgh Tool along Beaver Avenue

These are the buildings that were most likely the Opalite companies – the Pittsburgh Tool buildings are not in this photograph, but were located to the right of these buildings.

This is the 104 inch grinder at Pittsburgh Tool Steel Wire Co. – 1964 (was to be replaced by a larger 168 inch unit).

———————

Imperial Manufacturing Company – south Monaca (by Pittsburgh Tube Co. which was at 2060 Pennsylvania Avenue
1906   Business was new in fall of 1906.

———————

Solar Electric Co. –
1914
          Completed their smaller factory in the summer of 1914.   Employed about 50 people when it opened.

———————

Hiram Hicks – was hired by borough to do all the laying of curbs (1906).

———————

Beaver County Light Company – they controlled the Monaca Electric Light Company of Monaca.
1900

———————

Monaca Electric Co. –
1901
          Secured right of way over the streets and alleys of Monaca and began the construction of an
                    electric light system in 1901.

———————

Crescent Oil & Gas Company – 1138 Pennsylvania Avenue
1912, 1918, 1931
> W. A. Eberle was the manager in 1912.   Their main office was in Pittsburgh.
> They supplied Monaca, Monaca Heights, New Sheffield, Colona, South Heights,
>   Wireton, and Glenwillard, PA.

_____

In 1903, the Freedom and Monaca Bridge Company and the Ohio Bridge Company merged and consolidated under the name of Ohio River Bridges Company.
> Andrew J. Jolly and John J. Allen were two of the new company's Directors.

_____

Pittsburgh Tube Company – 2060 Pennsylvania Avenue
1902, 1929, 1953, 1978, 1998
> Built in 1902.
> Ran an ad for a master machinist in the Feb 1913 paper.
> Spent thousands of dollars in rebuilding in late 1914.
> Officially founded in 1923.
> Originally known as Pittsburgh Tube Company of Delaware -   "of Delaware" was dropped.
> 1929 – was adding two additional factory buildings.
> John P. Gangwisch purchased a small mill next door to his plant in Monaca; together Mr. Gangwisch and four other men completed arrangements to take over the name, business, assets and liabilities of the Pittsburgh Tube Co. Company; it was later named PTC Alliance Corporation.
> Sep 1966 – a portion of the former Monaca Lumber Company (purchased in 1965) was used to construct a new 80 x 360 foot building.   This lumber company building was across the street on Pennsylvania Avenue.
> Late summer, 1978 – fire caused damage to the Pittsburgh Tube Co.
> Jun 1990– still in business in Monaca (ad for stenographer).
> Jul 31, 1998 - closed the "antiquated" 75 year old manufacturing plant. This particular plant would have to had been completely dismantled to be modernized and therefore once again productive. 50 percent of the employees were eligible for retirement at the time of closing and were going to receive packages that included severance pay, life insurance, and health insurance for life; others were to receive severance packages and benefits extending a period beyond the date of the plant closing.
> The Beaver County Corporation for Economic Development (BCED) purchased the large building and planned to utilize it as a multi-tenant facility.

photo by Adam Rust

Sept 1966 - This is part of the expansion with workmen drilling at the site of the new building
Pittsburgh Tube Co. was constructing for its specialty division.   It was to be a one
storey structure used for production only.

———

The Penn-Monaca Steel Products, Inc. – welding services - 1746 Pennsylvania Avenue
1927, 1944, 1954
Organized and began operations May 1927.
Advertised for help – 1944.
They made ornamental and miscellaneous iron.

**Penn-Monaca Steel
Products Co.**

1746 Penna. Ave.,   Monaca, Pa.
Tel. Roch. 1604

Light Structural Work
Fire Escapes—Railings
Sidewalk Doors—Gratings
Welding of All Kinds
Both Acetylene and Electric

C. C. McCREARY   1928

Moor Industrial Park   Side view of Penn-Monaca Steel.

Torn down 2013/2015 – as of 2016, just an empty lot.

_____

United States Sanitary Mfg. Co. (aka Tub Works) – 1729-1731 Pennsylvania Avenue
1901, 1912, 1943

Organized in 1901 as a partnership by three brothers - Charles F., James W., Jr., and
　　Albert E. Arrott.

Located in south Monaca (called Colona) – was surrounded by high fence in 1902/03.

It was close to the east Rail Road.   Property had streets and alleys on it and was by
　　the Pgh. Tube Company and the Pgh. Screw and Bolt Co. and the P & LE RR.
　　All in the Third Ward area of Monaca.

Property was from the river to the railroad tracks and the plant was to cover the entire
　　plot.   The plant was adjacent properties of Opalite Tile and Colonial/Colona Steel –
　　both considered to be in Colona.   It employed about 125 men in the beginning and
　　as the plant expanded, so did the workforce.

Operations started on Jul 1, 1902 when the first ladle of iron was poured.

The company was incorporated in 1907.   Owned more than 13 acres located closer to the
　　river, by the Beaver Valley Traction Company's tracks; 4 acres was under roof in 1907.

In 1902 there was a large lawsuit between the Standard Sanitary Manufacturing Co. for James
　　W. Arrott and his sons James W., Jr. and Charles F. Arrott.   The two sons bought major
　　portions of stock in the United States Sanitary Mfg. Co. and all 3 were already heavily
　　involved with Standard.   Not that it was, but Standard felt this was wrong and brought
　　them all to court.

Arrott Bros. & Co. of Pgh purchased eight and one-half acres and began erecting a large plant for
　　the manufacture of sanitary goods.

Manufactured a complete line of cast-iron enameled plumbing fixtures.

Their products are known from Maine to California and are exported outside the United States.

Article in Monaca News said that the United States Sanitary works shut down on Dec 13, 1907,
　　indefinitely, which put a large number of men out of employment.

The company manufactured civilian products until Jun 1942 when the facilities then became
　　devoted to production of war work where possible.

Dec 3, 1943 – Company and stock were sold to The Richmond Radiator Company of
Uniontown – a subsidiary of the Reynolds Metals Company, under the supervision
of E. A. Hibler who had been associated with US Sanitary for 10 years.

Photo courtesy Beaver County Historical Research and Landmarks Foundation

Then U S Sanitary became...............

Richmond Radiator Company of Monaca – 1729 Pennsylvania Avenue
1943, 1959, 1989

Installed $200,000 heating in warehouse.   Was a one storey concrete brick structure.
1954 – Bernard O. Knowland was personnel manager.
The Borough agreed that if the company would furnish all terra cotta pipe and materials, the
borough would furnish all the labor and tools necessary to install a sewer extension on
the company's property so they could expand.

Richmond Radiator added to its production capacity.

1954   Richmond Radiator in process of expanding.

Beaver Valley Alloy Foundry Company – Pennsylvania Avenue Ext. and/or Atlantic Avenue Extension
1919, 1953, 1967, current
>   Built in 1919, was organized and started operations in Feb 1920.   W. L. Forster – founder.
>   The address above reflects entrance to the plant from the "boat launch area."
>   There is another roadway right on other side of 2nd RR bridge leaving Monaca, too.
>   A large fire at the company the first of Jul 1924.   Machinery was saved, damage to building only.
>   A barrel of oil upset and touched off a fire Feb 24, 1967.   The fire was started in an annex to the main
>   plant on Atlantic Avenue Ext.; the plant was heavily damaged by the fire.

1956 view – listed address as Atlantic Avenue Extension.

———

Pittsburgh Hanger Company –
1944, 1965
>   Incorporated - 1944.

———

Monolith Steel Company – Pennsylvania Avenue
Feb -1909, fall of 1911, 1912
>   Manufacturers of steel reinforcing bars for concrete work; girder bars and spiral banded columns.
>   1910 - They received contract for supplying the reinforcement required in the construction of
>   the Columbia Paper Mill Company's new plant in Washington D. C.

———

Superior Drawn Steel Company   aka   Standard Steel Specialty Co. – 1585-1600 Beaver Avenue
1925, 1942, 1954, 1963, 1965, 1983, 1992
>   Founded as Superior Drawn Steel Company in 1942.
>   Closed the business in Monaca Aug 31, 1992.
>   Parent company was Standard Steel Specialty Co., West Mayfield.

In May 1925, the Superior Steel Company, along with Pittsburgh Tool Steel Wire Co. and
the American Wire Company had to suspend operations for a day due to the large
fire at Mecklem Lumber that was adjacent to their companies' locations.

The Superior Steel Company plant was located along Beaver Road and Railroad Road because
it was mentioned in a few articles "on the hillside above the present site of the Superior
Products Company plant."

The Bakers, Morris, Mellon, Baldwin, Alcorn, Eckert, Jackson and Ferguson farms had all
been adjacent or in the immediate area of this location.

There was a strike at the company which ended in Oct 1983.

SUPERIOR DRAWN STEEL CO.
MONACA, PENNSYLVANIA

Producers of Cold Finished Steel

ROUNDS, SQUARES,
HEXAGONS, FLATS,
AND
SPECIAL SECTIONS

Carbon and
Alloy Grades

The four natural gas-fired Car-Type Furnaces
as shown above are used for stress relieving
and annealing carbon and alloy steel bars,
over a temperature range between 600° F.
and 1750° F.

1955

BVHT Inc.   aka   Beaver Valley Heat Treating Inc. – 1585-1600 Beaver Avenue
1992,

Began business in Monaca on Sep 1, 1992.   Metal Heat Treating.

They were a subsidiary of Moltrup Steel Products, Inc. of Beaver Falls.

Took over when the Superior Drawn Steel Company left on Aug 31, 1992.

They used the atmospheric controlled annealing furnace, formerly operated by Superior
Drawn, moved in and employed a new work force.

Moltrup Steel Products, Inc. (Beaver Falls) purchased the facility and Beaver Valley Heat Treating
Inc. making the BVHT a subsidiary.   They operated the atmospheric controlled annealing
furnace, formerly operated by Superior Drawn. When they moved in, they employed a new
work force.

Colonial Steel Company – east Monaca
1901, 1953, 1962

    Built plant in 1901.

    Located near Opalite Tile and US Sanitary Company by RR tracks.

    A group of prominent Pittsburgh capitalists started the process and made application to locate the new company in Monaca.   Charter members: James W. Brown, George A. Howe, T. Howe Childs, Chas. M. Brown and Louis B. Hays.

    Specialized in tool and die steels.

    They moved their general offices from Pittsburgh to Monaca, Nov 1, 1903.

    John Auth started with the company at age 17 helping clear off the site for construction of the mill. During his employment, he invented two improved processes, one for the manufacture of cooper-clad products and the other for removing cores from drilled rods.

Merged with Vanadium in 1928, making it a division of Vanadium-Alloys Steel Co. of Latrobe, PA became known as……….

Colonial Steel Division of the Vanadium Alloys Steel Co.

    In 1962, the company made extensive improvements; added a new sheet mill.

In the picture above, is a view of the mill from the river side. At the very top of the picture would be the row of homes built by the company for employees. The current 4 lane highway replaced the two lane that is in this picture (along top)

The picture below is the way the company's property would have looked from the road way in 1995. All is now owned by the Beaver Valley Industrial Park Corp.

from c 1907 postcard – Colonial Steel plant

This photo was taken showing the front of the mill that faced the road way. The houses in the lower right were built by the company for their employees due to the lack of available housing. (See Location Section for additional information on these houses and those built in Colona Heights.)

Using the hammer to forge a cylinder.   U L S Archives Service Center

Teeming ingots.   U L S Archives Service Center

Colona Transfer – 100 River Road / 1755 Pennsylvania Avenue – coal supplier
    aka   River-Rail Terminal

The Colona Transfer property is a series of large industrial buildings located along the Ohio riverfront. Originally it was part of the Colona Steel Mill. The property is partially utilized for small scale industrial activities and warehousing.

One of the few river-rail terminals in Beaver County was found at Monaca, on the bank of the Ohio River. Constructed at a cost of thousands of dollars by the Pittsburgh and Lake Erie Railroad Company, the terminal was used to transfer cargoes from river barges to freight cars for shipment.

It was also called the Colona river-rail terminal and was built by the Pittsburgh and Lake Erie Railroad in the 1920s. It was used as a transfer point to move coal to Republic Steel facilities in Ohio. Quality Aggregates bought the terminal in 1988 and used it mostly for handling coal. Beginning in the mid 1990s, the company tried to attract manufacturers of different commodities to the site.

In 1997, the Morton International Inc. chose the Colona Terminal as its northeast distribution hub and moved more than 20,000 ton of salt to the 5,000-square foot warehouse at the terminal. In 1997 there were about seven people employed at Colona Terminal. In 1997, it was a part of the Port of Pittsburgh network and handled about 45 million tons of cargo a year.

Article of Oct 8, 1930, stated "The P & LE RR's new $500,000 river-rail terminal along the Ohio river at Monaca is to be constructed on land recently acquired from the Colonial Steel Company. The old docks of the company are to be remodeled and altered to meet the demands of the railroad."

In the summer of 1932, the river-rail transfer plant at Colonna was placed in operation. It was constructed for the purpose of transferring freight, principally coal, from barges to railroad cars for further shipment via railroad.

Front and side views of buildings – 1755 Pennsylvania Avenue
(between 1729 Pennsylvania Avenue – Moor Industrial Park and Metcon plant)

Little Beaver Historical Society   Colona river rail transfer whirly.

Little Beaver Historical Society

Colona river rail transfer 1931.   *Print in lower right corner says "P & LE RR – COLONA*
River-Rail Transfer Plant....." and is dated Oct 21, 1931

Little Beaver Historical Society   Colona River Rail transfer 1931.
Print in bottom right – *"P & L E RR – COLONA   River Rail Transfer Plant   Ice Breaker No 1"*

———

Rheem Manufacturing Company–Home Products Division plant - (their office area was on Pennsylvania
Avenue)

1901, 1965, 1967
    Began operating the Home Products Division in 1902.
    Rheem was one of the largest manufacturers of steel shipping containers, too.
    The foremost producer of automatic storage water heaters for homes and commercial use, as
        well as related lines of central heating and air conditioning equipment, bathroom/
        laundry/ kitchen fixtures.
    In Mar 1973 a New Jersey firm purchased the former site of the Rheem Co.
    The Moore Industrial Park, Monaca, the former Rheem Manufacturing Co. plant on Pennsylvania
        Avenue, was sold.   The industrial park property was formerly owned by Moore Properties, Inc.   The
    article stated that Rheem used it for manufacturing purposes from 1956 until 1967.

———

Doyle Factory - Phillipsburg
1881

Jun 1881 – lamp chimney factory was built.

Sep 1881 – factory opened by Joseph K. Doyle and his son William, Phillipsburg.

In Feb 1884, the Phoenix factory was destroyed by fire.   Fall of 1885 - Phoenix Glass Co. took a lease for this glassworks and it became factory No. 3 of Phoenix at that time.

This company faded away and just seemed to melt into the Phoenix Glass Company.

In 1933, I found some information and a statement referring to Phoenix Glass.........
"It has been said that Monaca lights shine brightly every hour of the 24 somewhere on the globe."
This statement was probably closer to the truth than not because in 1933, Monaca led the world in the production of glass for illumination purposes.

Phoenix Glass Company – Monaca

Organized and began manufacturing in Aug 1880 in Phillipsburg.

Located along the railroad tracks between about Eighth Street and Ninth Street.

Andrew Howard, President; William I. Miller, Secty and Treasurer.

Andrew held the position of President until his death in 1904; his son succeeded him as President until Oct 1964.

Operated one ten pot furnace for lamp chimneys and reflectors.

Originally they made flint chimneys and shades.   They continued to make chimneys exclusively until 1883.

Chimneys made by two processes, one known as the hand process and the other the iron mold process.

The 2nd plant was built down in the area between about Twelfth and Thirteenth Streets – again, along the railroad tracks.

1883 - Part of the plant was turned over to the production of gas and electric shades and globes.   Phoenix was the first in the U.S. to make a line of gas and electric globes west of the Allegheny mountains.

Between 1883 – 1894 Phoenix Glass had great success in art glass.

This was due to Joseph Webb, Jr. who became plant superintendent for Phoenix and was very knowledgeable in glass and no other company but Phoenix could produce what was being made during this time period.

Phoenix obtained the rights to manufacture "The Celebrated Webb Glass" thanks to Joseph Webb's affiliation with T. Webb & Sons.

Phoenix Glass was out of the art glass production within a year after Mr. Webb's leaving Phoenix.   This may have been due to the lack of his involvement then OR the fact that tariff was reduced from 60% to 35% in 1894 -?

FIRE - Feb 1884 - the factory was destroyed by fire.

This is when the Doyle factory was leased (became Factory #3 of the Phoenix Glass Co.).

The plant worked on 3 shift days - eight hours each - midnight Sunday thru Saturday at noon.

They manufactured lamp chimneys, reflectors, gas and electric globes.

When rebuilt after this fire, it was equipped to manufacture etched and decorated glassware.

Andrew Howard – founder.

1885 - The demand for their products increased necessitating erection of a 12-pot furnace.

The lamp chimneys were discontinued and production of a higher grade of illuminating glassware was increased.

Phoenix became the forerunner in production of high grade etched and decorated glassware, being the most well-known producer of this glassware in the U.S.

1891- The company began manufacturing incandescent bulbs at the old Doyle factory, having already purchased this property.

The manufacture of incandescent bulbs was abandoned after a number of years to meet the demands for making the regular line of illuminating glassware.

In 1892/93 and 1898 – Andrew Howard was President; A. H. Patterson was vice president; E. P. Ebberts was the secretary and treasurer. F. J. Duffner was Manager & Sole Agent

FIRE - Early in 1893 – once again, the factory was destroyed by fire. This fire destroyed a 10 pot furnace which was razed to make room for improved manufacturing facilities for the plant. They made temporary quarters in the old Dietrich plant in New Brighton for two years while a new plant was completed in Monaca. The new plant was much larger in every department/area.

The 3rd plant being constructed again after fire #2 and was built between about the 1000 block and on down past Ninth Street, close to Eighth Street. This plant has been expanded and updated over the years, purchasing acres of land and buildings and putting in parking lots to accommodate workers.

In 1898, the directory stated they had their factory office in Monaca, PA – General Offices were at 413 Pennsylvania Avenue, Pittsburgh, PA – their General Show Rooms were at 42 Murray Street, N.Y. and 107 Madison Street, Chicago, Ill.
Andrew Howard-Pres.; E. P. Ebberts-Sec'y. and Treas.; A. H. Patterson-V. Pres. & Mgr.; F. J. Duffner-Manager and Sole Agent.

Mar 1902 -The company took over a 14-pot factory in Washington, PA, and made illuminating glassware there for more than 11 years. It was eventually sold and the employees were transferred to the Monaca plant.

The 12-pot furnace was torn down and replaced with a 14-pot furnace.

In 1904 - A small 8-pot furnace was erected about 200 yards above the No 1 factory.

During WWI, Phoenix became a "war plant" and was engaged in the production of glassware for the United States government producing a very large volume of the needed product. They received special approval from the government to be in full operation. 83% of what was produced in the plant during this war time was made for the government. Girls and women were given employment that had previously been done by boys and men; it should be noted that they did the work equally as efficiently as the men. (see War related information section)

1914 - Extensive improvements were made—the erection of an additional 16 pot furnace in No 1 factory.

1919 - T. H. Howard, Edgeworth, PA–President.   E. P. Eberts, Pittsburgh–Secty. and Treas.
G. F. Wehr, Rochester, PA–General Supt.   E. H. Peck, N.Y. – Sales manager.
T. W. McCreary, Monaca – Supt.
The General Office of the company was located in Pgh; General Sales Offices was located in N.Y. City; Branch Offices were maintained in Chicago, N.Y., and Boston.
Phoenix Glass was credited with being a great aid during WWI. Even during the "essential" work ruling, the products made by Phoenix for the war effort were so important that they utilized their employees and work was done by night and day shifts.   Records of the county also show that the employees made 100 percent contribution to the First, Second, Third, Fourth, and Fifth Liberty Loans.
(See Monaca War Effort section for information.)

1920 - Phoenix Glass Co. purchased three frame houses at Ninth Street and Pacific to be used to accommodate employees who were experiencing trouble finding homes due to the scarcity of houses in Monaca.

1970 – Anchor Hocking acquires Phoenix Glass Company of Monaca.

FIRE 1978 – Jul 15 - The Phoenix / Anchor Hocking is destroyed by fire.
1987 – Jul 2 - Anchor Hocking was acquired by the Newell Corporation.
2004 – Anchor Hocking was purchased by Global Home Products (GHP).

Miscellaneous................
When the company started in 1883, it mainly produced gas globes which were in demand in that era. The company's products and buildings changed with the demands – it produced light bulbs, along with a general line of residential, commercial and industrial lighting, as well as engaging in all phases of silk screening, decorating, hand cutting, etching, hand decorating, and heat treating many types of glassware.

From a small, but solid beginning in 1883 with one 10 pot furnace, the company gradually increased and became known as the largest producer of exclusive illuminating glassware in the world.

In local news articles when Phoenix Glass was mentioned, several departments or factories were recognized within the whole plant. They were given names for recognition purposes since for many years, only parts of the factory/plant would shut down for a week or more during any given month or year. Some of those names were *No. 1 factory*, *No. 3 factory*, "*Carrie Nation*," "*Swamp Angel*," "*Kitty*."

Little Beaver Historical Society

There is no information on this photo, but I would have to make an educated guess that it was some type of dedication or celebration by the apparel of all the people and where some of the people are located (in doorways, on top of the railroad car, at the entrance, etc.)

Little Beaver Historical Society

This photo was taken looking over Phoenix Glass Rochester Tumbler works. The river is in the back ground and this picture would have been taken from far end of the Monaca Heights area. There is print on the light brick building, to the right, in the foreground – "The Phoenix Glass."

Beaver Historical Society   1900s – woman working on assembly line.

1920 working conditions at Phoenix Glass Co.

The fire on Mar 28, 1964 caused approximately $500,000 in damages.
Work continued at the plant with little interruption while repairs were being made.

These photos were taken from the other side of the river.   The Jul 15, 1978 fire
at the Phoenix Glass Co. plant caused an estimated $20 million damage; it nearly
destroyed the entire plant.

Phoenix soon rebuilt the plant after this fire and expanded at a cost of about $95 million.   With this expansion,
there were approximately 90 properties purchased surrounding the area of the plant.

2015

Samples of popular early Phoenix Glass products:

This was a promotional paperweight from about 1894 to 1898.   This one has Pittsburgh, PA on it,
but shows the type of craftsmanship they put out even before the turn of the century.
This paperweight had a white background, all the lettering and designs were in a royal to dark blue,
and there were splashes of a rose coloring shadowing the lettering of "Phoenix."

Antique Phoenix Glass Florentine Floral Brocade Acid Etched Cameo Amber Light Shades – c. 1920s

This is one of their promotional ashtrays from 1930.

1930s large Phoenix glass pillow vase w/geese – white on soft blue.

In Sep 1980, the mayor of Monaca presented Phoenix Glass with a resolution of appreciation for their contribution to the community with the decision to rebuild in Monaca following the fire in Jul 1978. The 500 Phoenix employees working at the new plant that started production in Jun 1980 had an opportunity to show off the new plant to their families on Family Open House day in Sep 1980.

Sep 1980

A resolution in appreciation of Phoenix Glass' contribution to the community will be presented to the company Saturday when its new plant is officially dedicated.

Michael E Reskovac, mayor of Monaca, will present the resolution on behalf of Monaca Council and townspeople who supported the company's decision to rebuild in Monaca following a fire in July 1978.

According to Reskovac, mayor at the time of the rebuilding, "We worked right down the line to keep Phoenix in Monaca. We went all out to have them here. It was a unanimous vote."

A series of public meetings preceded the vote by council with residents and merchants voicing their opinions of the project. In the end, Reskovac said, "The majority were in favor of giving up their homes." More than 90 properties were affected by the decision to build the new and larger plant on a 19-acre site that will allow for future growth.

The community gave its support in tangible ways to allow Phoenix to resume production just six days after the fire in temporary headquarters. After cleanup, the salvaging of some euqipment production continued in the furnace area of the old plant.

Then the Scanlon building in Moor Industrial Park was leased and a decorating department set up while warehousing was handled in the former Laidlaw Wire Co. Building. Production and clerical people were housed in the former Monaca Five and Ten.

Tractor-trailers shuttled the glass back and forth and were able to park on land owned by the Monaca No. 1 Volunteer Fire Department.

Other organizations turned over their parking lots for employees' cars, including the American Legion Post 580, the Monaca Turners, the Veterans of Foreign Wars Post 4653 and Penn Supermarket.

While Anchor Hocking and Phoenix personnel worked at setting up and keeping production lines going, employes worked in less than ideal conditions and governmental officials were pursuing ways to secure financial help for the new plant construction.

The Beaver County Redevelopment Authority with Steve Petz as executive director coordinated these efforts. With its help and the help of many others, Phoenix Glass received grants and loans totaling $10,-700,000.

A loan of $5 million was received from the Pennsylvania Industrial Development Authority; the Urban Development Authority issued a $1 million loan; the state Department of Community Affairs loaned $750,-000; $1 million came from Community Block Grant Funds and from the County of Beaver, $50,000.

These funds were used for land acquisition, the construction of the building, for machinery and equipment, and administration.

The 500 Phoenix employees working at the new plant where production was started in June will have an opportunity to show it off to their families on Family Open House day Sunday. With many Monacans employed, the town of Monaca can be proud, along with Phoenix and Anchor Hocking personnel, of its accomplishments.

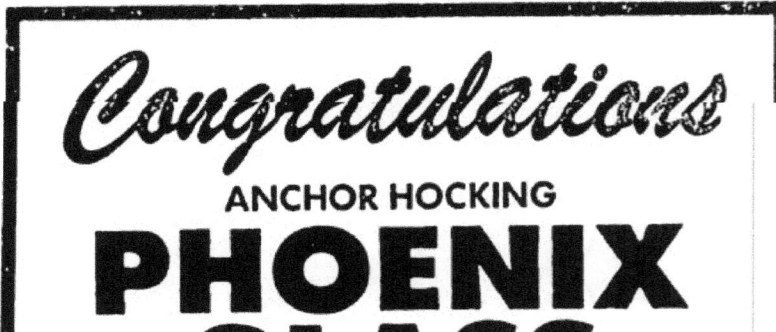

There were quite a few public meetings with merchants and residents voicing their opinions of the project and how it would change and affect the lives everyone and the look of Monaca. In the end, the majority were in favor of giving up their homes and businesses affected by the decision for Phoenix to build a new and larger plant on a 19 acre site, also allowing for future growth.

METCON – metal finisher - 1816 Pennsylvania Avenue

Titanium services for surface conditioning; metal finishing services to the specialty metals industry.

A division of Platte River Equity - Headquartered in Monaca, PA, MetCon has developed and patented a metal finishing process that provides cost savings and yield-enhancement improvements to producers of titanium and other high value metals.

Pennsylvania Metal Cleaning Co. – 200 Seventeenth Street
1978, 1986, 1991, Current

      Founded in 1978.   Paint stripping on metal or wood, rust removal, repair and refinishing furniture.   Some may have even met 3 former "security force" dogs – Brandy, Delilah, and Pacer.   Fire did damage to a one-storey building on Nov 18, 1986.

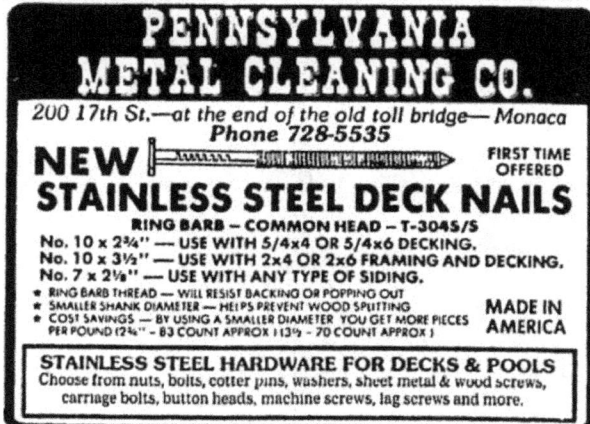

PENNSYLVANIA METAL CLEANING CO.
200 17th St.—at the end of the old toll bridge— Monaca
Phone 728-5535

NEW
FIRST TIME OFFERED
STAINLESS STEEL DECK NAILS
RING BARB – COMMON HEAD – T-304S/S
No. 10 x 2¾" — USE WITH 5/4x4 OR 5/4x6 DECKING.
No. 10 x 3½" — USE WITH 2x4 OR 2x6 FRAMING AND DECKING.
No. 7 x 2½" — USE WITH ANY TYPE OF SIDING.
★ RING BARB THREAD — WILL RESIST BACKING OR POPPING OUT
★ SMALLER SHANK DIAMETER — HELPS PREVENT WOOD SPLITTING
★ COST SAVINGS — BY USING A SMALLER DIAMETER YOU GET MORE PIECES PER POUND (2¾" - 83 COUNT APPROX) (3½ - 70 COUNT APPROX)
MADE IN AMERICA

STAINLESS STEEL HARDWARE FOR DECKS & POOLS
Choose from nuts, bolts, cotter pins, washers, sheet metal & wood screws, carriage bolts, button heads, machine screws, lag screws and more.

1990

The McClymonds (Colona) Coal Transfer Facility -   100 River Road
Closed as of 2015

      This facility was listed as a "Temporary." It was a large scale bulk coal transfer operation and considered controversial in that its original approval was granted partially under the concept that it would not be permanent. Even though listed as "temporary," the facility was in operation for more than two decades and even expanded since 2005.   Residents in the downtown and riverfront areas complained about the amount of coal dust that blows off the site from the tall coal piles into the adjacent residential neighborhoods.

Moor Industrial – 1729 Pennsylvania Avenue

      Moor Industrial (Former Colonial Steel) rents out to different industrial tenants. Only approximately 50% of the site is developed.   The Moor Industrial Park was once part of the former Colonial Steel Mill Complex.   There have been several owners over the years, one of the latest being called Monmouth Reality. (See further for information on Monmouth Real Estate Investment Corporation.) Monmouth Reality's also owns several out-parcels, located towards Seventeenth Street, most of which are cleared and vacant, however, some include smaller industrial structures.   There were 12 industrial buildings and a significant amount of vacant land. Several of the larger industrial buildings are currently leased by tenants including Datatel Resources Corporation and NF&M International. The existing buildings include operating cranes and the site included a 100,000-gallon water tank on a 75' high tower for the complex's fire suppression systems; the tower once was a visual landmark in the town. The tower and tank were torn down in 2014 or 2015.

      All the property is adjacent to the Monaca-East Rochester Bridge.   Private developers have expressed interest in redeveloping the site for a mixed community and hotel complex with river frontage.

Moor   Metcon   former Polish Club   then   Swink's

Moor Industrial Park   Metcon

Left side of buildings in Moor Industrial Park

Roadway is to extreme left of Moor Industrial Park – called "Ohio River Trail" on the maps.

View of former water tank that was on property; it was torn down in 2014/15.

_____

Scanlon business or building – Moor Industrial Park – was used by Phoenix glass in late 1979/early 1980 after there was a fire at their plant – they leased this business/ building and set up the decorating dept.

_____

DART – 1729 Pennsylvania Avenue – Moor Industrial Park
        Moved here in Jun 1987.
        A shared ride service, operated by the Lutheran Service Society of Western Pennsylvania. (For the Beaver County Transit Authority.)   They were in Rochester, but needed additional storage and maintenance space for their vehicles.

_____

C.C.B.C. held one of their continuing education classes in the Moor Industrial Park
1982   Auto Body Repair – Beginning class – spring of 1982.

_____

Datatel Resources Corp – 1729 Pennsylvania Avenue
1955, Current
        Fabricate business forms, documents, and computer supplies.   Began business in 1955.

_____

N F & M International – 1729 Pennsylvania Avenue – metal fabrication
Current
        Manufacturer of titanium billet and bar stock for aerospace and medical industries.
        NF&M recently spent approximately $4 million on improvements to its production facility.

_____

Pittsburgh Logistics Systems - 2060 Pennsylvania Avenue
1997

Located at former Pittsburgh Tube headquarters on Pennsylvania Avenue.

Opened for business in Monaca on May 21, 1997. There were very few novations needed to the two storey building before moving in. The company helps companies transport their products. The company was developed because many companies were beginning to want relieved of bothering with arranging to have their products shipped by truck, rail or barge, so Pittsburgh Logistics does it for them.

———

Ambridge Mobile Welding & Fab. - Welding Equip. Repair Service – 1990 Beaver Avenue

Opened in 1982; owned by Robert N. Urda, Jr.

They were first located at 1742 Pennsylvania Avenue; in Apr of 1989 they requested rezoning by Monaca Borough Zoning Board for a variance so they could construct a new building at 1990 Beaver Avenue. Currently located at 1990 Beaver Avenue, but it is not a new building. They specialize in fabrication and erection of hand railing, guard rails, stairs, caged ladders, and other miscellaneous metal products.

ATI Precision Finishing / Rome Metals Inc. – 2070-76 Pennsylvania Avenue – metal fabrication shops.

Processes anything from ingots to finished products using titanium, zirconium, stainless, nickel, and cobalt-based super alloys.

———

A & D Transfer Inc. – 1901 Beaver Avenue

Local trucking without storage. Freight services/hauling.

———

Ciccone Welding Company - 2450 Beaver Avenue
prior to 1982

They gave public notice of dissolving the business the first of Aug 1982.

———

Trucking and Contracting Co. –
1940, 1953, 1954

Improvements and addition done in 1953/54.

———

Morton International Inc. – salt Division
1997

In Dec 1997, Monaca's Colona Terminal was chosen as their northeast distribution hub for its industrial salt business. There would eventually be as much as 20,000 tons stored at this terminal by 2002. The salt must remain dry once it is shipped in by Morton, remaining on site until a customer requests it. The salt came from Morton's mine in Louisiana to Monaca.

———

ALLVAC – 2060 Pennsylvania Avenue – metal fabricating / metal specialties business

_____

C F Manufacturing – steel / forging - 1817 Pennsylvania Avenue

_____

Discovery Acquisition Service LLC – Surveying and seismic drilling - 10 Industrial Park Road
Provides front-end seismic services. Created through the combination of multiple companies-seismic and drilling.

_____

Mulch Manufacturing, Inc. - 1555 Beaver Avenue
S. E. U. S. S. Division - Pittsburgh R & D Lab.

(Mulch Factory Outlet in Ohio has the same company symbol as found above the door on this company.)

_____

Beaver Valley Industrial Park - 1 Industrial Park Rd
Former site of Colonial Steel business

This business is listed (2016) with approximately 30 acres, brick and metal mill type buildings, totally fenced in area, very large parking area, overhead cranes, 14 truck doors with load lifters, Conrail available at property line, barge loading availability.

_____

Monmouth Real Estate Investment Corporation– various properties
Monmouth Real Estate Investment Corporation is a Maryland corporation operating as a qualified real estate investment trust under Sections 856 through 859 of the Internal Revenue Code (the "Code"). Formed in 1968. They seek to invest in well-located, modern buildings leased to creditworthy tenants on long-term leases and derive their income primarily from the rental of those facilities. They focus on single-tenant, net-leased industrial properties on long-term leases, to investment. They state "an appreciation for all that has been built in the past and a focus on continuing to deliver sustainable long-term results for many years to come."

_____

Beaver County Corp for Econ Development
This is a non-profit corporation; a Commonwealth of PA certified economic development organization. They are governed by a pupil-private partnership that includes business leaders, community leaders and the Beaver County Commissioners.

_____

William Quinn's rope making

One of the earliest settlers in what would become known as Phillipsburg/Monaca was William Quinn. He built his log cabin on the hillside overlooking the Ohio River (was part of the land that became that of the Sanitary Manufacturing Company). William grew flax and became quite skilled at making rope from the flax. He not only made a rope walk for his home, he also became quite well known for the cordage he made and it was sought after by many others. When Commodore O.H. Perry was building his fleet on Lake Erie, the government bought all the rope Mr. Quinn had at the time and it was taken to the lake by ox team in heavy wagons built for that purpose. William not only supervised the work, but helped rig the ships and was present at the Battle of Lake Erie in 1813; he received commendation from the government for his service.

In 1806, William married Margaret Jacobs, daughter of Samuel Jacobs of New York city. They crossed the mountains in a wagon drawn by four horses and settled in what was to become Phillipsburg. In about 1832, Mr. and Mrs. Quinn eventually moved to Ohio where he lived until his death; he was buried with military honors. All of their ten children grew to maturity. One daughter, Eliza was married to John M. Srodes; they had two children - Ann Eliz married Captain W. J. Bickerstaff. One of their sons, William had a son - Rev. John J. Srodes, pastor of the Presbyterian Church of Monaca from 1892 to 1897.

————

*** *** *** *** ***

Although the following companies were actually in Moon, Center, and/or Potter Townships, I have included them in this book because so many of Monaca residents were employed in the businesses and they greatly impacted Monaca and its economy. (There is additional information on all of these businesses in my book on Center Township.)

Kobuta aka Koppers aka Sinclair–Koppers aka NOVA
1942, 1953, 1969   400 Frankfort Road/Rte. 18 - Potter Township

One of the major industries in the Monaca area was the Kobuta plant of the Koppers Company, Inc. The Beaver Valley Plant of Atlantic Richfield began in the early years of WWII. After the invasion of southeast Asia by Japanese troops, even before officially entering the war, the United States government was formulating plans for developing a synthetic rubber industry. The U.S. government realized that this invasion caused the loss of the U.S.'s major source of rubber. Koppers Company of Pittsburgh was chosen by the Defense Plant Corporation since they had a strong background in assembling chemical plants that specifically processed by-products of coke industries. The site along the Ohio River for the Kobuta plant was chosen for this production of styrene and butadiene. Styrene and butadiene are two of the essential ingredients for making Buna S rubber, which was the best type of synthetic rubber at that time. The name of "Kobuta" was formed from Koppers and butadiene. The plant was built in a very short time period due to the pressure of the war; they "fired up" the first boiler at the plant just one year and a day after the ground had been broken on Jun 22, 1942. Only eighteen months later, the plant was in full operation. The total cost to build Kobuta was $61 million. There were more than 20,000 men and women who helped build Kobuta. In the summer of 1943, as many as 7375 people were employed. When the original plant was built, a whole community was also developed and also called Kobuta. See the *Specific Areas* section for additional information on this community.

Two years after the war was won, in spite of all the labor and time to build Kobuta, it was totally shut down. In 1946, the plant was sold by the government (Reconstruction Finance Corporation) to the Koppers Company for one dollar. The plant continued to produce styrene which was used to make polystyrene plastic. The demand and market for plastics grew; Unit 3 of the plant was put back into operation about January of 1951; it had been "put in mothballs" since the war ended. By the mid 1950s, Koppers was expanding and producing many types of products including introducing high density polyethylene.

The Sinclair Oil Company purchased a one-half interest in the former Kobuta plant from Koppers in 1965. This purchase resulted in the formation of a merger that benefited both companies and the newly merged company became known as Sinclair-Koppers. Both former companies' trademarks were modified and the new trademark became a "SK" surrounded by Koppers' familiar octagon. Former Kobuta employees were able to continue to work for the new business since there was little change with them after the merger.

BCHR&LF

There was a major fire at the plant in March 1951 that did about half a million dollars in damages. The Federal Bureau of Investigation and State Police fire marshals began an immediate probe to the cause of the fire to determine if it was intentional or accidental since the government owned the plant. There were more than a dozen fire companies from the surrounding areas, including Pittsburgh, who were called in to help battle this fire. There was even an appeal to volunteer fire companies that was made over the Beaver Falls radio station WBVP. The Koppers Company also had a styrene plant it owned that was located nearby, but it was not involved or damaged by the fire.

This plant was one of the key producers in the WWII synthetic rubber program. It had large quantities of butadiene, made from high proof alcohol. Each unit of the plant, when in full production, could convert more than two million gallons of alcohol into five million pounds of synthetic rubber in just one month. Ethylene is derived from crude oil and benzene is a coke oven by-product. With such flammable materials throughout the plant, the plant took great precautions against fire, even before the Korean war. Workmen entering the plant were required to leave behind all matches or anything else that could start a fire.

In 1970, the Atlantic Richfield Company (ARCO) purchased the bulk of the assets of Sinclair Oil and Kobuta was feeling the effects of this ARCO purchase by 1974. As ARCO continued to purchase shares, eventually Koppers' share of Sinclair-Koppers, Inc. were bought up and once again the plant's identity changed. The sign at Koppers was also changed to reflect the new name and read "Beaver Valley Plant, ARCO Polymers, Incorporated."

In mid June 1996, Nova Chemicals, Inc. announced they were going to be purchasing ARCO Chemical Company's plastics business; this included the Beaver Valley Plant in Potter Township. Since 2009, Nova had been a subsidiary of International Petroleum Investment Co. of Abu Dhabi, United Arab Emirates. Nova had about 2,400 employees worldwide. The company planned on acquiring Royal Dutch Shell's styrenics business which would make NOVA Chemicals the largest producer of plastic resins in the hemisphere and the second largest producer in Europe. The plant in Potter, Monaca, PA was then producing plastic resins used in packaging, insulation, and beverage cups. Nova completed the planned sale of the facility to PFB International of Calgary, Canada, in May 2012.

———

St. Joseph Lead Company – 300 Frankfort Road - along the south bank of the Ohio River, Potter Twp.
1920s, 1931, 1953, 1980

1920s the Zinc Smelting Divisions were erected (original company was from Missouri).
Mr. George F. Weaton was the first Division Manager. 1931 until 1936, the principal product produced was zinc oxide. A permanent shut down for Jan 1980 was announced Nov 1, 1979.

BCHR&LF

In 1953 there were several hundred Monaca area residents of the approximately 900 employees at St. Joseph Lead Company in Potter Township. It was one of the major industries of the county. They had recently done a huge expansion program. Zinc metal, cadmium metal, sulphuric acid, and zinc oxide were produced at the smelter.

———

Horsehead Zinc Smelting Plant – 300 Frankfort Road, Potter Township

Bought the St. Joseph Lead Company plant and property in 2003, the former site of St. Joe Minerals/Lead.
Producer of specialty zinc and zinc-based products and a leading recycler of electric arc furnace dust.
Sold the plant and land to Shell in 2015.

Poor Farm   Horsehead Plant

HORSEHEAD
CORPORATION
Leading the World in Zinc Recycling

A E S Beaver Valley Cogeneration Plant – Frankfort Road (Potter Township)
1942 to 2015

A coal-fired plant, built in 1942. It was originally built to serve as a power generator for the
       Koppers plant; it was built as a "bomb proof facility" since it was built during war time.

Once employed more than 100 people and provided power to nearly 100,000 homes.

At one time, considered the world's largest global power company.

Most recently supplied electricity to West Penn Power and steam to Nova Chemical and
       BASF Corp.   AES, founded in 1981 - Headquarters in Arlington VA - bought the facility
       in 1981 with an agreement between NOVA.   AES employed approx. 40,000 people
       around the world.

Was to close in 2017, but this was accelerated and was closed in 2015.   NOVA had the responsibility
       of demolishing the plant; the 10 acre site was to be converted to a sustainable Brownfield Area.
       It was expected to take until 2018 for the last of the demolition of the external buildings to be
       completed.

View of AES from the river.

***   ***   ***   ***   ***

***   ***   ***

ORGANIZATIONS

ATHLETICS / SPORTS

FUN FACTS AND SNIPPETS OF INFORMATION

PEOPLE AND FAMILIES

ORGANIZATIONS

As in most other towns, townships, cities, and areas, there are clubs, organizations, and societies that form. Society in general benefits greatly from their social relations and influence; it is a fact that society is more cultivated in any community or area if there are social activities. These societies, clubs, and organizations all have various aims and objectives in the social lives of the residents.

Each club or society in Monaca had/has their aims, too. Some were formed solely for pleasure, others to benefit society, and some for profit only. There were numerous organizations, clubs, and societies throughout the many years of history of Monaca. I have captured as much information and included as many of these as I could find; but understand that there will be others that are not included here. I apologize for all that are omitted and do not mean to discriminate or intentionally not include any.

Water Cure Lodge Knights of Pythias No. 99
1885, 1911, 1940
> Instituted Oct 21/28, 1885 – of the Grand Lodge Knights of Pythias of Pennsylvania.
> This organization was listed as a "Secret Society." The Order was founded in Washington D.C.
> > on Feb 19, 1865 and was the first organization to be granted a Charter by the Congress of the United States; founded by Justus H. Rathbone. An international non-sectarian fraternal organization which engages in many benevolent activities. The Pythias web site states: "The object of this organization was the moral uplifting and purification of society. Strict morality, absolute truthfulness, honor and integrity were thoroughly inculcated in the minds of its membership."
> It is a Fraternal Organization founded on the principals of Friendship, Charity, and Benevolence.
> When the town was named Monaca, the Lodge was named Water Cure Lodge, No. 99, Monaca.
> Still in existence in 1940 but not one of the charter members was living.
> They met every Thursday evening in the Business Block.
> > First officers of this organization were: Edward Kaye-Past Chancellor; James Huggins-Chancellor Commander; J. W. Moorehouse-Vice Chancellor; David Kay-Prelate; William Wagner-Master of Exchequer; J. B. Zitzman-Master of Finance; Charles Abel, Jr.-Keeper of records and seals; William Urwine-Master at Arms; J. A. Burgen-Inner Guard; J. W. Weigle-Outer Guard; William Hunter-Representative to Grand Lodge.
> There were several Pythias companies – one of those was the Fort McIntosh Company, No. 53, Uniformed Rank. They had their headquarters in the Bank Hall of Monaca; would perform in "full dress" at parades (1904).

Monaca Mission League –
1883, 1903   Started in 1883.

Pastime Athletic Club
1907
> Had a baseball team and played other teams in the valley.

Trilby Club
1900

_____

Monaca Lodge No. 1115, Independent Order of Odd Fellows   aka   Monaca I.O.O.F.
      Instituted Sep 16, 1899.
      This was considered a "Secret Society" and they met every Saturday evening in the
            Business Block (Citizen's Bank building).   Then they had their own hall…..but I guess
            they kept good secrets because I found no address for it.
      This organization stood for Friendship, Love, and Truth; they were also known as The Three
            Link Fraternity because …………..

*Fun facts: The original men who founded the organization used to go about in their community
and help out anyone in their community that needed anything.   They would also anonymously
leave food on the doorsteps of needy people.   No one could figure out who was behaving in
such a seemingly impractical yet generous manner.   People would refer to them as "odd fellows";
this is how the name was formed.   This organization was officially founded in 1819 in another
state.   They were also the first national group to include both men and women when it adopted
the Rebekah Degree in 1851.   The Odd Fellows and Rebekahs were the first fraternal organization
to establish homes for our seniors and orphaned children.*

*The most recognizable symbol for them is an open hand with a heart in the middle of it.   A program
on the History channel made small references to items that have been found from old, defunct groups in
various areas of the United States.   Some of the information they shared was they would put leather
"hoodwinks" on an incoming member during the initiation ceremony and there would be a half sized real
or papier mâché skeleton inside a half sized casket held up right in front of them – the eye covers on the
hoodwink would be opened and the incoming member would be face to face with the skeleton and would
be told that this is what he would become………..so he had to do good now.   They also had mesh masks that
had eyebrows, beards, mustaches, and/or weird hair on them that were worn so a member could not be
identified for various reasons/at various times.   It is also said that many of the Odd Fellows' rituals (ancient
secret handshakes, special songs, and ceremonies) disappeared from most lodges decades ago.
Regardless of their rituals and secret procedures, this organization of men and women did very good things
for many people and communities.*

*The Odd Fellows and Rebekahs both currently continue to exist with nearly 10,000 lodges in 26
countries.*

Hoodwinks

_____

Monaca Castle No. 17, Knights of the Golden Eagle
1909, 1911, 1912
      In 1912 they met alternate Wednesday nights in Business Block (Citizen's Bank building).

_____

The Sons of Temperance –
1904

_____

Local Union, No. 36, A. F. G. W. U of Monaca
1903

_____

In Jan 1907, P. F. Lewis added a third storey to his new brick block building on Eighth Street and was going to have it "fitted up" as a lodge room.   Lodge room for whom -???

_____

Allaire Club, of Colona
1910

_____

Monaca Tent No. 335, Knights of the Maccabees   (K. O. T. M.)
1900, 1906, 1911, 1912
      This group was considered a "Secret Society."   They met the 2nd and 4th Monday evenings
          in Block Building (Citizen's Bank building).
      A fraternal organization whose aspects included low-cost insurance to members; in the society's
          earlier years, it also provided other final-expense related benefits such as society
          cemeteries.   The Knights of Maccabees motto was the Latin phrase "Astra Castra Numen
          Lumen" - translated it means "The stars my camp, the Deity my light."   In 1941 the
          group gained control of the Michigan Union Life Association which furthered the
          transformation from a "benefit society" into a modern, legal-reserve insurance company.
          In 1962 the name was changed to the Maccabees Mutual Life Insurance Company. In
          the 1990s it was sold to the Royal Insurance Group and operated under the name Royal
          Maccabees Life Insurance Company.   In 1999 it was sold once again to Swiss Re which
          merged it into its subsidiary, Reassure America Life Insurance Company.

Ladies auxiliary was called Monaca Hive -   Ladies of the Maccabees, Hive No. 203
1911, 1912   They met the 2nd and 4th Monday evenings in Business Block.

_____

Women's Benefit Association – formerly Monaca Review No. 203 - which in turn had been organized
          from the Ladies of the Maccabees of the World.
      Organized Jun 16, 1900.
      From this organization, the following clubs were fostered:

Pioneer Women's Club	West Way Girls' Club	Veritan Girls' Club
Jolly Juniors Club	Girls and Boys Club	Past Presidents' Club

      First officers were: Ida Kaye-P. Co.; Annie Sweet-Com.; Janette Allen-L. Com.; Mollie
      Sweet-R.K.; Annie MacDonald-C.; Lydia Johnston-L.A.; Margaret Smith-Sgt.; Cora
      Adams-S.; Ida Bittner-P.

_____

"The Boys"
      Club of 10 old Bachelors who had meetings and outings.   They were a bit secretive in their
      activities but always claimed to have good times.   They would spend Sundays at *Hickory Bottom*.
      (*I found reference to a Hickory Bottom in Connellsville, PA, but have no idea if this was where they went.)

_____

Beaver County Home for the Aged
1913
      The Monaca Auxiliary to the Beaver County Home for the Aged began in 1913.
          o   They raised funds toward the maintenance of the home and keeping up the room which it
            furnished at the time of the opening of the home.

_____

Workingmen's Sick and Death Benefit Association
1911, 1913   Had meetings in 1912 (in members' homes).
                    They met on Sixth Street near Pennsylvania Avenue.

    and / or ……..

Sick & Accident Association Hall – Sixth Street
1919   Held dances here.

————

Monaca Turn Verein (Turners) – started at 819 Pennsylvania Avenue in a small one store frame building;
1883 to Current
    Organized Apr 9, 1883; erected and dedicated their first building in 1893.
    "Turnverein" comes from: German *turnen* – "to practice gymnastics" and *Verein* – "club, union."
        It was an association of gymnasts founded by the German teacher and patriot Friedrich
        Ludwig Jahn in Berlin in 1811.
    The group started meeting in a small one storey frame building at 819 Pennsylvania Avenue.
    They moved to 699 Pacific Avenue (corner of former Seventh Street and Pacific Avenue - back
        toward the railroad tracks).
    Their first structure was a two storey frame building the was completed and dedicated
        Nov 29, 1893.   The building was enlarged in 1901 with a 30 by 20 foot addition added
            on the back of the building.   In 1915 the building was again enlarged with a one
            storey, 20 by 100 foot, brick structure on the front of the building.   This
            addition included two bowling alleys. They purchased land from Marie Bimber in
            1929.   Another one storey brick building, 50 by 100 feet, was added in 1938 and
            three more bowling alleys were added to the previous addition.
    Turners occupied the building on Seventh Street and Pacific Avenue until 1980 when Phoenix
        Glass expanded and purchased the property.
    They had a gymnastics team beginning in the earlier 1900s which consisted of only men – no
        women or children.
    1920 – Michael Uyak was proprietor of the Turnverein – he was living at 699 Pacific Avenue.
    Had bowling leagues in 1939 – Women's ---- they used the Turners' alleys.
    In Jan 1981, erected a modern new building and moved to 1700 Brodhead Road, Center Twp.
        This new building includes a bar room, dining room, regulation size gymnasium, kitchen,
        banquet hall, racquetball courts, and six bowling lanes.

        First officers of the club were elected Apr 9, 1893:
        W. A. Miksch-President; Gustave Friebe, Sr.-Vice President; Gustave Fitz-Recording
        Secretary; Rudolph Berchthold-Corresponding Secretary; Robert Werner-Financial
        Secretary; Cosmos Gaube-Treasurer; Ralph Langer-Gymnasium Instructor.   Trustees
        were: George Bechtel, Cosmos Gaube, Robert Werner, W. A. Miksch, Adolph Langer, and
        Paulus E. Koehler.

I apologize for the poor quality of the picture below; it was the only one available to me.
This picture shows the front of the brick portion of the club facing Pennsylvania Avenue.

The front section is seen in the previous picture and would be to the right of this picture. This was the continuation / rear portion of the building at 699 Penna Avenue.

Photo courtesy Beaver County Historical Research and Landmarks Foundation

The building in the background is the former Turners. The older, two storey portion (to the left) was built in 1883 and considered at the corner of Seventh Street and Pacific Avenue (699 Pacific Avenue). The brick portion, to the right was added in 1915 and was then considered the social hall and main entrance. The back (original 2 storey) portion became the gymnasium and activity part of the club. The front, brick addition changed the address to 699 Pennsylvania Avenue (corner of Seventh Street and Pennsylvania Avenue).

The roadway you see in this picture was a section of Pacific Avenue; Seventh Street ran paralell on this side of the building.

These buildings no longer exist, nor does Seventh Street or a great portion of Pacific Avenue. As stated previously, in 1981 Turners constructed a new building in Center Township at the corner of Brodhead Road and Chapel Road (1700 Brodhead Road).

_____

Phillips Council No. 24, Jr. O.U.A.M.   aka
        Phillipsburg Council No. 24 of the Junior Order of the United American Mechanics
1882, 1898, 1911, 1940
    Instituted and organized Jan 6, 1883 – chartered Dec 1882.
    They moved their meeting locations - met in Lay Building, Sparling's, Wagner's, back to Lay's, then
        to the City Hall, and finally Bank Hall.
    As of 1940, this group was assisted by Monacatootha Post 580, American Legion, and other
        fraternal organizations.
    Known as.........Phillipsburg Council No. 24, Jr. O.U.A.M.
        They endeavored to foster the principal objects of the Order: a) Promote the interests of
        Americans; b) pay sick and death benefit to members and families; c) Uphold the public
        schools and encourage the reading of the Bible therein; d) Care for their orphans by
        maintaining national homes (which in 1940 were in Tiffin, OH and Lexington, N.C.).
    The first Councilor was John M. Johnson and the first Secretary was Charles M. Wagner.

_____

The Protected Home Circle
1911

_____

Good Will Council, No. 921 - Royal Arcanum of Monaca
1898, 1912   They were considered a "Secret Society" and had meetings as called by members.

_____

The Monaca Athletic Club – headquarters in the basement of the Keystone Block Building
1911
Organized several years prior to 1911.
Had various gymnastic appliances and a well-equipped reading room.

———————

Monaca Cornet Band / Band Room Club – 1199 Pacific Avenue
1898, 1964 Current
Their beginnings were with a German men's club. It is Beaver County's oldest community band.
Edward Swansey was the first Director; Jimmy Sebastian served as Director the longest – from
    1935 to 1985; Jimmy Rubbo was Director from 1985 to 1995; Jean Busack then became
    the Director.
It was an all-male group until into the 1950s and 1960s when several women joined.
Had the original name of Monaca Silver Cornet Band (see *Fun fact* below).
Received their charter Dec 21, 1898 which was a few years after they organized.
Used to meet in one of the buildings on Sixth Street, then moved to 1199 Pacific Avenue.
The band performs for parades, concerts, and in 1964-they played at Pittsburgh Airport
    to greet President Johnson.

Pacific Avenue on left   Twelfth Street is along the side of The Band Room building

Oct 1952

Fun Fact: The Economite and the Silver Cornet Band was the
predecessor of the Monaca Cornet Band.

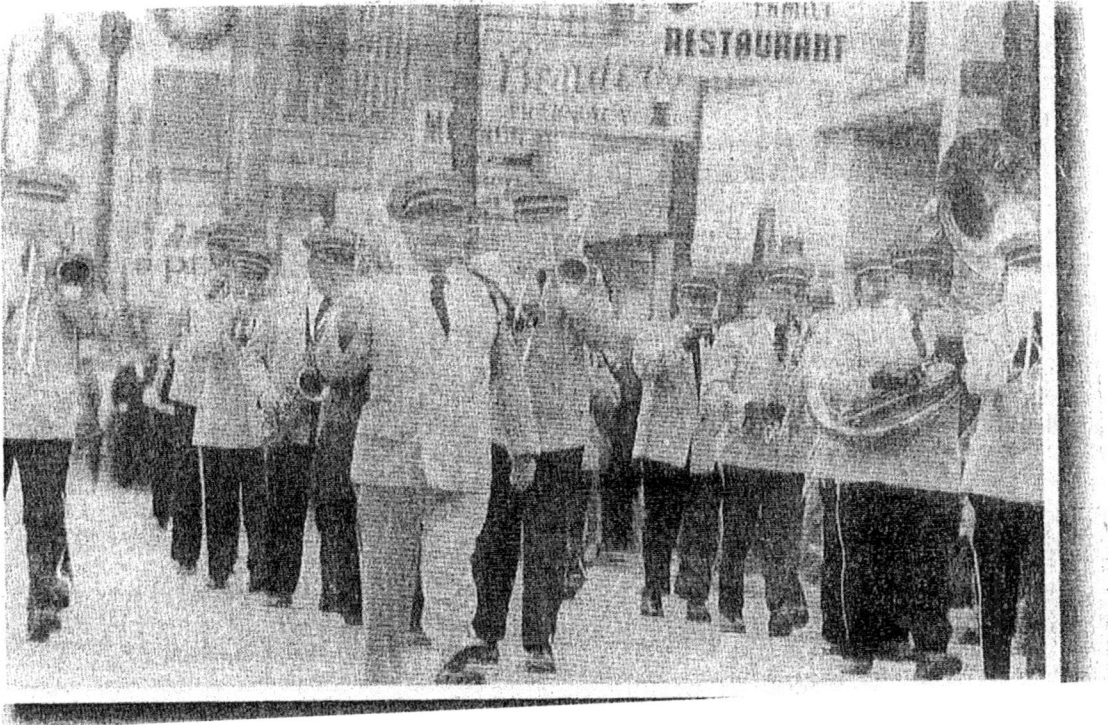

1975 - Jimmy Sebastian leading the Cornet Band in parade; he was well known in Monaca.

———————

Monaca Aquatic Club (1916) – 799 Atlantic Avenue
1916, 1922   Held dances and functions to raise money to improving the local bathing beach.

———————

Monaca Chess Club
    Used the Lay Building at corner of Eighth Street and Indiana Avenue after selling their
        club house.
    1907 article states original club house <u>was</u> on Pennsylvania Avenue near Sixth Street.
        It was built in 1901 on Pennsylvania Avenue – sold it in 1907 to Mateer Bros., but the
        club planned to build another soon.
        This first club house was purchased by John and James Mateer in Mar 1907 for
        investment purposes.   The Mateers planned on moving the building to a lot they own on
        Penna Ave, near Eleventh Street. The Mateer Bros. didn't move the building because in
        Jun 1907, they rented it out to a number of young men from town who organized a social
        club and leased the building after doing some remodeling. (See Belmont Club)

———————

Fancy Work Club – met in members' homes
1909

———————

Bowknot Club – met in members' homes
1906   Devoted to fancy needle work.

———————

Young Men's Christian Association of Monaca   aka   YMCA – Used the large building on the corner
1901, 1902, 1903, 1907   of Eighth Street and Indiana Avenue
        Organized in 1901.
        Closed their doors in Aug, 1907.
                This association had a few different meeting places.....
                        – Corner of Eighth Street and Indiana Avenue (in 1902/03).
                        -In 1903 they moved into the old skating rink – Pennsylvania Avenue.
                        -Apr 1903 -- the new Association Hall on Pennsylvania Avenue is nearing completion; the
                                front of this building was to be divided off and fitted up as a store room to be rented out.
                Had an educational and game room in Dec 1903 – had it renovated and painted.
                Had a membership contest in mid Nov 1903.
                Did a number of improvements in 1904 – added bathroom, two shower baths, 30 private lockers,
                        water heater (Opalite Tile Co. donated the tile).
                Throughout the very early 1900s, they went by full name Young Men's Christian Association
                        in all news articles.
                Oct 11, 1906 -- they had a formal opening of the YMCA's social rooms.
                Had their own gymnasium, basketball team, held roller skating parties, dances.
                1907 – the Board of Directors decided to close up the hall on Pennsylvania Avenue, pay off the
                        indebtedness and dispose of the paraphernalia – all due to lack of interest in the work of
                        the association.
                There was a "farewell skate" on Aug 31, 1907 for all those interested before the hall closed permanently.
        Although this group was only in Monaca from 1901 to 1907, they were a VERY active group and
                seemed to have multiple activities going on each and every week during this time period.
                They were always in the news and advertising one event or another.

The South Branch YMCA – 1300 Taylor Ave
1978, 1980, 1984
        Opened Dec 1, 1978 on Monaca Heights.
        Monaca YMCA by the water reservoirs – Sokol Lodge – Taylor Avenue/1019 Grove Street.
                o   The Sokol Lodge had a large gymnasium and meeting rooms.
        It was discussed to have a YMCA in Monaca as early as Jul 23, 1935.
        The South Branch of YMCA in Monaca was offering classes in Apr 1980 and to make reservations
                calls were to be made to the South Branch office at 1300 Taylor Avenue.
        Their gymnasium was going to be used for disco roller skating beginning Apr 25 1980.
                ▪   Skaters had to have their own skates with wooden or plastic wheels that would
                        not leave marks on the floor.
        I did not find many articles or many ads for this South Branch.
                        Also see Assembly 124 of the Slovak Gymnastic Union Sokol in this section.

        _____

Belmont Club – Pennsylvania Avenue (near Sixth Street)
1907
        Young men of Monaca formed a new club.   They leased the former Monaca Chess Club building
                and formed a social club.   They met in Jul 1907 to elect officers.
        Also in 1907, a well-known wrestler, Paul Bowser, rented the gymnasium room at the Belmont
                Club headquarters so he could train for the fall wrestling bouts.
        (It appears they leased this building from the Mateer Bros.)

        _____

Order of Buffaloes aka   Royal Antediluvian Order of the Buffaloes
1901
        Organized in 1901.   It did not offer sick benefits and was purely of a social nature.

        _____

The Monaca "Ladies" Five Hundred Club
1911

Their meetings were held in members' homes. Membership was made up of women well known in Monaca society circles.   Five Hundred card game was played during the afternoon and at each meeting refreshments were served.

————

The Jolly Twelve Club
1911

Composed of women prominent in the social life of Monaca.
Met two evenings a month.   Cards and social intercourse were the meetings' diversions.

————

Monaca Aerie, No. 1412, Fraternal Order of Eagles – 1199 Pennsylvania Avenue
Instituted May 26, 1906.
Met the 2nd and 4th Monday evenings of each month in the Eagle Hall at 612 Pennsylvania Avenue in 1912.   Held meetings in Bank Hall, Sullivan Building (Pennsylvania Ave), Chess Club.   Then had a club house at 612 Pennsylvania Avenue by 1912.
This building was occupied by the South Side Club next.
Jul 10, 1919 – the Hamilton Hotel building was purchased - 1199 Pennsylvania Avenue.
   o   1923 the adjoining house and lot were bought – 1135 to 1197 Pennsylvania Ave.
The Dec 26, 1919 article said they bought a 2 storey frame building, lower(612) Pennsylvania Avenue, owned by Mateer Bros. and formerly occupied/rented by the Eagles.
This order paid a weekly benefit to the sick and disabled members and funeral benefit in death.
Were at 1199 Pennsylvania Avenue in 1919 and until 1967.
Harry Murchland was the steward in the club.
They were closed and no longer had members in 1994.

First officers were: David J. Mitchell-Worthy Past President; George V. Mullen-Worthy President; Timothy Kaye-Vice-President; Edward M. Johnston-Chaplain; H.W. Feurhake-Secretary; Henry Weirich-Treasurer; Dr. J.J. Allen-Physician; Joseph Schachern, George Lais, Jr., and William Swansey-Trustees.

————

Monaca Circle No. 569 – Protected Home Circle
1912   Met alternate Thursday evenings of each month in Business Block.

————

The Senior Society
1911   Made up of married men and women of various churches.   Meetings held in members' homes every month.   Games were played and usually a lunch was served.

————

The Young People's Social Club
1911

Of the Methodist church and of other denominations.   A committee of 6 entertained the club each week.
Both the Senior Society and The Young People's Social Club were organized to raise money for the Methodist Church debt.

————

Daughters of Liberty
1911   They were considered a "Secret Society" and would meet every Friday evening in the Business Block (which was better known as the Citizen's Bank Building).

————

Monaca Business Men's Industrial Association
1911   They held their meetings at the Hotel Monaca.

_____

Spojeni Bratia Assembly No. 526 of the National Slovak Society of the United States of America
      Established on Jan 28, 1906.
      The main National Slovak Society of the United States of America was established Feb 16, 1890.
      The purpose of the organization was 1) to protect its members in misfortune, distress, sickness,
            and death by maintaining funds for payment of benefits; 2) to educate and instruct them
            in English and Slovak languages and support them socially and morally; 3) to fit them for
            the duties of life and citizenship with English speaking people; 4) to educate and to care
            for the future of the Slovak youth; 5) to preach and practice the gospel of true
            brotherhood of man.
      First officers were: Stefan Huraj-President; John Vavra-Vice President; John Silorsky-
      Secretary; Josef Pajtas-Treasurer

_____

Analoc (Analog) Club -   Held meetings in the Stephen Phillips Homes community hall.

_____

The Slovak Evangelical Union Assembly No. 130 – 1019 Grove Street– Monaca Heights
      Established May 22, 1904.
      Had a Women's Union Branch – No. 37 - organized Sep 20, 1908.
      Also called The Peter Markovich Assembly No. 130 of the Slovak Evangelical Union of America.

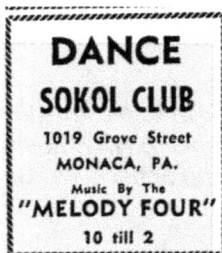

DANCE
SOKOL CLUB
1019 Grove Street
MONACA, PA.
Music By The
"MELODY FOUR"
10 till 2

1960

(It is confusing to the differences between the above and below...............)
These were evidently considered two separate organizations for the most part – one a club with memberships and
one an organization to support physical culture among its members.
Both locations are within a few 100 feet of each other.   The 1019 Grove Street structure must have been closed
and all activities were moved to the 1300 Taylor Avenue building(s) - ? -

Monaca Slovak Sokols   aka   Assembly 124 of the Slovak Gymnastic Union Sokol
                                                            1300 Taylor Avenue – Monaca Heights
            Organized May 20, 1907.   Closed in 1984.
            Met first in the old bank building on Ninth Street.
            Moved to Monaca Heights.
            In Mar of 1970, the gym club was broken in to; about 15 bottles of liquor and an
                  undetermined amount of money stolen from a pinball machine.

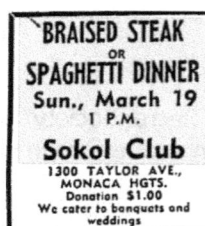

BRAISED STEAK
OR
SPAGHETTI DINNER
Sun., March 19
1 P.M.
Sokol Club
1300 TAYLOR AVE.,
MONACA HGTS.
Donation $1.00
We cater to banquets and
weddings

1967

This property became available to the borough at no cost – now used for public works building by the reservoirs on Taylor Ave.

(2015)

This structure is most likely new, but this is the area the clubs/gymnasiums were located.... 1300 Taylor Avenue.   Note - 1019 Grove is just behind where I was standing to take this picture.

First officers were: Joseph Goza-President; Paul Karcis, Sr.-Vice President; Paul Kermiet, Sr.-Recording secretary; Paul Hecio-Financial secretary; Steve Hurray, Sr.-Treasurer; Mathew Hiebo, John Sochor, Michael Bednasz-Trustees

_____

In the early 1900s and 1911, I found mention of various fancy work clubs that held sessions at regular intervals. Basket picnics were common among Monaca women as a summer diversion.

_____

Various Church organizations included....
1911

        The Christian Endeavor Society   The Luther League   Epworth League

_____

The Club – Eckert Building – Pennsylvania Ave
1911

        This group had a few rooms – well-furnished and in them a library and piano.   "The Club" would camp two weeks each year at Conneaut Lake.
        Members were "male only," but receptions on certain evenings were held for their lady friends.

_____

Monaca Fife and Drum Corps
1903

        Organized Dec 21, 1903.   There was an "old Monaca drum corps" that existed prior to Dec 1903 which was reported to have dropped out of existence; but was revived again.   The former members were contacted and formed a new group.
        Surviving members of the old Monaca drum corps served as a nucleus for this new organization.

_____

Monaca Tennis Club – (last location) corner Eleventh Street and Atlantic Avenue
1924

        Work of grading of the new site began spring of 1924. The site extends to the bottom hand along the Ohio River and they planned on a bathing beach to be opened also.
        The former location of the club's court was on the site of the new school building at the corner of Tenth Street and Indiana Avenue.

_____

Young Men's Republican Club

Was formed in 1938.   Orin W. Hughes-President; O. H. Sayre-Vice President; Oliver T. Berkman-Secretary/Treasurer.

_____

The German Six Benefit Association of Monaca, Pa   - 410 Sixth Street
1902 to 2015

Organized Jul 1, 1902.

Purpose was to create social activity among Saxon people and to work in harmony with other small organizations; this corporation also stood for the maintenance of a society for beneficial or protective purposes to its members from funds collected therein.

Granted charter Oct 26, 1903 under the name *German Sick Benefit Association of Monaca, PA.*

First met at the Singers' Society Hall on Monaca Heights prior to 1910.

Prof. Fred Bechtel owned a lot on the North Side of Sixth Street near the Siebenberger's Hall \ (see Saxon Club).

In Nov 1910, Prof. Bechtel purchased the old Pittsburg and Lake Erie passenger depot which was located on Sixth Street (and had been abandoned for several weeks since the new depot was at Fourteenth and Pacific Avenue).

Prof. Bechtel had the old depot moved about a half block and placed on his lot – it was a frame structure and was going to be remodeled and be a permanent headquarters for the Union; instead, another structure was built adjacent tò the relocated depot.

In 1936 – the charter was changed, then became known as.......................

Siebenberger Sachsen Kranken Untersteutzungs Verein, Branch 29, Monaca

Received the nickname of..............

Monaca Saxon Club – Branch 29 – 410 Sixth Street

Transylvanian Saxon Germans came to Monaca about 1900 and as a group started the Saxon Club.

The vast majority of Saxons were farmers, with many others actively engaged in mining, forestry, artisanry, military service, monastic priesthood, and merchant commerce, so when they emigrated and settled in the Monaca area, it was not a totally difficult transition for them.

Although I have no roster or list of names, some of the most likely persons among the first members of the Saxon club may have included Peter Petrus, Steven Vahs, Sam, Andrew, John Zoppelt, Tom Moldovan, Charles Clark, George Lesch, Joe Fenik, Joseph Galia, John Lang, John Mainer --- all were from Transylvania.

First officers were: George O. Miller-President; Stephen Depener, Sr.-Vice President; Andrew Meiterth-Recording Secretary; Andrew Schenk-Treasurer; Michael Fleischer, Michael Depener, Jr., and John Welter were trustees.

Model Train Museum   Saxons

_____

Acme Club
Organized in Sep 1901.
First met in the Morris Barnett building which was built on corner of Ninth Street and
Pennsylvania Avenue.
Moved to 711-713 Pennsylvania Avenue.

1906 – changed the name to…………..

Monaca Rod and Gun Club
The club maintained a summer camp in Oak Grove on the James Mateer farm, Center Twp.
They limited their membership to 40 members.
Each year, members would summer camp in the Canadian woods.

Photo from Milestones magazine – BCHR&LF

An early photo of members of the Rod and Gun Club of Monaca. Back row: Fritz Bechtel,
Billy Meanor, Henry Miksch.   Front row: Joe Fisher, Joe Stein, Bill Bechtel, Carl Mattauch,
Walter Buchholz

_____

Junior Christian Endeavor Society of the First Presbyterian Church

_____

The South Side Club – 612 Pennsylvania Avenue
1920, 1930s
Purchased a building for clubhouse from Mateer Bros. in Jan 1920.
Formerly occupied by Frat Order of Eagles.
Front room on 1st floor was being made into athletic room with fully equipped gymnasium.
In the rear of the room would be a pool and billiard room.   A parlor and reading room on
the 2nd floor.   It was a 2 storey white frame building with front porches on the 1st & 2nd floors.
The American Legion building was on the right of this building, with the former
Stoop's Livery on the left side of the club building.   Stoop's became the S & S
Garage.   Both the garage and the club house were razed.
They produced one of the better semi-professional football teams in the Pittsburgh district in the
1930s.   They met with many of the best football teams in Western Pennsylvania and
Ohio on the barred field.

_____

Monaca American Social Club –
1900, 1958

_____

American Legion – 600 Pennsylvania Avenue
1920, 2010s

Organized Nov 15, 1920 – chose the name Monacatootha Post.

Formed by 29 former vets.

Aims: to further the promotion of good fellowship and friendly relationship among all people, to support, advocate and maintain the principles of true Americans, and good citizenship.

1923 the American Legion had their post in the basement area of the Citizen's National Bank building – it was just renovated for the Legion – had reception room/parlor, bowling alley, rifle range, card and pool room, and other equipment and conveniences for the Legion.

1928 – transferred its headquarters from the Citizens Bank Building to Paulus Koehler property across the street (beside the old Hotel Monaca site --- Koehler's house was behind the Citizens Bank Building at 826 Washington Avenue). Their meetings were held at this location until -?-.

May 1931, purchased Dr. Allen residence at 802 Washington Avenue and Eighth Street as the Monacatootha Post No. 580 American Legion Home and still had meetings there in 1940. There is a small two storey brick building in the rear of the lot that goes with this house; it is not known if this building was used for anything or possibly just rented out.

Early Jun 1953, this house (corner of Eighth Street and Washington Avenue) was up for sale. Their new building was at the corner of Pennsylvania Avenue and Sixth Street; still the home to American Legion Post as of 2016.

Auxiliary to the American Legion

A group of Monaca women began meeting in the home of Mrs. J. R. Gormley following W.W. I.   On Nov 29, 1921, they formed the organization.

They were granted a charter on Jan 17, 1922.

This Auxiliary group was invited to use the lodge room of the Monaca Fraternal Order of the Eagles.

They began to hold their meetings in the 2nd floor of the new Legion home on Washington Avenue in 1931.

This group worked toward aiding disabled soldiers and made contributions to Child Welfare, scholarship funds, and presented a medal each year to an outstanding girl and boy in the eighth grade of Monaca schools.

First officers: Mrs. Philip Faust-President; Mrs. J. R. Gormley-Vice President; Mrs. Ralph D. Houser–Secretary; Mrs. Leroy Potter-Treasurer; Mrs. Joseph O. Ault-Historian; Mrs. Lawrence Griffin-Chaplin

The Fathers and Sons Council was organized in 1936 under the sponsorship of Monacatootha Post No. 580, American Legion, Monaca. Their purpose was creating better fellowship among the fathers and sons and also to instill greater interest in furthering the objectives of the American Legion.   Thomas W. McCreary served as the first president, and Eddis Hood was secretary.

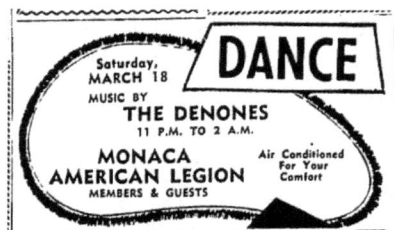

Saturday, MARCH 18 / DANCE
MUSIC BY
THE DENONES
11 P.M. TO 2 A.M.
MONACA
AMERICAN LEGION
MEMBERS & GUESTS
Air Conditioned For Your Comfort

1967

Monaca American Legion Has Fine Home

Meeting place of Monacatootha Post, No. 580, American Legion, the Ladies' Auxiliary and other Legion units of the Southside community is the fine Legion Home, pictured above. Located at 802 Washington avenue, the home was purchased in 1931. It was formerly the home of Dr. and Mrs. J. J. Allen.

1940

American Legion Home

2½ story brick building, with forced air heat, centrally located in Monaca, at corner of 7th Street and Washington Ave., near bus facilities for upper and lower Valley. This building is suitable for doctor's office, funeral home, club rooms, office building or apartment building. Also a two-story brick building on lot in the rear.

1953

(side from Eighth Street - 2015)

1955

2015

Women's Club of Monaca

Began meeting Jan 19, 1921.

Apr 7, 1921 – became a member of the Pennsylvania State Federation of Women's Clubs.

Jan 1940 – a garden club committee was appointed and this eventually became the Monaca Garden Club or Garden Club of Monaca.

First officers were: Mrs. D. C. Locke-President; Mrs. D. J. Mitchell-1st Vice President; Mrs. Mary Jenkins-2nd Vice President; Mrs. C. M. Wagner-Recording Secretary; Mrs. J. H. Martsoif-Corresponding Secretary; Mrs. Charles Houston-Treasurer; Mrs. E. M. Callaghan and Mrs. E. H. McMahon-delegates to the county Federation

Monaca Garden Club
1941, 1965   Organized Apr 14, 1941.   This group grew out of the Women's Club of Monaca.

_____

Monaca Junior Women's Club
    Nov 6, 1933 - Organized from the Women's Club of Monaca.
    On Apr 4, 1934 the club was federated with the PA Federation of Women's Clubs.
    The Monaca Junior Women's Club's main project was the Monaca Public Library.

        First officers were: Miss Emma Werner-President; Miss Elizabeth Lepper-Vice president;
        Miss Veda Measel-Recording secretary; Mrs. Venetta Loudon Brakenridge-Corresponding
        secretary; Miss Genevieve Sowash-Treasurer.

_____

Monaca Barracks & Auxiliary No. 738, W.W. I
1956, 1957, 1965
        Local group was organized in 1956.   The ladies Auxiliary was organized in 1957.
        Barracks in Beaver, Midland, and Rochester were organized from the local Barracks 738.

_____

Beaver County Children's Aid Society
    The Monaca Auxiliary to Beaver County Children's Aid Society was organized Aug 25, 1932.
        o   They made garments for needy children, provided glasses for Monaca children, provided
            clothing for Monaca children in foster homes, and gifts at the holiday season.

        First officers were: Mrs. W. R. Leigh-President; Mrs. Robert N. Embree-Vice President;
        Miss Vera V. Grant-Secretary; Mrs. Harold M. Williams-Treasurer

_____

Touchdown Club
1944
    Newly organized in Sep 1944 – held their meetings in the borough building.
    The purpose of the club … to back all Monaca athletics.

_____

Monaca-Center Lodge No. 791 Free and Accepted Masons – corner Pacific Avenue and Fourteenth Street
1961 - current
        Constituted on Mar 11, 1961.
            The Lodge purchased the old, dusty, abandoned station from the railroad in 1969; after over
    10,000 man hours of labor donated by Lodge members, family, and friends, the new lodge
    became home of Monaca-Center Lodge No. 791.   This railroad station was built in the 1900s and
    in April 1910 it was moved from its original site at Colona (Monaca area) to this current location
    on the corner of Fourteenth Street and Pacific Avenue.   Lodge No. 791 was holding its meetings
    in the Masonic Temple in Rochester before moving into this new location in 1970/71.

            The furniture for this Lodge was donated by Grand Lodge; there are hand carved benches and
    chairs that date back over 135 years and had been used in the "New Masonic Hall" in Philadelphia
    between 1855 – 1873.   Bright crimson upholstered furniture and a rich blue carpeting adorn the
    60 by 28 foot Lodge Room.   (See Railroad Station section for photographs of the former station
    and the current Lodge.)

_____

American Croatian Social Club – 1543 Pennsylvania Ave
1943, 2009

> Chartered May 26, 1943.   The club building was erected shortly after they were chartered.
> Additions to the club and bar were done over the years.

(Pennsylvania Avenue looking toward downtown)

former Potter's (small building) & Echo Point Restaurant   Croatian Club
Johnstone off picture, on the left

Monaca Sportsmen's Club

> Organized in Nov 15, 1939.
> Affiliated with the Beaver County Sportsmen's League.
> They met once a month in the Monaca Polish-Alliance hall.
>> *First officers were: Ralph Aumack-President; Frank Sephton-Vice President; Arthur H. Brown-Secretary/Treasurer*

Beaver Valley Sportsmen's Club – 698 Calder Avenue (1956) - 1001-A Grant Street, Monaca Heights
1930 - current

> Organized -   Aug 1930. Meetings were held in a rented one room building 698 Calder Street
>> which served as the club house.   Jun 2, 1934 became incorporated by the State of
>> Pennsylvania.   Purpose of promoting sports and protecting fish and wildlife.
> In Jun 1934, the club was incorporated by the State of Pennsylvania.
> Ladies Auxiliary was organized Mar 8, 1939.
> Nov 1939 - purchased the ground and building of permanent club home.
>> (but still had 698 Calder Avenue address in 1956 in an ad -???? --- maybe just the
>> ladies were still using the old rented room then -?????)

> *First officers were: Jerry Conners-President; Daniel Liston-Vice president; Elmer Gantz-Secretary; Daniel Slater-Treasurer; Frank Rambo, Hugo Elder, and Charles Herman-Trustees.*

2015

Harmony Lodge, No. 56, Order of Italian Sons of Daughters of America
> Organized Dec 10, 1932.
> They held their meetings at St. John's Catholic Church hall.

The Sons of Italy Lodge No. 1348 / Loggia "Colombo" No. 1348 – 1115 Pacific Avenue
        Instituted Jan 18, 1925 – held meetings in St. John's Hall.
        1926 – constructed a building at 1115 Pacific Avenue.
        1953 – enlarged building adding new social and club rooms.
        It fosters a sick and death benefit and maintains an orphan's home.

        Charter members were: Charles Alexander, Frank Pacciti, and Joseph Setting

Wahl Street would be a few houses down to the left of picture
where Pacific Avenue now ends.

_____

Monaca Veterans of Foreign Wars Post 4653   aka   Monaca V F W
1945 to 2014
        Organized in 1945.   The Post disbanded in 2014.
        The first building was erected at the corner of Seventh Street and Pennsylvania Avenue / 701
                Pennsylvania Avenue.   This original building was razed with the redevelopment project
                of Phoenix Glass in 1979/80.   They moved to a building at 310 Sixth Street.

BCHR&LF
It was located on Pennsylvania Avenue and Seventh Street, then...

At 310 Sixth Street (corner Washington Avenue and Sixth Street).

_____

Polish Falcons of America – Nest No. 87 – 1098/1099 Pacific Avenue
                aka   Polish National Alliance/Group No. 841 –1752 Pennsylvania Avenue
Nest No. 87 of the Polish Falcons of America and the Polish National Alliance
        Group 841 were organized jointly in Rochester – Jan 13, 1907.
1924 – these organizations moved to Monaca.
Feb 16, 1931 – the Falcons became a separate organization.
The purpose of the organization was to promote better social conditions among the Polish
        people in America.   They carried a sick and death benefit insurance and maintained
        their own Junior College and Technical School at Cambridge Springs.
Had the Polish Women Alliance of America No. 594.   Was instituted Jan 14, 1930.
The first meetings were held in the home of Frank Pietrowski; plans were made to provide their
        own meeting place. They purchased properties on Pacific Avenue.
In 1940, the club had their meetings held at 1099 Pacific Avenue.
                o   This building was purchased from the ZNP organization in Jan 1958.
        This building was the former first St John's church building (which was built in 1888) and
        was moved to 1099 Pacific Avenue to be used as the Polish Falcons building in c1930s.
The Polish Club building was beside the Nu-Way Cleaners. All were razed as part of the Phoenix
        Glass expansion project.   (Would have sat almost across the street from the current
        (2015) S.O.I. building on Pacific Avenue).

DANCING
THIS SATURDAY — 10 P.M. 'TIL 2 A.M.
'Lil Ronnie and his Carousels
Special Guests "The Jumping Jacks" From Buffalo
Polish National Alliance
MONACA—MEMBERS & GUESTS INVITED

1967

The organization made their next location at 1752 Pennsylvania Avenue (by Swink Autos)
        This occurred in approximately 1957. (In the 1940s it was listed as the location of the roller
        skating rink).

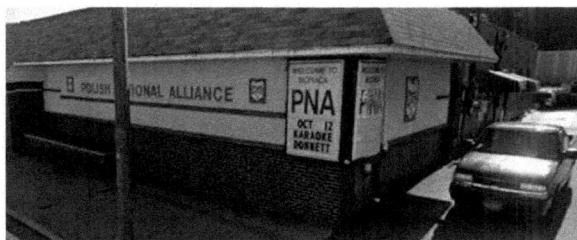
facing Pennsylvania Avenue in 2014

Swink's Auto   building was razed in 2015

This is a photo of the original church building that
was moved to Pacific Avenue and became the Polish
Falcons club building.

*First officers were: Julian Olozewski-President; Stanislau Staszkiewic-Vice
president; Jan Zimiting-Treasurer; John Tomasze-Financial Secretary; Jan
Korecki-Recording Secretary; Michael Balamut and Michael Zrodjeliski-Trustees.*

Center Township Grange – 125 Center Grange Road, Center Twp.
Organized Jan 19, 1921.   This group first met in the Simon Field School house.
New hall was built and dedicated Aug 4, 1926.   H. C. Hartenbach donated the property for the
Grange.   The Grange sponsored annual local fairs. First known as the Produce Show,
but the name changed as additional attractions were added each year.

 2015

Center Youth Club
Organized Aug 1939.   A social organization made up entirely of Grangers.
Meetings were held each month in the Grange hall.

*** *** *** *** ***
*** *** ***

ATHLETICS / SPORTS

Opalite Park aka   Monaca Park - was located in East Monaca
1902, 1909, 1911, 1913, 1919, 1922

It took up almost a whole block.
- —width wise….. beginning at Eleventh Street (on track side) and went toward a bit past Wahl Street (2015 – about from Fountainhead Café to about Main Street Barbers).
- -Depth…..from Pennsylvania Avenue to almost the railroad tracks.

All type of sporting events were played on this area/field from baseball to football.

Large community events and many other affairs were also held here.

The Monaca football team used this park in 1908.

Apr 24, 1913 – local league team completed work on the new bleachers at Opalite park
- Max Barnett, Pennsylvania Ave, was erecting a backstop at Opalite park for the benefit of the local league team.

In Jul 1919, an article stated "at the Opalite grounds, recently known as Monaca park."

In Sep 1922, the park was still referred to as Opalite park.

In 1919, there was a parade that started at Sixteenth Street and Washington……went on Washington to Sixth St…Sixth Street to Pennsylvania Avenue…Pennsylvania Avenue to Opalite park.

Prior to Nov 1922 - The property was sold and was to be used for building purposes.

Property at the foot of Fifteenth Street located on the river bank was to be seriously considered for new site.

Twelfth Street is here for orientation purposes.

Eleventh Street is here for orientation purposes.

To orient where the park was once located……the pointers are showing Twelfth Street (at the very top left corner) and Eleventh Street (the bottom left). Pennsylvania Avenue is printed and the railroad tracks can be seen on the top right corner.   The third pointer indicates the field area.

Colonial Steel Field / Colonial Field –
1931, 1948, 1953, 1954, 1965

     1937 – high school team played on "the Monaca Heights field" – where was that -???

     In 1940, for the centennial celebrations, it was stated that a lack of a field was the reason there
          would be no celebratory baseball game.

     Curiously, in 1945 it was referenced as "the old Colonial Steel field" -???

     It was stated that it wasn't used extensively for baseball for several years and had to be cleared
          of trees and brush, scraped and dragged and would be in fine condition by Jun 9, 1945;
          with a back stop erected and foul posts installed.

     As of 1945 in addition to the Colonial Steel field, there was also the Sportsmen's field and the
          Colona Heights field.

     In Apr 1953, the Monaca street department was instructed to move the portable department
          from the high school's football stadium to the Colonial Field prior to May 4.   These
          portable bleachers were evidently moved at will between the football stadium and
          Colonial Field since in the spring of 1954 permission was granted for 1 ½ sections of the
          portable bleachers to be moved to the Colonial field again for the summer.

     Dugouts were constructed in Apr 1953.

     A 1963 article stated that the Monaca recreation Board leased a 5-acre site of Stone Quarry Field
          along Ridge Road in Colonna Heights for making a permanent recreation area. The field was
          to be used by recreation soft ball league. The property was near the Marshall Road School – 20.8
          acres.   Stephen Phillips Homes are now located in this area.

The field was reconditioned in the spring of 1964.

*** *** *** *** ***
*** *** ***

Clubs and Teams

In the early years of Monaca, there were many different clubs and just as many different sports teams that formed in Monaca. If pictures of any athletic club building were found, they have been included in this category or with the listings of Organizations.

There were MANY different clubs and teams throughout the years, too many to actually list.   Many were just teams that formed from different men living on specific streets, some from different types of businesses, others were from various organizations.   I listed just a couple that were found more frequently mentioned than others to give readers an idea of what there was for the athletic minded to be involved in.

There was the *Monaca Athletic Club* which had semiprofessional players, as did other Beaver County areas. 1903 to 1922

1907 – (Aug) Colonial Steel Works - baseball team.

1911 – football team called the Monaca Scholastics.

1913 – (Apr) – Monaca Regulars.

1913 – (May) – Monaca Lyceums – believe they were a baseball team.

1922 – (Sep) – baseball team was called *Monaca* and it was in the *Beaver County Baseball League.*

1922 – (Sep) – there was another county league called the Harry Davis A.C. of Monaca.

1922 – (May) – Monaca Orioles.

Monaca Athletic Association

1911, 1928   The object of this club was to develop the weak and provide pleasant hours of recreation for the strong.   The hall had rooms in the basement of the Keystone building. They had various gymnastic appliances set up and a well-equipped reading room.

_____

Young Men's Christian Association

Started their first baseball team in 1904.   They had many athletic teams while associated in Monaca.

_____

Monaca Athletic Club

1903, 1904   Had a football team that played surrounding area's teams at the Opalite Park. They also had a baseball team who used the Riverview Park in 1904.

_____

Pastimes Athletic Club

1906, 1907   Played games with other local towns' teams.

_____

Rag Time Athletic Club of Monaca

1901

_____

Colona A.C.

1922

_____

Monaca Southside Club – 612 Pennsylvania Avenue

1920s to 1940s

This club had a semi professional football team in the Pittsburgh district.   Although the club is said to have disbanded in 1925, there were articles stating that they were still holding games into the 1940s - ? –   Their club house became an apartment building situated between the S & S Garage and the current American Legion.   This building was razed with the Phoenix Glass revitalization project.

_____

The list of the many, many different groups that supported the athletic persons/events which came and went over the years could go on and on.   Many of these athletic organizations did not have designated buildings for their groups.

*** *** *** *** ***

As stated in the section on bridges, the Monaca-Rochester Bridge aka Rochester-Monaca Bridge was an object of bragging rights depending on which team was considered champion. Even the announcements of games between the two teams would reflect the rivalry:

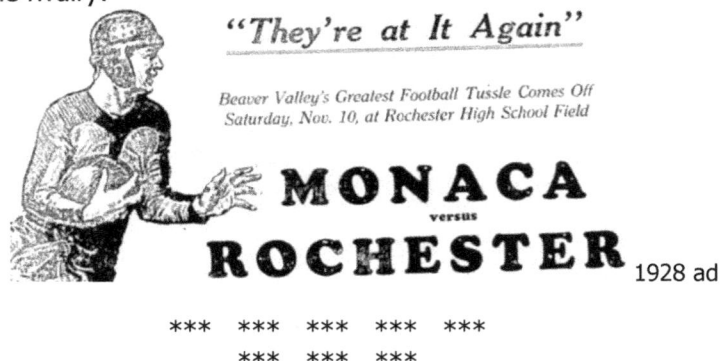

*** *** *** *** ***
*** *** ***

Noted Athletes of Monaca

This list in no way depicts all the athletic persons of Monaca. Since there could be a separate book put out on all the persons from Monaca who excelled in athletes, in this book, you will find I have only highlighted a fraction of these athletes.

Tom Alexander – was a three-year football letterman; he also lettered in basketball and baseball while attending Monaca High School. He continued his football skills while attending Bucknell University. Tom served in the US Army in Europe and played football while there. He began a 23 year coaching career in 1965; he was head football coach at Center and a line coach at Hopewell and Ambridge.

Don Bailey – he never played on any level of organized baseball but yet he was known as "Mr. Baseball" in Beaver County from 1941 until he died at age 77 in 1974. He started his occupation as an umpire at the age of 13 in Ohio. He officiated throughout Beaver County. Don is tied to Monaca because he opened a photography studio in Monaca.

Stan Berkman – he played three sports in high school while at Monaca, but was known for a long and successful career as a high school basketball, football, and baseball coach. He was a quarterback at Slippery Rock State College and the University of Pittsburgh during the 1920s. He then coached basketball and football at Monaca High School from 1935 to 1944. He moved on to be head basketball and football coach and assistant baseball coach at Wilkinsburg High, then going to Clarion. He left Clarion to become superintendent of schools at Baltic, Ohio, where he died at age 70 in 1974.

Paul Bowser – once famous wrestler – began in Monaca 1908 and retired in 1915
Known as "the Beaver Valley Whirlwind"
In a 1912 directory, Paul had wrestling listed as his only occupation.
Paul and Beryl lived at 999 Washington Avenue

Lenny Clarke – played basketball at Monaca under Larry Bruno in 1950s. Lenny then played as a guard at Geneva College. After college, he spent a year as an assistant coach at South Side H.S. before going to Grove City High School where he also coached golf.

Brad Davis – played very well for Monaca High School. In junior year at the University of Maryland, he applied for the NBA draft and was taken by the Los Angeles Lakers. In 1980, Brad signed with the Dallas Mavericks and played with them for the next 12 years, named most popular Maverick five years in a row. He retired in 1992. He was the first player in franchise history to have his number retired.

Edward J. "Mickey" Davis – was an outstanding basketball player while at Monaca High School. He continued on to Duquesne University where he received considerable recognition. He played both guard and forward while at Duquesne; opted to forgo his senior season and signed with the Pittsburgh Condors. He was picked up by the Milwaukee Bucks in 1972; they released him in 1976. Brad and Mickey Davis were brothers.

Dick Deluca – was a guard and lineman while attending Monaca High School. He went on to play nose guard on defense and an offensive lineman with Penn State Nittany Lions. He became assistant football coach at Freedom and Rochester; was also a baseball umpire from 1978 to 1995.

Bruce Fleming – earned eight varsity letters in sports while at Monaca High School; 4 in Basketball and 4 in football. He broke the school's all-time leading scoring record previously held by Brad Davis. Bruce went on to the University of Miami where he continued to play football as a linebacker. Upon graduating, Bruce became a teacher and coached junior high football and basketball in Arizona.

Jerry Ford – starred in football and baseball at Monaca High School and at the University of Pennsylvania. He was named athletic director at Penn in 1953, a position he held for 14 years.

Mark Grater – played both basketball and baseball while attending Monaca High School. While in college, he earned awards for his pitching ability. He signed with St. Louis in 1986 and continued in his career of pitching until he signed with the Cardinals as a pitching coach in their system in 1997.

Franklin Hood – had his career from 1919 through 1931 in football. He played for teams in Monaca, went to an all-star team in Texas and played for the Univ. of Pittsburgh. He also played one season with the Rooneys of Pittsburgh.

Jim Irons – started his career in basketball with Monaca High School. He played for Geneva and on into independent leagues until the age of 40. He played both basketball and football while at Monaca. Jim coached basketball at the high school level for 16 years and was named Coach of the Year several times.

Adam Karcis – played high school sports for Monaca and became a collegiate star at Geneva College. He coached a variety of sports at Rochester Jr. and Sr. high schools for 31 years before retiring from coaching in 1982.

John "Bull" Karcis – member of the New York Giants professional team. He began his football career at Monaca High School in 1923 as a lineman and a fullback position, receiving All-County and All-District honors. After playing for Carnegie Tech, Bull played a year of semi pro and in 1932 made his debut in the National Professional League with the Brooklyn Dodgers. He played for this team from 1932 through the 1935 season. He was transferred to the Pittsburgh Pirates at the start of the 1936 season and stayed with Art Rooney's club until 1938. He was then traded to the New York Giants. He was still under contract with the Giants in 1940, was married and living in Pittsburgh.

Chris Lindsay – career in professional baseball.   He began to play baseball as a boy and even at a young age he became such an excellent player that he had an infield position with a fast independent club in Beaver Falls in 1900.   He played with this team for three years and then played an infield post on the famous Homestead Mill team in 1904. Even though the Homestead club was not officially in organized baseball, many players moved from there directly into the Big Leagues, including Chris. He was sold and then played for the Detroit Tigers in 1906; then to Indianapolis in 1907 & 1908; sold to Denver in 1909 where he spent the remainder of his baseball career.   He was forced to retire from baseball when he suffered a broken leg in 1913. Chris began as a third baseman early in his career, but while with Indianapolis and Denver, he played first base and other infield positions.   His home was on Virginia Avenue.

Mike Linkovich – was a basketball star at Monaca High School before serving in the Army from 1942 to 1946.   Mike became the head trainer at Bowdoin College in Maine, worked at the U.S. Olympic Training Center at Colorado Springs in 1979 and served as a trainer in the 1980 Winter Olympics at Lake Placid, NY.   He was recognized as one of the top trainers in the country and was inducted into the National Athletic Trainers Hall of Fame in 1982.

Alex Makowiecki – played the position of tackle while at Monaca High School. He attended Geneva College and then won a scholarship at Florida State University.   After serving in the military, Alex returned to play sports again, but a severe knee injury ended his football career in 1957.

Dave Nichol – he starred in football, basketball and baseball while attending Monaca High School.   Dave was a quarterback for two years at Geneva College and Tarkio College in Missouri.   He then was long time coach of both a baseball and basketball for Monaca.

Ernie Pelia – in 1936, Ernie dropped out of school and enlisted in the Army at the age of 16.   He began boxing while in the Army.   In 1937 Ernie returned home when the Army discovered he was too young to have enlisted. He then played football for Monaca High School but quit the team in 1939 to concentrate on boxing. Although he never won a major professional championship, he still fought many of the best national and local fighters before retiring in 1948. Ernie died in Dec 2002.

Otto Pritchard –was an excellent basketball player for Monaca High School and also for Geneva College.   He returned to his alma mater as a teacher and took over basketball coaching duties for the 1958-59 season.   He coached for the next 15 years.

Paul Pupi, Dr. – he starred in both football and basketball at Monaca and also played baseball in the 1950s.   He attended Geneva College and earned 4 letters in football, 4 in baseball, and two in basketball. After his football career, Paul practiced general, thoracic, and vascular surgery.

Jack Pyecha – played baseball while in Monaca High School. While a freshman in college, Jack signed a professional baseball contract with the Chicago Cubs as a pitcher.   Arm trouble ended his career in 1955.

Matt Raich – brother to Mike, was quite involved in sports and served as an assistant coach for the Pittsburgh Steelers.

Mike Raich – brother to Matt. While attending Monaca High School in the 1950s, he played football, basketball, and baseball.   He received a scholarship to Cornell Univ. and was a three-year starter for their football team. He earned various honors in football over the years.

Bill Reigel – He had a very successful career as a basketball player at Monaca High School.   He played basketball all through his college years, earning various titles.   After college, he played for the Louisiana AAU and Goodyear AAU Cagers from 1957 to 1962.   He became a coach in 1957 for the Louisiana AAU team and completed his coaching career in 1978 at White Cloud High where he was also an English teacher.

Alex Scassa, Sr. – was raised in Monaca and then resided in Rochester and Beaver Falls for many years.   He began boxing in the 1920s with Teddy Yarosz as a sparring partner.   He became a trainer, manager, and second of boxers.

Leland Schachern – He became a star quarterback and safety of the Geneva College football team in 1920, 1926, and 1927.   He took a break in his education and came back to be a coach for Monaca, went back to Geneva, then became coach at Aliquippa, Hopewell, East Liverpool H.S. and also at Geneva. He coached baseball for 18 years at Beaver Falls High School and became head football coach there between 1943 and 1952.   He resigned as both a coach and teacher in 1964.

Jos. Schachern – a professional baseball catcher in the later 1800s
Jos. was the father several sons who inherited some of their father's athletic abilities.   Merle was well known in Monaca and another son, Leland was a Monaca high football coach.   Jos. played professional baseball with the New Orleans, LA. Club in the summer of 1889.   He also played for clubs in the following order: New Haven, Conn.; Austin, Texas; Portland, Oregon; Johnstown Club; Danville, PA; Austin Texas-as catcher and manager; Lansing, Mich.; Battle Creek, Mich.-as manager; Hornellville, N.Y.; and Baltimore, MD of the old National League. He was forced to quit after an injury to his knee; the injury was so bad that he was advised by the specialists that his leg may have to be amputated.   He returned home and took a very long rest period and the knee injury healed well enough to permit him to play with the old Water Cure Lodge team of Monaca in 1903.   His home was at 1106 Atlantic Ave.

Howard S. Shanks – He started his baseball career as a catcher in Monaca and was shifted to outfield.   His baseball career covered about 32 years; 14 of those years in the major leagues.   After high school, he played with two semi pro clubs.   In 1911 he was signed by the Washington Senators and in 1912 he was pinch hitting for Dixie Walker in the big leagues.   He was a regular in May 1912.   He played every position except catcher and pitcher.   In 1922 he suffered a broken finger and by 1923 he was traded by the Senators to the Boston Redsox.   In 1926 he was traded to the Yankees. His active playing career ended in 1926.   In 1928 he went to Cleveland as a coach and utility player under Roger Peckinpaugh.   Between 1934 and 1938, Howard was out of baseball, but in 1938 he was managing a Beaver Falls club of the Penn State League and in 1939 was coach and manager with New Orleans of the Southern Assoc.   Howard was married to Wilhelmina Wagner who spent a lot of time traveling with her husband.

Al Vlasic –after setting records while playing on the Monaca Indian's team, he became one of the many Monaca natives who starred on Geneva College Basketball teams.   Al served in the Marines from 1942 to 1945 and played service basketball in China.   He also played with the Philadelphia Spas on a national tour with the Harlem Globetrotters.

Huber "Hube" Wagner / Dr. J. Huber Wagner – became one of Pitt's all-time players. He graduated from Monaca in 1910 and began college at the University of Pittsburgh that fall, establishing himself as a star there.   He played every position except quarterback. He was elected to the National College Football Hall of Fame in 1973. Upon graduation, he became a prominent surgeon in Pittsburgh, retiring in 1975.

Hal Woodeshick – once pitched a perfect game at Monaca High School.   He played six seasons of minor league ball and in 1956 started with the Detroit Tigers. Before retiring, he pitched for the Tigers, the Houston Colts (Astros), the Cleveland Indians, the Washington Senators, and the St. Louis Cardinals. He was a relief pitcher for the St. Louis Cardinals in the 1967 World Series (who beat the Boston Red Sox in seven games).

Eddie Yarosz – older brother to both Teddy and Tommy was on his way to a career in boxing also.   When his father died in 1926, Eddie was 19 years old and had to assume the family responsibilities. He gave up his own career, but became a manager and trainer, developing his two younger brothers, too.   Eddie was born in 1907 and died in 1974.

Teddy Yarosz – former world middleweight boxing champion.   Teddy was Monaca's most famous living athlete until his death in 1974.

Tommy Yarosz – was the younger brother of Teddy, although he never got a title bout, he compiled an impressive record.   The Yarosz family resided at 1516 Pennsylvania Avenue.

Larry Zigerelli – he starred in basketball at Monaca from 1973 to 1976, also lettering in baseball. Larry then went to Yale where he was a point guard and had a very successful basketball career at Yale.

Bill Zopf – graduated from Monaca in 1966 and starred at Duquesne University. He then played a season with the Milwaukee Bucks in the NBA. After being drafted into the National Guard, he rejoined the Bucks but was released.

*** *** *** *** ***

HOW YAROSZ AND DUNDEE COMPARE

The Champion

The Challenger

VINCE DUNDEE

TED YAROSZ

Sep 1931 ad

1934

Local Folk See Fight Pictures

Beaver county fight fans and followers of Teddy Yarosz, Monaca boxing idol and new middleweight champion of the world, witnessed the showing of moving pictures of his championship fight with Vince Dundee at the Oriental theatre, Rochester, Friday and today.

While it lacks many of the characteristics of the original fight staged Tuesday evening at Forbes field, a good blow-by-blow view of the fight is afforded.

The theatre patrons settled in their own minds at least the fact that Yarosz won the fight by the big lead piled up in the early rounds.

Reports that moving pictures of the title fight would not be shown in the Roxy Theater, Monaca, published in a Pittsburgh newspaper, were branded as false today by the theater manager. The fight pictures will be shown at Monaca next Wednesday and Thursday.

Howard S. Shanks

FUN FACTS AND SNIPPETS OF INFORMATION

Monaca man becomes director of Buhl Planetarium

Mr. C. V. Starrett was born in Monaca in 1899. He served in France during WW I, had a bachelor's degree in English from the University of Pittsburgh, and was a former director of the Buhl Planetarium from 1940 until 1964. Mr. Starrett was also the president of the Western Pennsylvania Historical Society from 1969 to 1979. He died early in 1989 at the age of 90.

Beaver County "part time resident" advocated for Daylight Savings Time

Robert and Eliza Garland emigrated to American with their family in 1877 and all settled in Pittsburgh, Allegheny County. Why am I mentioning this Allegheny County family and/or Center Township residents you ask..... One reason is that a very small portion of the property owned was considered in the Boro of Monaca. Another reason is that one of the original owners to the property purchased by the Garlands was formerly that of James Welch who owned and operated the Welch Brick company and the clay mines in the area, as well as to give some back ground to a few of the "part time residents" - one credited with being the father of daylight savings time in the United States.

Two of the Garland sons, John W. and Robert, wanting to escape the pollution of the city, found the area that is still known as Sylvan Crest to be a very desirable place for their summer homes. Beginning in the early 1900s, Mr. Welch and family sold their home and moved to Pittsburgh. A brother-in-law to John W. and Robert Garland, Robert Tener, purchased the home and property and was using the home as a summer retreat. Once the Garlands eventually owned the entire elevated area, local residents and enumerators began to call it Garland Heights. The Garlands named their summer estates' area Sylvan Crest and this name was retained by the developers of the housing project after the Garlands sold their land; the name just seemed to have been passed down through the years.

Robert and John W. Garland and Robert Tener all married Bailey sisters. The three men's wives came from a very prominent and wealthy family and then the men themselves built their own fortunes with business transaction over the years. Robert Tener was the first to have his summer estate on this area of land; he purchased the former James H. Welch 15 room, 2 storey buff brick mansion. John W. Garland was the next to purchase acreage, built his own mansion/summer home (also 15 rooms). R. W. Tener sold his home to John W. Garland and then Robert Garland purchased John W.'s former home. All these mansions and estates were strictly "secondary" homes where the families held many social gatherings and events.

While R. W. Tener and both Garland brothers continued to prosper in their industrial occupations, Robert Garland had many other interests; he was invested in the betterment of Pittsburgh and held many offices, and he had long advocated the advantages of advancing the clocks one hour during the summer months in order to take advantage of the longer period of daylight. Through his efforts, the Boreland bill in the Congress of the United States was enacted into law on Mar 18, 1918; therefore giving him national recognition as the American father of Daylight Saving time. In one his addresses on the subject, he included the following information which I chose to include for those who are interested or to those who may say "why do we have to change our clocks":

Mar 7, 1917, Robert Garland addressed the Washington (PA) Board of Trade with the advantages of implementing daylight savings time.

Daylight Saving, in a nutshell, is to put the hands of the clock forward one hour simultaneously throughout the country in the different time zones, this to be accomplished by act of Congress. Thus, while the working hours are, for example, from eight to five, under this principle one would still go to work at eight by the clock (seven o'clock sun time) and would quit at five by the clock (four o'clock sun time). Those who work until six P. M. would still quit at six by the clock, but at five by the sun, the advantage being that one more hour of daylight would be enjoyed.

The ancient Romans divided their period of daylight into twelve divisions of equal length, which they called hours, and according to the time of year these hours varied from about forty-five to seventy-five minutes each. The various occupations of the day were arranged with reference to sun rise. The Romans welcomed the rising sun, and shut their doors and turned their backs on the setting sun. They were very early risers. A school-boy was often on his way to school, munching his breakfast roll, by the light of a lantern.

Many men got up in the middle of the night to start the day's work.

The result was that the Romans accomplished a great deal of work in a long morning, leaving the afternoon for recreation, exercise, and care of the health. In the afternoon, the prominent men of the day invariably took exercise. They usually played ball, something akin to our modern tennis. We read of one man who, at seventy-seven years of age, walked four miles daily and played a vigorous game of ball, afterwards taking a warm bath, a cold plunge, and a rub down. It is therefore no wonder that the ancient Romans could indulge in a good dinner, as according to all accounts they generally did.

In the Merry Wives of Windsor, we find Shakespeare saying, "We burn daylight." So far as we can find it recorded, it was Benjamin Franklin, however, who first in a practical manner called attention to the burning of daylight, our own Franklin, who wrote: "Early to bed and early to rise Makes a man healthy and wealthy and wise."

What I found more interesting than who helped introduce Daily Light Savings to the area, was that once it was introduced, not every area, town, or even company/business had to accept or use it. What do I mean – well – In Apr 1922, Ambridge, Woodlawn, and Aliquippa were working on Daylight Savings; Ambridge was the first of these three to adapt. But not all towns in the Beaver valley were as willing to change. Jones and Laughlin plant in Woodlawn waited till the moment to vote to also use the plan. Rochester turned down the daylight saving proposition. Although the whole Borough of Monaca did not change to Daylight Savings – Phoenix Glass Company and Pittsburgh Tool Steel Company did decide to operate under the plan. Can you imagine the confusion with getting to and from work in a timely manner!

BCHR&LF

John W. Garland built this summer home, then after purchasing the former Welchmont home from his brother-in-law Robert Tener, he sold it and it became Robert Garland's summer home in Sylvan Crest. This picture is from c 1970s/1980s. The front of the house faced the Ohio River.

BCHR&LF

This was the entrance to the former Welchmont home and then the Garland estate. This was the only way to access these summer resorts and homes and the area when first named Sylvan Crest. When new roadways like Wagner Road and Stone Quarry Road gave access to the area, this roadway was no longer used and just seemed to almost totally disappear, especially after the improvements and additions were created to Rte 18, coming from the Beaver Valley Mall into Monaca. This entrance was removed with the improvements to the main highway; it had been about 100 yards south of the railroad tresstle as you were leaving Monaca; behind the photographer of this old postcard would be the viaduct and beginning of Pennsylvania Avenue.

(There is extensive information and additional pictures on these families and the estates in my book on Center Township.)

So think about Robert Garland next time you pass by the Sylvan Crest area or have to reset your clocks - *Spring Ahead* or *Fall Back.*

*** *** *** *** ***

*** *** ***

PEOPLE AND FAMILIES

Miscellaneous

In doing researching, I found this very early marriage Phillipsburg/Monaca:
In the Beaver Argus – Nov 7, 1834 edition
Marriage –

  "In Phillipsburg, on the 2d inst. By the Rev. Mr. Daubort, Mr. Jacob Wagner to Miss Christiana Haet."

————

FIRST GROUP OF SETTLERS TO THIS AREA

I am repeating this information which is listed in Vol. I.   Listing it again will give some clarity to why some of the families are being listed below.

In 1795 the Greenville Treaty was signed, making safe the settlement of the Northwest Territory. One of the last acts of the old Continental Congress was the passage of the "Ordinance of 1787." This defined the manner and form of land grants in this territory.   Questions of ownership became a leading problem since much of the lands involved were already possessed by individuals from the first wave of settlers who were capable of purchasing large tracts for exploitation.

Many of this first group of settlers to this vicinity were of the family names:

Blaine	Baker	Bruce	Quinn	Temple	Tod(Todd)
Srodes	Phillips	Graham	McConnell	Potter	LeGoullon

Phillips and Graham holdings were purchased by Maximillian who brought in the Germanic group from Economy in the very early 1800s.

Many of the names from this group of families were:

Authenreith	Frank	Fath	Lay	Lais	Trumpeter	
Schaefer	Knapper	Davis	Shule	Schmidt	Zutie	Erb
Hahn	Heydil	Fischer				

Of these, some spread over the farm lands, but the majority settled in Phillipsburg and were dominant families until the coming of the industries.
Another group of family names that either came from Economy later or came directly from Germany were:

Botts	Blatts	Bimbers	Bechtels	Erbecks	Ackers	Huffs
Merkels	Markeys	Bickerstaffs	Vollhardts			
Muellers (Millers)						

Sampling of Prominent People / Families

There were references and information available for the following families, so I wanted to share what I found.   My goal for this publication was to go back in time and show the diverse amount of businesses and trades from Phillipsburg and Monaca and not to do a genealogy study of the residents.   Since I do enjoy doing genealogy and family trees and had the following information available, I found no reason not to share.   Please understand that the names of individuals and/or families below are by no means close to being the only prominent families of Monaca, they are just ones that I easily found available information.

Acker

Dr. Edward Aug. Acker of the Water Cure Sanitarium

> He was b Jan 8, 1809 – d Oct 25, 1853   He is buried in the German Cemetery, Monaca
> Married first to Mary Haskell; they had 6 children.

Dr. Acker's first wife must have died close to 1850 by the birth of a son in 1848 and she is not listed on the 1850 census.   He married 2nd to Widow Christina Smith (or Schmidt) Wagner and they had 2 children, 1 surviving—Louis Acker who became a druggist in Allegheny County.

What a shame......Christina found herself widowed a second time by 1853 and now had NINE children (Acker and Wagner) with her ranging from ages 19 years to 6 years old!   Christina had given birth to the last child shortly before she had to bury her 2nd husband.   All 9 children were living with her on the 1860 census.   Christina never married a third time, and by the 1870 census, all the children had moved out except the youngest, who at age 16 was still living with his mother.   Over the years, she also had to bury eight of the children she either gave birth to or raised as her own from Dr. Acker's first marriage; some quite young, and others not seeing much of their adult life.

Mrs. Christiana Smith Wagner Acker – b 1818 Germany– died on 28, 1905. She had been the oldest resident of Monaca at the time of her death and the last member in Monaca of the original Economites who seceded from the Harmony Society at Economy, coming to Phillipsburg in 1832.   She was living in a house on Atlantic Avenue, where she had lived since 1839; it was once used as a headquarters by Count de Leon.   She was also a pioneer member of the German Lutheran Church in Monaca.   She married first to Simon Wagner and they had 4 children.   Simon died between 1845 and 1850.   With her 2nd marriage to Dr. Edward Acker, she became step mother to 6 more children.   Then she had 3 more children with Dr. Acker – one dying in infancy.

Christiana and Simon Wagner's daughter, Wilhelmina was married to Phillip Lay.

> Phillip was a shoemaker in the 1870s.   They had 4 children.
> Wilhelmina was also a widow by 1900.   She was living in the house beside her mother in 1900; by 1910, she was living on Fifth Street.

―――――

Allen

John J. Allen – b Ireland; he married Elizabeth Weiley and they had 3 children.   John J. became a well-known doctor in Monaca. He married John Armstrong's daughter Jeannette (Nettie). Nettie was an accomplished musician and art student.   They had 2 children. John J. was 3 months old when his family came to America from Ireland.   Dr. Allen began his practice when Monaca was still known as Phillipsburg.   He was one of the strong supporters of a bridge being erected in Monaca and was a stockholder in the bridge company.   He served on the school board for 7 years, held a position on the poor board; was a member of the staff of the Beaver Valley Hospital. John J. belonged to Royal Arcanum; Woodmen of the World; Knights of Pythias; and Rochester Masonic Lodge.

―――――

Barnett

Morris Barnett was born in 1863 and married Anna Bernstein b 1865.   They had ten children.   The Barnett family members all moved from Monaca to surrounding areas, most settling in the Pittsburgh areas about the 1920s.   Morris and Anna were most likely living above their storeroom on Pennsylvania Avenue in 1900.   When they were living in Monaca in 1910, Morris was a proprietor of his own clothing store and was evidently providing for the family nicely since they soon owned a home at 799 Indiana Avenue (free of mortgage) and had a servant living with them.

Morris was in business with "Jimmy" Davis at Pennsylvania Avenue and Eighth Street – a general store that opened in 1887; but was destroyed by fire in 1893. Morris Barnett and James M. Davis were among the first of the businessmen in Phillipsburg/Water Cure/Monaca.   In 1893 Morris built the large two storey brick building for his own clothing/department store.   This store was located on the corner of Ninth Street and Pennsylvania Avenue and had an address in the 800s Pennsylvania Avenue.   (It would have been located on one of the corners leading into Phoenix Glass Co.) Max, Morris's son, joined in business with his father (see further). In 1906, son Harry opened his own small storeroom in the same building and sold shoes.

There was an ad in the May and Jun 1917 papers stating Morris Barnett was closing out the Monaca store and would only have the Rochester storeroom on Brighton Avenue (it was next door to the 5 cent and 10 cent store there). Morris retired from business in 1935 and resided in the Pittsburgh area.

Harry, s/o Morris, married and they were living with their children and his wife's parents in 1920.

Max H, s/o Morris, was born in Monaca and was a clerk in his father's clothing store from a young age.   In 1910, Max joined in business with his father. Max owned a home at 808 Indiana Avenue prior to moving to Rochester in about 1930.   In the fall of 1914, he rented the lower storeroom of the new Campbell's building in Rochester and moved his store room there; his younger brother, William, took charge of the Barnett Shoe Store in their father's building in Monaca.   Max married and they were living in Rochester where he had a shoe store.

At age 21, Max was elected a member of Monaca borough council; in 1911, that meant he was the youngest councilman in the state of Pennsylvania.   As a member of council, he was on the light and street committee and in 1913 the old street gas lights were abolished and replaced with electric lights.   Max was a veteran of WW I.

William Barnett, s/o Morris, was born in Monaca. He was associated with the Barnett Shoe store in Rochester and the Quality Boot Shop in Beaver Falls, too.   William never married; died in 1946.

————

Bechtel
George Bechtel was born in Germany where he learned mercantile business. He came to America in c1863 and at the age of twenty first settled in Pittsburgh. When he came to Phillipsburg, he engaged in mercantile business, keeping a general store.   He married first to Emelia Knapper (d/o Anthony Knapper). She died shortly after they married.   His second wife was Mary Miksch; they had 2 children. George filled several town offices. (See Knapper further.)

————

Biddle
Robert Biddle lived on Atlantic Avenue and an article on him stated he was 83 years old in Sep, 1911.
He followed the river for years, coming to Phillipsburg/Monaca in the mid 1860s from W. Va. In the 1870s, Robert gave up his career as a river man (due to the railroads entering Monaca), and he began to do gardening on a large scale (20 acre garden), supplying New Brighton and Beaver Falls with his produce. He served two years during the Civil War in the Transport Service. He married Mary Hayward.   They lived in a house on Atlantic Avenue, overlooking the river. Robert is credited with planning and developing Phillipsburg east of Ninth Street.

————

Bimber
Henry Bimber was born in Germany. He came to America in 1854, settling in Phillipsburg.   He returned to Germany in 1870 on the occasion of his father's death; remaining there until 1884.   He married Josephine Acker (d/o Dr. Acker); they had four children.   Henry was a teacher in the German school of Phillipsburg, listed as a lumber merchant, and was an active worker and superintendent of the Sunday-school.   The Bimbers lived at the site of the Veterans Home on Pennsylvania Avenue.

————

Blaine
Ephraim Blaine was a Virginian. He served in the Revolutionary War. Previous to coming to Phillipsburg. he served at Valley Forge, then with the Eighth and Thirteenth VA regiments, came to Western PA to help in forts against Indian attacks.   He received a conveyance of a parcel of land called "Appetite" from William A. Lungen as early as 1769. He secured the title to the land in 1787. Appetite became the land that Monaca now sits on.   Ephraim later removed to Brownsville where he died some years later.

————

Blasche

Wenzel R. Blasche was born in Austria and died at age 96 in the fall of 1981. He lived at 701 Atlantic Avenue; a resident of Monaca for 78 years. Wenzel owned and operated the Blasche Barber Shop for 72 years, retiring in 1975. He learned the tonsorial trade from Paul Mattauch of Pennsylvania and Fourth Street, and was employed with him until 1909 when he opened his own business. He married and had 7 sons and 4 daughters. Fritz Blasche, Wenzel's son, was also in the barber shop business and had his own business in Monaca. He was born in Monaca and died at age 84. He also had his own barber shop and was self-employed for over 61 years on Pennsylvania Avenue. It appears that Fritz never married.

————

Blatt

Aug. F. Blatt married Margaret __, both were born in France. They first settled in Pittsburgh after immigrating to America, then came to Phillipsburg in 1853. They purchased a frame house at 387 Atlantic Avenue (which their daughter, Sophia, occupied until her death). This building had once been the Strumm Tavern and is still standing today. They had 5 sons and 2 daughters.

————

Emil Bott

Emil was born in Wurttemberg, Germany, in 1927 and was brought to America by his father, Aug. Bott. Aug and Emil were part of the group that came to Phillipsburg with Count de Leon. Emil grew up and received his schooling in Phillipsburg. He returned to Germany to study painting, then returned to America several years later. Emil taught drawing in a private school in New Brighton from 1848 to 1856. Many people started to notice the work he was doing and an 1849 Pittsburgh newspaper wrote an article on him making comments and giving high praise of an oil painting he did. Bott was hired to make a painting of an area near Beaver that Marcus Gould and others were planning to develop. Before the years of the Civil War, Bott moved from Phillipsburg to Pittsburgh and had his first exhibition of his art work in 1859 in the first show of the Pittsburgh Art Association. Emil was proving to be a successful artist and had a downtown studio between 1865 and 1867. Emil's art works could be found in different places in Mississippi and even on packet boats that traveled the Mississippi River, most likely because he sold them on the river fronts to boat passenger stopping at the different ports.

Before leaving Phillipsburg, Emil married Emma Bocking and they had Clara, and two other children who unfortunately died within a few months after birth in 1861 and 1862. Clara was one of the first five students to graduate from Thiel College while it was located in Phillipsburg. He returned to Phillipsburg about 1880, buying a home on the lower portion of Atlantic Avenue so he could watch the river and paint. Emil became crippled as he aged; even with the aid of a cane, he walked with great difficulty. Emma died in 1899; Emil died Feb 17, 1908; both are buried in the German Lutheran Church cemetery. Only five paintings are known to have survived as of 1983 even though he completed many of his wonderful art works. Two of these could be found in the New Brighton's Merrick Art Gallery – one of a man walking in the moonlight and the other of the upper Beaver River. Penn State University's art gallery also has a Bott painting of the upper Beaver River. The remaining two paintings were last known to be at the Westmoreland County Museum of Art in Greensburg (of the Ohio River-Lake Erie Canal and canal boats) and as of 1983, a local Monaca man had *Fenterman's Crossing* which was of the upper Beaver River in 1850. Mr. Batchelor did the majority of the research found here on Emil and accumulated quite a collection of information on Emil and his life and art work.

Though not printed here in color as it was originally painted, here is a black and white copy of the 1850 – Beaver River Landscape and a picture of Emil.

————

W. M. Boyle

Mr. Boyle retired from the Colonial Steel Company May 1, 1907. He was born in 1847 and started work with the Colonial Steel Company in 1863 when he was only 15 years old. He retired after 45 years with the company. He purchased a nice farm along the Montour road in Allegheny county and planned on spending the remainder of his days in peace and quiet on this farm.

_____

Brown

Capt. Joseph Brown was born in Switzerland in 1826 as Josef Gigande. He came to the Pittsburgh area in 1843, later settling in Phillipsburg. He died in 1884 at Phillipsburg. Joseph was one of the pioneer river men, a steamboat pilot. I imagine his name was difficult to pronounce in America, so he changed it to "Brown." Joseph married Thirza Schaefer (d/o Jacob and Catherine (Staiger Schaefer) and they raised 5 children in the Brown home. This brick home was built in 1837, at the corner of Sixth Street and Washington Avenue; it was last home of the VFW hall. Joseph became employed in the boating business, first floating rafts, and later as a pilot and master of riverboats. He was a pilot on the U.S. Ram *Lioness* (gun boat) during the Civil War. He had a license that extended from Pittsburgh to New Orleans. Capt. Brown was instrumental during the Civil War with both himself and Capt. John Shrodes in assembling the eight boat ram fleet by Memphis, Tenn. When the battle ended, the Confederate boats withdrew and the river was opened to the Union forces. Joseph's boat, the *Lioness*, was the first boat to pass the blockade.

_____

Bryan

James P. Bryan was the former "village smithy" back in the horse and buggy days. He was the son of John Bryan of Hookstown. He learned his trade at the Patterson-Blackmore blacksmith shop and worked in Clinton, Bavington, and Midway before coming to Monaca. James's old blacksmith shop was razed in the 1930s. He became owner of the shop in 1901 which formerly belonged to Justus Merkel in 1840 and became the business of William Wagner and his brother-in-law David Fisher. James closed the shop in 1915 when he became elected Sheriff of Beaver County. He re-entered his profession which he then carried on until 1926. In 1927, the Bryans moved from Monaca to Beaver where he became the post master. John B. Potter, a general building contractor and liveryman in Monaca was James' first customer back in 1901.

_____

Burry

Jacob Burry started his business in Phillipsburg, as a barber, on Aug 2, 1881. He was still following this business as of Sep 1911. In 1911, Jacob was the oldest living business man in Monaca.

_____

Carey

Daniel Carey b 1827 married Adaline. Adeline was a widow with three children when Daniel married her. He was a farmer in 1850 and they were living in Moon Twp. In 1860, they added 2 boys and 2 girls to their home. In 1870, Daniel was still a farmer and they were still in Moon Twp. but only had 3 children with them. Daniel was a retired farmer in 1880, 53 years old; both he and his wife had moved and were living with one of the children on Fourth Street in Phillipsburg (now Pennsylvania Avenue).

In 1900, their son, Martin was in the grocery business, living on Pennsylvania Avenue and his father, Daniel, was living with them. 1910 – Martin and wife were still in the grocery business. 1920 – Martin was widowed and still had all but one of their children living with them. Martin was still a grocer and running the store at age 79 in 1930. A directory indicates that in 1931, M. W. Carey still had the business. The 1940, 1941, and 1942 tax lists show no Careys at 899 Pennsylvania Avenue (location of the store and residency; but, Minerva Dress Shop was listed at #899.

The grocery store that Martin owned and operated was located at the corner of Ninth Street and Pennsylvania Avenue (899 Pennsylvania Avenue). The store was very familiar to everyone and the Careys were such a noted family in Monaca that the location became known as "Carey Corner." After the death of Martin, the store was owned by Max Sobel and called Sobel's Quality Clothes (in 1940s). After Sobel closed the store, it became known as *Monaca Inn/Monaca Hotel* and was known for its friendly atmosphere and good foods.

_____

Davis

John Marston Davis – b 1818 Monaca, s/o Samuel and Anstis (Day) Davis – first married to Mary (?) and they had 9 children – 3 sons and 6 daughters; all living with them in 1860 and 1870.   By 1880, his wife, Jennie, had died and only one daughter was living with him in Phillipsburg.   He then married again after 1880 to Jennie Taylor Wilson.   John M. was a shoemaker by trade and known in the community as "Yankee" Davis.   The family lived in a frame house on the hillside that became the approach to the bridge over the Ohio river.

John M.'s son, Millard F. Davis – b 1848, married Anna A.; they lived at 900 Pennsylvania Ave; had 5 children.   In 1870, while still living with his parents; Millard F. was a cigar maker and was still in that trade in 1880 after he married.   In 1900, the census states his occupation as *day laborer*.   In 1920, Millard was 71, he had a new wife – and only one son living with him; he was working in a glass plant, as was the son.   In 1930, at age 82, Millard was finally retired; he had a son and daughter (and her family) living with him.

_____

Davis

This Davis family was most likely not related to the previous (John M.) Davis family.   This family migrated from the Philadelphia/New Jersey area.   Tracing back farther than 1756 with William has proved difficult and with there being no further ties to either family over the years, my conclusion is that there is no connection – but I have been proven wrong may times ☺   William Davis b 1756 d 1834; a Revolutionary War soldier; married second to Izabella Scott; he fathered 10 children.

John Davis – b 1804; lived in Independence Township, then Moon Township; married Margaret Flanegin.

They had 12 children.   One of those children was Henry Davis who lived in Moon Township.   Henry's son James McLean Davis, not wanting to farm, moved to Monaca and began his own business.

James owned and operated a confectionery and ice cream parlor on Pennsylvania Avenue.   "Jimmy" started in business with Morris Barnett sometime between 1886 and 1887, but in 1893, the building they had on Pennsylvania Avenue and Eighth Street was destroyed by fire.   Morris then built a large brick two storey brick building on Pennsylvania Avenue (near Eighth Street) and began his own business.   "Jimmy" bought a new building and had many improvements made to it over the years ---- Dec 1900, enlarged the store, put up new steel ceilings and repainted --- Apr 1904, had a new box sign placed out front ---- Oct 1906, added three new show cases in the front.

Although Jimmy Davis had a few properties in Monaca, he was a boarder in either the Hotel of Cimotti or the Central Hotel in 1900.   He suffered a severe stroke of paralysis in mid Aug 1907 and was taken to the home of his uncle Hugh Davis in Moon Township (Center) and another uncle, Dr. Smith Davis of Pittsburgh, was called to come and attend to him.   James unfortunately never recovered and died.   Charles (Charley) Lindsay was employed by James M. since 1901 and conducted James' business until after the estate was settled.   Harry B. Barnett of Monaca bought the building and business (Harry already had a clothing and gent's store in Aliquippa, but conducted both businesses).   The building James had for his store was listed as one of the oldest in Monaca.   It became the property of James Hicks and was eventually razed in May 1927.   The property the building sat on was owned by the Wagner heirs.

_____

Dietrich

John E. Dietrich was born in Germany in 1841.   During the Civil War he engaged in making boots and knapsacks for the Union army.   For a time, John stopped the manufacturing of shoes and engaged in the liquor business.   He moved to Monaca in 1884, returned to his trade and had his shoe business at Eighth Street until his death in 1907.   John was married to Anna C. (Truber) Dietrich in Germany and they came to America in 1847 settling first in Allegheny County.

John's son, George, Sr., was born in 1880 in Allegheny County.   He apprenticed to learn the plumbers' trade.   George then rented in the rear of his father's business building on Eighth Street and started a plumbing and heating business.   After his father's death, George, Sr. converted the shoe store into his plumbing business. George, Sr. then moved the business to 817 Pennsylvania Avenue.   George's sons, George, Jr. and John took over the plumbing and heating business; it remained in the family for over 85 years until George, Jr. sold the business in 1984 about a year after his brother John died.

_____

Dockter

George Dockter was born in 1835 in Germany; he married Eva Elizabeth Ebert. They were living in Butler County in 1860 and soon moved to Moon Township (Center), purchasing a large farm. They had 7 children. Eva and George still had their farm in Moon Township in 1900. In 1910, George was widowed, living on his farm and had his 90-year-old sister and one of his sons with him; he still listed his occupation as *farmer* even though he was 75. By 1920, George was 84, retired, and living with his daughter in Moon Township; whether this was his property or his daughters, I am not sure.

The Dockter farm was located in the far side of Monaca Heights and when the property was sold and divided into lots it became known as Dockter Heights. A few of the streets in the Dockter Heights area are Grant Street, Speyer Ave, Kay Ave, some of Bechtel Street.

Eckert

John H. was born in 1828 in Germany and came to American in 1843. John H. first owned a farm in Economy Twp. and then went into butcher business in Pittsburgh. In 1868, he purchased the house and farm where his house stood in Monaca. The Eckert house was at the top of the Eckert Road, Fourth Ward, and gave a splendid view of the surrounding towns in the valley. John H. and Charlotte (Koerner) had 9 children. John H. was widowed in 1920 – age 92 and living in the same home.

A few of their children remained in Monaca and established their own well-known businesses:

Henry J. became owner of the Monaca Rolling Mills.

Henry's son - Charles R. Eckert became a prominent attorney. He married Clara H. Wagner* of Monaca. Charles moved to Beaver where he then had his law office with Mr. Sohn.

*Clara was the d/o Christian and Philipena (Wagner) Erbeck and gd/o Jacob Wagner – all well-known and respected Monaca residents.

Erbeck

Christian Erbeck was born in Jan of 1835 in Germany. He came to America about 1917 at the age of 19 and followed his trade of saddler and upholstery in Pittsburgh and Rochester by working in car shops. Christian married Philipena Wagner; they had 4 children. He retired from this business due to health reasons and did farming and butchering in Moon Township, eventually giving up butchering and only engaged in farming. His wife, Philipena was the daughter of Jacob and Christine Wagner of Monaca. They lived in a large frame house, now razed to make room for a service station at Fourth Street and Pennsylvania Avenue. Christian was a member of the town council several times and was also a member of the school board for 15 years. Christian and Philipena are buried in the German Lutheran Cemetery in Monaca.

Fischer

George Fischer was one of the original settlers in Monaca, when it was still Phillipsburg. Their son, Christian Fischer, Sr. was born on the high seas in late 1818 as his parents were sailing to America from Germany. Christian came to Phillipsburg and was employed as a river man. He married Anna Barbara Schroeder and they made their home at 609 Washington Avenue that they purchased in 1854. Christian and Anna had 4 children. One of their sons, Christian, Jr. was a partner of his brother-in-law William Wagner in the hardware business.

Folland

Peter and Mary Folland were longtime residents of Phillipsburg/Monaca, living in the same home since 1855. Their homestead was an old frame house at the corner of Pennsylvania Avenue and Fourth Street, built by seceders from the Harmony society. Mrs. Mary Folland was still alive, at 80 years old, in 1911. She came to America from Germany when only 3 years old. She lived in Uniontown until she was 15, then the family moved to Monaca. She first lived on Pennsylvania Avenue, formerly in a house near the present home on the corner of Pennsylvania Avenue and Fourth Street. When being interviewed about growing up in Monaca, she stated that she watched the town grow from a group of crude huts to become a noted town in the county. Her husband, Peter followed his

---

trade of wagon-maker.   Mary and Peter reared a family of three sons and three daughters.   Mary's home was originally intended and built for a large granary, a store house of crops harvested by the Harmony society pioneers. Since it was too large for the purpose intended, it was soon afterward converted into a residence.   There were heavy rafters, hewn from giant oaks, which supported the ceilings. A wide hallway extended from the front to the rear entrance. On either side of the stairs were two big rooms with high ceilings.   Every nook and cranny showed the care and precision the builders took in their work.

_____

Frank

The Frank family has the distinction of being not only among the founders of Monaca, but also of being one of the families and earliest settlers of the United States.   Rheinol Frank was one of the original Economites, coming to Monaca in 1832, eight years before the town was incorporated. He married a lady named Catherine "Kate" Raup Frank and withdrew from the Economite Society, settling in what is now Monaca.   Rheinol and Kate had ten children.   Reinhold/Rheinol stated he was a farmer, even in 1870 at the age of 71.

Their son, Edward Frank, was born in Monaca in 1851.   He married Jennie Wilbur of Pittsburgh and they had three children. Their home was on Pennsylvania Avenue.   Edward followed the trade of stone mason.   He was born in a house at the corner of what was back then First Street and Garden Street – now named Atlantic Avenue and Fifth Street.   To add to the great distinctions, Edward's wife, Jennie was a direct descendant of William Bradford, second governor of the Plymouth Colony of Massachusetts.

_____

Hahn

Leonard Hahn was born in 1823 in Germany and emigrated to America with parents. The family joined the Economite Society when Leonard was quite young.   Adulthood brought about "love" into his life when he met Katerine Scheid of Pittsburgh.   The Society had laws stating that any person unmarried must remain so or sever his membership, so.........Leonard left the Society and he came to Phillipsburg with his new wife where they had seven children. Their son, Henry, was in the furniture business all his life with Joseph I. Reno. (Predecessors to Batchelor Furniture Company.)

_____

Hamilton

Oscar Hamilton was born in 1829 of Beaver County; he married Catherine Craig; they moved to Monaca in 1884. Oscar and Catherine had 7 children.   Their son Samuel was a well-known resident of Monaca for many years. He taught school for several years and then became a painter for at least 15 years in Monaca.   In 1903 Samuel erected the Hotel Hamilton on the corner of Pennsylvania Avenue and Twelfth Street.   The former hotel building is still standing today (2016).

_____

Harbison

George J. Harbison was born in South Beaver Township. He married to Ida Bell Wentworth of Pittsburgh. They moved into the old Anshuts house at Third and Buffalo Streets in Beaver.   A few months later, they moved to 901 Pennsylvania Avenue and made this their home. At ages 71 and 70, they celebrated their 50th anniversary in 1932. George was in the general contracting and building business as well as serving three terms on Monaca council and four terms as a member of the Board of Education.

George J. was awarded many of the contracts for erecting and remodeling many of the building in Monaca over the years. Since he was a carpenter, I am sure that George built many of his own investment properties in Monaca since the Harbisons owned many homes in Monaca.   A few of these included – one on Indiana Avenue and Tenth Street (#1001) and the house right beside it, one on Tenth Street, their house at 901 Pennsylvania Avenue and the two adjoining properties (these were located between Ninth Street, going toward Phoenix and the Municipal Building – 2015).   When George died, all the properties owned by the Harbisons in Monaca were being sold by 1944.

_____

Herbert

Carl Herbert came to Monaca in 1911. He started in the wholesale liquor business in Pittsburgh for 10 years before coming to Monaca. He became the proprietor of the Hotel Monaca. He married Mary Kuth and they had 4 children.   It is apparent that Mr. Herbert had great interest in the welfare of Monaca and must have been well informed; his suggestions and opinions were held in regards because there was one publication that stated......"*Mr. Herbert is a factor to be reckoned with in the political affairs of the community, and his opinions are listened to with deep interest and close attention.*"

Hughes

Andrew Hughes settled in Monaca in 1880 and took a position in a brick yard for 3 years, then was employed 8 years at Phoenix Glass.   In 1901 he fulfilled his desire and opened his own very successful grocery store at 1416 Pennsylvania Avenue.   He built and owned the store (which in 2016 has the business *Geared Up* occupying the building). He married Ida Radcliffe and they 2 children.

Hunter

William Hunter was born in 1850 in New Sewickley Township. At age nine he left home, worked as a farmer laborer for three years, then on a canal for a season, afterward learning the carpenter's trade.   He followed this trade until 1880.   In 1880, he took a contract to build the Phoenix Glass Works.   William stayed connected with Phoenix Glass; after the original building burned in 1883, he erected the next structure and was a foreman in the etching department.   He married Barbara Bloom and they had eight children.

Irons

James A. Irons was born in 1837, the son of Hopewell residents John and Ann (Moore) Irons.   James was a blacksmith before and during the war.   He served on the ram "Lioness" on the Mississippi as an assistant engineer and blacksmith. While he was in Virginia in 1870, he served for three years as a local minister of the Methodist church; in 1873 he was in Washington and was a sub-contractor on the James Creek Canal for six months.   James returned to Phillipsburg after the war and followed his trade on a part time basis because he became active in the real estate business.   He was justice of the peace beginning in 1883 and served multiple terms as burgess.   James married Margaretta Quinn (granddaughter to William Quinn) and they had four children.   He belonged to the Equitable Aid Union and the Rochester Post G.A.R.

Jackson

Thomas Jackson was born in 1826 in Brighton Township. His parents moved to Industry Township when he was very young.   Then the family moved to a farm in Moon Township. Thomas farmed this property until later in 1900 when he sold the land to Colonial Steel Works, Monaca.   He married his wife, Melinda, and they had three sons and one daughter.   Thomas and Melinda were living on Atlantic Avenue in 1911.   Their son Thomas S. lived and helped work the family farm until later in 1900 when he built his own grocery business on Pennsylvania Avenue; married Florence S. Cummings and they had a son. By 1920, Thomas no longer had his grocery store and was working in one of the mills.

Jolly

Dickerson A. Jolly was born in 1826 in Washington County, Ohio. He worked on his father's farm as a young lad.   When still living with his parents in Ohio in 1850, the census had him listed as a *boatman*.   He had been a resident of Monaca since 1851 and steam boated on the Ohio River before the Civil War.   He began as a deck hand and finished his river career as a mate after railroads crippled traffic by boat.

When he first came to Monaca, he lived in a small house on Eighth Street, which is referred to as "the lower end of town."   After he retired from his river boating career, he accepted a position as toll man at the Monaca end of the Rochester Monaca bridge, and after 3 years at this job, he retired permanently.   D. A.'s first wife died in 1856.   He then married to Ellen __ by 1860. Dickerson A. Jolly was also a toll collector in 1902/03 according to the Monaca Directory and he was living on Atlantic Avenue at that time.

D.A. was very well known for the Jolly Bakery that was run from their home at 216 Sixth Street.   With such a successful business, he never listed himself as a *baker* for his occupation on the censuses, but rather either a *river mate* or *toll keeper*.   He no longer had the bakery business in the early 1900s.

From his marriages, he fathered 7 of the 9 children living with D.A. and Ellen.   In 1860, I deduce Ellen had previously been a widow because the children with them were listed with a different last name.   On the 1870 census, along with all previous children to the couple, there were 4 more children listed.   He was living with two of his daughters on River Road in 1900; then with a daughter on Washington Avenue in 1911 at age 85.

Kaye

David Kaye was born in 1859, son of David Kaye.   He married Ida Hogan and they had 3 children.   He worked as a glass blower in the Phoenix Glass Works until 1906 and then became the postmaster of Monaca until he died.   Mrs. Kaye became the assistant post master.   In 1900, he established "The Only Drug Store" remaining an active manager of it until 1906.   The Only Drug Store was located at the corner of Sixth Street and Pennsylvania Avenue, then relocated in the Keystone Building by late 1903.   After David died, Ida remarried continued to live in Monaca.

David's son, Walter D. Kaye helped at his father's drug store.   Walter became the manager in 1905, then bought the business from his father and was a pharmacist on 1910 census.   Walter married Lucy Marg Kidd who died in her mid-twenties.   He was widowed and had moved to Beaver Falls and working as a pharmacist by 1920.

David Kaye

Kemmer

Adam Kemmer was born in 1850; came to America in 1866 and settled in Pittsburgh; then moved to Monaca.   Adam was a tinner by trade.   He owned and operated a hardware store on Pennsylvania Avenue.   He owned quite a bit of property on Pennsylvania Avenue.   Adam married Elizabeth Littinger and they had a daughter.   After Adam died his wife and daughter continued to conduct the business.
Their daughter, Elizabeth married Christopher Lindsay who was a carpenter and professional baseball player; they made their home at 1101 Indiana Avenue.

Kerr

Thomas G. Kerr was one of the early residents in Phillipsburg.   He was employed by Phillips & Graham as a blacksmith building boats.   He moved with the company to Freedom when the land was sold.   The 1850 census shows him living in Freedom beside the Charles and John Graham families; age 41; an *accountant*; married to "Grizzy;" they had two sons who both became ship carpenters.

Knapper

Anthony Knapper was one of the early settlers to the Monaca area.   He was a trustee in the organization of the New Philadelphia Society.   After Maximilian departed, Anthony was chosen as one of the four trustees to manage affairs of the community when it dissolved.   (The other 3 trustees were Adam Shule, Jacob Wagner, and Jacob Schaefer.)   He was a merchant and had his business and home on what is now Fourth Street (in the vicinity of the Monacatootha apartment building's parking lot).   His home eventually became known as the *Bechtel home*.   Anthony was also the postmaster of the town from 1858 to 1877.   There are no official documents to reference, but it is presumed that Anthony died in 1877, as his son-in-law, George Bechtel succeeded him as postmaster at that time (George held that position until 1881).

Koehler

Paulus E. Koehler was born in Apr 1856 in Germany.   Paulus chose the trade of decorator of porcelain. He immigrated to the United States in 1881, went to Ohio, and then settled in Monaca about 1883 where he took a good position with Phoenix Glass Co.   Paulus had the honor of decorating the first piece of work ever turned out by the firm.   Paulus was a brilliant scholar. After the fire at Phoenix in 1884, he started a shop of his own, doing work for various glass firms. He built the first clay kiln ever constructed for firing decorated glass; the previous kilns had all been made of steel.   He reemployed with Phoenix until 1897 but gave up the profession due to failing health.   Beginning in 1897, he began to deal in real estate and had extensive real estate interests in Monaca.

Paulus was one of the organizers of the Citizens' Improvement Company, which was active in developing the interests of the community.   In 1898 he built the four storey *Hotel Monaca* (corner of Washington Avenue and Ninth Street) which opened in 1899.   He sold his interest in the hotel in 1905 and focused in dealing real estate. He purchased an 84 acre farm with river frontage formerly being the farm of Frank D. Barnes of Moon Township. This farm had good buildings, choice fruit trees, an excellent view of the Ohio Valley, and adjoined the proposed state improved road; was excellent for sub division.   (* the farm lots may have been what Nichols Wire & Sheet Company who moved from Rochester purchased when they moved onto Paulus E Koehler's property at Pennsylvania Avenue near Seventeenth Street (1923).   The company purchased 2 other properties, too).   The American Architect and Architecture Vol. 70 publication from Oct-Dec 1900 stated P. E. Kohler & Co. built a business building in Monaca but it did not state which building they meant.   By the date, it was most likely referencing the Hotel Monaca structure.

Paulus was a member of Monaca Council, Burgess, appointed Justice of the Peace, and was the tax collector in Monaca for 22 years.   He was also a member and/or officer in many social clubs – R.A., K. of P., Woodmen of the World, B.P.O.E, Syria Temple, A.A.O.N.M.S., and Masonic Order in Rochester Lodge.   He was a stockholder of the bridge company since he was active in his efforts to secure a bridge across the Ohio River.   Paulus married Mary Henrietta Schilling and they had 13 children; five of their children did not live past 1900.   They lived at 826 Washington Avenue (the remodeled house is still standing – 2016); it is right behind/beside the Hotel Monaca. Paulus purchased a lot and house from George W. Stoffel in Jul 1902.   With him so involved in real estate, it is difficult to know if it was the house at #826 or another one.   In 1930, their son, Howard lived right next door at 822 Washington Avenue and was a machinist with his own shop. (#822 is also still standing in 2016.)

Hotel   #826   #822
This is a view from Washington Avenue going toward Ninth Street.

Paulus E. Koehler

Lais

David Lais came to Phillipsburg in 1832. He lived with his mother in Lancaster County for a time, then came to Economy, later moving to Phillipsburg and they lived there their remaining years. He was born 1817/19; married Catherine Steinbach.   David was a weaver by trade and worked in the silk factory in Economy; he then learned the carpenter's trade.   They had 8 children.

Their son George H. Lais was born in 1841. He was a carpenter by age 16 and active in business as contractor/builder by age of 25.   He was awarded many contracts in Monaca; a few of them being in 1922-Ninth Street for M. Theil's Tailor Shop, Monaca First Ward School building in 1882, and even the Presbyterian Church in New Brighton.   George H. went west for 10 years, returning to Monaca in 1901.   He married first to Ellen Stewart and they had 4 children. After Ellen died, he married 2nd to Anna Butchly and they had 4 children. Once again he was a widower when Anna died; he married 3rd to Elizabeth Shaneman and had 3 more children with her. Henry and Elizabeth lived in the same building as his business at 714 Washington Avenue. The home was still standing in 2016 (corner of Eighth Street and Washington Avenue).   G. Henry had a successful business all his life, beginning c1870.

Eighth Street is on left - Washington Avenue runs in front

George H. Lais

Lay

George Lay, Sr. was born in 1819. He was one of the many young men who came to Phillipsburg with Maximilian. George married Mary Baker (granddaughter of Anthony Baker) and they had two sons. In 1850 George, Sr. was a shoemaker. In 1860, George, Sr. was a boot and shoe maker; his son Felix was in the same business. In 1870 and 1880 George, Sr. was a *laborer.* They were living on Third Street (became Washington Avenue) in 1880.

George Lay, Jr. (son of George and Mary) was born in 1844; he married Dora Letzkus and they had 2 daughters. George, Jr. was marked as *married* and NOT *widowed* on the 1880 census and the two girls were living with him at his parents' – no Dora though? I believe this was an error by the census person because....... On 1900 census it states George, Jr. was married in 1882 to Mary E. (they never had any children together).

In 1880, George operated a hotel and restaurant at the corner of Eighth Street and Indiana Avenue and was listed as a *saloon keeper.* This building was from then on referenced as the *Lay building*. It is still standing in 2016 – 800 to 804 Indiana Avenue. It served not only as a hotel and restaurant, but was used for school rooms, home to the Chess Club, and Charles Brown had his business out of the building (Charles was a *gardener* which means he probably sold produce). This same building is currently occupied as apartments. George, Jr. was a well-known citizen of Monaca. He served on the council and school board, was active in many borough events. He was president of the Monaca National Bank for 24 years, from the onset of its organization. George's obit stated he was a widower and his home was at 810 Indiana Avenue which is still standing next door to the *Lay Building*.

Phelix/Felix Lay (son of George, Sr. and Mary) was born in 1841. He married to Wilhelmina Wagner; they had 3 children. Phelix was a boot & shoe maker at age 19 in 1860 and again, a shoemaker in 1870. Their home was on Atlantic Avenue in 1900 and 1910 with Phelix listed as a mould maker.

Their grandson, George E. Lay was appointed postmaster in Monaca, 1934 and again in 1939 succeeding George Weinman. George E. was a councilman and served for 3 years before resigning upon his appointment as postmaster.

George E. Lay

LeGoullon

Francis R. LeGoullon was born in France in 1802. He married Ernestine Dorothea L. Hihne of Germany. They came to America on their wedding trip and settled in Phillipsburg in 1831, one year before the Economites arrived. Francis and Ernestine had 7 children.

Francis R. was one of 100 during the Civil War being appointed to look after the women and children of enlisted soldiers. He was the first Burgess and Justice of Peace in Phillipsburg and was the manager of the seminary. He was also known for his penmanship and wrote the first deed that was put on record in the Beaver County Court House. Francis R. was one of the first merchants, having a general merchandise store at Indiana Avenue and Fifth Street; he was owner for 50 years. (This property was occupied by the Sephtons in 1840).

Lindsay

Charles K. Lindsay was born in 1887; married Clara Dixon; they had 4 children. Charles first worked for "Jimmy" Davis, then owned the Lindsay parlors on Pennsylvania Avenue and was well known for his confections and ice cream. C. K. opened his own parlor on Pennsylvania Avenue in 1907. He also made a specialty of sporting goods. The Lindsays were living in Monaca in 1935; by 1940, their residence was in Beaver with his occupation still as *newspaper and confections.*

McCreary

Robert and Mary McCreary and family came to Monaca from Pittsburgh in Jul 1882. Their son, Thomas W. McCreary immediately became associated with the Phoenix Glass Company, starting to work there in Sep, 1882. Thomas started as a carry-in boy and progressed up the ladder within the company, becoming the vice president and general superintendent in the company by 1937. He became the chairman of the Manufacturers' Exhibit committee for the Monaca Centennial.

Thomas W. McCreary

McKinley

Dr. Andrew Stewart McKinley was born in 1881. Dr. McKinley came to Monaca and started his physician's practice in 1908. He was still in practice in 1956.

Mateer

The Mateer family was really from the Moon/Center Township area; but were also very closely tied to
Monaca with their businesses and other family members.
Michael Mateer was born in 1804; came to America in c1826 and lived in Pittsburgh. He was in the Monaca/Center area by 1832 where he owned a farm on Center Grange Road. He married Margaret (Rook); they lived in Moon/Center Township during their married life; Michael was a farmer. They had 7 children. Two of their children became prominent businessmen in Monaca; they had the Mateer Bros. Meat Market at 1000 Pennsylvania Avenue from about 1900 until the 1930s.

> James M. was born in 1878; he married Elizabeth Todd by the 1920 census. They had 11
> children. In 1930, James M. and Eliz. were living in Center Township with 10
> children and James was listed as a *butcher - cattle dealer.*
> John R. Mateer was born in 1876. He was a teacher in 1900. In 1902, John R. was in business
> with his brother James for quite a few years; had a meat market on Pennsylvania Avenue.
> In 1920, John R. was living with his sister and brother-in-law and family and he was listed as
> *proprietor of Meat Market.* John R. was married to the widow Clara Streit Miller and this family
> was living at Pennsylvania Avenue in 1930; John was still in the meat business.

Merkel

Justus Merkel was born on May 3, 1824 in Germany and died on Apr 20, 1907 in Monaca. Justus was apprenticed to learn the blacksmith trade while he was living in Germany. He came to America in 1847, landing in Philadelphia, migrated to Pittsburgh, and finally came to Phillipsburg in 1850. He lived in a brick house at 705 Pennsylvania Avenue, but has since been torn down. He operated the blacksmith shop on the corner of Eighth Street and Pennsylvania Avenue (this building has been torn down also). Justus spent his monies wisely and acquired a large amount of real estate. He sold portions of these properties from time to time and made considerable profit each time; then he would re-invest the profits. Justus married (first) to Margaret Mateer; they did not have any children. At age 71, he married (second) to Marie Elstner; he was over 40 years her senior; they had 4 children.

Miksch

Wenzel A. Miksch was a glass decorator and worked at American Glass Specialty Company. He invented a new process which was said to possibly revolutionize the art of glass decorating. He was a native of Bohemia where he received his education. In 1881 he came to America and located in Monaca about a year later. He remained in Monaca for 3 years, then removed to Pittsburgh in 1885 where he worked as a foreman for 13 years in the Thomas Evans Company (glass). While in Pittsburgh, he purchased 10 acres of land in Monaca.

Wenzel became one of the organizers of the Metropolitan Glass Company of Monaca and held his interest in the company from 1897 till 1898. At that time he went into partnership with his brother Charles Miksch, in the American Glass Specialty Company. Only two companies in American were using Wenzel's invention for decorating glass as of 1899. They built a new structure for the American Glass Specialty Co. in 1898 – two storey building, 26 x 90 feet. They had two kilns that operated on natural gas. By 1899, Wenzel owned the property and building of the American Glass Specialty Company, the building of the Metropolitan Glass Company, and the house in which he lived. He was a member of Germania Blue Lodge, Duquesne Chapter, F & AM.

James A. Miller

James A. came to Monaca with his family from Pittsburgh in about 1904. He was first employed by the United States Sanitary Manufacturing Company, then was an employee of the Monaca Borough for 25 years before ill health forced him to retired in 1939. He held the position of street commissioner, later serving as the day custodian in the municipal building after it was remodeled. Mr. Miller was very interested in the affairs of the borough and was one of the best-known residents of town. In 1940, at age 86, in spite of his illness, he sat on his porch on Atlantic Avenue and enjoyed all activities he could see.

Morgan

Silas Morgan died many years prior to 1900. He married Cassie Fischer (born in Monaca) and they lived in a four room structure on Fourth Street. She was the daughter of George Fischer, pioneer settlers of Phillipsburg. Silas and Cassie had 3 children. Cassie Morgan was 89 years old in 1937 and was living with her daughter and family. She was a lifelong resident of Monaca, being born in the First Ward; coming to live in the First Ward of Monaca continuously.

Fun note: Even at age 89, Cassie (Fischer) Morgan could read without the aid of glasses.

Murphy

William George Murphy was born in 1877 in Allegheny County He was a Superintendent of the foundry department of the US Sanitary Manufacturing Company for 6 years; then engaged in business independently.

Peirsol

Scudder H. Peirsol was born in 1828. He was first employed in 1856 by the government as the organizer and teacher of a school for the Wyandot Indians in Kansas. He returned to the area soon after the end of the Civil War and became principal at Soldiers' Orphans' School until it was destroyed by fire in 1876. Scudder then established Peirsol's Academy in West Bridgewater and conducted the same until his death in 1903. I find no evidence that Scudder lived in Phillipsburg or Monaca; his only connection was the orphans' school. Scudder married first to Elizabeth Weaver and they had 4 children. After Elizabeth died, he married Mary Maxwell Chambers. Mary was an assistant teacher at the Orphan's School); they had Scudder H. who became a doctor and practiced in Rochester after receiving his education at his father's academy.

Quinn

William Quinn built a log house on the slope overlooking the Ohio River on land that was occupied by the Sanitary Manufacturing Company. He raised flax and made rope. Commodore O. H. Perry was building his fleet on Lake Erie and bought all of William's stock and took it by ox team to the lake. William supervised all the work and was present at the battle, receiving commendation of the government. He eventually moved to Ohio to live out his life. William was buried with military honors. His daughter, Eliza, married another Monaca resident, John M. Shrodes (see Shrodes).

Schaefer

Jacob Friederick Schaefer was born in 1801 in Germany. He came to America in 1806 with his widowed mother and two sisters, then became a member of the Harmony Society, Butler County.   He learned the trades of carpentry, weaving, dyeing and machinery.   Jacob dyed the first silk woven in Old Economy (Ambridge), the colors of which are still bright more than 150 years later.   Jacob was born with a well-developed mechanical and mathematical mind, and the society found him most useful as a result.   Once he reached adulthood, he held many positions in town. When still the New Philadelphia Society, he was selected as one of the 12 trustees and then was on the committee to settle up its business when it dissolved.   Jacob was then one of the first 3 members of the town council, one of the first two school directors, a manager of the first woolen mill at Phillipsburg, trustee of the seminary; in general, Jacob had an active part in the building of the town. The *Schaefer House*, as it was known in those days, was at 609 Pennsylvania Avenue.   Jacob married Catherine Christine Staiger in 1832 and they had four children.   Jacob died at Phillipsburg.

————

Shrodes

The Shrodes family (spelling varies – Shrode, Shrodes, Shroads) left Strasburg, Germany; the father and mother died of "ship fever" and were buried at sea.   Coming with a William Penn expedition were also their sons, Jacob (see below), Henry, and William.   All three boys were bound out and raised by the Quakers.

Jacob Shrodes settled in Pittsburgh when it was still a borough. The majority of his family settled throughout Allegheny County.   Jacob married _?_ .

His son George Shrodes/Srodes married Mary Minor and they reared a large family.
Of their children --- George became a County Commissioner; Margaretta became the wife of John B. Potter of Monaca; and William was County Commissioner and Steward at the Beaver County Home.

John Shrodes/Srodes, Sr. was born in Beaver County in 1777 and settled in Beaver County; he died in Phillipsburg.   He was a soldier under Mad Anthony Wayne in War of 1812. He is buried in the old Baldwin Cemetery, east of Monaca. John married Catherine, the widow of Christian Hettick who was a great Indian fighter.   John and Catherine had 6 children.

Miscellaneous mentions of other Shrodes/Srodes family members.............

William G. Shrodes/Srodes was a designer, builder, and captain of steam boats. In 1845 the engine of the Monrovian blew up (one of the ships he designed) and Capt. Srodes was the only life lost in the explosion.

John M. Shrodes was born in Pittsburgh in 1809. He married Eliza Quinn; and they had 7 children.   After Eliza died, John remarried to widow Nancy Galbraith Chase (who died in 1892). John M. died of paralysis at his home on the Ohio River bank in Phillipsburg.   John M. was a boat pilot by occupation. He was a captain in the Mexican War and also a captain in the Civil War (in command of the U.S. Ram *Lioness*).   He later became owner of the Shrodes Hotel, which became the Point Breeze Hotel.   He operated the hotel for many years before selling it to Tommy Lee (who in turn sold it to Samuel Love in 1891).   John M.'s granddaughter related to others how he would tell the story about his childhood. This story was that he got angry at his brothers one day and ran away. He was captured by some Indians, and his brothers could not find him. Although quite young, he knew to pretend to like the Indians in order to escape, while in reality, it seems that he actually did enjoy living with the Indians since he stayed with them for two or three years. John M. finally did go back home when an opportunity arose to do so. He would sit and tell his stories about when he lived with the Indians and it is said that he would even teach their language, life, and customs.

John M. Shrodes

————

Shule

Adam Shule was one of the four trustees chosen to manage the affairs of the community after Maximilian left. The other three trustees were Jacob Wagner, Jacob Schaefer, and Anthony Knapper.   With no information to be found, it is presumed that Adam died childless as no trace of his family has been found.   He was quite instrumental in the development of the community.

————

Simpson

John Simpson was one of the last Civil War veterans in Monaca. He died at age 92 in 1936. He married Josephine __; both John and Josephine were born in Pittsburgh and came to Monaca in 1881.

————————

Taylor

William Graham Taylor was born in 1820, Pittsburgh. He became a Presbyterian minister, but took a job as asst. editor of a publishing co. After he became ill, he went to New England to recover. William returned to Pittsburgh for a while and was engaged in manufacturing and mercantile. He attended the ministry, then went to Beaver Falls to revive a church there. From Beaver Falls, he went to a church in Tarentum in 1861, then to Mt Carmel Church, Aliquippa. Mt Carmel had been without a pastor for twenty years and lacked unity.   Dr. Taylor restored harmony and left there with it in better condition. From there he revived another church in Pittsburgh. He was then called to Phillipsburg and the Soldiers' Orphans' School. He was appointed president, manager and superintendent. He donated $50,000 of his own money to starting up the school. When the school closed, he engaged in the real estate business in Beaver County. In 1897 he moved to Beaver and lived there until he died.   William married Charlotte Thompson and they had 8 children. *See Soldiers' Orphan School's information for more on the school.

————————

Trumpeter

John Trumpeter, born in Germany and died in Phillipsburg.   The family joined the Harmony Society where John learned the trade of a carpenter. He came to Phillipsburg with Maximillian in 1832. He married in 1832 to Agatha Wolfert/Wolfram. He married 2nd to Dorothea Fischer in 1843.

Gilbert Trompeter - s/o John and Agatha - was born in Phillipsburg in 1833. Gilbert was the one who changed the spelling from TrOmpeter to TrUmpter. He became a teacher in the public schools and engaged in market gardening. He also became the owner of a great deal of real estate and eventually was a real estate dealer.   He laid out the first plan of lots in Phillipsburg. Gilbert married Elizabeth Mechem; they had at least 12 children.....

Gilbert's son, Nelson was one of the organizers of the CAMMAR Bldg. and Loan Assoc. He was a borough council secretary, school board member, and auditor of the borough and school district. He married Emma Volhardt; then after her death, he married Fannie Scott.   He had a son to Emma, and then 4 children to Fannie.

Gilbert's son, John was engaged in market gardening with his brothers until 1901. The Colonial Steel Company purchased one of their farms, so in 1903 he established his own grocery business at 1299 Indiana Avenue and continued there until his death in 1934.   He married Emma Preece; they had 4 children.

Another son of Gilbert, also named Gilbert was born in 1869. He also engaged in market gardening with his brothers until 1901. The brothers used 5 wagons to deliver their produce.   He then entered into the real estate and insurance business at 1216-18 Pennsylvania Avenue which he continued until his death.   He married 1st to – Lydia Barton and 2nd to Marie Muller.

William Trumpeter, fourth son of Gilbert, was born 1876. Like his brothers, he was in market gardening with his brothers and 1901, he engaged in the grocery business and had his store at 1119 Washington Avenue.   He was later employed by the Standard Sanitary Manufacturing Co. and J. & L. Steel.   He became the first custodian of the Sr. High School in 1924 and remained as such until his death. He married Rosa Mabel Carey, d/o John Carey.

————————

Vetter

Alvin C. Vetter was the proprietor of the Sanitary Barber Shop in Sep 1911. This shop was located at the corner of Pennsylvania Avenue and Ninth Street.   In 1911, A. C. was also the corresponding secretary of the Barbers' Union of the Beaver Valley and secretary of the Central Labor Council of Beaver County.   Alvin was born in Pennsylvania about 1886; he married Yetta Holler; they had 3 children. The family lived on Atlantic Avenue in 1930 and Alvin's occupation stated *steel mill*.

————————

Volhardt

Henry C. Volhardt was born in 1825; lived in Beaver Borough in 1860 and came to Phillipsburg by 1870 where he was a ferry man and followed his trade of shoemaking.   Henry was married to Rosenia in Germany and they had 11 children. Henry C. drowned in 1880.

One of their children, William C. came to Monaca with his parents in 1863.   He worked on steamboats in 1969; took charge of the ferry after his father's death and operated it for about 35 years.   William sold the ferry business and engaged in the liquor business for 5 years, then was a yard foreman of the U.S. Sanitary Works for 7 years.   He also had charge of an ice wagon for a short time and started work with the American Specialty Company of Monaca in 1912.   William married Jessie Springer and in 1908 they built a house at the corner of Washington Avenue and Eighth Street.   They had 2 children.

_____

Wagner

Jonathan Georges Wagner was born in Germany and married Anna Marie Huber. They emigrated to American in 1804.   Jonathan and Anna had five children.   The entire family, except one daughter, came to Phillipsburg with the Count de Leon in 1832.

Their son, Jacob J. was born in 1801, and was but 3 years old while en route with his parents to America.   His parents and the children gave up their way of life and possessions and joined Father Rapp in the Harmony Society. He married Christine Heydl and they had 6 children. Jacob was one of the leading influences in the movement and settling of the New Philadelphia Society coming to the soon to be Phillipsburg.   The family finally settled in and lived at 403 Atlantic Avenue.   Jacob was a well-respected citizen.   He was selected for transacting business matters with the outside world; he was also one of the trustees to settle up the affairs of the New Philadelphia Society. He was also selected by the owners of the woolen mill as an agent and president, as well as holding offices in the church, school, and civic affairs.   He was a farmer all his life. Of their children:

Phillipena was born in 1835; married Christian Erbeck who was a saddler & upholster, then a farmer in Moon Twp.   They had 4 children.

Israel was born in 1842 in Phillipsburg. When of age, he first lived in Allegheny County, then in 1874 he moved to Moon Township and engaged in farming and stock raising. He was involved in the community also and served as supervisor and school director.

Another son of Jonathan, David was born in 1803; married to Catherine Zuntle, a former Economite. David and Catherine moved to Missouri where they raised 7 children. In 1862 they moved to Oregon where David died.   Most of his family remained in Oregon.   David was a locksmith.

A son of David, William was born in 1848.   While in Oregon, he learned the trade of his father, locksmith. William worked with his father in this trade until his father's death. At that time, he decided to travel to France upon an invitation from his uncle Jonathan where he planned to further his education in music.   William stopped at Phillipsburg to visit the cousins before leaving for France and he met Wilhelmina Fischer (d/o Christian Fischer).   After this meeting, he chose to stay in Phillipsburg; he married Wilhelmina and went into business with his brother-in-law, Christian Fischer, Jr.   William then purchased the Justus Merkel property cornering on both sides of Eighth Street and Pennsylvania Avenue, which included the former Merkel shop. David Fischer was working in the blacksmith shop at the time and he lived with William and Wilhelmina (his sister) in 1900. William and David eventually worked together in the blacksmith shop.   William and Wilhelmina had 8 children.   William was also active in public affairs serving on council, school board, and trustee of his church.

Their son, John Huber "Hube" was born in 1891 and spent his youth in Monaca. He then attended Geneva College and played on their football team. Col. Joseph Thompson, Pitt coach, had his eye on Hube and took him in. He graduated with credit from the medical course there; took a course in brain surgery in Philadelphia, and began his practice in Pittsburgh.

_____

Welch

James H. Welch was born Jun 1846 in England and came to America in 1867. He started the Welch-Bright Fire Brick Co., Monaca in 1878. It was one of the first big businesses in Monaca. James was the proprietor and general manager of the prosperous company. Bricks from his company were used in Madison Square Garden in New York City. He also owned a brick works at Vanport, PA. as well as being a member of the firm of Welch, Gloninger, and Maxwell of Welch, PA.

He owned a very nice home in Moon Township which stood upon an elevation above the town and was called "Welchmont" (the Sylvan Crest area). Not only did his home have an excellent view, he had acreage to go with it. He also owned a 354 acre dairy farm (Borie Twp.); it reflects that he evidently had wealth. James H. operated coal and clay mines beneath the hill where his home stood; as well as close to his large brick manufacturing plant. He married first to Lizzie J. Moffet, and they had 4 children; then he married #2 to Julia Beech, who gave him a son. James and family lived in Pittsburgh in 1880 and even at that time he was evidently doing well financially having a servant with them. In 1900, he was still providing quite well in the brick business since they had two servants living with them in Welchmont/ Moon Township. James, Julia, and family moved to Pittsburgh about 1905/1906; James was retired and their son became a salesman in the brick business by 1910. The home and property in Moon Township were sold. It was then used as a summer home by R.W. Tener and then John W. Garland before it eventually became known as the Valley View Hotel.

Photos courtesy Beaver County Historical Research and Landmarks Foundation

Front and rear views of Welchmont after it was converted into the Valley View Hotel.

James H. petitioned Monaca Borough for a street railway franchise and started the Monaca Heights Street Railway Company. James H. was the President, W. G. Moffett was the Secretary, and Fred Bechtel was the Treasurer. They were incorporated in 1903. James H. would have had an interest in this company being developed because he owned extensive acreage and had what became the Welch Plan of homes in Monaca Heights. I do not know much history of this railway company, but it was listed in various reports in 1903, 1904, 1905.

Zigercal / Zigerelli

Joseph Zigercal built the Zigercal Block building in 1909 at 1308 Pennsylvania Avenue. Joseph came to Monaca in 1901 and was a tobacconist and confectionery merchant. He was born in Italy; married Carmella Crebarr and they had 6 children. In 1920 he was listed as a merchant with a grocery business. In 1930, Joseph and some of his family were living at 910 Pennsylvania Avenue and he had retired from his business.

Joseph's son, John F. was a barber and owned his shop at 1414 Pennsylvania Avenue in 1920, 1930, 1940. John's son, John "Dud" lived his entire life in Monaca, was active in community affairs, Monaca athletics, became a teacher, then was principal in former Center Area Schools (now Central Valley).

*** *** *** *** ***

*** *** ***

ENTERTAINMENT and RECREATION

Nickelodeons

Theatres

Leisure and Recreational

Amusement and Picnic Parks

Swimming

Golfing

Roller Skating

Various other forms of entertainment

Nightspots /Recreational Sites

NICKELODEONS and THEATRES

Nickelodeons

The word "nickelodeon" comes from a combination of the admission cost and the Greek word for "theatre." Nickelodeons were the first to provide a type of exhibition activity held indoors and were dedicated to showing projected motion pictures.   Most businessmen interested in opening a nickelodeon did so by converting a storefront or portion of a storeroom into the small, simple theatre area.   They were most popular from about 1905 to 1915.

Example of more elaborate nickelodeon

Example of a small-town nickelodeon

European and American inventors, including the likes of Thomas Edison, had been working on developing movie cameras since late in the 1880s.   By the late 1890s, not only were the early films being viewed as peep shows, but methods to allow them to be projected onto a screen were being refined. With the growth of the number of nickelodeons opening and the demand for "moving" pictures, Henry Miles of San Francisco started to rent films which set the format for today's distribution system of movies.

These nickelodeon movies were no longer than 5 minutes, most often only 30 seconds to a minute or two.   These short films were not the highlight of a performance, they were called "chasers" and shown at the end of the live acts of slap stick comedians, animal acts, or freak shows that were brought in to perform as the main attraction.

A nickelodeon would offer several performances a day or evening; depending on its location and the population of the area, sometimes quite rapidly moving patrons in and out to accommodate the next group of customers. Along with the usual five cent admission charge, those in attendance were entertained with live piano or organ music accompaniment since all were "silent movies" at that time, not having the technology to have sound added to them yet.

Technology in the early 1900s was primitive.   Prior to the advancements made in more developed theatres, a projectionist in a nickelodeon usually use carbide tanks to produce light and water loaded with salt to conduct electric current.   The films themselves would be run through the projector and would pass out the front of the projector into a bag that hung in front of the machine.

Even though there are most likely no true nickelodeons to be found today, movie theatres and the films are now both so advanced and much more refined, that as with many inventions, the importance of those first storeroom nickelodeons will never go away.

Examples of the first movie projectors

Fun facts:

Pittsburgh is credited with starting the world's film industry in 1903. It all began in a dingy storeroom nickelodeon and the thrill of seeing moving pictures.

Harry, Al, Sam, and Jack Warner (the Warner Brothers) opened their first movie theatre in Pennsylvania in 1903, a converted storeroom, they named the Cascade Theatre, in New Castle. They were familiar with this area since they were living in Youngstown, Ohio, at the time. They showed movies that other people had made. This first theatre was so successful that they soon built /opened many more theatres in the United States. The brothers also began to make movies themselves to show in the many theatres they had built/owned. They revolutionized the film industry with the adding of sound to their movies.

The early movie studios were called movie "factories."

Nickelodeons were soon springing up across the country, including Monaca. They would usually offer live vaudeville acts and have the short films as the added attraction. It is said that by 1907, over 2 million Americans had made a visit to a nickelodeon. They remained the staple of indoor entertainment until being replaced about 1915 to the 1920s with what at that time were considered the large more modern theatres.

Monaca had their share of nickelodeons to entertain residents in the early 1900s. There was even one family of actors that lived in Monaca. I only found this family listed on the 1860 census though. They were all from the same family but there was no name of a specific nickelodeon or theatre they performed in or exactly what type of "acting" they actually engaged in.

Joseph Foster – age 60 – theatre manager
Louisa Foster – 35 – actress
Charles Foster – 34 – actor
Osman Foster – 27 – actor
James Foster – 17 – actor
Francis Foster – 14 – actor
Edwin Foster – 9 – actor
Ada Foster – 6 – actress
Julia Foster – 4 (not listed as an actress)

———

W. L. Treiber (of Beaver) was a Nickelodeon owner (no specific name of this business) - in the Keystone Block Building on Pennsylvania Avenue in 1907.

———

Dixon's Nickelodeon – Pennsylvania Avenue (near Twelfth Street)
1906, 1907

W. L. Dixon – owner. W.L. Dixon also had a tailor shop in 1906.
He closed up the business the first of Sep 1907 and rented the room to Jack Curry
of Rochester who planned on opening a restaurant in the building.

———

Nickelodeon and Family Theatre – Pennsylvania Avenue
1907, 1909

Opening performance was on Oct 7, 1907.
Nicholas Wurzel already had a penny arcade at this location – he had the room in the rear of the
building enlarged and a stage was erected to accommodate the moving pictures
and for it to be a vaudeville house.
Evidently a great feat at that time, it was advertised that 1000 feet of moving pictures would
be shown at Wurzel's Arcade.
Admission was 5 cents. (end of Dec 1907).
Jan 1909 - N. Wurzel, Jr. sold out his interest in this theatre to his son Cornelius (Corny).
"Corny" had helped his father since the theatre was built; "Nick" was also going to continue in
the restaurant business at his old stand. (no address for either)

———

Finn's Nickelodeon – Pennsylvania Avenue (near Twelfth Street)
1918

Abel Finn owner.
Closed by 1919 and Julius Carper opened a garage in the building.

———

End of Sep 1911 – Motion picture show was removed from the Bank Building and young people
planned to form a club to hold weekly dances there since it was available. This may have been
more of a community type picture show since there is no available name on it (nor was there
any mention of the name of the club or if the club was ever actually formed).

Theatres

Monaca may have been a smaller town compared to some of the surrounding towns and cities, but the business-minded and residents kept up to date when it came to progress and offerings of products and activities. With the development of more modern movies, the need to provide better theatres was a must and Monaca rose to the challenge.

On September 24, 1900, the Monaca borough council passed an ordinance granting a right of way through the borough for a branch of the Consolidated Street Car Company to have a line running up Ninth Street from the Ohio River Bridge to Pennsylvania Avenue and thence east along Pennsylvania Avenue to the Opalite Tile Company's plant. Council saw the need to expand the service to keep moving forward and grow with other towns. This means of transportation would help bring in more business to those associated in the "entertainment" field.

At the same meeting, it was approved to erect a new business building with the front facing Ninth Street and adjoining the Hotel Monaca building. It would be a three storey building constructed of iron, brick and stone. The basement would contain three storerooms, a room for dynamo, engine, and heating apparatus, and three cellars. The first floor would contain three large storerooms (18 x 70); the third floor a lodge room (55 x 57), necessary anterooms, and closets. The 2nd floor the second floor would contain a stage and large auditorium theatre and would be "one of the coziest little play houses found in Western PA." The 2nd floor would have two entrances – one from Ninth Street and one from the side.

Other local businessmen took this new building as a lead-in to bigger and better things and wanted in on the business of entertaining residents. With this line of thinking, more theatres began to spring up throughout the town which slowly phased out the once popular, less modern, nickelodeons.

Beginning in the mid to late 1920s, sound was added to movies. The first step in the process was incorporating synchronized dialogue, more commonly known as "talking pictures" or "talkies." It was the task of the projectionist to properly start the sounds and movies to synchronize it all. These early "talkies" would tend to be quite static sounding. This technique was added exclusively to short films with the longer length feature movies having a recorded sound that included only music and effects. It was still more common for theatres to still be using live piano or organ music and some were now also adding other musicians to accompany the longer movie features.

Novelty Family Theatre – Pennsylvania Avenue
1907,
>Opened first of Oct 1907.
>George S. Challis, Manager of this new play house.
>>(He was evidently in the "theatre business" because he was also the lessee of the Grand
>>Opera House and manager of the new Majestic theatre elsewhere.)
>Mrs. Leonia Thompson of West Bridgewater was pianist; Miss Jemima Romigh of Rochester was in
>>charge of the ticket office.
>Opening performance was given by the Hill-Edmunds Trio, "Baby Florence"-child artist,
>>Miss Virginia Foerstige-singer from West Bridgewater, and a moving picture show.
>It was described as one of the "coziest little family theatres in the county."
>Was decorated by Daniel Leary of Monaca.
>Had a "good sized stage with drop curtain and all the equipment necessary for
>>putting on a good show."

_____

Bank Hall Theatre was the auditorium portion (2nd floor) of the Citizen's National Bank Building on Ninth Street
(beside the Hotel Monaca building).
>There were movies and entertainment programs held in this theatre a year or two
>>prior to 1907 and several years later.

_____

Dreamland Theatre – Bank Hall / Citizen's Nat'l Bank building – Ninth Street
1907, 1909
　　　　J. B. Boyd – Manager in Sep 1907.
　　　　　　　There was also a Dreamland in Freedom – D. C. Craig proprietor.
　　　　The wood floor was often used for roller skating in Bank Hall in 1907.
　　　　James Boyd of Monaca rented the Bank Hall; had the Boyd Family Orchestra furnish music for
　　　　　　　roller skating parties.

DREAMLAND
THEATRE
—
BANK HALL -- MONACA
—
**Pictures Changed
Every Day**
—

The latest and best in Moving Pictures. Open every evening. Special
vaudeville acts every Friday and
Saturday. Special attention given
lady and children patrons.

Vaudeville feature for Friday and
Saturday will be Miss Florence Geneva in her fancy dances.

Absolutely complying with all the
fire laws.

One price--every night—five cents
to all.

1909

_____

Mercer Theatre – Pennsylvania Avenue
1912, 1913
　　　　Dec 24, 1912 – and article stated that "the work on the new Mercer Theatre on Pennsylvania
　　　　　　　Avenue was progressing and would soon be ready for occupancy."
　　　　Was often referenced as "the new Mercer theatre" in Dec 1912.
　　　　Admission was 5 cents in 1913.

_____

Olympic Theatre – Pennsylvania Avenue
1913, Dec 1916
　　　　J. W. Mercer, Proprietor in Mar 1913.
　　　　In Nov 1916, there was an ad "For Sale – Moving picture theatre equipment, price reasonable"
　　　　　　　and they were to inquire at the Olympic Theatre ……..
　　　　　　　　　but……………. in Dec 1916, they were looking for a piano player and usher…..so either
　　　　　　　it was bought and it was the new owner doing that advertising, or they decided not
　　　　　　　to sell -?

_____

In Jan 1913, it was noted that the new theatre on Pennsylvania Avenue was nearing completion and would be
ready for occupancy.   Exterior was painted and the interior decorated.   Was to be occupied about Feb 15th.
　　　　Mr. Mercer was the manager.
　　　　　　　(He was the manager of a few theatres….)
Which theatre is this?   Could this have been for the Duquesne or the Mercer Theatre?   It may have even been
the Monaca Theatre since Mr. Mercer eventually bought this business from Mr. Mellon in Mar 1913.   - ? -

_____

Monaca Photoplay Theatre – 900 to 920 Pennsylvania Avenue (near Ninth Street)
1912, 1917, 1922, 1925
     Apr 1925 - Louis Stoll was listed as proprietor of the Monaca Photoplay Theatre.

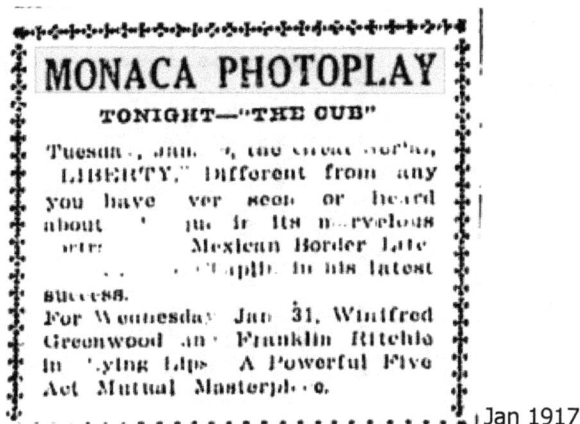

MONACA PHOTOPLAY

TONIGHT—"THE CUB"

Tuesda., Jan. , the Great North, LIBERTY." Different from any you have ever seen or heard about . . . u. ir its m..rvelous seri. Mexican Border Late . . . .aplin his latest success.
For Wednesday Jan 31, Winifred Greenwood an Franklin Ritchie in .ying Lips A Powerful Five Act Mutual Masterpi..e.

Jan 1917

Eventually became known as ......

Monaca Theatre - lower 900s on Pennsylvania Avenue
     Pre-1913 – Attorney W. J Mellon – owner.
     1913 to 1917 – J. W. Mercer – owner.
     1917 to 1922 – John R. Sturgeon – owner.
     1922 to ___ - F. J. Tepper.

Up until Mar 1913- the building was owned by Attorney W. J. Mellon, then he sold to J. W. Mercer.

Mar 26, 1913 article stated "Attorney W. J. Mellon has sold to J. W. Mercer his new theatre on Pennsylvania Avenue at a private consideration. Mr. Mercer will at once take charge as manager and owner and will continue the same high standard of amusement features that has been noted in the past."

May 23, 1917 – John R. Sturgeon of Beaver Falls purchased the Photoplay theatre in Monaca. Mr. Sturgeon planned to remodel the playhouse and install a new machine. He was taking possession before the end of May.

Mid Jun 1919 – the properties beside the Monaca Theatre were purchased by the Monaca Nat'l Bank but the bank never did erect their new building here. The theatre building was left standing since Louis Stoll purchased property beside it in 1926 and the bank was built at 999 Pennsylvania Avenue in 1922/23.

Louis Stoll is also listed as leasing the building of this theatre (no set dates – only 1925 was verified). Mr. Stoll was also listed as the proprietor of the Beaver Theatre in Beaver.

The Monaca Theatre was listed as the only theatre in town early in 1926.

In May 1926, property between the Monaca Theatre and the municipal building was purchased and the new theatre was being built.   See the *Penn Theatre* information.
The adjoining Monaca Theatre was to be remodeled by the Mellon heirs and converted into a mercantile building.

Coming!
America's Greatest Star
Billie Burke
in
GLORIA'S ROMANCE
Supported by HENRY KOLKER.
A MOTION PICTURE NOVEL BY MR.¹ MRS.
RUPERT HUGHES

By Arrangement With F. Ziegfeld, Jr.,
Beginning
Thursday, January 11
At The
Monaca Photoplay
MATINEE 1:30 TO 5:00
EVENING 6:30 TO 10:30.

Jan 1917

MONACA
THEATRE
MONACA, PA.

WEDNESDAY

World's Championship
Wrestling match between
Joe Stecher and Earl
Chaddock

EDDIE POLO
—in—
"THE CRADLE OF
DEATH"

Century Comedy
"PALE WINDS"

1920s

Liberty Theatre – unknown location
1919

It appears this theatre was only used during the war time years. It doesn't appear that it was a formal theatre building and most likely was set up in an empty store room or another meeting place.

Liberty Theatre, Monaca

THURSDAY

The Third and Last Official Government War Picture

"Under Four Flags"

Nowadays every newspaper, magazine or book you pick up contains some description of the late fighting front. To understand them fully you should see this picture. To see an enemy airplane actually shot down, is alone worth the price of admission.

1919

Penn Theatre – 922 Pennsylvania Avenue   (beside Borough Building)
                    (in 1955, it was listed as 92**4** Pennsylvania Avenue -?)
1926, 1931, 1934
   Louis Stoll was owner of the *Penn Theatre*.
        Louis Stoll b 1877 Germany – d 1943; moved to Monaca in 1926; married Sara__;
        4 children; lived at 931 Washington Avenue in 1943.   Louis Stoll, Jr. was a locally
        known organist.   Louis, Jr. died in 1982.
   May 1926 - Louis was erecting a new theatre / amusement house on property he purchased
        between the Monaca Theatre and the Municipal Building on Pennsylvania Avenue.
        The Monaca National Bank owned the property and it was one large vacant lot that was
        adjacent the municipal building and another lot beside it that had a two storey frame
        building on it that was said to be one of the oldest structures in Monaca – the "ark."
        The "ark" property adjoined the current Monaca Theatre property which was owned by
        the W. J. Mellon heirs. The ark was occupied as a Chinese laundry (being run by Ping
        Fong) and was his dwelling until a few days prior to May 7th.   The 2 storey "ark" was
        scheduled to be razed at once, followed by clearing the site for the new theatre.
        The adjoining Monaca Theatre was to be remodeled by the Mellon heirs and converted
        into a mercantile building.   The construction of the theatre was to start at once.

        The new theatre was being built of red, rough faced brick and was a two storey building.
              It had two storerooms on each side of main entrance with a theatre in rear
              (54 wide x 113 deep).   The theatre had 600 seats of leather upholstery, oil
              heating system, two toilet rooms, 2 side exits and 2 in the rear.   The 2nd floor
              contained office rooms.
              R. Twain of Pittsburgh was the architect. The planned opening date was Oct 1.
   Oct 1926 – work on the new Monaca theatre was progressing and was on schedule.
   Nov 1926 – Louis C. Stoll – owner of newly completed Penn Theatre.

   There were many congratulatory wires sent to Louis upon the opening of this new theatre.
   This was the only theatre listed on tax list in 1930.   The Penn Theatre building was between the
        present Municipal Building and the Monaca Theatre building.
   The Monaca Theatre was supposedly closed at this time because articles state that the
        new Penn Theatre was "the only amusement house in the town" at that time.
   The Penn Theatre was dedicated Wednesday, Nov 24, 1926.

   Jul 1929 – showing a movie using a synchronized sound and music to make it "as real as
        life itself."
   1930 –There was a fire at 9:15 pm on Aug 4, 1930 – more than 200 people escaped.
        o   Owned and operated by Louis C. Stoll at the time.
        o   Flames were discovered burning in the wall above the stage and crept toward the
            platform.
        o   Fire was confined to the front of the auditorium.
        o   Offices and apartments on the 2nd floor of 2 storey building were not damaged;
            interior of theatre was badly damaged by fire, smoke, and water.

   Dec 1930 – Santa Claus arrived in Monaca and landed on the Penn Theatre roof –
        escorted to the ground by the new aerial ladder of the fire department.
   Louis Rottenstein of Aliquippa was leasing the theatre from Louis Stoll – Oct 1931.
   Oct 1931 – It was remodeled, redecorated, and new sound equipment. Article stated:
        "The New Penn Theatre in Pennsylvania Avenue, which has been
        closed for several weeks to permit extensive improvements....."
   Mar 29, 1934 – still showing movies.
   The "Penn Theatre" or "New Penn Theatre" was not used by Feb 1935 because the Roxy Theatre
        was advertising movies; ads said "under new management"; then a Roxy ad in Feb 1936
        stated "Formerly New Penn – Monaca" ......BUT ....
        there were still references to the building as being the "Penn Theatre bldg." for several

years after 1935.   I have no explanation to why this occurred since it is verified by tax records and Roxy's own ads they occupied the very same edifice as the former Penn Theatre, with both being located beside the Municipal Building and at 922* Pennsylvania Avenue.

922 Pennsylvania Avenue would have been where the site/ property of parking lots and the newer 12-sided building at 900 Pennsylvania Avenue now stands (2016).

Photo from Beaver County Times -1953

This 1953 photo of the Penn Theatre building had Thad's Jewelry store on the left. Not in the photo is a dry-cleaning shop on the right of the theatre entrance.   The Municipal Building, at that time, would have been just to the left of the picture.

Municipal   Penn / Roxy Theatre bldg   Grater's
Bldg

This photo is calculated to be in the late 1950s since Thad's Jewelry is not on the left of the buiilding any longer and Grater's appears to still be in business.

PAY A VISIT TO MONACA'S NEW $75,000 MOVING PICTURE THEATRE

The first moving picture theatre in Pennsylvania to be equipped with the latest type Superior Projector. You will find everything here to be according to the latest developments of the cinema art.

Latest and best film features, projected upon the famous Minusa De Luxe Special Screen—no eye strain—the finest screen made for moving pictures.

This ad was for the Penn Theatre in Nov 1926.

SPECIAL! THANKSGIVING DAY ATTRACTION

The Comedy Hit of the Current Season—a Wonder Film You Will Enjoy

"YOUNG APRIL"

With JOSEPH SCHILDKRAUT, BESSIE LOVE and RUDOLPH SCHILDKRAUT

ALSO A GOOD COMEDY AND NEWS REEL

Milds Orchestra — Popular Prices

600 SEATS . ROOM FOR ALL

(There is a picture and some information on the Martin Mild Orchestra further on in the *Various other forms of entertainment* section.)

Fun Fact:
  Note in the actors and actress in the above ad. Bessie Love and Joseph Schildkraut were two of the people who sent a congratulatory wire to Louis Stoll on the opening of his new theatre.

A few of the congratulatory wires that were sent to Louis Stoll when he opened the new theatre:

In Culver City, Calif., Nov. 22, 1926.
Louis Stoll:
    Penn Theatre, Monaca, Penn.
    Accept my congratulations on the opening of your beautiful new Penn Theatre. The erection of such theatres is definite proof of the great success being made by this industry of ours. As my pictures come to you I will appreciate frank criticism from you and your patrons. Sincere best wishes.
             Cecil B. DeMille.

(Cecil B DeMillie was producer in Calif)

In Culver City, Calif., Nov. 22, 1926.
Louis Stoll:
    Penn Theatre, Monaca, Penn.
    It is pleasant to note how theatre building has kept pace with all other improvements in motion pictures. The people of Monaca would best know their fortune if you could only recreate for one night the unpleasant nickelodeon of twenty years ago. Sincere congratulations.
             Marie Prevost

In Culver City, Calif., Nov. 22, 1926.
Louis Stoll:
    Penn Theatre, Monaca, Penn.
    It is always a thrill to us in the acting profession to see erection of splendid theatres like yours built especially to house our products. I will look forward to frank criticism from your patrons and yourself on my performance in Young April as it is only by frank criticisms that we can hope to become better actors. Please know you have from me every good wish for a splendid future with the Penn Theatre.
             Joseph Schildkraut.

In Culver City, Calif., Nov. 22, 1926.
Louis Stoll:
    Penn Theatre, Monaca, Penn.
    As a native of France it is a constant wonder to me why my own country, the earliest home of the cinema, has not developed theatres of the class you are giving the people of Monaca. My sincere congratulations to you.
             Jetta Goudal.

In Culver City, Calif., Nov. 22, 1926.
Louis Stoll:
    Penn Theatre, Monaca, Penn.
    You are to be sincerely congratulated on the opening of a playhouse which without doubt will act as a model for scores of other homes of entertainment. As I came to you in Young April I will appreciate the reactions of yourself and patrons to my performance.
             Bessie Love

In Culver City, Calif., Nov. 22 1926.
Louis Stoll:
    Penn Theatre, Monaca, Penn.
    Sincere thanks for backing our efforts to please and entertain by the erection of such a beautiful playhouse as the Penn Theatre. Congratulations and best wishes.
             Leatrice Joy

In Culver City, Calif., Nov. 22, 1926.
Louis Stoll:
    Penn Theatre, Monaca, Penn.
    I love Los Angeles but I would give everything to be in Monaca to see the lights twinkle on for the first time in front of your Penn Theatre.
             Vera Reynolds

All those sending these wires were actors, actresses, or film makers of the day. As bustling of an area as California was in 1926, they still took notice of the small town of Monaca!

Penn Theatre

MONACA, PA.

Mon. & Tues., Dec. 15-16

See and Hear the Human Document
Written in Pictures and Words
That Will Sear Their Way Into
Your Memory Forever.

"ALL QUIET on the WESTERN FRONT"

Wed. & Thurs.   Fri. & Sat.
"Animal Crackers"   "Tom Sawyer"

Dec 1930

THE NEW
PENN
Theatre — Monaca

Louis Rottenstein, Mgr.
Adults 25c, Children 10c

Nov 1931

NEW PENN

THEATRE • MONACA
Admissions - 10c and 20c
Book Tickets - 6 for $1.00

TUESDAY
TODAY and

The Most Beautiful Love
Story the Screen ever Told

BERKELEY SQUARE

with
LESLIE HOWARD
HEATHER ANGEL
Directed by
Frank Lloyd

Mar 1934

THE NEW
PENN
Theatre — Monaca

Louis Rottenstein, Mgr.
Adults 25c, Children 10c

Today—Last Time

CLARK GABLE
in

"Sporting Blood"

with MADGE EVANS and
ERNEST TORRENCE

SCREEN SHORTS

FRI. & SAT.—

Charles Bickford in
"East of Borneo"

5c Matinee Every Saturday

PENN THEATER

MONACA, PA.

FRIDAY AND SATURDAY

"Here Come The Marines"

With The Bowery Boys

PLUS ."CRIPPLE CREEK"
With George Montgomery

SATURDAY MATINEE

JUNE 6th AT 2 P.M.

Bugs Bunny Cartoon
Our Gang Comedy

Two Giant Feature Attractions
Plus Chapter No. 1 of
"Son of Geronimo, The
Apache Avenger"

Come Early to Get a Seat
Also FREE CANDY till 6 P.M.
for Each Child

both of these were from 1953

PENN
THEATRE
924 Pennsylvania Avenue
MONACA, PA.

Ends Tonight—Wayne Morris
"Two Guns and a Badge"

"Meet The Monster"
Bowery Boys

Starts Sunday — 3 Days Only
ACADEMY AWARD WINNERS

BIG AS THE OCEAN!
THE CAINE MUTINY
HUMPHREY BOGART · JOSE FERRER
VAN JOHNSON · FRED MacMURRAY
ROBERT FRANCIS · MAX WYNN· TECHNICOLOR

MARLON BRANDO
On The Waterfront

Jun 1955 - Note the address is now 92**4** -???

Going by the ads where the theatre is being called "Penn Theatre" again in 1953, it is confusing as to the name of the theatre.......the Roxy advertised in 1938 as "formerly The New Penn," so why in 1953 is the *Penn Theatre* still advertising? There were also ads as late as 1955 for the apartments on the 2nd floor that stated "inquire Penn Theatre" if in fact the theatre had become the Roxy -??

Perhaps since Louis Rottenstein was simply leasing the building from Louis Stoll, Stoll didn't permit the official name change; but Rottenstein tried to make it his own, to give distinction of it being under new management by giving it a new name "to go by?" When Carl Broidi was the Manager in Jun 1944 or when Tony Albino was the manager prior to 1952, one of these men may have gone back to Louis Stoll's original name of "Penn Theatre." This scenario would be the best educated guess because in doing my initial research, not having any pictures yet, and trying to pin down a location of the theatres, I had a couple comments from former residents and frequent visitors to Monaca who said they were not sure where the "Roxy" was since no one before them frequented it much due to the type of entertainment and atmosphere associated with it in the 1930s – so.................... eradicating the name "Roxy" and going back to the name of the more reputable "Penn Theatre" would have made good business sense.

As for the address differences between 1926 and 1955, this could easily be an error, especially since the Municipal Building was the building adjacent to the theatre building on Pennsylvania Avenue at that time.

Mateer's Meats   Municipal Building   empty lot

This picture is included again only to show the area of Pennsylvania Avenue before the Penn Theatre was erected. It was built to the right side of the Municipal building and the property it was built on included the empty lot shown here.

———

Roxy Theatre – 922 Pennsylvania Avenue
1931, 1936, 1941, 1943, 1955
        Louis Rottenstein (of Aliquippa) was the Manager.
        Sep 7, 1931 – The newly remodeled Roxy Theatre had a grand opening. The Roxy was newly
                remodeled after being closed for a few days – painted, new interior decorations, electric,
                and sound equipment was done. Carpeting extended from the commodious foyer
                through to the orchestra pit. Modernistic style interior. Lobby frames for attractive
                displays of popular features.
        Opened by Feb 15, 1935 under new management.
        Ad in Oct and Dec 1938 stated "Visit the beautiful new Roxy."
        Still in business May 1940 with ad for movies and ad congratulating Monaca on Centennial.
                There was new carpet laid throughout in early Dec 1941. The theatre had a foyer, lobby
                In 1940, admission was 20 cents & 10 cents daily and Sundays.
        Aug 28, 1942 – they were selling war bonds and stamps at the Roxy Theatre.

Carl Broidi, Manager in Jun 1944.
In 1946, the movie "The Gay Cavalier" was showing.
Tony Albino was the manager of the Roxy Theatre prior to 1952.
I found no more mention of or ads for the Roxy starting in the late 1940s/mid1950s.

In April of 1938 the ads for the Roxy stated "Visit Western Pennsylvania's Most Modern Theatre."
Sunday Matinee prices at that time were - adults 20 cents and children were 10 cents.

Note – this ad states "Formerly New Penn" --- yet the Penn was still advertising in the 1950s -?????

ROXY THEATRE
FORMERLY NEW PENN—MONACA
This theatre is glad to announce that we now employ union operators. Signed: The Management.

TODAY – LAST TIMES

THE SCREEN'S THOROUGHBRED LAUGH CHAMPION..!!

WILL ROGERS
'IN OLD KENTUCKY"
— DOROTHY WILSON
RUSSELL HARDIE • BILL ROBINSON
A FOX PICTURE

1936

Monaca Theatre Will Show Dance Pictures

Moving pictures taken at the 'Hollywood Ball" sponsored by Beaver Valley Lodge, No. 4, Fraternal Order of Police, will be shown at the Roxy Theatre, Monaca, police lodge committees announced today. The special attraction will be shown along with the full feature program at the theatre Friday and Saturday, March 11 and 12. The pictures were taken of the Grand March and dance scenes at the ball held at the Junction Park pavilion February 28 and March 1.

Mar 1938

ROXY

Princess Yvonne, one of the leading psychics of the stage, will be at the Roxy Theatre tonight and Tuesday, in an extraordinary engagement. You may ask any sensible question you like about your business affairs, vacation trips, love affairs, money matters or lost articles and the psychic wonder will give you an answer.

Duquesne Theatre – 1144 Pennsylvania Avenue
1912, 1913,

This theatre underwent remodeling in May 1912 with the front changed to conform with the warm weather conditions.

Duquesne Theatre

Penn'a. Ave. and Twelfth St.
MONACA.
J. W. MERCER, Proprietor.

TONIGHT:

"ON BURNING SANDS"
Powers, 2 reels.

"RAGS AND RICHES"
Imp.

Admission 5 Cents 1913

Still only charging 5 cents
for admissions

TONIGHT:

Three Independent pictures at the

Duquesne Theatre

Penn'a. Ave. and Twelfth St.

—and—

Three Association pictures at the

Olympic Theatre

J. W. MERCER, Proprietor.
MONACA.

1913

(see previous for Olympic
Theatre information)

*** *** *** *** ***
*** *** ***

LEISURE AND RECREATIONAL SITES

So many of the residents of Monaca could enjoy many summer days visiting the surrounding entertainment sites in the area. Monaca itself provided many social clubs and activities including its own roller skating rinks and theatres. The railroad and street cars opened the doorway to accessing and traveling to places and would have seemed quite a luxury in the day; steamboats provided transportation and excursions to many of the sites, too. I've included this section just for the readers' entertainment; to also show the variety of activities and places where people could go and enjoy spending a fun filled day, weekend, or longer.

There were numerous excursion boats that made the journey from Monaca to Rock Springs Park during the summers of the 1930s. Just a few of the steamers making such trips were the *Greater Pittsburgh*, the *Julia Belle Swain,* and the *Morning Star*. It would have been quite a good time with fun at the park all day, not to mention the ride with dancing on the luxurious steamer in the traveling to and from the destination. It was not unusual for the whole community to participate in such outings with stores and businesses closing for the day and the town coming to a standstill; many people from all parts of the county joined the Monacans, boarding at the Monaca wharf (located by the pump house). One such outing made claim to ten or twelve hundred people in attendance on the boat. Typically, they would leave between 9 and 11 am in the morning, returning to Monaca about 9 pm that same day. You will find pictures of some of the local steamboats in a different category of this book.

Not all the outings were made by steamer; the P & L E railroad had many excursion specials for Monaca residents to enjoy. One that was interesting was advertised to Washington, D.C. the first of Mar in 1901 to attend the inauguration of President McKinley. There were also excursion trips to New Orleans, Mobile-Alabama, and even Pensacola-Fla, all offered at low fare, so I am sure there were residents who would have joined in the annual Mardi Gras festivities and many other events that once were just a dream.

*** *** *** *** ***

There were many events held in Monaca over the years. Here is just one example from Jul 1965.

This is a miscellaneous picture of an excursion steamboat.   Note the tall smoke stacks. When necessary, they could be bent down for passage under certain bridges.

The stern wheel above is the *Homer Smith*. This steamboat was an excursion boat that operated on the Ohio River.   She was mainly used for brief excursion trips to the amusement parks and other entertainment areas.   She was sold to Pittsburgh Amusement Co. and renamed *Greater Pittsburgh* in 1928.   She was built in 1914 and used until she burned at Pittsburgh in Apr 1931.

AMUSEMENT and PICNIC PARKS

I was tempted to include a large section on information of the many, many surrounding amusement parks and areas that Monaca residents would have visited, as well as many that are still in operation. Instead this information was omitted since the main objective of this book was on concerns with Phillipsburg and Monaca.

For this book, I have limited information and pictures, keeping both to a minimum and only mention a few better known parks or recreation areas that earlier residents would have frequented.   During many of the earlier years, most of the parks listed here would have been accessed via trolley cars, steam boats, and/or trains.

From a Jun 1924 paper....

DO YOU KNOW

That you can go to your choice of five parks by electric street cars?

JUNCTION PARK

Local cars direct to the Park.

MORADO PARK

Local cars direct to the Park. An ideal spot for Sunday School and exclusive Club picnics. Special car service if desired.

FALLSTON BEACH (Brady's Run)

A place to swim. Run water well dammed and safe. Take your own suit— a 10 cent charge for checking your clothes. Take a street car to the Junction—just a short walk over the bridge. Plenty wading room for the children—Good picnic spot. Special cars if desired.

CASCADE PARK

New Castle, transfer from local car to Harmony at Fifth street, Beaver Falls.

ROCK SPRINGS PARK

Chester, W. Va., transfer from local car to the Yellow Car line at East End avenue, Beaver.

STANTON PARK

Steubenville, via, same route as if going to Rock Springs, but no transfer at East Liverpool.

We want you to consider the convenience of the trolley for your outing. It's a clean, safe and comfortable way to go and you are free from all worries.

GO BY TROLLEY

COMMERCIAL DEPARTMENT

Beaver Valley Traction Company

Pittsburgh-Beaver Street Railway Company

The *Greater Pittsburgh*, *Senator*, and *George Washington* were the three most used excursion steamboats that took Monaca's and other local residents to the parks and picnic areas.

*** *** *** *** ***

Aliquippa Park – Aliquippa, PA
On July 1, 1880, the Pittsburgh and Lake Erie Railroad developed an amusement park on Crow Island, just off the shore from Logstown, Aliquippa – West Aliquippa. West Aliquippa was once known as just Aliquippa and Aliquippa proper was referred to as Woodlawn. Crows Island was privately owned and eventually sold to J & L Steel who maintained it for the employees of J & L. The Liberty Gardens developed on the island during the Great Depression with J & L Steel giving residents seeds and plots of land for planting. During WWII, the name of the gardens was changed to Victory Gardens. As with most smaller parks, Aliquippa Park also became defunct and what once was a place of fun and relaxation, along with gardens, became industrial land.

Courtesy: B.F. Jones Memorial Library

Barges serving as a bridge to link residents of West Aliquippa and Woodland to Crow Island.

_____

Rock Point Park – Ellwood City
The park opened about 1885 and officially closed in 1912. The site the park was located on what is now the Rock Point Nature Area and is open to the public. Rock Point Park was like so many others, built as a "trolley/railroad park." People were known to dress up, take the New Brighton & New Castle Railroad (or later the Beaver & Ellwood Railroad) train and spend the day at the park. The life of this park was short due to a spark from the train's engine starting a fire that destroyed most of the park. Rock Point Park was known as *Felician Park* for a short period of time.

_____

Junction Stretch aka Junction Park

Junction Park was considered a "trolley park" because it was built by a trolley company, the Beaver Valley Traction Company.   Many of the trolley companies found it profitable to construct amusement areas within their line of business and not only gain a strong income from the passengers that used their trolleys, but found the monies spent at the parks to be a great source of income, too.   Local people didn't have to travel too far once the bridges, street cars, and railroads became a more common factor of life.   Junction Park, located between Rochester and New Brighton, was full of entertainment ventures for persons of any age.   This entertainment area had it all – roller coasters, carousel, fun house, toboggan slide, automatic swings, dance hall, dinner theater, athletic fields, picnic areas, swimming pool, and most of all – easy access for local people. Many old timers used to recall and tell the story of how in 1909 Ringling Brothers Circus came to town, unloading 26 elephants from the train and parading them down the street to announce their arrival and promote attendance to the circus.   Many organizations held events and activities in the park.   Junction park area was even used as a training camp for WWII soldiers.

————

Morado Springs Park – Beaver Falls, PA

This park sat on thirty-two acres; in 2015, this would be the area where a defunct small open mall sits, by Caputo Insurance Agency, Inc, and across the road from C. J. Rombold Engine Builders – all along the Big Beaver Blvd./ Rte. 18.   It was considered a getaway place for the townspeople of Beaver Falls and surrounding areas, with Monaca residents among the frequent visitors.   The Beaver County Traction Company opened Morado Park in 1891.   They would run open-air summer cars to and from the park, especially during the 1920s.   It was primarily a picnic ground, but folklore tells of it having a carousel although no evidence has proven it. The park was also known for its mineral springs and waters.   It is said that there was a swimming area in the Beaver River even though the river would have been heavily polluted at that time.   No park would be complete without a dance hall, and Morado had one.   The park closed in 1937.

————

Conneaut Lake

Many summer days were enjoyed at Conneaut Lake and the Conneaut Lake Park.   In 1892 the park was opened as Exposition Park.   It was built as a permanent fairground and exposition for livestock, machinery, and industrial products from Western Pennsylvania.   It was previously land used as a boat landing. Exposition Park also included several hotels, a dance hall, a convention hall, and a bathhouse.   The park's first mechanical ride was a carousel which opened in 1899 and shortly after other rides and a midway were added.   The park was renamed Conneaut Lake Park in 1920.

————

Cascade Park – New Castle, Lawrence County

Levi Brinton started off with 70 acres of wooded land, planning to clear the land and make improvements using portions of it as picnic groves. He named the property *Brinton Park*. He sold the entire plot to the New Castle Traction Company which began to turn the property into a park with several amusement rides and a streetcar extension to the park. Since there was a water fall within the park, it became named Cascade Park and opened on May 29, 1897.   As with most of the urban amusement parks, it began its decline in the 1930s and 1940s. With the attendance on a slow and steady decline throughout the 1960s and 1970s, Cascade Park was doomed to close. Several groups began to restore Cascade Park in the late 1980s and with many of the old midway rides removed, existing buildings repaired and/or remodeled, a new playground, and renovation of the public swimming pool, the park was making a comeback.   This was one great recovery effort for the park that survived through it all and is now called a nature park and former amusement park.

————

Idora Park – Youngstown, Ohio

Idora Park was built by the Youngstown Park and Falls Street Railway Company and opened May 30, 1899, with the name of *Terminal Park*. By the end of 1899, it was renamed *Idora Park*. This park was very popular, but with much larger and newer parks within the area, attendance began to decline. A fire in 1984 caused millions of dollars' worth of damage. The ballroom escaped the 1984 fire and remained open for various events until Memorial Day 1986 when it also was closed. On Mar 5, 2001, a suspicious fire starting in the basement of the ballroom building also destroyed that landmark building.

———

Rock Springs Park – Chester, West Virginia

In 1857, it was known as Rock Springs Grove; was donated by the Marks Farm for church picnics. It consisted of mere hiking trails, picnic pavilions, and a small dancing platform. On Jun 26, 1974, the last dance at Virginia Gardens (the dance hall) was held as the final event at Rock Springs Park before the project of rerouting US Rte. 30 began. Structures were auctioned off, the site was cleared, the lake was drained, and all traces of the park were soon gone.

The *Greater Pittsburgh* steamer was one of the steam boats that would frequently take Monaca residents to Rock Springs Park. In Jul 1930, Monaca residents were among about 1,000 people who traveled via the steamer and even more went by street car or automobile with over 200 from Monaca in attendance at the park. This park was a very popular venue for many local family reunions.

———

White Swan Park – 1 ½ miles from Pittsburgh Airport

White Swan Park was a very small park compared to many others in the area that operated for 34 seasons. It opened in 1955 and had seven rides. It sat on 40 acres and eventually featured a kiddie park and 15 rides. After the park's 1989 season, the Pennsylvania Department of Transportation bought the park to make improvements on the roadway. All the amusements and other artifacts were sold at auction and White Swan Park joined the ranks of being defunct.

———

Kennywood Park – Pittsburgh, PA

Kennywood Park would have been one of the big attractions for the residents of the Beaver Valley. It was considered one of the small trolley parks when it was founded in 1898 on a 40-acre plot of land in Allegheny County, PA. The Monongahela Street Railway Company, controlled by Andrew Mellon, built the park. Two of the park's original buildings still stand – the carousel pavilion and the restaurant, originally called the Casino. School picnics became quite popular in the 1950s and again many rides were added, especially to Kiddieland. Monaca was just one of many of the schools that did enjoy celebrating their annual school picnics at Kennywood beginning in the later 1930s and into the 2010s. The Monaca High School and Center High School Bands both participated in many of Kennywood Festivals over the years.

MONACA PICNIC IS ATTENDED BY 2,500

An ideal day, with not a single accident reported, aided in making the annual Monaca School-Church picnic held at Kennywood Park, Pittsburgh, Monday one of the most successful outings ever held. Approximately 2,200 students, parents and others were aboard the two special picnic trains. Between 300 and 400 others drove to the park in cars.

Jun 1939

Monaca Picnic Tickets Go On Sale Tomorrow

Tickets for the annual Monaca school, church and community picnic at Kennywood Park, McKeesport, Monday, June 17, will go on sale at the Monaca high school office Friday morning at 9 o'clock and continue until Saturday evening at 8 o'clock.

Monaca merchants will close their stores Monday for the picnic.

Jun 1940

Monaca Folk At Annual Picnic

School students and adults boarded two trains this morning at the Pittsburgh and Lake Erie Railroad station for Kennywood Park, to attend the annual Monaca school picnic.

A number of other Monaca folk plan to drive to the park this afternoon.

Monaca stores and the First National Bank were closed for the day. The Monaca Federal Savings and Loan Association closed at noon.

Jun 1949

Buttermilk Falls   aka   Homewood Falls — Beaver Falls (Homewood)

This nature park is sometimes referred to as a hidden oasis.   It obtained its name from the Homewood sandstone quarry near its waterfall. Stones were quarried to be used in nearby tunnels, roadways, and Western Penitentiary in Pittsburgh.   The quarry can still be seen if you make your way to the bottom of the waterfall. Although known most recently as the Buttermilk Falls, it was referred to by locals in the area as Homewood Falls and even earlier as *Smiddy's Falls*. The name Buttermilk is said to have begun about 1870 because of a group of Civil War veterans who enjoyed picnicking in the area while enjoying their choice of beverages – buttermilk.   There are two other waterfalls located very close to this location that also go by the name *Buttermilk* – one near the southern end of 5th Ave in Koppel and the other along Wampum Run in Wampum.   The area has been landmarked for its historic value since it was the site of the headquarters of General Israel Putnam, Commander in the Highlands in 1779.

Many residents from all the local towns and areas would have come to the site to enjoy hiking, swimming, and summer picnics.

Frankfort Mineral Springs   and Raccoon Park – Hookstown, PA -Rte. 18 from the south & north or US 22 & US 30 from the west

The very small borough of Frankfort Springs grew out of the Mineral Springs Resort that once was present in the area.   It was advertised in 1843 as a small village near a cool, romantic glen, thickly studded with forest trees and a mineral spring.   Mineral Springs Resort soon became known as Frankfort Mineral Springs.   The springs are located by the entrance to Raccoon State Park.

It developed into a Victorian era health resort, Frankfort Mineral Springs and Resort.   With the mineral spring water containing 15 different minerals, it was believed to have had curative powers, curing everything from kidney ailments to indigestion.   The area that was originally the site of the resort is now part of the Raccoon Creek State Park.   Frankfort Mineral Springs and Resort closed in 1912. The state park is considered to have opened in the early 1930s.

During the great depression, Raccoon Park was established as a Recreational Demonstration Area with the Civilian Conservation Corps (C.C.C.) constructing its earliest buildings in 1935. The park area and buildings were added to the National Register of Historic Places in 1987 for their distinctive architecture, their role as parts of a recreational area, and reflecting the federal government's attempts to resolve the poverty of the Depression.

Brady's Run Park – off Route 51, Brighton Township

This nature park area was established in 1947. It is located in Brighton Township and is a county-owned park. Brady's Run Park is currently considered one of Beaver County's largest parks consisting of almost 2000 acres. The park opened with just usage of the grounds and pavilions, then additions of swimming, fishing, walking and jogging trails, a lodge building, playground area, horse arena, 5 softball fields, 2 basketball courts, ice area, electricity, charcoal grills, and restrooms. In recent years, this is home to the annual Maple Syrup Festivals and Festival of Trees, too. Another annual event at Brady's Run Park is the stocking of the lake with fish for new fishing seasons' opening day.   The lake in the park now encompasses 28 acres. It is a man-made lake which was built by Beaver County in 1948. It had an average depth of 7 to 10 feet with a few areas being up to 21 feet; but after it was drained once again in 2011 and more silt removed, the depths increased.

In 1976, construction of the enclosed ice skating area was started; it was completed in 1977. The park has "cleaned up" the lake several times over the years. This involves having to remove several feet of silt from the bottom of the lake which tends to choke off aquatic life.   They added small improvements over the years such as boat docks, a bath house, fresh sand for the swimming beach area, paving once dirt roads, upgrading the pavilions, adding charcoal grills, wiring the park with electricity to the pavilions, etc.

Fun Fact: Although I have no idea what happened to these geese, I found it interesting to put as a fun fact.   Late in 1987 there were two Egyptian geese who favored Brady's Run Lake with their presence.   This may not sound like news, but this breed of geese is native to Africa. At the time of their identification at the park in 1987, it was unknown how they came to settle in this area. They did not "socialize" with the other geese at the time, but kept to themselves.   As I stated, I do not know how long they stayed, nor the fate of these geese; they may even still be residents of the area.

Brush Creek County Park – off Glendale Road, Beaver Falls

This park is also a nature park. The county bought 645 acres in the 1960s; the Beaver County Commissioners established the area as a public park in 1969. The park was dedicated in 1972. There is no electricity or modern plumbing.   It has 10 picnic areas, charcoal grills, 2 outdoor tennis courts, horse trails, 2 softball fields, 3 soccer fields, walking and jogging trails, a tiny tot playground, fishing, and large grassy play areas. There is a covered bridge within the park, too.

Allaire Park aka   John A. Antoline Park

Monaca Residents could and still enjoy picnicking at Allaire Park.   Property on Jackson Street (directly behind the Fifth Ward School) was donated to the Borough of Monaca in 1936 by the Allaire Land Co.   It was partially cleared and used as a park with improvements made in Apr 1964.   It was donated to the Borough with the stipulation that it would not be used for anything other than recreation or park use.   The first work on the area was done by the W.P.A. and help of some interested citizens in 1936.   The waterslides opened in 1984 and had a 34-foot vertical drop into a landing pool.

The slides were built by a Coraopolis based Water Adventure, Inc. and were the beginning operators of the slides.   The borough maintained ownership of the property.   Water Slides of Monaca Inc. took over the lease of the slides in 1999.   The waterslides at Allaire Park aka John A. Antoline Park were closed in 2002 and dismantled in Aug 2005.   They fell victim to 1) a property dispute between the borough and the owner of the adjoining property; 2) the abandonment by the most recent operator – the Aliquippa based Water Slides of Monaca, Inc.

Former water slides were constructed in 1984.

*** *** *** *** ***

SWIMMING

Monaca Beaches

Monaca had two municipal beaches and bath houses at one time. One was located where the current pump house is and referenced as "Monaca Beach" and sometimes "Eighth Street Beach." The second beach area was a little further up river by Twelfth Street and appropriately called "Twelfth Street Beach." Many people used the Ohio River for their swimming area in the earlier 1900s. I will remind you that the river was not as deep and dangerous back in the late 1800s and earlier 1900s as it is today. In those days, the deepest part of the river by Monaca was probably 10 feet and that would be in the middle of the river where the large boats would travel AND during rainier seasons. Along the shore lines, the Ohio River was much shallower as you can see in the pictures further; look how far from shore the swimmers have gone. In 1916, a citizens committee raised money to put the Monaca beaches in good condition. Money was raised and an offer was received for the concession stand to provide refreshments. There was a nice large area by the pump house that was shallow enough for wading out into the river to cool off and swim – again, nothing like it is today (2015). As mentioned, these accessible beach areas of Monaca went by many names through the early years. A few of the names were Municipal Bathing Beach; Eighth Street Beach; Twelfth Street Beach; and most often, regardless of the exact location, just Monaca Beach or bathing beach. These areas that were accessible for people to use as bathing/swimming beaches also had a large area for picnicking, corn roasts, camp fires, camping out, using and storing canoes and row boats, and even beach houses. Local bands and musicians would come and provide added entertainment.

During the 1910s, the entire community would join in a corn roast and have beach parties. The bath houses and bathing beaches were used daily during the hot summer days into the 1920s. Edward Mahan of Pittsburgh leased the municipal bathing beach at Twelfth Street and had the area cleaned up and put in shape for the 1917 summer season. The bath houses were remodeled, other improvements were made, and new equipment was added. Mr. Mahan expected to make the beach the most popular resort in Monaca's section of the county with it opening on May 26, 1917.

In the spring of 1926, council was approached and asked approval for use of the currently abandoned beach houses to be used by the Monaca Aquatic Club. The fact that there were abandoned beach houses tells me that residents were no longer so fond of using the polluted Ohio River as a place to swim. I found no resolution to the first request, but only a few months after this request was made, there was a petition by the Monaca citizens presented to the town council asking for once again, a permanent park and bathing beach to be available to them. This petition also made the claim that in previous years, Monaca was the first to have a bathing beach in the county; they wanted their bathing beaches restored. In the 1930s, the Boy Scouts would hold events on the Ohio, starting from the Monaca beach, going by row boats across the river to the Beaver beach area and then rowing back to Monaca. Residents that lived along the Ohio River in Monaca would improve the shoreline along their properties adjacent to the river, too. These all had their own names, too – one was a Neal Henry Beach aka Henry's beach (1940s), a Olshansky Beach, and others.

The popularity of swimming in the river dropped drastically when it was proven how unhealthy it was to be swimming in the heavily polluted waters of the Ohio River. The waters were increasingly polluted due to the growing industrial and mine pollutions; also remember that in the earlier days of the 1900s, it was a common practice for sewage lines of all communities to be drained into the Ohio without being processed or cleaned as is required today. This was happening all up and down the Ohio River, so the cumulative results were probably quite hazardous. With that last statement being said – "yuk" - can you only imagine how polluted the rivers and streams were then!

It is puzzling that with all the fondness and activities of the Ohio River, that it took an attempt by a man in 1980 to commit suicide by jumping off the East Rochester-Monaca bridge for Monaca to recognize the need for a boat launch area. In the rescuing of this man, the only access to the river by the rescuers was at the public boat launch in Rochester. Monaca Council made the decision at that time to have the Fish and Game Commission build a boat launch at Monaca for both emergency and recreational use.

BCHR&LF

Eighth Street Beach (located by the current pump house)
1910, 1936, and ____
    The swim suits and caps are just adorable.   It was evidently uneventful to see the steam boat
    passing up or down the river since most seem unconcerned with it.

***
OPEN PICNIC GROUNDS.
The Monaca Aquatic club will open a picnic grounds on the site formerly known as the Aquatic club bathing beach at Eighth street and the Ohio river front. The ground will be fixed up and equipped for picnic purposes and will be an ideal place for picnics and outings during the summer months.
***

Jun 1919

BATHING BEACH
    Stating that it was his intention to revive the bathing beach at Monaca, Elmer Folland asked the approval of council for the use of the bath houses located on the borough's property on the beach at Eighth street. The bathhouses were abandoned, it was said, by the Monaca Aquatic Club. Pending further investigation by council no definite action was taken in the matter.

May 1926

Monaca Aquatic Bathing Beach   (Note the trolley on the bridge.)   BCHR&LF

There are many people in the river swimming in this photo. Due to the poor quality of this photo, they are difficult to see. Also, note, there are many people up on the bridge looking down, too.

Fun fact:
Monaca's beaches were well known. An article in the Pittsburgh Press in Aug 1918 stated that Pittsburghers made the trip down to use the beach in Monaca and swim.

1920s   Photo from Monaca Borough

Twelfth Street Bathing Beach   (along the river's edge at the end of Twelfth Street)
1916, 1917

BATHING BEACH AT MONACA ASSURED

At a recent meeting held in the interest of the Twelfth street Municipal bathing beach at Monaca, committees composed of citizens of the Second and Third wards, decided to take steps for raising money to put the beach in good condition for the coming summer. They reported that so far $100 had been subscribed and that an offer has been received for the refreshments concession at the beach during the summer. They expect to hold several benefit motion picture plays in various theatres in the near future to assist in raising the money needed

Feb 1916

TO IMPROVE BEACH

Edward Mahan, of Pittsburgh, who leased the Municipal bathing beach at Twelfth street from the town council, was in Monaca yesterday making preliminary arrangements for improving the beach. Mr. Mahan looked over the boat landings along the Monaco beach. He stated that he expected to run boat excursions from Pittsburgh to Monaca during the coming summer. He also said that some dredging would be done at the beach to permit of a deeper swimming pool.

Jan 1917

·MONACA BEACH·
(Foot of 12th Street)

Now Open for the Season

Bathing Suits 35c
Individual Lockers 10c
Individual Towels 5c

Refreshment Stand
(Well Stocked)

For Picnic Dates Call or Write

E. D. MAHAN
MONACA, PA.

Jun 1917

Another article from Jul 1917 stated that between 1200 and 1500 persons enjoyed Sunday bathing at the Monaca beach at the foot of Twelfth Street; and the attendance included a large number of people from out of town, too.

*** *** *** *** ***

Monaca Swimming Pool – Sixteenth Street and Indiana Avenue
1953   to   1991

> Located on a tract of land between Washington and Indiana Avenues and between Fifteenth and Sixteenth Street.
> Discussions for a swimming pool in Monaca were made as early as 1937 but was not approved until 1953.
> Aug 1954 the pool was nearing completion – consisted of the pool, bath houses, concession stand and surrounding grounds.   The swimming pool itself was an L-shaped construction with the deeper diving area in the smaller portion of the "L."   It had a lower diving board and a high diving board.
> Dec 18, 1954 newspaper article stated that the project cost $130,000.   The work was finished too late for 1954 usage, but the pool would open for residents in the summer 1955.
> 1982 – the pool had extensive repairs approved.

Since the pool was originally built on land that was filled at one time, the settling was taking its toll on the property and the pool itself.   There were extensive repairs needed to keep the pool in operating and most of all, safe condition.   The Monaca council found it not feasible to repair the pool and unfortunately approved the closing of the only public pool in the borough.

> The pool was closed in 1991.

> Jul 7, 1995 – bid was awarded to have the L-shaped cement pool filled in and grass planted over the site.

There were many citizen meetings after the pool was closed and opinions are still being presented to the Monaca Borough to consider the building of a new community pool for the borough.

> 2015 – the concession stand is still standing; the remaining property is an open grassy area.

> *Fun fact – Mr. Nichol would give life guard lessons and certify life guards at the Monaca pool. I took life guard lessons at this pool from Mr. Nichol and worked as a life guard there for three summers in the earlier 1970s.   It was a fun job and attendance was very good; the pool was always full of swimmers, even on the cloudy days.*

During construction of new swimming pool in 1954.

High dive   Regular dive   Bath houses   Indiana St.

*** *** *** *** ***
*** *** ***

GOLFING

Raccoon Golf Course   aka   Pettibon's Golf Course – Center Township, Monaca

The property where the Beaver Valley Mall and its environs now stands, was, prior to 1937, basically farm land, as was most of Center Township at that time. This made it possible for Arthur Pettibon to turn the land into a plush golf course in no time.   A complete 18-hole golf course was built in two stages.   Mr. Pettibon also donated some of his first land purchase to the township's water department which built a tank at the south end of the golf course. This was a smart move for Pettibon since obviously it was a source of water that was much needed if the grass conditions were going to be improved.

The actual land the entire golf course was created on involved two major purchases for Arthur and Hazel Pettibon. They eventually purchased a total of 174 acres of land to complete the 18-hole golf course.   Per a deed dated March 7, 1938, a 76.05 acre portion of the land was purchased from Miss Bernie Orpelli of Beaver Falls.   Tom Schmoutz/Schmautz has been listed in the mix of being the owner on this same farm land.   In 1910 and 1920, I found Caroline Schmoutz (widowed) owning a farm with her son Thomas (farmer) in that area. With this information, I can only theorize that the mention of Thomas Schmautz may come from the fact that they were "known" to own the property for a number of years, while Miss Orpelli would not be as well known for referencing. Regardless of my theory, Mr. Pettibon did develop the first 9 holes and then the actual proof of him purchasing the property occurred almost a year later with Miss Bernice Orpelli the seller in 1938.   Even though the final paper work was not dated until 1938, the Raccoon Golf Course was advertising for memberships to the golf course in 1937 and the local newspapers stated the "grand opening" was held on Jul 3rd, 1937.

By 1941, Mr. Pettibon wanted to expand/complete the original 9-hole golf course to an 18-hole course. Mr. Mateer had owned the property Mr. Pettibon wanted to purchase since 1926 and although neither he nor his family actually lived on the property, he did maintain the many, many fruit trees on the property.   In 1941, James Mateer, whose health was failing, was not properly attending to this farm land adjacent to the then 9-hole golf course, so he made the decision to sell his 98-acre farm to Arthur Pettibon and the deed was entered Aug 11, 1941. This acreage is the right portion of the land area of the current BV Mall.   Arthur and Hazel Pettibon now owned 174 and plans were being formulated for an 18-hole golf course.

Golf enthusiasts may recognize some of the more famous golfers of the area including the likes of Vasile Daniel of Monaca, Stan Namola of Chippewa Township, Pete Vuckson of Beaver and Bill Gabal of Baden, then Aliquippa.   A pro golfer, Ken Sumner of Erie also played there in the summer of 1954 and became the resident pro advisor succeeding Mitch Lewis, Bob Dawson, Bert Whitehead, and Glen Welsch.   Russ Franks, a junior at Monaca High School in 1954, was serving his apprenticeship at Raccoon Golf Course as Mr. Sumner's assistant. Mr. Sumner continued to worked there until it closed.

Along with the first club house, Mr. Pettibon included tennis courts and even a grove of trees was turned into a picnic ground to cater to valley churches and other social groups; the club house was completed in the summer of 1937.   The Pettibons also erected a very nice two storey brick home for themselves at the edge of the property. The home formerly sat approximately where the Silo business is located; the house was eventually sold in the late 1980s or earlier 1990s and moved; it is still a private residence and sits off Brodhead Road on Wilhelm Drive, behind the Center Car Wash-2016.

The course was completed for 18 holes of golf by about 1945, Mr. Pettibon had also erected the 2nd club house for the golf course.   Once the new club house was completed, he sold some of the acreage of the front corner of the original 9-hole area of the course, along with the 1st club house to Elton and Elsie Tate.   This acreage and former club house were purchased by the Tates in Nov 1946; all located closest to the current large intersection (now the site of Hampton Hotel).   Elton and Elsie Tate were my grandparents, so I can relate quite a bit of information on the former club house since it was converted into their home.

The majority of the property (what was left from the subdividing and sale of the club house, the government's portion for the location of the intersection, and other sales) was purchased by mall developer Bill Sullivan of McKeesport in 1965. It was noted at the time of that sale that Raccoon Golf Course was considered the most appealing public course in the county.

Fun Fact: Edward Gallagher, Monaca Heights was the first to get a hole in one on the 185-yard sixth hole at the Pettibon's Raccoon Golf Course in Jul 1938. He was playing with Earl Cookson, Bud Pettibon, and Paul Vollmer.

This picture shows the tee for the first hole with a sand trap to the left. To the right of the sand trap is the green of the ninth hole. If you look very carefully, you can see the club house hidden behind all the trees in the middle of the picture.

***   ***   ***   ***   ***

ROLLER SKATING

A view of a typical roller skating rink in the 1950s   (NOT from Monaca)

In the late 1800s and early/mid 1900s many buildings were multi-purposed by the Monaca people and businesses. An example of this can be found below with the some of the listings of events. Before the official skating rink was built in 1908, other buildings with large wooden floors were not just used for athletics, and/or dances, but were also used for roller skating. Before Oct 1907, residents and guests still enjoyed the sport of roller skating in these make-shift rinks. Two men, D. J. Mitchell and George V. Mullen recognized the need for a permanent roller rink; they formed a partnership and took the opportunity to invest in that business. On Apr 18, 1913 Messrs. Mitchell and Mullen sold their lease on the Monaca roller skating rink to Walter M. Degraw of New Brighton. Mr. Degraw continued the same policy established by Mitchell and Mullen.

Roller skating always seemed to be quite popular and people were finding every place they could to enjoy the activity.   In early 1907, it was reported that the employees of the J. S. Mitchell & Sons company cleaned and swept the second floor of the planing mill and started to use it as a skating rink.   There were also many occasions of roller skating in the gymnasium of the Young Men's Christian Association in Monaca prior to 1907; the association's gymnasium was located somewhere on Pennsylvania Avenue and was called *Association Hall.*   Other examples of the popularity and how various buildings were being used for roller skating would be when a part of the Bank Hall and the Young Men's Christian Association gymnasium both had skating parties on different evenings in Jan 1907 and it was stated that large crowds were in attendance at both.   In late Feb 1907, the Eagles fitted up a rink on the first floor of their building, under the social rooms, for roller skating.   The YMCA was closing its door for good in Monaca and an article in the Aug 31, 1907 newspaper stated that the association would keep the hall open that "evening to give those who desire to have a farewell skate the opportunity."

Monaca Roller Skating Rink aka   Silver Slipper Roller Rink - Pennsylvania Avenue
1907, 1936, 1938, 1940, 1948, 1950

VALENTINE PARTY
THURSDAY NIGHT
MONACA SILVER SLIPPER RINK
Candy Prizes For Sweetheart Skates
Action Pictures Taken by Shiflet Studio
Skating Until 12 O'clock

Feb 1946

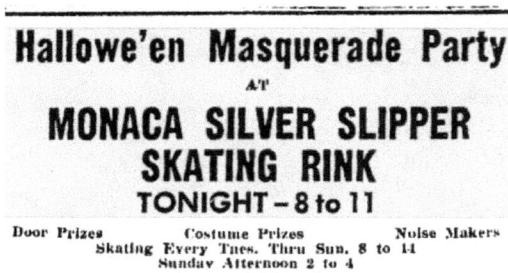

Hallowe'en Masquerade Party
AT
MONACA SILVER SLIPPER
SKATING RINK
TONIGHT – 8 to 11
Door Prizes   Costume Prizes   Noise Makers
Skating Every Tues. Thru Sun. 8 to 11
Sunday Afternoon 2 to 4

Oct 1948

This was named "Monaca Silver Slipper Rink;" the name *Monaca* being added because there was another *Silver Slipper Roller Rink*; it was located in Hookstown, PA, under the management of M. K. Berger in the summer of 1946.

As stated, roller skating was one of the most popular recreations, along with dancing, for many years in Monaca and surrounding communities.   Research on the Monaca Silver Slipper Skating Rink / Monaca Skating Rink proved a bit frustrating with no solid answers on the location of the rink; folklore indicating it was anywhere from being in the location of the 2016 Municipal building to along the avenue now vacant of buildings in front of the Phoenix glass plant. The only common fact known is that it was definitely located on Pennsylvania Avenue.

The Monaca Silver Slipper Roller Rink had a new hard wood floor laid in Sep, 1908.   An article in early 1908 stated the firemen's "carnival in the <u>old</u> rink building was largely attended," indicating a designated building was being used prior to 1908 primarily for skating.   This article did not indicate where this old rink building was located, nor could I find any other mention of this building.   The same paper stated that the roller skating rink would open within the next two weeks and that the new hard wood floor in the rink would have been laid --- this leads me to believe there were two were separate buildings.   With no surviving Monaca local tax records or other documentations, this is all the information I can provide at this time.

The Monaca Roller Skating Rink on Pennsylvania Avenue was still being used as of Feb 1933, Oct 1937, Sep 1938 and Jun 1940, Oct 1948 evidenced by advertisement of skating parties and events on those dates.   The Rink was listed on the 1940 and 1941 mercantile tax lists at 1752 Pennsylvania Avenue.   This would place it on the lot that became the Polish Club (now torn down). An unexpected heavy snow fall of between 40 and 48 inches on Nov 24, 1950 caused the roof of the skating rink to collapse.   Fortunately, there was no one in the structure when the collapse occurred.   No further mention of the skating rink can be found after this roof collapse.

A local announcement in 1916 stated that the Monaca Skating Rink would be open every Saturday night until further notice.   Along with many different types of roller skating events and parties, numerous other activities took place over the years in the Monaca roller skating rink, too.   Local organization and small clubs, the Red Cross, the police department, and church groups are some that would hold skating parties throughout any given year.   There was live music provided at many of the roller skating events, most orchestra's being local. Also among the non-skating activities were boxing matches of various levels. One such exhibition was sponsored by the Monaca and Colona Athletic Club in the spring of 1912 with Patsy Maley of Colona winning over "Fighting Dunn" of Ambridge.   The Monaca Roller Rink had Dorothy and Elmer Besnicker of Evans City give a demonstration of fancy roller skating in Dec of 1930.   The police had a dance in the building in 1946 to raise money for a two-way radio communication set.

Monaca also had roller skating teams and a Monaca Roller Polo Team used the skating rink in 1930.   Other towns had roller polo teams, too since the Monaca team had a match with the Evans City team late Dec 1930.   Mr. and Mrs. Andrew Stauffer took first place in the novice division of an interstate competition held in the Greater Pittsburgh roller rink in the spring of 1959.   In the early 1940s there was a Johnnie's Skating Club in Monaca.

From all this information, I have determined that one of the first recognized places of a formal roller rink in Monaca most likely would have been.........

1890s   – 823 Pennsylvania Avenue
         In 1924, 823 Pennsylvania Avenue became The Public Motomart.
         1929 – 1931 S. P. Kohlman's retail business was at this address.
         Other business in this building were: Paul's garage,   L & M Market,   Mesta Roofing, Inc.)
1909/10 to 1930 - Various locations: usage of gymnasiums, clubs, and other large business building areas.
1931   - 1814 Pennsylvania Avenue (per Mercantile Tax List).
1940 to 1950   - 1752 Pennsylvania Avenue (per Mercantile Tax List).

*** *** *** *** ***

Fun Fact:

To Race For Championship.
    For the roller skating championship of the Valley, Raymon Wubbeler, of Beaver Falls, and Hubert Wagner, of Monaca, will meet this evening in a mile race at the Monaca roller skating rink. Both men are trained to the minute for the event and the rivalry is intense.

1909

*** *** *** *** ***
*** *** ***

Various other forms of entertainment

There were many places that the residents of Monaca, Moon/Center and Potter could go to relax and enjoy themselves, but please note that I have only included a fraction of these activities and locations.   Although I have not included any additional information on Presque Isle on Lake Erie and Geneva-on-the-Lake, Ohio, they were mentioned frequently as places where families would spend a day, weekend, or longer.

Raccoon Creek in Potter /Raccoon Townships
There were places like Hober's Beach and Lubert's Beach that were used frequently for picnics and outings.   The creek provided excellent swimming and plenty of space for other activities.

Many people from Monaca owned property along the creek and would camp there during the summer time. Hunting in the area was also a frequent activity.

As use of the Ohio River became less attractive due to pollution, late in the 1900s a very popular location on Raccoon Creek for swimmers and families to gather was called Sandy Beach.   The water of the creek was not only very clean and clear, but at Sandy Beach and a few other areas there were quite deep pools that people could even enjoy doing some diving.

Mr. Bitner caught many turtles for his famous turtle soup in Raccoon Creek.

———

Mc Cracken's Lakes – located off Cochran Drive, Center Township
This was an ideal local spot for some quiet, relaxing time and great fishing.   They would stock the two lakes with fish. Anglers were invited for a small fee in 1940s, 1950s, 1960s, 1967.   The lakes were operated by James and Alice McCracken of Center Township.   The end of Dec, 1967 is the last mention of McCracken's Lakes I could locate.

Hall's Lake   and   Lyon's Lake were two other once popular small lakes in Center Township the public was invited to frequent in the mid 1900s.

———

Even with the nation emerging from the Great Depression people found they still wanted to have fun and sought out entertainment. There were several local establishments that provided such entertainment in the area.   I have listed some of the more local places that Monaca residents would have been more likely to have attended.   I purposely did not even attempt to include all the recreational activities or sites in the area; but wanted to give a taste of some of the more popular and frequently visited attractions.

Bell's Grill – 920 Pennsylvania Ave
Had Ralph Miller provide entertainment in the mid to late 1930s.

Frank's Place – 2000 Beaver Avenue
Offered "DANCE" every Thursday and Saturday with music by Jack Kennedy's Orchestra.

Bandroom - 1199 Pacific Avenue (corner of Pacific and Fifteenth Street)
Had many events and dances as well as several with Joe Elmer providing entertainment.

Palm Gardens – Ninth Street
1925, 1945

       Opened at least by 1925 and no further mention of it after 1945.

       It was mostly considered a dance hall, but also many other types of affairs were held here.

       Feb 15, 1945 a Monaca Youth Canteen opened in Palm Gardens.

       Located on one of the floors/areas in the Opera House (the building that held the Callaghan's Drug Store - better known as the Citizens National Bank Building which was also later known as the Campbell/ Mayflower building).   With the dances, club meetings, events, and celebrations held in the Palm Gardens and also the canteen stating they had 300 youths in attendance at their grand opening. I would have to deduce the Palm Gardens was either on the second floor of the Citizen's old bank building – this 2nd floor formerly was built with a large auditorium and stage; or it was on the third floor which originally contained a lodge room with smaller side rooms and closets.

Vanity Fair Dance Hall – Ninth Street in the Citizens National Bank building -   1936

Blue Bird Dance Hall – Brodhead Road, Center Township

       This hall was there at least by 1930 and then 1941.   By the spring of 1933, the name changed and it became the Golden Chain.   May of 1958 it was referred to as "the old Bluebird Dance Hall."   It was also used for public meetings in Center Township during the 1930s and 1940s; Center's first fire department also used this hall.   This dance hall was located near Lincoln Drive and former site of the Golden Dawn Supermarket.

Local land owners and farm owners always had an "open door" for company and fun. Barns were used for dances and the farm land provided plenty of room for all types of activities; as well as many having access to water ways, ponds, streams, and/or lakes.   The articles I found with businesses going for picnics and "a day of fun" were too numerous to list.   There is so much truth in making the statement that the area was very friendly and willing to break bread and share and enjoy the company of others.

I had sent out many random requests for information on Phillipsburg and Monaca for anyone interested in sharing. A copy of the picture below was sent to me anonymously, so I have no one to give proper credit to for sending this to me, who the photographer was, or where it originated from, but it was very noteworthy in my opinion, so I decided to include it in this section.

There was no mention as to where this picture was taken, just that it is of Martin Mild's Band of Monaca in 1912-1916.   This was a very popular group that played at many events and affairs in Monaca and Moon/Center Township. There were only a few names of members listed along with this picture......Back Row: Martin is in the middle; Samuel Gref is to the left of him; Michael Weiss is to the right of him. Front Row: John Gref is by the small drum.

Monaca Memorial Recreation Association

The association was in existence for many years; organizing in 1933 as the Monaca Recreation Board.

The Stone Quarry Club leased five acres to the Monaca Recreation Board, but WWII interrupted plans for the development of this property. This association erected a recreation area in 1960 adjacent to the swimming pool. It was to be used for year-round programs of supervised recreation for Monaca area residents, such as tennis, badminton, volleyball, basketball, and shuffleboard as well as the area becoming an ice skating rink in the winter months. This association received support from the Borough Council and Monaca School District. Council supplied funds for maintenance and new facilities; the school district met the cost of supervision. The United Fund and several Monaca service organizations and clubs also financially supported the association.

Dedication, determination, and many hours of volunteering made the whole program work. An article in Jan 1962, recognized and named the Association officers: Mrs. Lester Patton-Pres., Mrs. Edward Garrity –Vice Pres., Regis Meehan-Secty. and Treasurer, Clarence Graeser-council rep., and Robert Prichard-school board rep. It was headed by John Nichol in 1963. The association had plans for construction of a building to house a concession stand, rest rooms, and areas for ice skaters to use while putting on their skates. Until the building was finished, there was a heated trailer donated by William Roorback, manager of Interstate Amiesite Corporation Monaca division.

ICE SKATING RINK

Several community articles made mention of ice skating on the area used for the basketball court adjacent to the water works building. Apparently over the years, it would purposely be flooded and allowed to freeze, then used for ice skating during the winter months.

In 1961, the Monaca Memorial Recreation Association built a new ice skating rink. It was located adjacent to Monaca's memorial swimming pool. There were lights installed for night skating, too. The rink was open, weather permitting, Sundays through Saturdays and on holidays, with different opening times, but closing by 10 pm each evening.

The rink was 210 feet by 130 feet and there was a maintenance supervisor and operator who was to see to the checking and re-glazing of the rink's ice surface.

*** *** *** *** ***
*** *** ***

Weather Events

Tornado

Major Snow Falls

Flooding

Ice on the River

Wind Storms

WEATHER EVENTS

In this section, I have listed only a few of the many weather events that have occurred affecting Monaca.   There were many that could have been listed in this section, but I chose to highlight only a few.

Tornados

Photo from another tornado in Beaver County in 1985 (not Monaca).

Jun 4, 1907

On Tuesday evening, Jun 4, 1907, at about 8:00 pm, there was a horrible wind and rain storm that passed over the lower Beaver Valley and did many thousands of dollars' worth of damage in Monaca. It was never classified as a tornado, yet the winds that came in with this storm did damages equal to those of a tornado.   It was compared to being more of a cyclone as far as insurance agencies and claims made as a result of the storm.

The United States Sanitary Company's plant, in South Monaca, sustained the greatest loss. One of the three storey brick buildings was blown completely in and parts of the roof was found on the river bank the next morning.   Another new 160 x 20 feet frame warehouse was razed to the ground.   Unfortunately, they did not carry insurance against cyclones and could not make any claims.   A house on Monaca Heights occupied by John Olsing was split in half by the storm; the Olsing's had no insurance to cover such a storm either.

Jun 28, 1924

On Saturday, Jun 28, 1924, the whole Beaver Valley was hit with what they called a *cyclone*. The Daily Times newspaper stated "Worst Cyclone in History of Beaver Valley.....". There were pounding rains, hail, winds; all leaving damage, destruction, and death where it hit.   One article stated that it looked like France after all the bombings.   Monaca was also among the areas hit hard by this storm.   There were porches and roofs blown off many homes as well as numerous windows being shattered and trees uprooted. Although there were thousands of dollars in damages done throughout the borough of Monaca, only one casualty was reported which was George Kane, a night engineer at the water works plant. He was badly bruised by falling bricks as a brick wall caved in when the roof was blown off.

The brick firewall of the Eagle's building on the corner of Pennsylvania Avenue and Twelfth Street caused damage to two cars when it blew over and fell on them.   Many of the houses were left roofless and/or sustained damages.   Boards, bricks, and other debris could be found scattered everywhere.   The fallen trees blocked the avenues and streets. With the electric power being compromised, the street car traffic was cut off, telephone service didn't work, and there were no electric lights.

Though it was not a common or legal practice, hardware store merchants opened their stores on Sunday to give people access to purchase window glass and other supplies needed to make repairs on their homes.   All the area towns and communities sustained severe damages from this cyclone.

<u>Sep 4, 1970</u>

A tornado hit the Center Township and Monaca area at little after 7 pm on Saturday, Sep 4, 1970.   It traveled from Center Township, passed over some of Monaca Heights and then traveled down Fourteenth Street Hill and on into Monaca.

It totally destroyed Marcello Block Co. and Mecklem Lumber Company (both in Monaca) and damaged more than 50 homes.

It may have lasted only 3 minutes, but it traveled over 2 miles and was 100 yards wide in some spots. The weather bureau had given repeated warnings in advance of the approaching tornado.

The tornado opened a gap in the residence of Joseph Marcello and tore down the office.

Damages to the grounds of Marcello Block Co.

Although a very poor grade of a picture, you can still make out the destruction to Mecklem's store.

Part of the siding from the second floor of the Roy H. Mecklem Hardware and Lumber Co. crashed into two garages at the rear of homes.

May 31, 1985

There was what was considered a "tornado outbreak" that passed through eastern Ohio and northwestern Pennsylvania on May 31, 1985. The Borough of Monaca, Center, and Potter escaped damages from the F5 tornado that began near Erie, PA and stretched to Beaver, PA. When all was said and done from this storm, 65 individuals had lost their lives in Pennsylvania alone. These storms developed, intensified throughout the day, and by evening the tornado warnings were up for all in the area. At some point during this storm, one was classified as a F5; this monster storm was nearly a half-mile wide. There was not just one tornado on this day in 1985; a report states that twenty-three tornadoes actually swept through the area. Some fizzled out as quickly as they developed, others caused significant damage before dissolving. The Monaca area was spared from all the destruction, while other close by areas were not so lucky.

*** *** *** *** ***

Major Snow Falls in Area

There have been many cases of heavy snow fall in and around Monaca, Center, and Potter.   Just some of these events are:

During the winter of 1944 there was 15+ inches of snow that fell in the area, paralyzing all the surrounding areas.

Nov 24, 1950

Depending exactly where you lived, 40 to 48 inches of snow fell in Beaver County and the surrounding areas in a totally unpredicted snow storm.   During the early morning hours on the day after Thanksgiving, the heavy, wet snow began to fall and 48 hours later, with high winds and frigid temperatures thrown into the mix, there was distress, property damage, and deaths.   The Silver Slipper Roller Rink's and Welch-Bright's roofs collapsed because of the heavy snow.   Businesses were forced to close with workers not able to get to work.   Cars and trucks were abandoned on most rural roads and even main streets in towns alike. Monaca Presbyterian Church offered their building to motorists and families who were in need of either heat or a roof over their heads or both.

Jan 1978

At least 25 inches of snow fell over 3 days crippling the area.

Mar 12-14, 1993

This storm was labeled "Superstorm."   The weathermen were predicting FEET of snow from this front as it moved through the area.   When the snow first started to fall, it was a much slower rate and many thought the weather people were making a much bigger deal of it all than necessary; but by midday, the predictions were proving true.   The slow snow fall quickly turned into heavy, wind-driven snow.   Some places received so much snow by the time it did finally stop that people were sequestered to their homes and other places for up to three days until roads and parking lots were eventually cleared.   The severe winds had caused massive drifting which seemed to add to the incredible amount of snow; some drifts were up to 15-foot high.   Not only had it snowed inches and inches, but then a layer of over an inch of sleet/ice was added, and yet more snow came down on top of that. This storm yielded 25.3 inches of snow.   Weight-wise, this snow fall was considered a lighter snow as opposed to the possibility of that much snow being considered wetter which would have made it much heavier. Had this snow been the heavier, "wetter" version, even more damage would have occurred.

Jan, 1996

A blizzard laid about 30 inches of snow that over most of Pennsylvania.   The snow amount was short lived though because about a week later, a freak weather condition occurred. The temperatures warmed seemingly overnight; then, with this same weather front, on Jan 19, 1996, there was a cloud burst where between 2 and 5 inches of rain fell in a matter of hours all over Pennsylvania. The rain melted the snow so rapidly that flooding was the only logical outcome. (See further under "Flooding" for more details.)

Feb 6, 2010

This weekend snow storm paralyzed many areas. The official accumulation at Pittsburgh International Airport was 21.1 inches, but many areas received even more.   This storm laid a very heavy and wet snow that felled trees and limbs and snapped electrical wires leaving over 130,000 customers without electricity for many days.   To add to the already troubling situation, there were temperatures in the single digits.   This storm was persistent in that throughout its duration there was an average of one inch of snow falling per hour.   Many meteorologists found this amount of hourly snow fall interesting from a scientific standpoint.

*** *** *** *** ***

Flooding

Monaca is just one of the local communities along the Ohio and surrounding rivers that has been plagued with flood waters. Monaca is one of the luckier areas though since for the most part it is situated a safe distance above the river, even in times of flooding. The residual effects of flooding has always affected the residents of Monaca though. It wasn't until the Pennsylvania Governors began to approve millions of dollars to complete dams along the rivers and main streams that the flooding became much more controlled. Still, with dams in place, there were and probably will always be severe flooding events throughout the river communities.

Feb 1884

Phillipsburg was among the many areas which suffered with the flood in Feb 1884.

Photo from History of Beaver County, Pennsylvania and Its Centennial Celebration

View of the bridge before the waters were totally receded.

Photo courtesy the Beaver County Genealogy and History Center

This picture is showing an opposite view of the damage to the very first Monaca-Beaver Pittsburgh & Lake Erie Railroad Bridge after the flooding of the Ohio River in Feb 1884. This picture is a view from Beaver looking toward Monaca. The Fallston and Bridgewater bridges were destroyed and the rushing waters hurled them against the P & LE RR bridge, in turn destroying it. It is fair to say that there have been ongoing flooding problems along the Ohio River over the years. If I were to do more in-depth researching, I am very sure that there would be evidence to show what averages out to be at least one flooding event of some degree of intensity per year since Beaver County and Monaca have existed. Following are some additional and more notable flooding events that impacted Monaca.

Mar 15, 1907

Extreme and rapid rain fall caused many of the local smaller creeks and streams to overflow their banks unexpectedly. Once these creeks and streams emptied into the rivers, the rivers in turn began to overflow their banks at an alarming rate.

Sep 16, 1911

The Ohio River was expected to reach flood levels and put the river over its banks at the lowest point by Monaca which would be at the Hotel Speyerer in Rochester. The water level was at 23-foot stage in Pittsburgh and would have to go to a 27-foot stage before it would move down river and affect Freedom, Rochester, Monaca, and others. The quickness of the rising waters due to the storm caused five empty barges belonging to the Ohio River Combine to break loose up river. They were caught by the *Exporter* and *Voyager* tow boats at dam No. 5.

The higher waters in the Beaver Falls area did cause the Beaver River to flood. Over a forty feet section of the woodwork at the Tenth Street Bridge in the Beaver River went down with a crash due to the volumes of water pressing against it. The middle section of the dam gave way also; the entire dam was considered weakened and was expected to give way at any time.

Jan and Apr 1913

1913 had a particularly wet start to the first part of the year. There were several occasions of localized flooding events. The worse of these ….

Mar 23, 1913

There had been periods of rain in the area, but on Easter Sunday, Mar 23, 1913, devastating rains hit the area. For two weeks previous to the rains on this day, the area had been victim to intense storms. With the rains that hit on that Mar day, the streams and soon, the rivers were all spilling out over their banks at an alarming rate. Bridges were threatened, roadways, railroad tracks, and properties were all underwater before anyone realized what was happening.

St. Patrick's Day Flood – 1936

When local people in 2015 make reference to a flood, it usually goes back to the "Great St. Patrick Day Flood" that occurred in 1936. Many share and relay tales of previous floodings to the local communities, but the 1936 flood is still the one where tales can be shared from personal experiences. That being said, it is not to diminish the severity of any of the floods; but the 1936 flood is often referenced as one of the worse to have occurred in Beaver County.

After a horrible winter freeze that still left the ground frozen solid, heavy Mar rains moved in and continued relentlessly. All the rain water along with the melting rushed into the creeks and from there into the rivers, causing the rapid rising of river waters.

This flood caused millions of dollars in damages and many deaths. More than 60 people died in Pittsburgh, 25 died in Johnston, and Beaver County reported one – a 17-year boy in Aliquippa. Monaca's Water Works building took yet another hit from the flood, but once again, the location of Monaca being well above most flooding stages, the town survived fairly well for the most part.

Mar 3, 1955

Due to high waters, 6 barges, each loaded with 900 tons of coal, broke loose from the Colona Dock at Monaca. Five were caught within a short time and returned to their moorings; one sank. Strong currents in the river caused the barges to break loose. They floated about three miles down the Ohio before being retrieved. The barge that sank hit a pier of the Monaca highway bridge and sank near the P & LE railroad bridge. The crew of the diesel boat, *Gateway*, owned by Bill Grimm Company of Pittsburgh was in the vicinity and caught the barges; the crew of the *LaBelle*, a Wheeling Steel Corporation diesel also helped.

Mar 6, 1963

High waters on Mar 6, 1963 once again caused a barge loaded with coal to break loose from docks at the Conway Yards and float down the Ohio River crashing into a pier of the Monaca-East Rochester Toll bridge.

Jan 19 and 20, 1996

A blizzard just a week before put down about 30 inches of snow that blanketed most of Pennsylvania; then a freak weather condition occurred. The temperatures warmed almost overnight and with that weather front, in a matter of hours on Friday, Jan 19, a cloud burst dumped between 2 and 5 inches of rain all over Pennsylvania. The rain melted the snow so rapidly that flooding was the only logical outcome. Ice jams were common with very large, car sized, frozen chunks of ice acting as battering rams and smashing anything in their path. By Saturday, Jan 20th, the rains had stopped and the main river levels actually dropped a little giving all the false security of relief. Ice jams in all the local streams had only begun to break up and let them flow though, and once their waters reached the main rivers, the second flood began and the waters rose so rapidly that even old-time river officials were amazed. Flooding and ice jams caused damage in downtown Pittsburgh and in several Beaver County towns along the Ohio River.

Nov 30, 2003

Heavy rains caused the Ohio River waters to rise and with that damages in the path of rushing waters. There were runaway barges that made their way down the river hurtling past several bridges and smashing boat docks. Twenty barges broke loose from their dock just outside Ambridge. Immediately, the police and firefighters were told to close down the Ambridge-Aliquippa Bridge, the East Rochester-Monaca Bridge, and the Rochester-Monaca Bridge while the sand and gravel filled barges tore down river past the bridges. None of the barges did actually strike the three bridges, but one barge bumped into the CSX Railroad Bridge but caused no damage. The Vanport Bridge was also closed as the barges continued down the river. The barges were finally rounded up by towboats in the Potter Township area of the river, none reached the Montgomery Dam and Locks. Inspection crews found no serious damage was caused.

Sep 19, 2004

Swollen rivers spill their banks in Sep 2004 after over 6 inches of rain fell due to the remnants of Hurricane Ivan.

Flooding of the Ohio River........this is the Monaca Water Works building with the Railroad Bridge in the back ground.

Photo from Monaca Borough

No date on this view of flooding. The picture is taken from the roof of the Water Works building in Monaca. Since the waterworks was refaced in 1936, the date of this photo has to be after that date.

*** *** *** *** ***

Ice on the Ohio River

Mar 1936 – Ohio River

1936 Ice jam near Monaca Rochester bridge (Monaca is in the back ground).

This wintry scene is looking down river toward Midland.

*** *** *** *** ***

Wind Storm

In Jul 1958, there was a considerable rain storm with high winds. There was a large tree by the corner of Pennsylvania Avenue and Tenth Street that was blown down and had to be removed. There were damages to cars with numerous other branches blown down and areas were without power due to electrical wires coming down in many areas from the winds of the storm. The First National Bank of Monaca is on the left of the picture. The Keystone Block Building is across the street from the bank. Note the building still standing in this picture that was beside the Keystone Block Building; also, the paved (bricked) Tenth Street.

*** *** *** *** ***
*** *** ***

Ads

Interesting Articles

Miscellaneous Information

ADS   INTERESTING ARTICLES   MISCELLANEOUS INFORMATION

1900 - there were taxes placed on having dogs and bicycles.

THE BICYCLE TAX.

The most difficult of all taxes to collect are those on bicycles and dogs. Just why this should be the case is difficult to determine, but such is the fact. Many people object to paying the bicycle tax because their wheel is old and worn out. In such cases the remedy is simple; give your wheel away or destroy it. Some profess to believe the law imposing this tax is unconstitutional, but you do not find any lawyers expressing such an opinion. The law is constitutional, and moreover, there is no lack of power to enforce the collection. The Act says this tax shall be collected "as county taxes are now collected." That means that in case you refuse to pay your property can be levied on and sold by the collector, or if necessary, you may be arrested and committed to jail,

there to remain until the tax and costs are paid. If you are wise you will pay all your taxes, including the bicycle tax.

We do not know how such a belief gained currency. but we find that many people have the idea that when the side-paths are constructed under the Act of Assembly, that no one except a member of the League of American Wheelmen can use them. This is an entirely erroneous idea. They will be free to all bicycle riders, and also pedestrians, but the former have the right of way; which is entirely proper, considering that the paths are built from the bicycle tax and primarily for the wheelmen. This being the case every owner of a wheel should pay his tax cheerfully.

One very cute notice in November 1928 edition of The Daily Times was….. "WOMAN, 84, CASTS VOTE FIRST TIME Setting an example for much younger women, and men, too, Mrs. John Doyle, 84, Monaca Heights, Tuesday journeyed to the polls and cast her vote for Herbert Hoover and the other Republican candidates for office. It was the first time that Mrs. Doyle had ever voted and she greatly enjoyed the experience according to friends."

It appears the tax faded away, but did you know that Monaca required persons to have bicycle licenses? Did Monaca have *that* many people on bicycles zipping around town or is it that bike pirating was just *that* popular -?

Monaca Issues Bike Licenses

Anthony Zaccari, Monaca police chief, is reminding Monaca residents that the police are conducting a voluntary bicycle licensing program this week. The program is being conducted in an attempt to curtail bike thefts.

A 50-cent fee will be charged to inspect the bike, record the serial number and issue a license sticker.

Bikes will be licensed from 10 a.m. to 4 p.m. at the playgrounds at the Third, Fourth and Fifth ward schools on Thursday, Friday and Saturday, respectively.

Zaccari is asking participation from residents in order to make the program work.

Monaca Issuing Bicycle Licenses

Bicycle licenses are available at the Monaca police station.

Police urge all bicycle owners to register their bikes as soon as possible. The registration fee is 25 cents.

Apr 1953

1974

From Beaver Valley Times – May 1949

1937 – from refrigerator ads....

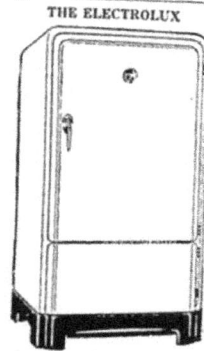

THE ELECTROLUX

HIGHWAYS or DIE WAYS — *It's up to you!*
DRIVE SAFELY
GOVERNOR'S HIGHWAY SAFETY COUNCIL George H. Earle Chairman John B. Kelly Vice Chairman

1937 ad   Note the outfit, boots, and cycle.

Flanders 20 and E. M. F. 30

1912 gas stove   1912 automobile

Advertisement from May 1909 -

You Stand by
Your Home Town —

When you buy from a town merchant.

When you patronize a town tailor

When you employ a town dentist.

When you encourage a town enterprise.

When you speak the town's praises.

When you subscribe for the town's newspaper.

Some citizens fail in some of these duties. A few fail in all of them.

HOW ABOUT YOU?

FOR SALE Milk only. Please return all empty milk bottles promptly to store or give them to any milk man delivering milk on your street. Your Milk Man.   4 24-29 inc

1944

This is either a more expensive way to drum up business, or a smart way to dispose of an unused lot and write it off on taxes.............

A beautiful building lot 25x150, on sunny Monaca Heights, given away free. Elvidge Service Station, Monaca. Get a ticket. Open all night.   5|21*

1925

Must have been a few slow news days ---- check these out.................

Mr. Jacob Burry, the Pennsylvania avenue tonsorial artist, while crossing the Ohio river bridge Tuesday, lost his hat as the result of a sudden gust of wind sweeping it away.

Apr 1903   (Wonder if he was walking, on a horse, or in a carriage?)

Paulus Koehler is sporting about with a new horse, which has quite a record. He secured it through a trade with a Rochester jockey.

Mrs. Rex Wilcox, of Braddock, Pa., arrived here last evening. Mr. Wilcox is employed as bookkeeper with the Frederick Webster Company. They will go to housekeeping in a flat in the new Keystone Improvement Company's building.

Sep 1903

Emmett McMillen has purchased a new Columbia bicycle and now rides to and from his work at the Ingram-Richardson Enameling works on College Hill, Beaver Falls, where he is employed as bookkeeper.

Aug 1907

Under the "Monaca News" section in May 1900 was included a statement that said John Hunter purchased "a handsome new buggy of which Monaca has not its equal."

I enjoyed finding many of the ads and articles. Some were more serious while others had a humorous flavor to them or may have just been included in the local news merely to fill space ....☺

A man who gave his name as Mc-Farland, hailing from Carbon county, who ha. imbibed too freely in the flowing bowl, was pinched Monday evening and lodged in Misery Hall. He was introduced to his royal highness Burgess Irons, yesterday, with whom he had a private interview, which cost him just $4.50 without refreshments.   1903 – under local news

Monaca Resident In 1846 Believed He Would Be "Crucified", But Fled

In 1846 a man from Ohio named Keil, then a resident of Monaca, announced that he was Christ and that he would be crucified on a certain day. The cross was prepared and a large crowd gathered near the site of the old P. & L. E. railroad bridge. In the meantime Kiel fled. It was afterward learned that he had located in the West.   1940

"Dead Man" Swears Loudly as He Awakens In Undertaker's Basket

Picked up on the road as dead and while being placed in a wicker basket, used by undertakers, Mike Maygak, 878 Beaver avenue, Colona, startled state police and driver of the Batchelor's ambulance, by violently swearing.

Corp. Marcus White and Private Philip Richards had rushed to the scene Sunday night, when told a man was lying dead along the road, near Colona. The Batchelor ambulance was also summoned to the scene.

Following the return to "life" of Maygak, police learned he had been struck and knocked unconscious by a "hit run" driver.

Chief of Police Gilroy of Aliquippa, later arrested Robert F. Hunter, 1014 Pennsylvania avenue, Monaca, and his companion, George M. Bozett, Pittsburgh. The right fender of the car, driven by Hunter, was bent and police say they found a pop bottle of moonshine on Hunter. Hunter was committed to the Aliquippa lockup on a charge of driving an automobile while drunk and failing to stop and render assistance.

Maygak was taken to his home instead of the morgue.   Jun 1928

'Bomb' Found Near Big Monaca Railroad Span Caused Excitement

Years ago when the new Pittsburgh and Lake Erie Railroad bridge was in course of construction a fever of excitement and fears of a "blackout" prevailed in Monaca when a large, deadly-looking bomb was discovered by some boys under an old "shack" that stood along "The Narrows."

John Shroads, then police chief, was notified and with the greatest care the bomb was removed to the Monaca police station, placed in a tub of water and the Pittsburgh Detective Bureau informed of the discovery. It was believed it was to have been used to blow up the bridge. The municipal building was given a wide berth, especially when a detective arrived from Pittsburgh and proceeded to stick a knife into the bomb, which proved to be one of a number overlooked during a fireworks display on the river front.

May, 1940

These 3 items were all listed together in Feb 1903....

Word has been received at this place by several friends of Harrison T. Will, who is sojourning in balmy Florida, that the irresistable "Harry" killed a 60-foot rattler in that place recently. The theory is advanced here that he evidently took him a few sample bottles of his celebrated "chess club" and was "just seeing them."

That we are in a century of moral advancement is exemplified by that fact that Saturday was pay day in all the shops and not one arrest was made.

The Luther League of the Evangelical Lutheran church will hold the annual election of officers at a meeting called for that purpose to be held in the church this evening.

*** *** *** *** ***

Flowery writings and words were often found in articles.........

A girl with a rounder on her mind generally has bags under her eyes.......
Rounder - a person who frequents bars and is often drunk.

A poke - a bag, a sack, sometimes even a larger wallet or purse is called "a poke"
Ever hear the phrase "a pig in a poke" -??

babushka - a headscarf tied under the chin.   Typically worn by women in most areas until the mid 1900s.

Fresco –the art or technique of painting on a moist, plaster surface with colors ground up in water or a limewater mixture.

Frescoed – have painted in that style

*** *** *** *** ***

How's this for an ad........

"Nov 20th, 1834.
Mr. J. King, Portrait Painter, late from Philadelphia, Pittsburgh, & c.
Respectfully informs the citizens of Beaver County, that he has taken lodgings at the house of Samuel M'Clure, Beavertown, where he will remain for a few days, to wait on the Ladies and Gentlemen, who may favor him with their patronage. The flattering encouragement which he has hitherto received, induces him to expect, that the citizens of this vicinity will improve the present opportunity, to secure correct likenesses of themselves and their friends; at prices far below the usual charges, for the same style of Painting. Ladies and Gentlemen of Beavertown, and the neighboring villages, are invited to call and examine for themselves, a number of specimens, and among others, several from Pittsburgh, Fallston, Brighton, & c.   For other particulars, Mr. K. is permitted to refer to Dr. C. T. Whippa, James Patterson, Joseph W. Meynard and M. T. C. Gould, of Brighton-in whose families he has just executed eighteen portraits; some of which through their politeness, he is now permitted to offer as specimens of his art."

*** *** *** *** ***

Can you imagine this type of ad, with such specifics listed, being in any publication nowadays?   Better yet, can you imagine the legal actions if it were published!

from the fall of 1944

As if women weren't having enough identity problems.......
Does this mean – no "shorter" or "thinner" women need apply?

*** *** *** *** ***

Plane crash in Ohio River   -   The Daily Times – Aug 1927

Mr. George Roth was a well-known Monaca man.   Mr. Roth purchased a Piper Cub airplane in about 1924 or 1925. He had a runway and kept his airplane on property in Center Township by the site of the Blue Bird Dance Hall (which would have been on the opposite side of Brodhead Road from the current Snowy White Cleaners).

Explosion Causes Craft To Nose Dive Into Ohio River Near Legionville

MANY PERSONS SEE FATAL CRASH WHICH WAS FIRST OF KIND IN BEAVER COUNTY

Two men were killed late Sunday afternoon when an airplane in which they were riding fell nose down into the Ohio river at Legionville after an explosion had wrecked the plane high in the air.

THE DEAD

GEORGE W. ROTH, 34, Monaca, pilot, who had been carrying passengers from the Roth field on the Brodhead road near Monaca for two years.

KENNETH B. HERCULES, 23, Martins Ferry, Ohio; said to have been a student aviator, and employed as a bricklayer at Ambridge.

Both bodies and the wrecked plane were taken from the river soon after the crash.

MANY SAW EXPLOSION

The explosion, which is believed to have wrecked the plane, was witnessed by many spectators and heard by hundreds of others at Woodlawn, Baden, Ambridge, Conway, and other places. The descent of the plane immediately after the explosion was witnessed by hundreds of people.

Just what happened and how it happened will probably never be known. The prevailing belief is, however, that the gas tank exploded, either from pressure or fire, disabling the plane. One side of the crankcase of the motor was broken, but other parts of the motor were found intact after the wreckage was taken from the water.

BODIES MANGLED

Roth's face was crushed against the instrument board of the plane. Both bodies were found strapped in their respective seats when the wrecked plane was lifted from the water. They were crushed, some believe, when the plane, nose down, hit the bottom of the river in ten feet of water.

After examination of the bodies, Coroner H. C. McCarter issued a certificate of death by drowning in the case of Roth, and death from injuries in the case of Hercules.

The body of Hercules will be sent to his home at Martins Ferry this afternoon. Both bodies were taken to Spratts mortuary in New Brighton last night. The body of Roth was later taken to Monaca.

ROTH EXPERIENCED FLIER

Roth was an experienced flier. He had been operating the field near Monaca for two years, carrying passengers and students. He was in the air several times yesterday about noon. His last and fatal trip started shortly after 5 o'clock. He owned his plane. He had installed a Liberty motor in the plane two weeks ago, doing the work himself.

He was a plumber by trade and had been in Monaca probably 15 years. John Roth, Beaver merchant, and Chief of Police William Roth, Rochester, are cousins. Godfrey Roth, Rochester township, is an uncle.

News of the wreck spread rapidly all

(Continued on Page Three)

EXPLOSION CAUSES CRAFT TO NOSE

(Continued From Page One.)
over the valley. A great traffic jam, extending for a mile along the public road and down to the river edge, resulted in a short time. State and local police soon took charge of the situation and opened up the jam.

MANY CONFLICTING STORIES

There were many conflicting stories of what had happened to the fliers and how it happened. Some declare they saw the explosion in the air and the fragments of the plane coming down. Others hold to the belief that the explosion did not wreck the plane. Some believe that Roth was bringing the plane to a safe landing in shallow water, after some trouble, and came in contact with a high tension wire, causing the plane to plunge suddenly, nose down, into the water.

It is generally agreed, however, that nobody will ever know what did happen.

SAW FLAME BURST

Carl Vollhardt, lockmaster at Lock No. 4, who saw the explosion and the fall of the plane, immediately ordered out a small boat with other equipment in the locks and had the wrecked plane lifted to the lock walls.

Hundreds of spectators who heard the explosion and saw the plane fall rushed to the scene. Soon there was a large crowd. Many fragments of the wrecked plane were carried away as souvenirs. It would have been torn to pieces and all carried away but for the arrival of state and local police, who placed a guard over the wreck during the night.

FATHER IDENTIFIES SON

It was not until after midnight that the passenger in the plane was identified. The identification of Hercules was made by his father, George W. Hercules, who has been employed with the son in Ambridge. The father said:

"We were going down to see mother at Martins Ferry. Kenneth had bought a ticket Saturday, and later decided that he would not go, but stay up with the boys."

It is stated at Spratts mortuary, where the bodies were taken, that the bodies were not burned.

*** *** *** *** ***

PRINTER'S NO. 1869

THE GENERAL ASSEMBLY OF PENNSYLVANIA

HOUSE RESOLUTION

No. 406 Session of 2015

INTRODUCED BY MATZIE, JUNE 23, 2015

INTRODUCED AS NONCONTROVERSIAL RESOLUTION UNDER RULE 35, JUNE 23, 2015

A RESOLUTION

Commemorating the 175th anniversary of the incorporation of the Borough of Monaca, Beaver County.

WHEREAS, The Borough of Monaca, Beaver County, borders the Ohio River and is located 25 miles northwest of Pittsburgh; and

WHEREAS, The land now known as Monaca was first settled by Native American members of the Iroquois Confederacy; and

WHEREAS, According to survey records from 1769, a 330-acre tract of land, now part of Monaca, was first recorded by colonists under the name of Smith Township; and

WHEREAS, According to records from April 15, 1785, this same 330-acre tract of land was surveyed by William L. Lungan, who named the tract of land Appetite; and

WHEREAS, On September 5, 1787, Appetite was first purchased through a patent from the Commonwealth for 42 pounds, 7 shillings and 6 pence by Ephraim Blaine, grandfather of American statesman James G. Blaine; and

WHEREAS, On June 17, 1801, Appetite was sold and purchased by Robert Callender, who died soon after and willed the land to John Wilkens, Jr., George Wallace and Alexander Addison; and

WHEREAS, On December 29, 1804, Appetite was sold and purchased by John Niblow; and

WHEREAS, On August 1, 1813, Appetite was sold and purchased by Frances Helvidi, a Polish nobleman who was exiled from his native country and immigrated to America and is said to be the first colonial settler of Appetite; and

WHEREAS, On August 30, 1821, Appetite was auctioned at a public sale and won by Frederick Rapp; and

WHEREAS, On April 24, 1831, Appetite was sold and purchased by Steven Phillips, the owner of the Phillips and Graham boat yards; and

WHEREAS, On July 21, 1832, a group of settlers known as the New Philadelphia Society, led by Count Maximillian de Leon, purchased 800 acres of land, including Appetite, to develop a community called Phillipsburg, named after Steven Phillips, by constructing 50 houses, a hotel, factories and a stone church; and

WHEREAS, On March 6, 1840, the Municipal Government of Monaca was first incorporated under the name of Phillipsburg; and

WHEREAS, In 1848, Dr. Edward Acker established the Water Cure Sanatorium in Phillipsburg which used hydrotherapy to perform medical treatment and is considered the first hospital in Beaver County; and

WHEREAS, Thiel College, then known as Thiel Hall, was founded in 1866 by William A. Passavant in Phillipsburg and then relocated to Greenville in 1870; and

WHEREAS, On September 20, 1892, the name of the borough was changed from Phillipsburg to Monaca, in honor of Native American Oneida Chief Monacatootha, who also served as a representative of the Iroquois Confederacy and supported George Washington during the American Revolutionary War; and

WHEREAS, Monaca's official flag was designed by a 7th grade student named Tammi Temple and adopted by the borough council in 1976; and

WHEREAS, On July 1, 2009, the Center Area and Monaca school districts merged to establish the Central Valley School District, which was the first voluntary merger of public school districts in this Commonwealth; and

WHEREAS, Due to its large natural deposits of fire clay, the borough's manufacturers have produced enameled porcelain ware, glass, tile, tubing, drawn steel and wire throughout its history; and

WHEREAS, Today, the Borough of Monaca is home to more than 5,500 people; and

WHEREAS, During the week of June 20, 2015, the residents of Monaca will observe the 175th anniversary of the borough's incorporation by holding a series of celebratory events, which will culminate with the Monaca 175th Anniversary Festival on June 27, 2015; therefore be it

RESOLVED, That the House of Representatives commemorate the 175th anniversary of the incorporation of the Borough of Monaca, Beaver County; and be it further

RESOLVED, That a copy of this resolution be transmitted to Mayor John P. Antoline and Council President John DiMarzio of the Borough of Monaca.

1785 to 1986 - YEAR BY YEAR OF INTERESTING HAPPENINGS

1785 – the area in Beaver County surrounding and including what is now Monaca was then a portion of a vaguely defined township called Smith Township in Washington County.

Jul 25, 1769 – Colony of Pennsylvania ordered a survey of lands in the wilderness since it was being claimed by the Colony of Virginia. Although this survey was ordered, it was not done until after the Revolutionary War.

Apr 25, 1784 or Apr 15, 1785 – William L. Lungan surveyed the tract of land along the Ohio River where much of Monaca is now. 330 acres – called it Appetite (the first recorded name of what is downtown Monaca – First, Second, and Third Wards).

Sep 5, 1787 – Appetite was patented to Ephraim Blaine.

Jun 17, 1801 – Blaine sold Appetite to Robert Callender.

Dec 29, 1804 – as instructed in Callender's will, Appetite was sold again -John Niblow the purchaser – who sold it in 1813 to Francis Hilvelti.

Aug 30, 1821 – Hilvelti lost Appetite due to a debt and Beaver County Sheriff James Lyon put it up for sale; it was purchased by Frederick Rapp, leader of the Economite Society for $1,960. When it was sold it contained two log houses, one kitchen, one large sheep house, shingle roofed, and one cabin roofed stable, with 84 acres cleared of which 16 were in meadow.

Between 1822-1832 – a successful boat building business was on an adjoining tract of land to Appetite was owned by Stephen Phillips – business known as Phillips and Graham.

Apr 24, 1831 – Stephen Philips and John Graham purchased Appetite from Frederick Rapp for $2,400. It began to be called Phillipsburg.

Jul 31, 1832 – the combined former boatyard and Appetite tracts (over 800 acres) was purchased by Count Maximillian de Leon and associates (seceders from Economite Society of Economy) for $22,000. The Count and about 250 adherents who were splitting from the Harmony Society at Economy moved to Phillipsburg. They intended to form their own utopian community, but it failed to materialize for various reasons. They called themselves New Philadelphia Society. The boat yards were moved to Freedom (on the opposite side of the river, about 1-mile up river). They built 50 houses, a hotel, and factories; as well as the first substantial stone church in Beaver County.

Aug 10, 1833 – The New Philadelphia Society dissolved. Numerous former adherents chose not to continue to follow de Leon, but to remain in Phillipsburg and make it their permanent home.

Mar 6, 1840 – decree was granted for the incorporation of the Borough of Phillipsburg.

Water Cure* was the name given by Edward Acker, M.D. to a hydropathic institute where he treated people with varying illnesses from mumps, dysentery, typhoid, battle wounds, childbirth or wasp stings. Patients were treated by being wrapped in warm, soaked towels for hours or days at a time. Water Cure was much like a health resort. Water Cure was located in the area of the current Monaca Water Pollution Control Center.

*for a short time in 1848 / 1856, the post office was changed from Phillipsburg to Water Cure in memory of the old resort and to clear confusion since there was another village in Pennsylvania named Phillipsburg. Phillipsburg was called such in honor of Stephen Phillips – it was laid out by Abner Lacock, county surveyor.

1865 –The old Water Cure and Health Resort building was sold to Dr. W. G. Taylor for the Soldiers' Orphan School. The school opened Mar 1866.
Aug 22, 1876 the school was totally destroyed by fire.

Sep 1, 1870 – Thiel College opened on Fourth Street (where the Monacatootha Apartments now stand).

1871 – Thiel College relocated to Greensville.

1877 – Pittsburgh and Lake Erie Railroad Company made the decision to construct a route between Pittsburgh and Youngstown, Ohio. This meant railroad tracks had to be laid through Phillipsburg.

Sep 21, 1878 – the first locomotive crossed the Ohio River railroad bridge.

Feb 1879 – the Pittsburgh & Lake Erie Railroad Company (chartered in 1875) opened its roadway for services between Pittsburgh and Youngstown.

Aug 1886 – Phoenix Glass Co. was organized.

1888 – the passenger station at Phillipsburg was destroyed by fire and a new station was erected.

Mar 21, 1892 – Borough of Phillipsburg was renamed Monaca – a shortened version of Monacatootha. The name change occurred due to the confusion with another town in eastern Pennsylvania also with the name of Phillipsburg.

1890 to 1930 – prime interest of Monaca was to improve streets, grading, and laying sidewalks, along with developing programs for the town.

1896 – the first vehicular/passenger bridge was under construction connecting Monaca to Rochester.

1896 – the first Monaca pump house plant was built.

1897 – the new suspension bridge was completed between Monaca and Rochester.

1898 – the new bridge was opened for traffic. This bridge was a little short of being the longest span of a bridge in the U.S.A. – that belonged to that of the Niagara Falls bridge.

1902 – Pittsburgh Tool Steel Wire Co. (aka wire mill and Pittsburgh Tube Co.) opened.

Nov 1907 – a new freight station, located at Seventeenth Street, was completed in Monaca – considered the Colona area. The ticket clerk stayed in charge at the old station.

May 1910 – new double track cantilever railroad bridge over the Ohio River between Monaca and Beaver was completed and opened for traffic and the old bridge (which was reconstructed in 1889) was taken down and river piers removed.

Nov 1, 1910 – new passenger station, with platforms, umbrella sheds, passenger and baggage subway, was put into use – located at Fourteenth Street, four tenths of a mile south of the former station. The new station, formerly Colona Station, was located just beyond Twenty-First Street and was moved to its present location. (corner of Pacific Avenue and Fourteenth Street)

1918 – there was a major influenza epidemic in the area.

Nov 13, 1922 – after a football game where Monaca had defeated Rochester High School, many Monaca fans began celebrating by marching across the suspension bridge, causing it to sway.   George Copeland, a Rochester police officers saw what was occurring and ordered all the people off the bridge – most likely averting a disaster.

Fun fact repeated: The original bridge over the Ohio River (Monaca-Rochester bridge) was made of wooden planks.   They had wooden barrels along the sides of the bridge incase it caught fire.   Since the wooden bridge would have burned rather rapidly, someone could use that water in the barrels to assist in putting it out until the fire departments could get to the fire.

1930 – a new cantilever bridge to Rochester was opened. (remained opened until 1982)

1931/32 – Moon Township was annexed to the Borough of Monaca increasing Monaca approximately two square miles of additional area; formed the Monaca Heights area.

During 1933 to 1936 – the W.P.A. project beautified the water front and water plant grounds.
    The hillside was landscaped, terraced, covered with grass and flowers.

1933 – W.P.A. project enlarged the 1889 wharf or boat landing in the river (opposite the Monaca pump
    house).   It was sometimes called the "hog back."
    Permission to construct a wharf along the Monaca river shore line was secured from the War
        Department which granted a maximum length of 1600 feet.   When completed, the wharf was
        800 feet long and the river wall was 21 feet high, the terrace wall was 14 feet high, and the
        wharf proper was over 60 feet wide.   It was constructed of approximately 7000 perch of cut
        stone.

1935 to 1937 – W.P.A. project was above the Monaca Water Works.
    Two old houses with the included land were purchased. The houses were razed to permit the
        straightening of Atlantic Avenue and Eighth Street. In the middle of the street near this
        section, a fountain surrounded by a circular wall of cut stone was built; along the sidewalk on
        the river side of the street, a neat stone wall was constructed; atop the terrace a lily pond with
        a fountain in the center was erected; and a band stand and grotto with retaining walls of cut
        and dressed stone were placed and arranged in an artistic effect.

1940 – Monaca celebrated its centennial.

1940 – the new 2 storey, stone faced pump house plant was completed – a W.P.A. project.

1943 – Monaca Roll of Honor for those serving in WW II was erected on Pennsylvania Avenue by
        students in a Monaca High School shop class – Stuart Lindsay was the shop teacher. It had stone benches
        erected and a flag pole in front of it, surrounded by shrubs.   It was moved in 1962 to Fourth Street and
        Pennsylvania Avenue to make room for the Monaca Post Office.

1959 – A Toll Bridge between Monaca and East Rochester was opened.

Mar 28, 1964 – there was a fire at Phoenix Glass Co. plant which caused about $500,000 in damages.

Sep 1, 1964 – Monaca High School – Ella Street (Monaca Heights) opened.

Sep 3, 1970 – tornado struck the southeastern part of Monaca.

Jul 15, 1978 – another fire nearly destroyed the Phoenix Glass Co. plant; caused about $20 million in
        damages. The plant was rebuilt and expanded at a cost of about $95 million. In expanding and
        rebuilding, the company bought about 90 properties near the plant to do the expansion.

Jun 17, 1982 – the Rochester-Monaca Bridge was closed by Penn Dot after a safety inspection
        showed that there was brittle steel that could cause it to collapse.

Nov 25, 1986 – a new bridge opened between Monaca and Rochester. Both towns held all day parties to
        celebrate the opening of the new bridge.

In conclusion........................

I sat down one afternoon to research a building I found referenced in an article. This building was called the "Business Block" in Monaca, Pennsylvania. The reference stated that this building was constructed from bricks made in the same town as a brick company owned by James Welch. From this one finding and the research I began to do to find more information on where this Business Block building was located and who was James Welch, as well as being a native of the area, came all the information found in both volumes of my book. The more I read, the more interested I became in businesses and people that I remembered hearing mentioned through the years while my parents and aunts and uncles visited with each other and would sit telling stories or discussing things. Each time I found one bit of information, another business would be discovered or another fact would manifest, until it exploded into a full out research of the town we all now know as Monaca. My accumulation of all the information on the Borough of Monaca was purely an act of love.

Without the once hearty flavor of the still standing historical buildings, communities and/or towns, including Monaca, there would be nothing to visually share of its past and its history. To let these buildings go unnoticed, or worse, to simply let them be destroyed and removed is the same as turning our backs on all the past. It especially erases the memories of the people, the very souls who put forth such an effort and so much hard work in the place they called "home."

Many towns and communities have realized this and had/have the insight to embrace and restore rather than destroy their history and past. Just look around at some of the most thriving communities and towns who have restored instead of destroying!

My vision for Monaca is that current and future officials and property owners also begin to embrace their own history. I strongly suggest that actions begin very soon to start restoring and revitalizing currently standing historical buildings. All should see to it that these buildings, including homes, be marked and recognized as historically important and that these same buildings be cleaned, repaired, and restored to their original beauty to entice new proprietors to bring the prosperity back and for people to want to be land/home owners.

The borough itself may have to step up at first to begin the process – put enactments in place and stop granting permits for these historical buildings to simply be torn down and/or turned into a "modernized" façade of a building. The borough should want to keep the "flavor," the history, the beauty of the past! This would begin the process of bringing awareness and a desire for businesses and residents to join in and display the proud past of Monaca. Town officials and the residents of a town who show pride in its heritage entice others to do the same and to be part of the quest.

Monaca officials and residents have only to observe other adjacent towns and communities to see that this process absolutely succeeds. It not only makes the whole town begin to prosper once again, but it aides in the success, and most importantly, fosters pride as a whole.

This Beaver County river town of Monaca has always been home to a diverse population of hard working, dedicated, and proud people. Many family names carry on, along with many businesses, as well as all the new families and business that now call Monaca home. Buildings have stood the test of time, so why simply remove or destroy them now? I would like to see the people and especially the officials begin to show their pride and **not raze**, but **instead restore** – bring in a new era of thinking, of awareness – bring back the prosperous historical town of Monaca.

Progress is inevitable and needed.......B U T it does NOT mean all the past has to be eradicated, erased, razed, removed. Progress can implement existing structures, embrace history, resurrect the past, and caress the future without demolition!

It is absolutely the responsibility of the current generations and all local governments to instill local history in the next generations. Local history is not taught in the classroom, it is related, shared, exhibited, observed, and embraced.

BIBLIOGRAPHY and/or REFERENCES
for both Volume I and Volume II

There are no footnotes or direct notations within the text of either volumes of this book for any of the references used. This was done on purpose mainly to keep the main book clean and free of clutter. Another reason was that many times there were multiple tidbits or clusters of information obtained from one source and it would have been repetitious and therefore used up too much space per page. I felt it was more relevant to include the facts and keep the pages of the book to a minimum which was accomplished by simply listing all bibliographies and/or references at the end of the book as I have done below.

1840 – 1940 Monaca Centennial program

1840 – 1965 Monaca Quasquicentennial program

1840 – 1990 Monaca Sesquicentennial program

Beaver County Centennial Directory

Beaver County Centennial - 1800-1900

Beaver County Bicentennial - 1800-2000

Beaver County Year Book

Newspapers:
> *The Evening Review* – East Liverpool, Ohio – May 23, 1929 issue
> *Allegheny Times* – Oct 1988 through Jan 2008
> *The Argus* – Mar 1855 through Jun 1906
> *The Beaver Times* – Jan 1900 through Oct 1906
> *The Beaver Valley Times* – Oct 1946 through Jan 1960
> *Beaver County Times* – Nov 1954 through Oct 2007
> *The Daily Times* – Oct 1906 through Oct 1956
> *The Pittsburgh Gazette* – Mar 1795 through Nov 1962
> *The Pittsburgh Press* – Jul 1819 through Jul 1992
> *Pittsburgh Post Gazette* – Mar 1916 through Sep 2007

1920s through 1960s Monaca Year Books

1850 through 1940 U.S. Census Enumerations

Weyand, W. J.; Patterson, James; Weyand, J. – *Weyand & Reed's Beaver County Centennial Directory* - Beaver Printing Co., Beaver, PA., 1876

Harper, Frank - *Pittsburgh of Today*, 5 vols., New York 1931 information retrieved at *digital.library.pitt.edu*

Hughes, Robert W. - *The Story of Daylight Savings Times*, Pittsburgh, 1936

Beaver County Biographies information retrieved at *historicpa.net/*

American Gas Engineering Journal – Jul 6, 1918 - Formerly American Gas Light Journal – information retrieved at https://books.google.com

Western Pennsylvania History Vol. 96, No. 3, Fall 2013

Home Guide Publications Private Collection information retrieved at *smithsonianeducation.org/*

Office of War Information National Archives and Record Administration information retrieved at *smithsonianeducation.org*

The National WWII Museum (New Orleans) information retrieved at *ameshistory.org*

Buildings and Structures in Allegheny County, Pennsylvania

Government Printing Office National Archives and Record Administration information retrieved at *smithsonianeducation.org*

Hawkins, Jay W. - *Glasshouses & Glass Manufacturers of the Pittsburgh Region 1795 – 1910* - information retrieved at *journals.psu.edu*

Beaver Valley Labor News – information retrieved at *archive.org*

Caldwell, J. A. - *Caldswell's Illustrated, Historical, Centennial Atlas of Beaver County, Pennsylvania*, published by J.A. Caldwell, Condit, Ohio – Engraved, Lithographed & Printed by Otto Krebs, Pittsburgh, PA – 1876

Companies in Monaca – information retrieved at *manta.com*

University of Pittsburgh Library

Carnegie Library of Pittsburgh

The Spokesman and Harnas World – Vol. 26 – Jan 1910 – information retrieved at *books.google.com*

Beaver County Genealogy & History Center's extraction from a larger directory in this original published by the Burch Directory Co., Akron, Ohio, 1892 - Published in *Gleanings*

Extractions from a larger directory that was originally published by the Burch Directory Co. Akron, Ohio, 1892. Published: *Gleanings*, Beaver County Genealogical Society, Vol. XXI No. 4 Jun 1997 and Vol. XXII No. 1 Sep 1997

Beaver County Genealogy & History Center - 1869 Beaver County Directory

Harris' 1841 Directory accessed at *ancestry.com*

Mill Creek Church – information retrieved at *genealogypitstop.com*

Hosck, Rev. James R. – *History of Mill Creek Church*

Barnes, Mark R. – *Locations and Origins of the Cemeteries of Beaver County Pennsylvania*

Welchley, Mark H. – *Beaver County Church History Data Base*

Personal family information on Braden family – *"Opening The Door To Our History"*

Book of Biographies – This Volume Contains Biographical Sketches of Leading Citizens of Beaver County, Pennsylvania – Biographical Publishing Company, Buffalo, N.Y., Chicago, ILL - 1899

Adams, Belle; *The History of Beaver County Schools* – Volume 1 –published by Beaver County Historical Research & Landmarks Foundation

Art Work of Beaver and Lawrence Counties, Pennsylvania – Chicago: The W. H. Parish Publishing Co. – 1894

Pennsylvania County Histories – *Historic PA.net*

Information accessed at *mccarrollfamily.com*

Information accessed at *files.usgwarchives.net/pa/beaver/bios/martin-john.txt*

Information accessed at *phlf.org*

Beaver County, Pennsylvania - Book of Biographies Buffalo, N.Y., Chicago, Illinois.: Biographical Publishing Company, 1899 – information retrieved at *archive.org*

Watson, D.R. - *Directory of All Business and Professional Men and Official Guide of Beaver County, Penn'a*, Publisher, Press of Rieg & Smith Printing Co., Conneaut, Ohio, 1898 information retrieved at *digital.library.pitt.edu*

Brick - a monthly magazine devoted to brick, tile, terra cotta and allied clay industries – Jul 1900 Windsor & Kenfield Publishing Company, Monon Building, Chicago *books.google.com*

Engineering News and American Railway Journal – Volume XXXIII – Jan -Jun 1895 Engineering News Publishing Co, New York -Linda Hall Library Digital Collections at *hldigital.lindahall.org*

Paving and Municipal Engineering – a monthly magazine – Volume VIII - Jan to Jul 1895 - *books.google.com*

Engineering Record and the building record Sanitary Engineer; Conducted by Henry C. Meyer – Volume XLIV – Jul -Dec 1901 – information retrieved at *onlinebooks.library.upenn.edu*

Clay Record –Volumes 33-34, page 76, 1908

Extractions of information accessed at *gowaterfalling.com*

Industrial World – Pittsburgh, PA   Jul 1910 – information retrieved at *books.google.com*

Jordan, LL. D., John Woolf; *Genealogical and Personal History of Beaver County, Pennsylvania, Volume I and II*, Lewis Historical Publishing Company, New York, 1914

Ambridge Trade Area Directory – The Daily Citizen, Ambridge, PA – The Citizen Printing & Publishing Company 1956 information at *archive.org*

Records of the Work Projects Administration (W.P.A.) accessed at *archives.gov/research*

Crockery and Glass Journal, Vol. 85, No. 1, Jan. 4, 1917 at Google Books

Pittsburgh Commodity Index, Compiled by Pittsburgh Industrial Development Commission, Copyright 1913

Extractions of information accessed at *dcnr.state.pa.us*

Clay Record – Volume 22 – Jan 1903 at Google Books

Clay Record – Vol. XXVII – Chicago, Jul 14, 1905 at Google Books

Economic Geology of the Beaver Quadrangle, Pennsylvania – by Lester H. Woolsey - Department of the Interior United States Geological Survey, Charles D. Walcott, Director, Washington, Government Printing Office, 1906

Department of Labor and Industry, Clifford B. Connelley Commissioner, Third Industrial Directory of Pennsylvania, 1919

Municipal Engineering Index, January-June, 1902, Volume XXII, Municipal Engineering Company, New York, N.Y.

The Clay-Worker, Volumes XLIII-XLIV, 1904, T.A. Randall & Co. Publishers, Indianapolis, Ind.

Brick, Volumes XXII-XXIII, 1905, Chicago, Kenfield Publishing Company

Industrial World – weekly publication – Pittsburgh, PA – No. 15 – Monday, Apr 13, 1914 at Google Books

Paving – Municipal Engineering, A Monthly Magazine, Volume VIII, Municipal Engineering Company, Indianapolis, Jan to Jul, 1895

Brick, Vol. II, No. 1, January 1895 -- Vol. XVI, No. 1, January 1902 -- Vol. XVII, No. 5, November, 1902 -- Vol. XVIII, January-June, 1903

Clay Record, Vol. XXVII, No. 1, July 14, 1905

Taylor, Nick; *American-made: The Enduring Legacy of the W.P.A. : when FDR put the nation to work* – Bantam Book, 2008

The Great Arrow Historical Association of Center Township and Monaca; *I Remember..... Monaca !* - published by the GAHA and Beaver County Tourist Promotion Agency, Court House, Beaver County, PA. 1976

Extractions of information *facebook.com/americanqueensteamboatcompany*

Mercantile Tax Lists from 1904, 1910, 1922, 1924, 1928, 1929, 1930, 1931, 1940, 1941, 1942, 1943

Brown's Directory of American Gas Companies and Gas Engineering and Appliance Catalogue – 1922 edition – Robbins Publishing Co, New York – information retrieved at *books.google.com*

Historic American Engineering Record, National Park Service, Northeast Region U.S. Custom House, Philadelphia, PA

Transactions of the American Society of Civil Engineers, Instituted 1852, Vol. LXXII, Sep 1911, New York, published by the Society, 1911 – accessed at *archive. org*

Cook, Richard J., *The Beauty of Railroad Bridges: In North America –Then and Now*, Golden West Books, 1987

Pittsburgh & Lake Erie Railroad Historical Society, Inc. accessed at *plerrhs.org*

University of Pittsburgh Archive Service Center

Extractions of information accessed at *riverboatdaves.com*

Extracted a phrase from the song Mike Fink – accessed at *traditionalmusic.co.uk*

Extracted information on steamboats from *cincinnativiews.net*

Electronic Classroom, extraction of information – accessed at *xroads.virginia.edu*

Steamboats.com

Steamboats Built in the Greater Pittsburgh Area – accessed at
    freepages.genealogy.rootsweb.ancestry.com/~ricksgenealogy/boat_pa.htm

Pennsylvania State University Journals – accessed at *journals.psu.edu*

Extractions of information accessed at *cdm16066.contentdm.oclc.org*

USA Today accessed at *usatoday.com*

Extractions of information accessed at *gowaterfalling.com*

Lawrence County Memoirs accessed at *lawrencecountymemoirs.com*

Rock Point Park – accessed at *4ockpoint park.com*

Cascade Park – accessed at *sbno.illicitohio.com*

The Idora Park Experience owned by Jim and Toni Amey of Canfield (building set up beside their home with artifacts and information on Idora Park

Rivers of Destiny – Denver L. Walton, Eugenia Walton, Bob Bauder – Beaver County Historical Research and Landmarks Foundation – for the Beaver County Bicentennial – Photos/Charles Townsend – 1999

Guide to Historic Landmarks – 2002 – published by Beaver County Historical Research and Landmarks Foundation – Denver L. Walton, Bob Bauder and Charles W. Townsend III

Pittsburgh Music History site

Pittsburgh History & Landmarks Foundation, Pittsburgh, PA

Robert Morris University news site at *rmusentrymedia.com*

Amusement Today News Site at *amusementtoday.com*

1902/03 Directory Transcript by Don Fraser, Katie Jan accessed at *pa-roots.com*

Beaver County Genealogy & History Center's extraction from Harris' 1837 Pittsburgh Business Directory of Beaver County

Bausman A.M., Rev. Joseph H. - *History of Beaver County, Pennsylvania and its centennial celebration*, Volumes I and II – The Knickerbocker Press, New York – 1904

Beaver County Genealogy and History Center, Beaver Train Station, 250 East End Ave, Beaver, PA 15009

The General Assembly of Pennsylvania House Resolution No. 406 Session of 2015 Introduced by Matzie, Jun 23, 2015 Introduced as Noncontroversial Resolution under Rule 35, Jun 23, 2015 – accessed at *legis.state.pa.us*

The Iron Trade Review, Vol. XXXV, January 1 to December 31, 1902

Little Beaver Historical Association, 710 Market Street, 803 Plum Street, Darlington, PA 16115
    http://www.bchistory.org/beavercounty

Beaver County Historical Research and Landmarks Foundation, 1235 3rd Avenue, Freedom, PA 15042
    http://bchrlf.org/

Milestones publications – Beaver County Historical Research and Landmarks Foundation

Monaca Borough, 928 Pennsylvania Avenue, Monaca, PA 15061

Beaver Area Memorial Library, 100 College Avenue, Beaver, PA 15009

Monaca Public Library, 609 Pennsylvania Avenue, Monaca, PA 15061

The Western Pennsylvania Historical Magazine -Volume 47 Oct 1964 Number 4

The Navigator, containing directions for navigating the Monongahela, Allegheny, Ohio and Mississippi
    Rivers.   Published by Cramer, Spear and Eichbaum, Pittsburgh, 1817

A Cement Age: a Magazine Devoted to the Uses of Cement, Volume 8, May 1909, page 415 at Google Books

1860 maps and landowner information at *http://ancestortracks.com/Beaver*

The American Contractor – The Business Journal of Construction – Volume XL – No. 27 – Jul 5, 1919

The Hotel World – The Hotel and Travelers Journal – Vol. 86, No. 1 - Jan 5, 1918

List of Charters of Corporations Enrolled in the Office of the Secretary of the Commonwealth – by the
    Pennsylvania Secretary of the Commonwealth – during the two years beginning Jun 1, 1905,
    and ending May 31, 1907.

*Harris' Pittsburgh business directory for the year 1837: including the names of all the merchants,
    manufacturers, mechanics, professional, & men of business of Pittsburgh and its vicinity* –
    1837 –Isaac Harris – Pittsburgh: University of Pittsburgh

Monthly Bulletin of the Dairy and Food Division of the Pennsylvania Department of Agriculture – Vol. 9 –
    No. 1 – Feb 15, 1911

American Agriculturist farm directory and reference book of Beaver and Lawrence Counties, Pennsylvania
Published in 1917; New York: Published by Orange Judd Co.

The Insurance Press – No. 1,1165, Vol. XLVI – New York, Jan 2, 1918

List of Charters of Corporation Enrolled in the Office of the Secretary of the Commonwealth - beginning Jun 1,
1905, ending May 31, 1907

The American Architect and Architecture, Vol. 70, Oct-Dec 1900

"Sweet's" - Catalogue of Building Construct for the year 1910 - The Architectural Record Co., New York

In Transit publication, *The Motorman and Conductor*– volume 13, Dec 1904

The Railroad Telegrapher, Order of Railroad Telegraphers (U.S.), Published at St. Louis, Mo. by the Order of the
Railroad Telegraphers, Volume 27, Number 7, July 1910

Twenty-Ninth Annual Report of the Board of Directors To The Stockholders, The Pittsburgh and Lake Erie Railroad
Company, for the year ended December 31 1907, Terminal Station, Pittsburgh, PA

Memorial to the Pioneer Women of the Western Reserve, published monthly under the auspices of Woman's
Department of the Cleveland Centennial Commission, Parts one, two and three – Volume I, July, 1896.

The Bulletin of The American Iron and Steel Association, Vol. XXXIV, Philadelphia, January 1, 1900, No. 1

If you do not already have Volume I ....

Volume I Table of Contents

GENERAL   and   MISCELLANEOUS BUSINESSES
     Larger ads Sol Ostrow's Clothing Store
RESTAURANTS and BARS
WHOLESALE LIQUOR   DISTRIBUTORS   BREWERS
     Local "trade wars"   Wholesale Dealers and Distributors
     Moonshine   Distributors and dealers of liquor in Monaca
GROCERY MEAT FISH   CONFECTIONERY   FLOUR   GRAIN
     Gardeners   Grocers
     Meat Butchers Fish Poultry   Flour – Grain - Feed
     Fruit Markets   Confectionery   Bakery   Ice Cream   Dairy
     MISCELLANEOUS GROCERY AND FOOD STORE INFORMATION
ICE BUSINESS
TEAMSTERS   LIVERY   BLACKSMITHS   WAGON MAKERS   TANNERS and   SADDLERS
     Teamsters and Livery   Saddlers
     Tanners   Wagon and Buggy Makers
     Horseshoers   Blacksmiths
TONSORIAL ARTISTS / BARBERS   SALONS   BEAUTY SHOPS
APPLIANCES
FURNITURE
HARDWARE   HOME IMPROVEMENT
BUILDERS / CONTRACTORS   and   TRADES
     TRADESMEN
COAL
GARAGES and   SERVICE STATIONS
AUTO SALES
TRUCKING
MISCELLANEOUS AUTOMOTIVE RELATED BUSINESSES
WHOLESALE   and   GAS COMPANIES
HOTELS   and   INNS
     Farmer's Hotel
     Hotel of Cimotti   aka   Water Cure Hotel of Cimotti
     Central Hotel
     Imperial Hotel / Hotel Imperial / Colonial Hotel
     Colonial Inn
     Colona Hotel
     Hotel Monaca
     Hamilton Hotel
     Monaca Inn   often called Monaca Hotel (not to be confused with "Hotel Monaca")
     Shrode's Hotel
     Point Breeze Hotel
     Valley View Hotel
     Kobuta Hotel
JEWELERS
INSURANCE and   REAL ESTATE AGENTS
TRAVEL BUSINESSES
ATTORNEYS AT LAW
BILLIARDS POOL ROOMS ARCADES BOWLING
NEWSPAPERS   NEWS STANDS PRINTING

www.ingramcontent.com/pod-product-compliance
Lightning Source LLC
Chambersburg PA
CBHW080642270326
41928CB00017B/3165